Henry Kamen is a Fellow of the Royal Historical Society and a professor of the Higher Council for Scientific Research in Barcelona. Author of many standard studies on Spanish and European history, his most recent work is a biography of Philip II of Spain

The

SPANISH
INQUISITION

AN HISTORICAL REVISION

Henry Kamen

A PHOENIX GIANT PAPERBACK

First published in Great Britain
by Weidenfeld & Nicolson in 1997
This paperback edition published in 1998
by Phoenix, a division of Orion Books Ltd,
Orion House, 5 Upper St Martin's Lane,
London WC2H 9EA

A CIP catalogue record for this book
is available from the British Library.

ISBN: 0 75380 488 3

Printed and bound in Great Britain by
Butler & Tanner Ltd, Frome and London.

CONTENTS

ILLUSTRATIONS

GLOSSARY

alfaqui	Muslim clergy who ministered to the Muslim/Morisco population
aljama	Arabic word for the community in which Muslims or Jews lived separate from their Christian neighbours; known in Castilian as a judería or a morería
alumbrados	an illuminist, a mystic who minimized the role of the Church and its ceremonies
anusim	Hebrew term for Jews converted to Christianity against their will
arbitrista	writer of arbitrios or proposals for reform
auto de fe	'act of faith', usually public, at which those tried by the Inquisition had their sentences pronounced
beata	woman who dedicated herself to a solitary religious life, inside or outside a religious order
calificador	assessor, usually a theologian, who examined evidence to see if heresy was involved; he might also act as a censor
censo	annuities from investments
Chancillería	the high court in Valladolid and Granada; other high courts were called audiencias
Chuetas	nickname given to the converso population of Mallorca
comisario	select local clergy who helped the Inquisition in administrative matters
Comunero	a participant in the Comunidades, the Castilian rebellion against Charles V in 1520
concordia	a contract or agreement

Conseller	member of the Consell de Cent, the city council of Barcelona
converso	a person converted from the Jewish or Muslim faiths, especially the former; applied also to all descendants of the same
convivencia	coexistence, in this case of the three religious cultures of Spain
corregidor	civil governor in the main Castilian towns
Cortes	parliament of each realm
Diputación	(Diputació in Catalan) standing committee of the Cortes, of particular importance in the crown of Aragon. Members were called Diputados in Aragon, Diputats in Catalonia
ducat	Castilian unit of coinage, equivalent to 375 maravedis or 11 reales
edict	declaration (of 'grace' or 'faith') read out publicly by the inquisitors or their officials, at the commencement of proceedings in a district
effigy	in some autos de fe, an 'effigy' or figure representing an absent or dead heretic might be burnt in his place
encomienda	in mediaeval Spain, a grant of land by the king, on condition of military service; the encomienda brought with it membership of the prestigious military orders
familiar	lay official of the Inquisition
fuero	local law or privilege
Germanias	'brotherhoods', applied to those who rebelled against Charles V in Valencia in 1520
Hermandad	a 'brotherhood' or organized police force in some Castilian towns; later given official status by the crown as the Santa Hermandad ('holy brotherhood')
hidalgo	one of noble rank

limpieza de sangre	'purity of blood', freedom from semitic blood
maravedi	medieval Castilian unit of account
Marrano	abusive word, of obscure origin, applied to *conversos*
meshumadim	Hebrew term for Jews who converted 'voluntarily' to Christianity
Moriscos	'Moorish', applied to the Muslims of Spain after their forced conversion in the 1500s
Mozárabes	Christians living under Muslim rule
Mudéjares	Muslims living under Christian rule
reconciled	the Inquisition received back into the Church or 'reconciled' some heretics, but imposed severe punishments to accompany this
relaxed	those condemned for heresy by the Inquisition were handed over or 'relaxed' to the civil authorities to be executed
sanbenito	penitential garment of the Inquisition
Suprema	central council of the Inquisition
taqiyya	the tactic of conformism permitted in certain conditions to Muslims living under an alien faith

PREFACE

The first version of this book, written when I was twenty-seven years old and preparing my doctoral thesis (on another subject) at Oxford, had some of the virtues and all the defects of a young historian's work. Twelve years ago it was reissued in a slightly modified edition. A best-seller in its day, it received the support of a whole generation of readers. Needless to say, very much in it has been superseded by subsequent research. Thanks to the quality of work done over these years by specialists, it is now possible to get a far more reliable image of the Holy Office of the Inquisition. In many key respects, consequently, I have been obliged to change my views. I am particularly grateful to Benzion Netanyahu's recent *The Origins of the Inquisition* for compelling me to look again in detail at the evidence.

In Spain the modern phase of research into the Inquisition was launched twenty years ago, when Marcel Bataillon, myself and other scholars were invited to participate in a conference in 1976 at San Sebastián directed by José Antonio Escudero. Since then, scholars throughout the West have collaborated in a fruitful series of conferences on the subject.

The present study, while based on the original text, has been extensively rewritten and recast, leaving untouched only sections not substantially affected by recent research. As in the preceding edition, the quantity of material has obliged me to exclude treatment of the eighteenth and nineteenth centuries, when the Inquisition was virtually inert. Though much of value has been published recently on the whole subject, the bibliography and references have been restricted to items directly relevant to my presentation. A very limited number of footnotes have been given, to justify the arguments offered. I have left monetary units in their original form (*maravedis* or *reales*), which are impossible to translate into modern equivalents, but have normally expressed their value in the more common unit of ducats, in order to facilitate comparison between periods. I have also usually translated the Spanish word *Moro*, which has too exotic a ring as 'Moor', by the word 'Muslim'.

Written principally for the general reader, this book pays due attention to the major scholarly themes that have dominated Inquisition studies. Its conclusions, though based firmly on documentary sources, will not satisfy everybody. My aim, however, has been to go beyond polemic and present a balanced and updated synthesis of what we know about the most notorious tribunal of the western world. Like its predecessor, my book is fundamentally a 'state of the question' paper and therefore still open to discussion. It is dedicated to all those who have helped us to look more dispassionately at the Holy Office of the Inquisition.

Higher Council for Scientific Research
Barcelona

1

A SOCIETY OF BELIEVERS AND UNBELIEVERS

Asked if he believed in God, he said Yes, and asked what it meant to believe in God, he answered that it meant eating well, drinking well and getting up at ten o'clock in the morning.

A textile-worker of Reus (Catalonia), 1632[1]

In the west: Portugal, a small but expanding society of under a million people, their energies directed to the sea and the first fruits of trade and colonisation in Asia. In the south, al-Andalus: a society of half a million farmers and silk-producers, Muslim in religion, proud remnants of a once dominant culture. To the centre and north: a Christian Spain of some six million souls, divided politically into the crown of Castile (with two-thirds of the territory of the peninsula and three-quarters of the population) and the crown of Aragon (made up of the realms of Valencia, Aragon and Catalonia). In the fifteenth century the Iberian peninsula remained on the fringe of Europe, a subcontinent that had been overrun by the Romans and the Arabs, offering to the curious visitor an exotic symbiosis of images: Romanesque churches and the splendid Gothic cathedral in Burgos, mediaeval synagogues in Toledo, the cool silence of the great mosque in Córdoba and the majesty of the Alhambra in Granada.

In mediaeval times it was a society of uneasy coexistence (*convivencia*), increasingly threatened by the advancing Christian reconquest of lands that had been Muslim since the Moorish invasions of the eighth century. For long periods, close contact between communities had led to a mutual tolerance among the three faiths of the peninsula: Christians, Muslims and Jews. Even when Christians went to war against the Moors, it was (a thirteenth-century writer argued) 'neither because of the law [of Mohammed] nor because of the sect that they hold to',[2] but because of conflict over land. Christians lived under Muslim rule (as Mozárabes) and Muslims under Christian rule (as Mudéjares). The different communities, occupying separate territories and therefore able to maintain distinct cultures, accepted the need to live together. Military alliances were made regardless of religion. St Ferdinand, king of Castile from 1230 to 1252, called himself 'king of the three religions', a singular claim in an increasingly intolerant age: it was the very period that saw the birth in Europe of the mediaeval papal Inquisition (c.1232).

There had always been serious conflicts in mediaeval Spain, at both social and personal levels, between Mudéjar and Christian villages, between Christian and Jewish neighbours. But the existence of a multi-cultural framework produced an extraordinary degree of mutual respect. This degree of coexistence was a unique feature of peninsular society, repeated perhaps only in the Hungarian territories of the Ottoman empire. Communities lived side by side and shared many aspects of language, culture, food and dress, consciously borrowing each other's outlook and ideas. Where cultural groups were a minority they accepted fully that there was a persistent dark side to the picture. Their capacity to endure centuries of sporadic repression and to survive into early modern times under conditions of gross inequality, was based on a long apprenticeship.

The notion of a crusade was largely absent from the earlier periods of the Reconquest, and the communities of Spain survived in a relatively open society. At the height of the Reconquest it was possible for a Catalan philosopher, Ramon Llull (d. 1315), to compose a dialogue in Arabic in which the three characters were a Christian, a Muslim and a Jew. Political links between Christians and Muslims in the mediaeval epoch are exemplified by the most famous military hero of the time, the Cid (Arabic *sayyid*, lord). Celebrated in the *Poem of the Cid* written about 1140, his real name was Rodrigo Díaz de Vivar, a Castilian noble who in about 1081 transferred his services from the Christians to the Muslim ruler of Saragossa and, after several campaigns, ended his career as independent ruler of the Muslim city of Valencia, which he captured in 1094. Despite his identification with the Muslims, he came to be looked upon by Christians as their ideal warrior. In the later Reconquest, echoes of coexistence remained but the reality of conflict was more aggressive. The Christians cultivated the myth of the apostle St James (Santiago), whose body was alleged to have been discovered at Compostela; thereafter Santiago 'Matamoros' (the Moor-slayer) became a national patron saint. In al-Andalus, the invasion of militant Muslims from north Africa – the Almorávids in the late eleventh century; the Almohads in the late twelfth – embittered the struggle against Christians.

The tide, however, was turning against Islam. In 1212 a combined

Christian force met the Almohads at Las Navas de Tolosa and shattered their power in the peninsula. By the mid-thirteenth century the Muslims retained only the kingdom of Granada. After its capture by the Christians (1085), Toledo immediately became the intellectual capital of Castile because of the transmission of Muslim and Jewish learning. The School of Translators of Toledo in the twelfth and thirteenth centuries rendered into Latin the great semitic treatises on philosophy, medicine, mathematics and alchemy. The works of Avicenna (Ibn Sina), al-Ghazali, Averroës (Ibn Rushd) and Maimonides filtered through to Christian scholars. Mudéjar art spread into Castile. No attempt was made to convert minorities forcibly. But by the fourteenth century 'it was no longer possible for Christians, Moors and Jews to live under the same roof, because the Christian now felt himself strong enough to break down the traditional custom of Spain whereby the Christian population made war and tilled the soil, the Moor built the houses, and the Jew presided over the enterprise as a fiscal agent and skilful technician'.[3] This schematic picture is not far from the truth. Mudéjares tended to be peasants or menial urban labourers; Jews for the most part kept to the big towns and to small trades; the Christian majority, while tolerating their religions, treated both minorities with disdain.

Mudéjares were possibly the least affected by religious tension. They were numerically insignificant in Castile, and in the crown of Aragon lived separately in their own communities, so that friction was minimal. Jews, however, lived mostly in urban centres and were more vulnerable to outbreaks of violence. Civil war in both Castile and Aragon in the 1460s divided the country into numberless local areas of conflict and threatened to provoke anarchy. The accession of Ferdinand and Isabella to the throne in 1474 did not immediately bring peace, but gradually the powerful warlike nobles and prelates fell into line. Their belligerent spirit was redirected into wars of conquest in Granada and Naples. Of the two realms of Spain, Aragon had been the one with an imperial history, but Castile with its superior resources in men and money rapidly took over the leadership. The militant Reconquest spirit was reborn, after nearly two centuries of dormancy. It still retained much of its old chivalric ardour: in the Granada wars, the deeds of Rodrigo Ponce de León, Marquis of Cadiz, seemed to recall those of the Cid. But the age of chivalry was passing. The wars in Italy provoked bitter criticism of the barbarities of the Spanish soldiery, and in Granada the brutal enslavement of the entire population of Málaga after its capture in 1487 gave hint of a new savagery among the Christians.

Apparent continuity with the old Reconquest is therefore deceptive. Military idealism continued to be fed by chivalric novels, notably the *Amadis de Gaula* (1508), but beneath the superficial gloss of chivalry there burnt an ideological intolerance typified by the great conquests of Cardinal Cisneros in Africa (Mers-el-Kebir, 1505 and Oran, 1509), and Hernán Cortés in Tenochtitlán (1521). It is also significant that the new rulers of Spain were willing to pursue an intolerant policy regardless of its economic consequences. In regard to both the Jews and the Mudéjares, Isabella was warned that pressure would produce economic disruption, but she was steeled in her resolve by Cisneros and the rigorists. Ferdinand, responding to protests by Barcelona, maintained that spiritual ideals were more important than material considerations about the economy. Though affirmation of religious motives cannot be accepted at face value, it appears that a 'crusading' spirit had replaced the possibility of convivencia, and exclusivism was beginning to triumph.

The communities of Christians, Jews and Muslims never lived together on equal terms; so-called convivencia was always a relationship between unequals. Within that inequality, the minorities played their roles while attempting to avoid conflicts. In fifteenth-century Murcia,[4] the Muslims were an indispensable fund of labour in both town and country, and as such were protected by municipal laws. The Jews, for their part, made an essential contribution as artisans and small producers, in leather, jewellery and textiles. They were also important in tax administration and in medicine. In theory, both minorities were restricted to specified areas of the towns they lived in. In practice, the laws on separation were seldom enforced. In Valladolid at the same period, the Muslims increased in number and importance, chose their residence freely, owned houses, lands and vineyards.[5] Though unequal in rights, the Valladolid Muslims were not marginalized. The tolerability of coexistence paved the way to mass conversion in 1502.

In community celebrations, all three faiths participated. In Murcia, Muslim musicians and jugglers were an integral part of Christian religious celebrations. In times of crisis the faiths necessarily collaborated. In 1470 in the town of Uclés, 'a year of great drought, there were many processions of Christians as well as of Muslims and Jews, to pray for water ...'[6] In such a community, there were some who saw no harm in participating with other faiths. 'Hernán Sánchez Castro', who was denounced for it twenty years later in Uclés, 'set out from the church together with other Christians in the procession, and when they reached the square where the Jews were with the Torah he joined the procession of the Jews with their Torah and left the processions of the Christians'. Co-acceptance of the communities extended to acts of charity. Diego González remembered that in Huete in the 1470s, when he was a poor orphan, as a Christian he received alms from 'both Jews and Muslims, for we used to beg for alms from all of them, and received help from them as we did from the Christians'. The kindness he received from Jews, indeed, encouraged him to pick up a smattering of Hebrew from them. It also led him to assert that 'the Jew can find salvation in his own faith just as the Christian can in his'.[7] There was, of course, always another side to the coexistence. It was in Uclés in 1491 that a number of Jewish citizens voluntarily gave testimony against Christians of Jewish origin. And Diego González, twenty years later when he had become a priest, was arrested for his pro-Jewish tendencies and burnt as a heretic.

We can be certain of one thing. Spain was not, as often imagined, a society dominated exclusively by zealots. In the Mediterranean the confrontation of cultures was more constant than in northern Europe, but the certainty of faith was no stronger. Jews had the advantage of community solidarity, but under pressure from other cultures they also suffered the disadvantage of internal dissent over belief.[8] The three faiths had coexisted long enough for many people to accept the validity of all three. 'Who knows which is the better religion', a Christian of Castile asked in 1501, 'ours or those of the Muslims and the Jews?'[9]

Though there were confusions of belief in the peninsula, there seems in late mediaeval times to have been no formal heresy, not even among Christians. But this did not imply that Spain was a society of convinced believers. In the mid-sixteenth century a friar lamented the ignorance and unbelief he had found throughout Castile, 'not only in small hamlets and villages but even in cities and populous towns'. 'Out of three hundred residents', he affirmed, 'you will find barely thirty who know what any ordinary Christian is obliged to know'.[10] Religious practice among Christians was a free mixture of community traditions, superstitious folklore and imprecise dogmatic beliefs.[11] Some writers went so far as to categorize popular religious practices as diabolic magic. It was a situation that Church leaders did very little to remedy.[12] Everyday religion among Christians continued to embrace an immense range of cultural and devotional options. There are many parallels to the cases of the Catalan peasant who asserted in 1539 that 'there is no heaven, purgatory or hell; at the end we all have to end up in the same place, the bad will go to the same place as the good and the good will go to the same place as the bad'; or of the other who stated in 1593 that 'he does not believe in heaven or hell, and God feeds the Muslims and heretics just the same as he feeds the Christians'.[13] When Christian warriors battled against Muslims, they shouted their convictions passionately. At home, or in the inn, or working in the fields, their opinions were often different. The bulk of surviving documentation gives us some key to this dual outlook, only, however, among Christians. In Soria in 1487, at a time when the final conquest of Granada was well under way, a resident commented that 'the king is off to drive the Muslims out, when they haven't done him any harm'.[14] 'The Muslim can be saved in his faith just as the Christian can in his',[15] another is reported to have said. The inquisitors in 1490 in Cuenca were informed of a Christian who claimed that 'the good Jew and the good Muslim can, if they act correctly, go to heaven just like the good Christian'.[16] There is little or nothing to tell us how Jews and Muslims thought, but every probability that they also accepted the need to make compromises with the other faiths of the peninsula.

Christians who wished to turn their backs on their own society often did so quite simply by embracing Islam. From the later Middle Ages to the eighteenth century, there were random cases of Spanish Christians who changed their faith in this way. The Moorish kingdom of Granada had a small community of renegade Christians. In Christian Spain it was not uncommon to find many of pro-Muslim sentiment. In 1486 the Inquisition of Saragossa tried a Christian 'for saying that he was a Muslim, and for praying in the mosque like a Muslim'.[17] Long after the epoch of convivencia had passed, many Spaniards retained at the back of their minds a feeling that their differences were not divisive. In the Granada countryside in the 1620s, a Christian woman of Muslim origin felt that 'the Muslim can be saved in his faith as the Jew can in his', a peasant felt that 'everyone can find salvation in his own faith', and another affirmed that 'Jews who observe their law can be saved'.[18] The attitude was frequent enough to be commonplace, and could be found in every corner of Spain.

The remarkable absence of formal 'heresy' in late mediaeval Spain may in part have been a consequence of its multiple cultures. The three faiths, even while respecting each other, attempted to maintain in some measure the purity of their own ideology. In times of crisis, as with the rabbis in 1492 or the Muslim *alfaquis* in 1609, they clung desperately to the uniqueness of their own truth. Christianity, for its part, remained so untarnished by formal heresy that the papal Inquisition, active in France, Germany and Italy, was never deemed necessary in mediaeval Castile and made only a token appearance in Aragon. In the penumbra of the three great faiths there were, it is true, a number of those who, whether through the indifferentism born of tolerance or the cynicism born of persecution, had no active belief in organized religion. But the virtual absence of organized heresy meant that though defections to other faiths were severely punished in Christian law, no systematic machinery was brought into existence to deal with non-believers or with those forced converts who had shaky belief. For decades, society continued to tolerate them, and the policy of burning practised elsewhere in Europe was little known in Spain.

All this was changed by the successful new Reconquest of Ferdinand and Isabella. It appears that the rulers, seeking to stabilize their power in both Castile and Aragon, where civil wars had created disorder in the 1470s, accepted an alliance with social forces that prepared the way for the elimination of a plural, open society. The crown accepted this policy because it seemed to ensure stability, but the new developments failed to bring about social unity, and the machinery of the Inquisition served only to intensify and deepen the shadow of conflict over Spain.

2

THE GREAT DISPERSION

Do not grieve over your departure, for you have to drink down your death in one gulp, whereas we have to stay behind among these wicked people, receiving death from them every day.

Juan de León, of Aranda, 1492[1]

'The kings and lords of Castile have had this advantage, that their Jewish subjects, reflecting the magnificence of their lords, have been the most learned, the most distinguished Jews that there have been in all the realms of the dispersion. They are distinguished in four ways: in lineage, in wealth, in virtues, in science.'[2] Penned by a fifteenth-century Castilian rabbi, the claim was a frankly starry-eyed vision of the past. Even had it been true, by the time he wrote it it was barely more than a memory.

Jews had been in the peninsula from at least the third century. In mediaeval Spain they constituted the single largest Jewish community in the world. Compared to Christians and Muslims, however, they were few. In the thirteenth century they very likely formed just under two per cent of Spain's population, maybe some one hundred thousand persons.[3] Many preferred to live in towns that, by modern standards, were small. The Jewish presence created, at least in Christian minds, a stereotype of rich town-dwellers. Most Jews, in fact, lived in the small villages which were typical of the mediaeval countryside. There they farmed, bred sheep, kept vineyards and orchards, and lived for the most part peacefully with their Christian neighbours. In the towns they often occupied professions which involved daily contact with Christians: as shopkeepers, grocers, dyers, weavers. Sometimes they made a profession their own: in Murcia in 1407 there were thirty Jewish tailors.[4]

This regular contact, called convivencia or coexistence by historians, was typical of the mediaeval period. It enabled Christians, Jews and Muslims to understand and respect, but not necessarily love, each other. It enabled Spaniards of different faiths to pursue their daily tasks together. 'In the commercial sphere, no visible barriers separated Jewish, Christian and

Muslim merchants during the major period of Jewish life in Spain. Christian contractors built Jewish houses and Jewish craftsmen worked for Christian employers. Jewish advocates represented gentile clients in the secular courts. Jewish brokers acted as intermediaries between Christian and Muslim principals. As a by-product, such continuous daily contacts inevitably fostered tolerance and friendly relationships, despite the irritations kept alive in the name of religion.[5] Christians could accept Jewish physicians without prejudice. 'I, Miguel de Pertusa', runs a private contract in Aragon in 1406, 'make this contract with you Isaac Abenforma son of don Salomon', to treat his son of a head wound; 'and I promise that even if he dies I shall satisfy and pay you' the fee due.[6]

The communities lived, for the most part, separate existences. Jews had different food requirements and religious observances, and did not normally intermarry with Christians. The separateness was, in time, made firmer by sporadic persecution. The first great Christian persecution of Jews occurred in the seventh century, and made them greet with relief the invasions by Muslims from north Africa. Under the subsequent Muslim caliphate of Córdoba, they prospered socially and economically. This came to an end in the twelfth century with the overthrow of the caliphate by the invading Almorávids, who persecuted Christian and Jew alike and destroyed their places of worship. Many Jews fled to Christian territory and under the tolerant eye of Christian rulers continued to prosper in their new surroundings. They were not, like Muslims, obviously at war against Christians, and were therefore looked on more favourably.

But political rivalry and economic jealousy helped to break down their security. From the thirteenth century onwards, anti-Jewish legislation became common in Europe. The Church Council of Arles (France) in 1235, for example, ordered all Jews to wear a round yellow patch, four fingers in width, over their hearts as a mark of identification. The decrees were never enforced in the Spanish kingdoms, though successive Cortes continued to call for action – in 1371 at Toro and 1405 at Madrid. In most towns Jews began to be restricted to their own quarter (called an *aljama* when it was organized as a corporate body). Each aljama was a separate society within the towns, with its own officials and its own taxes. It was exempt from most municipal obligations except the duty to defend the town. It paid taxes only to the crown, under whose direct control it came. In practice, the crown had few resources with which to protect the aljamas against hostile municipalities.

In time the Jewish situation worsened throughout western Europe. The

Church began to take a more aggressive attitude both towards its own heretics and towards minorities. In 1290 England expelled all its Jews, and in 1306 France followed suit. In Spain convivencia managed to hold out. Hostility continued, however, to come from different groups: from urban elites who owed money to the Jews, from the ordinary Christian population who lived beside the Jews but resented their separateness, and from some rural communities that considered the urban Jews as their exploiters.

In the mid-fourteenth century the civil wars in Castile gave rise to excesses against the Jewish community in some towns. Religious fanaticism, stirred up in southern Spain in the 1370s and 1380s by Ferrant Martínez, archdeacon of Ecija, lit the spark to this powder keg. In June 1391, during a hot summer made worse by economic distress, urban mobs rioted, directing their anger against the privileged classes and against the Jews.[7] In Seville hundreds of Jews were murdered and the aljama was destroyed. Within days, in July and August, the fury spread across the peninsula. Those who were not murdered were compelled to accept baptism. In Córdoba, wrote a Hebrew poet, 'there was not one, great or small, who did not apostasise'. In Valencia during July, some two hundred and fifty were murdered; in Barcelona during August, some four hundred. The major aljamas of Spain were wiped out. Royal authorities in both Castile and Aragon denounced the excesses and tried, in the major cities, to protect the Jews. A Jewish contemporary, Reuben ben Nissim, reported that in the crown of Aragon, 'many of the governors of the cities, and the ministers and nobles, defended us, and many of our brethren took refuge in castles, where they provided us with food'.[8] In many places it was not the mob but the upper classes who were the perpetrators. The city of Valencia blamed 'men both of the country and the town, knights and friars, nobles'.[9] Many unprotected Jews were forced to become Christians. From this time the *conversos* came into existence on a grand scale.

Converso (or New Christian) was the term applied to one who had converted from Judaism or Islam. Their descendants were also referred to as conversos. Given the forced nature of the mass conversions of 1391, it was obvious that many could not have been genuine Christians. At least in the crown of Aragon, royal decrees made it plain that the forced conversions were unacceptable. Jews could, if they wished, return to their own religion.[10] But circumstances had changed and in many places, such as Barcelona and Mallorca, the converted felt it safer to remain in their new religion. Their adherence to Christianity was, within this context, voluntary. It posed problems, as we shall see, both for their former co-religionists as well as for the Christians. The conversos were inevitably regarded with suspicion as a fifth column within the Church. Terms of opprobrium were applied to them, the most common being *marrano*, a word of obscure origin.[11] Though no longer Jews in religion, they continued to suffer the rigours of antisemitism.

Even in the pluralist society of mediaeval Spain, Jews had always suffered discrimination. Like any other unprivileged minority they were excluded from jobs and professions exercising authority (for example, in town government or in the army), but served in a broad range of middle and lesser callings.[12] They still managed to play a role in public life in two main areas: medicine, and financial administration. They also on occasion had a significant cultural role as translators from Arabic, a tongue the Christians had difficulty in learning.

Doctors were in short supply in late mediaeval Spain, and Jews stepped in to meet the demand. Royal and aristocratic circles relied heavily on them as physicians. In the kingdom of Aragon 'there was not a noble or prelate in the land who did not keep a Jewish physician',[13] and a similar situation also existed in Castile. In many towns the only practising doctors were Jews, who received correspondingly favourable treatment. In Madrid in the 1480s one of the Jewish doctors was exempted by the grateful town council from certain laws and taxes.[14]

Popular hostility to Jews was based in some measure on their financial activities.[15] In specific times and places their role could be important. In the thirteenth century, under Jaime I of Aragon, some bailiffs of royal revenues in the major cities were Jews. Henry II of Castile told the Cortes of Burgos in 1367 that 'we farmed out the collection of the revenue to Jews because we found no others to bid for it'.[16] In 1369 a Jew, Joseph Picho, was 'chief treasurer and manager of the revenues of the realm'. In 1469 the Cortes of Ocaña complained to Henry IV that 'many prelates and other ecclesiastics farm to Jews and Moors the revenue and tithes that belong to them; and they enter churches to apportion the tithe among the contributors, to the great offence and injury of the Church.'[17]

The number of Jewish tax officials was, in proportion to Christians, always small. By the fifteenth century they served in the lower grades of the fiscal system, as tax-gatherers rather than as treasurers. In the period 1440–69 only 15 per cent (seventy-two persons) of tax-farmers serving the crown of Castile were Jews.[18] But a few Jews also played a significant role at the apex of the financial structure. Under Ferdinand and Isabella, Abraham Seneor was treasurer of the Santa Hermandad, David Abulafia was in charge of supplies for the troops at Granada, and Isaac Abravanel administered the tax on sheep, the *servicio y montazgo*. The tax-farming company headed by the converso Luis de Alcalá, which included among its members Seneor, rabbi Mair Melamed, the Bienveniste brothers and other Jews, played a prominent role in Castilian finance for some twenty years of this reign.[19] Not surprisingly, a foreign traveller commented on Isabella that 'her subjects say publicly that the queen is a protector of Jews'.

In size and numbers the aljamas shrank dramatically after the massacres of 1391, and indeed in some cities aljamas no longer existed. In Barcelona, the mediaeval Jewish *call* (street) was abolished in 1424 because it was deemed unnecessary. In Toledo, the ancient aljama consisted by 1492 of possibly only forty houses. It appears that by the end of the fifteenth century Jews were no longer a significant middle class.[20] They were not, on the whole, rich (their annual tax contribution to the Castilian royal treasury in 1480 represented only 0.33 per cent of its ordinary revenue), and had negligible social status. Their great days were undeniably past.

Within the changed circumstances, however, Jewish life maintained its equilibrium. Living in a region where the Jews had preferred the protection of the big towns, the chronicler and curate Andrés Bernáldez commented later that they were

> merchants, salesmen, tax-gatherers, retailers, stewards of nobility, officials, tailors, shoemakers, tanners, weavers, grocers, pedlars, silk-mercers, smiths, jewellers, and other like trades: none broke the earth or became a farmer, carpenter or builder, but all sought after comfortable posts and ways of making profits without much labour ... They never wanted to take jobs in ploughing or digging, nor would they go through the fields tending cattle. Nor would they teach their children to do so: all their wish was a job in the town, and earning their living without much labour while sitting on their bottoms.[21]

This picture, sometimes used to set a contrast between rural Christians and urban moneylending Jews, was not entirely true. Jews certainly lived in towns, where they shared much the same professions as Christians. In fourteenth-century Saragossa they were traders, shopkeepers, artisans, jewellers, tailors, shoemakers.[22] But there is ample evidence that from the fourteenth century the Jews had put less confidence in the cities and had moved out into the villages, where their relationship with Christians was normal and peaceful. By the late fifteenth century, contrary to what Bernáldez asserts, Jewish farmers and peasants could be found throughout Spain, but above all in the provinces of Castile. In Toledo, a considerable proportion of Jews seem to have worked their own lands. In Máqueda (Toledo) there were 281 Jewish families to only fifty Christian.[23] Even when they had lands and cattle, however, for practical reasons of religious observance and security the Jews tended to live together, usually in a town or village environment. In Buitrago (Guadalajara), members of the prosperous Jewish community (which in 1492 boasted six rabbis and even a town councillor) owned 165 fields of flax, 102 meadows, 18 market gardens, a large amount of pasture and a few water rights.[24] In Hita, in the same region, they had two synagogues and nine rabbis; the major investment was in wine, with Jews owning 396 vineyards totalling no fewer than 66,400 vines.[25] Even in the Andalusian countryside, from which Bernáldez came, there were Jewish farmers owning lands, vineyards and herds of cattle.[26]

In the crown of Aragon the Jews also engaged in agriculture, but on a much smaller scale. The lands they possessed were smallholdings rather than big fields. For reasons of security, they lived in and limited their activity to the towns.[27] In some areas their holdings may have been more ambitious. In Sos in Upper Aragon, birthplace of King Ferdinand himself, Jews were 'cultivators of vines, flax and cereals, and their business relations with Christians contributed to fraternal amity', their main callings being as peasants or as moneylenders.[28]

There was considerable variety in the social position of Jews in the peninsula. In many areas convivencia went on even while the storm-clouds were gathering. In Ávila, which was untouched by the fury of 1391, the Jews survived as perhaps the biggest aljama in Castile, constituting nearly half the city's population of 7,000.[29] In Zamora, also untouched by 1391, the small Jewish population actually grew in size. On the eve of the 1492 expulsion the 300 Jewish families there represented one-fifth of the population.[30] In general, it has been argued, 'relations between Jews and Christians remained extremely cordial throughout the century' in many parts of Castile.[31]

The reduced number of Jews after 1391 did not necessarily imply a cultural decline. The communities preserved their identity, legislated for their people (a comprehensive law was drawn up in 1432 in Valladolid), enjoyed the protection of leading nobles as well as of the crown, and coexisted pacifically with Christians.[32] In Aragon the crown itself, first with Alfonso V and then with Juan II, favoured the recovery of the aljamas, which paid taxes directly to the royal treasury. In 1479 Ferdinand expressly confirmed the autonomy of the Jewish community in Saragossa.[33] There were also many rich Jews, among them the financiers who enjoyed royal favour. Seneor in 1490 had a good fortune worth some six million *maravedis* (16,000 ducats), which included wheatfields, vineyards and a dozen houses in Segovia and Andalusia; Melamed had property worth over three millions, including houses and lands in Segovia and Ávila.[34]

Pressures and tensions were, inevitably, also present. In Castile a 1412 decree, inspired in part by the zealous Valencian saint, Vincent Ferrer (who shares some responsibility for the vents of 1391), and the converso Chancellor, Bishop Pablo de Santa María, deprived Jews of the right to hold office or possess titles, and prevented them changing their domicile. They were also excluded from various trades such as those of grocer, carpenter, tailor and butcher; they could not bear arms or hire Christians to work for them; they were not allowed to eat, drink, bathe or even talk with Christians; and they were forbidden to wear any but coarse clothes. In practice, extreme legislation of this type was unenforceable, and was either ignored or revoked.

In Catalonia in 1413–14 Vincent Ferrer helped to organize a top-level debate between Christian and Jewish scholars, which Pope Benedict XIII ordered to be held in his presence at Tortosa. At this famous Disputation of Tortosa[35] the chief star on the Christian side was the recently converted papal physician Joshua Halorqui, who now took the name Jerónimo de Sante Fe. The Disputation brought about more conversions, including members of the prominent Aragonese family de la Caballería and entire aljamas in Aragon.

Though the Disputation had threatened to extinguish the Jewish community in Aragon (some three thousand were baptized), it also had a favourable sequel. Vincent Ferrer took his campaign north to France in 1416. In Aragon a new king, Alfonso V, guided by the now Christian members of the Caballería family, reversed all the anti-Jewish legislation of the Ferrer epoch. From 1416 onwards the Aragonese crown protected the Jews and conversos firmly, rejecting all attacks on them.[36] In Tortosa in 1438 the crown insisted, against the protests of the bishop, that Jewish and Muslim doctors could visit Christian patients if the latter wished.[37] Restrictions on the movements and rights of Jews were lifted.

A policy of separating Jews from Christians had frequently been attempted. But the Castilian legislation of 1412, which required separation, was never enforced; and in Aragon the crown under King Alfonso refused to sanction ghettos. Subsequent local measures met the same fate. In Seville in 1437 Jews were ordered to live only in their quarter, but by 1450 they could be found in different parts of the city.[38] Separation orders in Soria in 1412 and 1477 were never observed.[39] From the 1460s Christian spokesmen in Castile – among them the general of the Jeronimite order, Alonso de Oropesa – returned to the theme, arguing that the conversos would be less tempted to maintain their Jewish links if Jews were clearly separated. In the 1480 Cortes at Toledo, the crown agreed to decree a general enforcement of separation in Castile. Jews were to remain in their ghettos, if necessary separated by a wall. This went the way of previous laws. In Soria in 1489 the richer Jews still had their houses outside the ghetto. In Orense the city authorities solemnly met in the synagogue in 1484 and ordered the Jewish community to 'observe the laws of Toledo', giving them three days in which to do so. In practice, on neither side were any steps made to observe the law. Four years later, in 1488, vain efforts were still being made in Orense to enforce separation.[40] In the crown of Aragon at the same period some cities, such as Saragossa, attempted to enclose the Jews, but both Isabella and Ferdinand came out firmly against such measures.[41] We should remember, in parenthesis, that separation was sometimes in the interests of Jews themselves, to protect them from harassment and to save the public authorities from the cost of repressing community riots.

In the century after the 1391 riots, therefore, there is ambiguous evidence of pressure on Jews. In many areas their situation was difficult, but this was nothing new. Repressive legislation, though decreed, was regularly unenforced. In 1483 Ferdinand ordered Jews in Saragossa to wear distinguishing symbols (a red patch), but there is no evidence it was observed. Moreover, the crown actively favoured Jews and former Jews. The reign was one in which the Jewish financiers Seneor and Abravanel flourished, and in which the Caballería family dominated politics in Saragossa.

The fall in numbers, all the same, left its mark. The mass conversions of 1391 depleted many communities. In the crown of Aragon, by 1492 there remained only one-fourth of the Jews of a century before.[42] The rich aljamas of Barcelona, Valencia and Mallorca, the biggest cities in these realms, had disappeared altogether; in smaller towns they either disappeared or were reduced to tiny numbers. The famous community of

Girona was, with only twenty-four taxpayers left, now a shadow of its former self.[43] In the realms of Castile, there was a mixture of survival and attrition. Seville had around five hundred Jewish families prior to the riots; a half-century later it had only fifty. By the time Isabella succeeded to the throne, Jews in Castile totalled less than eighty thousand.[44] By 1492, the communities were scattered through some two hundred centres of population. In some former centres, such as Cuenca, there was no Jewish presence.

From the beginning of their reign in 1474, Ferdinand and Isabella determined to maintain between Jews and Christians the same peace that they were trying to establish in the cities and among the nobility. The monarchs were never personally antisemitic. As early as 1468 Ferdinand had a Catalan Jew from Tárrega, David Abenasaya, as his physician, and both he and Isabella continued to have Jewish doctors and financiers as their closest collaborators. In both Aragon and Castile they followed the policy of their predecessors: taking the Jews under their direct personal control on the same terms as other Christian and Muslim communities which were in the royal jurisdiction. 'All the Jews in my realms', Isabella declared in 1477 when extending her protection to the community in Trujillo, 'are mine and under my care and protection and it belongs to me to defend and aid them and keep justice.' Likewise in 1479 she gave her protection to the fragile Jewish community in Cáceres.[45] Given that Jews were constantly on the defensive against powerful municipal interests, the interventions of the crown in local politics present an impressive picture of the monarchy protecting its Jews. In 1475, for example, the city of Bilbao was ordered to revoke commercial restrictions it had placed on Jews in the town of Medina de Pomar; in 1480 the town of Olmedo was ordered to construct a gate in the wall of the *judería* to give Jews access to the town square.[46] The monarchs intervened repeatedly against municipalities that tried to eliminate the commercial activity of the Jews.

Royal policy, however, had to contend with social tensions. In 1476 the Cortes of Madrigal, on the initiative not of the crown but of the towns, passed sumptuary laws against Jews and Mudéjares, enforcing the wearing of a distinctive symbol and restricting the practice of usury. Jews were inevitably unhappy (in Ávila they refused to lend any money until the regulations on usury were clarified), but it was not until the legislation of the 1480 Cortes of Toledo, which tried to put into effect a policy of separation and restricted Jews to aljamas, that real hardships were suffered.

There is no doubt that anti-Jewish groups in the municipalities were responsible for such measures. In Burgos in 1484 Jews were not allowed to sell food; in 1485 they were ordered to shut the aljama on all Christian feast-days; in 1486 a limit was put on the number of Jews in the ghetto (the order was subsequently annulled by the crown).[47] In Saragossa during the late fifteenth century there was an unmistakable rise in anti-Jewish pressure, fomented by the clergy. The penalties against Jews for not paying respect to the religious procession on the day of Corpus Christi, increased threefold within a short period of ten years.[48]

The anti-Jewish measures of the period did not represent any qualitative worsening of the position of Jews. In fact, the totality of existing legislation in Castile, had it been put into practice, was already highly prejudicial to them.[49] We need to look beyond the laws. Only then, in the realm of what really happened, is it possible to appreciate the extent to which community tolerance, administrative laxity, and royal policy combined to guarantee the survival and viability of the minority faiths.

The position of Jews, not intrinsically bad, was unfortunately affected by the converso problem. The monarchs became firmly convinced that a separation of Jews from Christians was the most effective answer to the situation, and in 1480 they set in motion a body whose entire concern was with judaizers: the Inquisition. Though the Inquisition only had authority over Christians, Jews quickly realized that they too were in the line of fire and all their worst travails date from 1480.

The existence of the Inquisition forced Jews to revise their attitude to conversos. When the great conversions took place at the end of the fourteenth century, Jews may have felt that the neophytes were still their brethren. A century later, the perspective was somewhat different. Jewish dignitaries, scholars and leaders had, not always under active persecution, voluntarily embraced the Catholic faith. The poet Selomoh Bonafed, writing in the wake of the Disputation of Tortosa, lamented how 'many of the most respected leaders of our aljamas abandoned them'.[50] Some converts, especially those who became clergy, became bitter persecutors of the Jews. The Jews of Burgos in 1392 complained that 'the Jews who recently turned Christian oppress them and do them much harm'.[51] A visible gap opened up in some communities between Jews and ex-Jews. In the early fifteenth century rabbis were still expressing the view that most of the conversos were unwilling converts (*anusim*). By mid-century they took the view that most were *meshumadim* (renegades), real and voluntary Christians.

Normal, friendly social relations between conversos and Jews could still be found at all levels.[52] But there were also ominous signs of tension.[53]

When the Inquisition began its operations many Jews found no difficulty in cooperating with it against the conversos. They themselves were, as non-Christians, exempt from its jurisdiction. By contrast, they could now pay off old scores. In small communities, the coexistence of Jews and conversos concealed long-standing tensions, even among those with close and apparently friendly family ties. In the town of Calatayud (Aragon) in 1488 one of the Jews, Acach de Funes, was scorned by both Jews and Christians as a liar and a cheat. He lived up to his reputation by bearing false witness before the Inquisition against several conversos of the town, whom he claimed were practising Jews.[54] In Aranda in the 1480s a Jewish resident went around 'looking for Jewish witnesses to testify before the Inquisition' against a local converso. The same Jew admitted confidentially to a Christian friend that 'it was all false' and that he was doing it out of personal enmity.[55] False witness by Jews in Toledo was reported by Hernando del Pulgar. They were, wrote the royal secretary, 'poor and vile men who from enmity or malice gave false testimony against some conversos saying that they judaized. Knowing the truth, the queen ordered them arrested and tortured'.[56] In Soria in 1490 a Jewish doctor testified freely against several conversos. He said that one converso, a legal official, had called Torquemada 'the most accursed man in the world, a vile heretic'. 'It really grieves me', the doctor told the inquisitors contritely, 'to say these things against him, but everything I have said has been the unvarnished truth'.[57] In the town of Uclés in 1491, a dozen Jews spoke freely to the inquisitor about conversos they knew to have observed Jewish customs.[58] The Inquisition itself, according to Rabbi Capsali, demanded that the synagogues should impose an obligation on Jews to denounce conversos.[59]

Cooperation with the Inquisition was not a tactic that brought any benefits. From the 1460s, as we have seen, some Church leaders had begun to advocate the separation of Jews from Christians. This policy, as adopted by the Inquisition, took the form of a partial expulsion of Jews, in order to minimize the contact with conversos. At the end of 1482, a partial expulsion of the Jews of Andalusia was ordered.[60] The exiles were free to go to other provinces of Spain. In January 1483 Jews were ordered to be expelled from the dioceses of Seville, Córdoba and Cadiz. The crown delayed implementation and they were not actually driven out from Seville until summer 1484. It is possible that the expulsions were in part motivated by fear of Jewish collaboration with the Muslim kingdom of Granada, then under attack by Ferdinand's forces; but the role of the Inquisition was paramount. In the event, the expulsions of these years were never fully carried out. A few years later, Jews were living without any problems in Cadiz and Córdoba.[61] In 1486 in Aragon the Inquisition issued an order expelling Jews from the dioceses of Saragossa, Albarracín and Teruel. The order was postponed, and later cancelled; no expulsions took place.[62] Meanwhile some towns carried out their own unauthorized expulsions, ignoring the protests of the crown.[63]

Though Ferdinand and Isabella intervened repeatedly to protect their Jews from excesses (as late as 1490 they began an enquiry into Medina del Campo's ban on Jews setting up shops in the main square), the monarchs appear to have been thoroughly convinced by Inquisitor General Torquemada of the need for separation of Jews. When the local expulsions had failed, after ten long years, to stem the alleged heresies of the conversos, the crown decided on the most drastic measure of all – a total expulsion of Jews.

Jews expelled by other countries in mediaeval times had been tiny minorities. In Spain, by contrast, they had for centuries been a significant, prosperous and integral part of society. Their fate was now in the balance, in a country where there was growing pressure against the other cultural minority, the Muslims. From 1480 the whole economy of the state was geared to the war against Granada. There was also less tolerance of Islam. In 1490 the Muslims of Guadalajara were accused of converting a Jewish boy to Islam. Though they claimed in defence that such conversions 'had been the custom in these realms', the royal council ruled that 'hereafter no Jew may turn Moor'; nor indeed could Moors turn Jew.[64] It had, of course, long been illegal (since at least 1255) for Christians to turn Jew or Muslim. When during the Granada war groups of ex-Christians were captured after the fall of Málaga they were immediately put to death.[65] By contrast, after the fall of Granada several ex-Christians there, who had turned Muslim, were accepted back into the Church.[66]

Ferdinand and Isabella hesitated for some time over the idea of expulsion. The crown stood to lose revenue from the disappearance of a community whose taxes were paid directly to the crown; and which moreover had helped to finance the war in Granada. Many people in Spain may have been anxious to get rid of the Jews for social and economic reasons: the Old Christian elites and several municipalities saw in them a source of conflict and competition.[67] The decision to expel, however, was the crown's alone, and it appears to have been taken exclusively for religious reasons: there are no grounds for maintaining that the government stood to profit, and Ferdinand himself admitted that the measure hurt his finances.[68] The king and queen were undoubtedly encouraged in their policy by the fall of Granada to their forces in January 1492, which seemed a signal of divine favour. On 31 March, while they were in the city, they issued the edict of expulsion, giving the Jews of both Castile and Aragon until 31 July to accept baptism or leave the country.

The decree gave as its main justification 'the great harm suffered by Christians [i.e. conversos] from the contact, intercourse and communication which they have with the Jews, who always attempt in various ways to seduce faithful Christians from our Holy Catholic Faith'. 'Over twelve years' of Inquisition had failed to solve the problem, nor had the recent expulsions from Andalusia been sufficient. It was now decided that 'the only solution to all these ills is to separate the said Jews completely from contact with Christians, and expel them from all our realms'.

When the news broke, a deputation of Jews led by Isaac Abravanel went to see the king. Their pleas failed, and at a second meeting they offered the king a large sum of money if he would reconsider his decision. There is a story that when Torquemada heard of the offer he burst into the monarchs' presence and threw thirty pieces of silver on the table, demanding to know for what price Christ was to be sold again to the Jews. At a third meeting which Abravanel, Seneor and the Jewish leaders had with the king, it became clear that Ferdinand was determined to go ahead. In despair they turned to the queen. She, however, explained that the decision, which she firmly supported, came from Ferdinand: 'the Lord has put this thing into the heart of the king'.[69]

The proposal to expel came in fact from the Inquisition. The king said so clearly in the text of the edict issued in Aragon, a ferocious document that was obviously drawn up by the inquisitors and reeks of a virulent antisemitism not present in the Castilian text.[70] There was more than a grain of truth in the story of Torquemada and the pieces of silver. The general expulsion was an extension of the regional expulsions that the Inquisition had been carrying out, with Ferdinand's support, since 1481.

The king confirmed the key role of the Inquisition in a letter that he sent to the principal nobles of the realm. The copy sent to the Count of Aranda on the same day as the edict explained the circumstances concisely:

The Holy Office of the Inquisition, seeing how some Christians are endangered by contact and communication with the Jews, has provided that the Jews be expelled from all our realms and territories, and has persuaded us to give our support and agreement to this, which we now do, because of our debts and obligations to the said Holy Office: and we do so despite the great harm to ourselves, seeking and preferring the salvation of souls above our own profit and that of individuals.[71]

Similar confirmation of the Inquisition's role was made by the king in other letters sent the same day. The inquisitors of Saragossa, for example, were informed that the prior of Santa Cruz had been consulted and that 'it has been decided by me and by him that the Jews be expelled'.[72] Though most Jews in Spain were under royal jurisdiction, a few were not. The local expulsions in Andalusia in the 1480s, for example, had not been applicable to Jews living on the territories of the Duke of Medinaceli. In 1492, therefore, the crown had to explain to the nobles, such as the Catalan Duke of Cardona who had assumed that 'his' Jews were not affected, that the edict was universal. However, seigneurs were granted the property of their expelled Jews as compensation. In Salamanca the royal officials were ordered not to touch the effects of Jews who lived on the estates of the Duke of Alba.[73]

It is possible that the monarchs thought mass conversions would be more likely than mass emigration. The rabbi of Córdoba was baptized in May, with Cardinal Mendoza and the papal nuncio as sponsors. In June the eighty-year-old Abraham Seneor, chief judge of the Jewish aljamas of Castile[74] and principal treasurer of the crown, was baptized in Guadalupe with the king and queen as his sponsors. Seneor, a prototype 'court Jew', had been a striking example of the way in which some Jews had rendered faithful service to the crown and in the process had managed to protect their community. He and his family adopted the surname Pérez Coronel; a week later he was nominated city councillor (*regidor*) of his home town of Segovia and member of the royal council. His colleague Abravanel took over as spokesman for the Jews and began to negotiate terms for the emigration.

The edict may have come as a shock to communities where Jews lived tranquilly. In some Christian areas, however, public opinion was well prepared for it. Stories of Jewish atrocities had been circulating for years. One concerned an alleged ritual murder performed on a Christian child at Sepúlveda (Segovia) in 1468. The converso bishop of Segovia, Juan Arias Dávila, is reported to have punished sixteen Jews for the crime. The most famous of all the cases concerned the alleged ritual murder of a Christian infant at La Guardia in the province of Toledo, in 1491. Six conversos and as many Jews were said to have been implicated in the crime, in which a Christian child was apparently crucified and had its heart cut out in an attempt to create a magical spell to destroy Christians. Such, at least, was the story pieced together from confessions extracted under torture, the culprits being executed publicly at Ávila in November 1491.[75] The affair received wide publicity: we find a printed account of it circulating in Barcelona shortly after. The timing was ominous, and there can be little doubt that it helped prepare many to accept the expulsion of the Jews. Atrocity stories of this sort, common in Europe both before and since – in England there were the cases of William of Norwich in 1144 and Hugh of Lincoln in 1255 – served to feed the most vicious antisemitism.

Spanish Jews could not have been unaware of the expulsions recently put into effect in neighbouring states. In Provence, soon to be part of France, an anti-Jewish movement was growing and led soon to expulsions; in the Italian duchies of Parma and Milan Jews were expelled in 1488 and 1490.[76] In any case, the Spanish decree – as they understood all too well – was not exclusively one of expulsion. The edict did not seek to expel a people, but to eliminate a religion.[77] Though the official text did not mention it, the edict offered Jews an implicit choice between conversion and emigration. This was demonstrated by the efforts of clergy in those weeks to convert the Jews, and by the satisfaction with which converts were accepted into the Church. Moreover, as the king stated expressly to Torquemada two months after issuing the edict, 'many wish to become Christians, but are afraid to do so because of the Inquisition'. Accordingly, 'you will write to the inquisitors, ordering them that even if something is proved against those persons who become Christians after the decree of expulsion, no steps be taken against them, at least for small matters'.[78]

The expulsion was a traumatic experience that left its impact for centuries on the Western mind. In that decade there were already prophetic voices which seemed to implicate the fate of the Jews in some greater destiny. Among some conversos, and presumably some Jews as well, there emerged a dream of leaving Sefarad (the Hebrew name for Spain) for the Promised Land and Jerusalem.[79] Among the Christians, the fall of Granada seemed to be (as it became) the omen for the conversion of the Jews. Was Ferdinand (always a firm believer in his own destiny) influenced by these voices? As a Catalan, was he influenced by the strong Catalan mystical tradition which identified the defeat of Islam in Spain with the destruction of the Jews?[80]

In giving the event its due importance, however, historians then and later exaggerated some of its aspects. They measured its significance in terms of great numbers. The Jesuit Juan de Mariana, writing over a century later, stated that 'the number of Jews who left Castile and Aragon is unknown; most authors say they were up to 170,000 families, but some even say they were as many as 800,000 souls: certainly a great number'.[81] Jews who took part in the emigration had no doubt of the dimensions of the tragedy. Isaac Abravanel wrote that 'there left 300,000 people on foot from all the provinces of the king'.[82] In fact, few reliable statistics exist for the expulsion. Those given in standard histories are based on pure speculation. Our first care must be to estimate the possible Jewish population of Spain in 1492. A judicious analysis based on the tax-returns of the communities in Castile gives us a fairly reliable total of around seventy thousand Jews in the crown of Castile at this date.[83] This accords with the estimate of under eighty thousand already mentioned above. The great days of a large and prosperous community were truly past. The situation was worse in the crown of Aragon, where Jews were reduced to one-fourth of their numbers as a result of the fateful year 1391.[84] In these realms, they numbered by the late fifteenth century some nine thousand.[85] In the whole of the kingdom of Valencia the Jews numbered probably only one thousand, most of them in the town of Sagunto.[86] In Navarre, there were some two hundred and fifty families of Jews. In total, then, the Jews of Spain on the eve of the expulsion in 1492 numbered just over eighty thousands souls, a far cry from the totals offered by their own leaders or by most subsequent scholars.

The sufferings of those forced into exile for the sake of religion are vividly detailed by Bernáldez, in a picture that has become all too familiar since the fifteenth century.[87] The richer Jews out of charity helped to pay the costs of the poorer exiles, while the very poor managed to help themselves in no other way but by accepting baptism. Many were unable to sell their possessions for gold or silver, for the export of these metals was forbidden; so they sold houses and property for the most desperate substitutes. 'They went round asking for buyers and found none to buy, some sold a house for an ass, and a vineyard for a little cloth or linen, since they could not take away gold or silver', Bernáldez reported. The ships that met them at the ports were overcrowded and ill-managed. Once they had put out to sea, storms drove them back, forcing hundreds to reconcile themselves to Spain and baptism. Others, not more fortunate, reached their desired haven in north Africa only to be pillaged and murdered. Hundreds of others staggered back to Spain by every available route, preferring familiar sufferings to those of the open sea and road. One of the exiles wrote that:

> Some travelled through the ocean but God's hand was against them, and many were seized and sold as slaves, while many others drowned in the sea. Others were burned alive as the ships on which they were sailing were engulfed by flames. In the end, all suffered: some by the sword and some by captivity and some by disease, until but a few remained of the many.[88]

Without minimizing the transcendence of the expulsion decree, it must be emphasized that only a proportion of the Jews of Spain were affected by it. There were several reasons for this. Aware that a choice of conversion was offered, a great many took the option. It was one that their people had endured through the ages, and there seemed little reason not to accept it now. Chroniclers then and later lamented the rapidity with which their people went to be baptized. 'Many remained in Spain who had not the strength to emigrate and whose hearts were not filled with God', reported one Jewish contemporary. 'In those terrible days', reported another, 'thousands and tens of thousands of Jews converted.'[89] The evidence suggests that possibly half of all the Jews of Spain preferred conversion to expulsion. The majority in Aragon, and possibly in Castile as well, entered the Christian fold.[90] A potent motive, obviously, was the fear of losing all their property. A converso woman resident in Almazán some years later observed that 'those who remained behind did so in order not to lose their property'.[91]

Many others went into exile. Possibly a third of the 9,000 Jews of the kingdom of Aragon emigrated.[92] They went in their entirety to adjacent Christian lands, mainly to Italy. The exiles from Castile went mostly to neighbouring lands where their faith was tolerated, such as Navarre and Portugal. For many the journey to Portugal ended in 1497, when all Jews there were ordered to become Christian as a condition of the marriage between King Manoel and Isabel, daughter of the Catholic monarchs. Several exiles, particularly from Andalusia, crossed over to north Africa. Others did so years later, after the Portuguese conversions of 1497. Navarre shut a door when it required its Jews to convert in 1498. Despite a persistent tradition to the contrary, no Jews are known to have gone to Turkey until very much later.[93] All these emigrations shared one thing in common: suffering. A Genoese diplomat, seeing the refugees who arrived in the port there, commented that 'no one could witness the sufferings of the Jews without being moved ... They could have been mistaken for wraiths, so haggard and emaciated did they look, undistinguishable from dead men ...'[94] Wherever they went the refugees were exploited or mistreated. Inevitably, many attempted to return.

In their exile in Africa, reported a rabbi from Málaga, 'many could not take it any more and returned to Castile. Likewise this occurred to those who came to Portugal and the kingdom of Fez. And it was the same wherever one went.'[95] Between those who converted and those who returned, the total of those who left Spain for ever was relatively small, possibly no more than forty thousand. The figures place many of the historical issues in a clearer perspective.

Many writers have assumed that the expulsion was motivated by greed and a wish to rob the Jews. There is little evidence of this, and it is highly improbable. The crown did not profit and had no intention of profiting. No one knew better than the king that Spain's Jews were a dwindling minority with few resources. By Ferdinand's own admission, he stood to lose some tax revenue; but the sum realized by the authorities from the sale of goods was negligible. Though Jewish communal property (mainly the synagogues and cemeteries) was seized by the crown,[96] it was in most cases handed over to local communities. Logically, the exiles exercised the right to take permitted wealth with them. Embarkation lists for the ports of Málaga and Almería, in Andalusia, show that many took substantial sums out of the country.[97] Several fortunate individuals were allowed to take most of their goods and jewels. One such was Isaac Perdoniel, granted the favour at the direct request of the last Muslim king of Granada, Boabdil.[98] Abravanel and his family were also given a special privilege to take their personal wealth with them. Others bribed officials to let them take treasure. In 1494 an official of Ciudad Real was prosecuted by the government for levying extortionate charges on Jews crossing to Portugal, and for 'allowing through many persons and Jews from these realms who were taking gold and silver and other forbidden items'.[99] Many individuals and corporations that had owed money to the Jews clearly benefited from the expulsion, but this was an incidental consequence of a measure that was primarily religious in motivation.

The effects on Spain were smaller than is often thought. The sultan of Turkey is reported to have said at a later date that he 'marvelled greatly at expelling the Jews from Spain, since this was to expel its wealth'. The statement is completely apocryphal, and comes from a later, uncorroborated Jewish source.[100] The Jews had played only a small part in the country's economy, and their loss had a similarly small impact.[101] In any case, in practice Jews had been allowed to transfer many assets to conversos. Those exiles who returned, such as Samuel Abolafia of Toledo,[102] were immediately given back their property. In Ciudad Real an official was obliged to give back to Fernán Pérez, 'formerly named Jacob de Medina', 'some houses that he sold to him at below their fair price, at the time that the Jews had to leave the kingdom'.[103] In Madrid in 1494 several expelled Jewish doctors who returned (as Christians) were welcomed back with open arms by the town council, which commented that 'the more doctors there are, the better for the town, for all of them are good doctors'.[104]

No less mistaken is the claim that the crown's purpose was to achieve unity of faith.[105] The king and queen were neither personally nor in their politics anti-Jewish. They had always protected and favoured Jews and conversos. They might be accused of many things, but not of anti-semitism.[106] Nor were they anti-Muslim. Ferdinand and Isabella made no move, until several years later, to disturb the faith of the enormous Muslim population of Spain, who in political terms were a far graver danger than the tiny Jewish minority.

Although the terms of the edict issued in Aragon were rabidly anti-semitic, the warm welcome given to returnees confirms that the expulsion was not motivated by racialism. The proportion of those who returned was high. They were, the evidence suggests, given back their jobs, property and houses. Those who had converted were protected against popular antisemitism. In 1493 the monarchs ordered people in the dioceses of Cuenca and Osma not to call baptized Jews *tornadizos* (turncoats).[107] The new converts and the old conversos continued to function in the trades and professions in which the Jews had distinguished themselves. The purely economic impact of the expulsion was thereby softened.

Contemporaries in Europe who heard of the expulsions reacted according to the information they received. Some congratulated the Spanish king on his action. Because it coincided with the expulsions, a new sexual disease (syphilis) which was identified during those months in Italy was dubbed by some 'the Jewish disease'.[108]

Many Christians in Spain, then and later, thought the expulsion wrong. Rabbi Capsali reported that after Ferdinand's death several Spanish officials criticized the king for banishing the Jews.[109] His information is supported by that of Ferdinand's own official biographer, the inquisitor Jerónimo de Zurita, who tells us that 'many were of the opinion that the king was making a mistake'.[110] The first historian of the Inquisition, the inquisitor Luis de Páramo, writing a century after the expulsion, was also firm on this point. 'I cannot omit to mention', he stated, 'that there were learned men who did not feel that the edict was justified'.[111] Criticisms were warranted by the curiously ambivalent policy of the crown after 1492. The practice of Judaism was forbidden in Spain and its colonies. But (a fact too little known) it was permitted in every other territory ruled by the Spanish crown in the early years of the sixteenth century. Not until a century after 1492 was Judaism prohibited in Milan (under Spanish control from the mid-sixteenth century). Not until nearly two centuries later was it prohibited in Spanish Oran, in north Africa.[112] This tacit acceptance meant that the Jewish religion continued to have some role in the consciousness of Spaniards who travelled through the empire, long after it had officially ceased to exist in Spain.

What Spain lost was neither wealth, for the Jews had not been rich, nor population, for few left. Some later commentators, writing at a time of economic difficulty, imagined that loss of wealth was the main consequence of 1492. But Spaniards who reflected on such things felt that the real loss was the failure of the crown to protect its own people. The crown turned its back on the plural society of the past, cut off an entire community that had been an historic part of the nation, and intensified the converso problem without solving it. The Jews had finally been driven into the Christian fold. 'In this way', wrote the curate of Los Palacios, Andrés Bernáldez, 'was fulfilled the prophecy of David in the psalm *Eripe me*, which says: *Convertentur ad vesperam, et famen patientur, ut canes; et circuibunt civitatem.* Which is to say: "They shall return at evening, and shall suffer hunger like dogs, and shall prowl round the city". Thus these were converted at a late hour and by force and after great suffering.'[113]

3

THE COMING OF THE INQUISITION

Keep yourself from the flames! the reverend fathers are coming.

A friar to a converso, Soria, 1491[1]

The expulsions of 1492 solved no problems, and only aggravated an old one. The small ex-Jewish community was now added to the already large community of converted Jews. A 'converso danger', which till then may have been an exaggerated product of the clerical imagination, now took on serious proportions.

Many Jews stayed and retained their property, but they were not always favourably accepted in communities where antisemitism had been stirred up. Emigrants had been allowed to transfer their property to New Christians, so that assets often continued to remain in the same family. In post-1492 Christian society, the new conversos occupied exactly the same social position as the Jews. As before the expulsion, they continued to be occupied as traders, tax-gatherers, moneylenders, farmers, tailors and cobblers. The populace found it easy enough to identify the New Christians with the old Jews, both socially and religiously. The process was helped by the conservative habits of the conversos, the survival of Jewish practices, and the difficulty many converts found in adapting themselves to Christian usage (particularly in diet).

The ex-Jews had to merge into an already existing converso society with which they did not necessarily have much in common. There were tens of thousands of conversos, most of them dating from 1391, who had played an active role in Christian Spain for well over a century.

At the upper social level, post-1391 conversos played a significant role in towns, the basic political unit in Spain. Towns were the focal point of rural communities, and also the key to royal authority. Many successful Jewish families by changing their religion became qualified to hold public office in the towns. The result was a growth of rivalry between newcomers and the older oligarchies. In some Castilian cities, such as Burgos (where ex-Jewish families such as the Cartagenas and Maluendas were prominent) and Toledo, conversos were influential on the municipal council. In others they used their tenure of public office to band together, contributing to the bitter and sometimes bloody clan rivalry that characterized Castilian political life in the late fifteenth century. The converso historian Diego de Valera reports that in Córdoba on the city council 'there was great enmity and rivalry, since the New Christians were very rich and kept buying public offices, which they made use of so arrogantly that the Old Christians would not put up with it'. In Segovia, according to the chronicler Alonso de Palencia, the conversos 'shamelessly took over all the public posts and discharged them with extreme contempt of the nobility and with grave harm to the state'.[2] In the city of Palencia in 1465 'there were great factions of Old Christians and of conversos', with the principal families of the city supporting the conversos.[3] The political role of conversos was evidently limited only to towns where Jews had been numerous; but in those few towns it could be significant. In Cuenca, converso families in the late fifteenth century occupied 85 per cent of the posts on the city council.[4] In Guadalajara the powerful patronage of the Duke of Infantado gave them a similar advantage.

Conversions became significant from the end of the fourteenth century and were substantial during the fifteenth. Converts from the Jewish elite had the advantage of being accepted on equal terms into the Christian elite. A decree of Juan II of Castile in 1415, addressed to his converso treasurer, states: 'Whereas I have been informed that members of your family were, when Jews, considered to be noble, it is right that you should be held in even more honour now that you are Christians. Therefore it is my decision that you be treated as nobles'.[5] Among the earlier converts was Salomon Halevi, rabbi of Burgos, who was converted along with his brothers in 1390, adopted the name Pablo de Santa María, took holy orders and eventually became bishop of Cartagena and then of Burgos, tutor to the son of Henry III, and papal legate. His eldest son Gonzalo became bishop successively of Astorga, Plasencia and Sigüenza. His second son, Alonso de Cartagena, succeeded his father in the see of Burgos.[6] In Castile the finance minister of Henry IV, Diego Arias Dávila (d. 1466), was a converted Jew who founded a powerful dynasty which produced one of the conquistadors of central America, Pedrarias Dávila. One of Diego's sons, Juan Arias, became bishop of Segovia, and a grandson became first Count of Puñonrostro.

In Aragon members of the powerful de la Caballería family converted in the wake of the Disputation of Tortosa. Other important first-generation converts were leading government officials belonging to the Santa Fe and Sánchez families. Of particular importance was the Santangel family, Christians since 1415 and employed as high officials of the crown of Aragon. It was a member of the family, Luis, treasurer of Ferdinand the Catholic, who put up the money that helped to finance Columbus's first voyage to America. At the end of the fifteenth century the principal administrators of Aragon were conversos. At the very moment that the Inquisition began to function, five conversos – Luis de Santangel, Gabriel Sánchez, Sancho de Paternoy, Felipe Climent and Alfonso de la Caballería – held the five most important posts in the kingdom.

Conversos continued to play a prominent part at the court of the Catholic monarchs. In Isabella's Castile, at least four bishops were of converso origin. Also of known converso blood was Cardinal Juan de Torquemada, uncle of the first Inquisitor General.[7] Three secretaries of the queen – Fernando Alvarez, Alfonso de Avila and Hernando del Pulgar – were New Christians. One of her chaplains, Alonso de Burgos, was a converso. Several other officials at court were known conversos, among them the official chroniclers Diego de Valera and Alonso de Palencia. Isabella's employment of both conversos and Jews was commented upon with surprise by foreign visitors.

Inevitably, many converso families continued in professions that they had previously exercised as Jews. Though the majority lived in urban centres rather than in the countryside, many also lived in the country. In the Seville-Cadiz area in the 1480s, about half of a sample of 6,200 conversos lived in the rural areas, where they were under the direct jurisdiction of the great nobles, who were more capable of defending their interests.[8] In the countryside, they worked the land. In Aguilar de la Frontera, near Córdoba, of the sixty *sanbenitos* (penitential garments of the Inquisition) hung up in local churches in the late sixteenth century, about nineteen belonged to converso peasant farmers (*labradores*).[9] In the towns, small independent callings attracted them. Of a sample of 1,641 Toledo conversos who were involved with the Inquisition in 1495, the majority were in modest urban occupations, but there was a significant number of jewellers and silversmiths (59), traders (38), tax-farmers (15) and money-changers (12).[10] The example of Badajoz, in Extremadura, shows that all the 231 conversos penalized by the Inquisition between 1493 and 1599 came from the professional and commercial classes. They held posts ranging from that of mayor and municipal official to the lesser occupations of physician, lawyer, trader, shopkeeper and manufacturer.[11] The same is true of Saragossa and other principal cities for which we have details. In Barcelona out of a sample of 223 tried during these years, one-fourth were traders and another fourth in the textile industry.[12] In Andalusia, a sample for the year 1495 shows that nearly half were occupied in textiles, and about a sixth in leather.[13]

Finance was a well-known area in which conversos excelled. It is memorable that, but for converso finance, Columbus's first voyage in 1492 would not have been carried out. The Aragonese conversos Luis de Santangel and Gabriel Sánchez protected and financed the expedition; Jews and conversos, including a Jewish interpreter, formed part of the crew; and it has been argued (on little secure evidence) that Columbus himself was descended from a family of Catalan conversos.[14] Several Spaniards were later to regret the expulsion of Jewish financiers in 1492, and in the seventeenth century we first meet claims by Spanish writers that the growing wealth of countries like Holland was due in great measure to the help of converso capital flowing into Amsterdam. At a later date, the mythical decline of Spain and the consequent triumph of its enemies were blamed on the international Jewish conspiracy. Among the first writers to take this line was the poet Francisco de Quevedo, who claimed that Jewish elders from all over Europe had held a meeting at Salonika, where they drew up secret plans directed against Christendom. The count duke of Olivares was accused, by Quevedo and others, of planning to invite the Jews back into Spain and so undo all the consequences of 1492.[15]

The other notable occupation of the conversos was medicine.[16] As with the financiers, their numbers and importance in this profession should not be exaggerated. The Inquisition in Logroño (Navarre) at the end of the sixteenth century found itself in need of a doctor, but could find no Old Christian with the necessary qualifications; finally it had to appoint a converso. The Inquisition in Madrid was consulted and decreed that the tribunal should keep him but give him no official status, in the hope that an Old Christian might some day be found. An equally embarrassing case occurred in Llerena, where the Inquisition in 1579 reported that for lack of Old Christian doctors the town authorities had appointed as their official doctor 'a man who was imprisoned by this Inquisition as a judaizer for three and a half years'.[17]

The crown regularly employed converso doctors. Francisco López Villalobos was court physician to both Ferdinand the Catholic and Charles V. Among other famous conversos we should mention Doctor Andrés Laguna (1499–1560), naturalist, botanist and physician, a native of Segovia and one of the great luminaries of Spanish science. The outstanding services of conversos to medicine are amply illustrated by the number of doctors who appear in the records of the Inquisition during the sixteenth and seventeenth centuries.

Following a long tradition, converso families gave many sons and daughters into the hands of the Church, to be brought up in the religious orders. Converso students were to be found in the universities of Spain, and choice benefices and episcopal sees went to them rather than to Old Christians. By the mid-sixteenth century it was maliciously reported that most of the Spanish clergy resident in Rome in search of preferment were of Jewish origin. Anti-converso publicists in the mid-fifteenth century had already suggested that New Christians were infiltrating the Church and threatening to take it over. Conversos, it was argued, had worked their way into the heart of Christian society, into the ranks of the aristocracy and the Church, and were planning to destroy it from within.

Infiltration of the aristocracy was, already in the fifteenth century, a known and accepted fact. In the wake of the anti-converso riots in Toledo in 1449, a royal secretary, Fernán Díaz de Toledo, wrote a report or *Instruction* for the bishop of Cuenca, in which he argued that all the leading noble lineages of Castile, including the Henríquez (from whom Ferdinand the Catholic descended), could trace their descent from conversos. The issue had, as we shall see,[18] considerable repercussions on Spanish society. Two sixteenth-century publications continued the controversy. In Aragon an assessor of the Inquisition of Saragossa drew up what became known as the Green Book (*Libro verde*) of Aragon,[19] a genealogical table tracing the origins of the nobility, from which it became clear that the most prominent families in the kingdom had not escaped converso infiltration. The document, set down in manuscript in the first decade of the sixteenth century, became a source of major scandal, for copies were passed from hand to hand, added to and distorted, until the government decided it could not tolerate the slander. In 1623, all available copies of the libros verdes were ordered to be burnt. But already a far more powerful libel had been circulating in secret. In 1560 Cardinal Francisco Mendoza y Bobadilla, angered by a refusal to admit two members of his family into a military order, presented to Philip II a memorandum, later to be known as *Tizón de la Nobleza de España* (Blot on the Nobility of Spain), in which he claimed to prove that virtually the whole of the nobility was of Jewish descent.[20] The proofs he offered were so incontrovertible that the Tizón was reprinted many times down to the nineteenth century, almost always as a tract against the power and influence of the nobility. At no time was even the slightest attempt at a rejoinder to these two publications made.

Questions of genealogy and blood came to the fore in politics. In an important memoir presented by the historian Lorenzo Galíndez de Carvajal to the emperor Charles V, it was reported that several of the most important members of the royal council were of converso origin. Among the exceptions, however, was Dr Palacios Rubios, 'a man of pure blood because he is of labouring descent'.[21] Purity (*limpieza*) from Jewish origins became an issue around which status struggles tended to focus.

The controversies over genealogy in the fifteenth century highlight the prominent role of converso intellectuals.[22] A handful of upper-class Jewish converts made, by the quality of their writing, a contribution to intellectual life out of all proportion to their numbers. Converso officials who wrote histories included Alvar García de Santa María (d. 1460), Diego de Valera (d. 1488), and Alonso de Palencia (d. 1492). Other conversos were well-known poets: among them were Juan de Mena (d. 1456) and Juan del Encina (d. 1529).

Several converso writers entered into the controversy over blood origins, but directed their work specifically against the Jews. Among them was Bishop Pablo de Santa María, with his *Scrutinium scripturarum*, written in 1432 but published posthumously. Another was the physician Joshua Halorqui, who adopted the name Jerónimo de Santa Fe, founded a powerful converso family and produced his anti-Jewish polemics in the form of a work called *Hebraeomastix*. A member of a third great converso family, Pedro de la Caballería, wrote in 1450 the treatise *Zelus Christi contra Judaeos*. These three converso productions, based on a solid knowledge of Jewish culture, resorted to polemic at a learned level. The anti-Jewish strain could, of course, also be found in the writings of many who were not of converso origin.

By contrast, there were polemics that were aimed at street level. The most significant of these was the *Fortalitium fidei contra Judaeos*, published in 1460, of the friar Alonso de Espina. Espina, a well-known Franciscan friar and confessor to Henry IV of Castile, used his position to stir up hatred against Jews and conversos. Though described by most historians as a converso, he was almost certainly not one.[23] The deliberate distortions and fabrications in his work betray a complete ignorance of semitic society. In the 1450s he was exceptionally busy in a campaign to bring about the forced conversion of the Jews, and his tract helped by its themes and language to contribute to race hatred. For Espina, the crimes of Jews against Christians were all too well known: they were traitors, homosexuals, blasphemers, child murderers, assassins (in the guise of doctors), poisoners, and usurers. What differentiates Espina from the converso apologists is the fact that his accusations were clearly racialist in character and purpose, whereas the anger of Santa María and the others was more explicitly directed against the stubborn unbelief of their unconverted brethren. Espina's tract has been viewed as a draft proposal which influenced the structure of the Spanish Inquisition,[24] but in reality his ideas were not new. The Spanish Holy Office, when eventually founded, was based rather on the concept of the mediaeval French Inquisition.

Though there was a generally peaceful coexistence between Old Christians and Jews during the fifteenth century, in some townships the presence of powerful converso families gave rise to struggles for power between Old Christians and conversos. Jews, normally incapacitated from office, did not feature directly. The first significant explosion of power struggles was in Toledo, ancient centre of Castilian Jewry and Castile's leading city. In 1449 there were serious disturbances here, directed in part against the minister of King Juan II, Alvaro de Luna, who was accused of favouring Jews. The Old Christian factions held court to determine whether conversos should be allowed to continue holding public office. Their leader, Pero Sarmiento, proposed a special statute (known as the *Sentencia-Estatuto*) which, despite opposition, was approved by the city council in June 1449. In this it was resolved 'that no converso of Jewish descent may have or hold any office or benefice in the said city of Toledo, or in its territory and jurisdiction', and that the testimony of conversos against Old Christians was not to be accepted in the courts.[25]

The immediate result was a bull issued by Pope Nicholas on 24 September 1449 under the significant title *Humani Generis Enemicus* (Enemy of the human race), in which he denounced the idea of excluding Christians from office simply because of their blood origins. 'We decree and declare', the pope went on, 'that all Catholics are one body in Christ according to the teaching of our faith.' Another bull of the same date excommunicated Sarmiento and his colleagues for alleged rebellion against the Spanish crown. Other Spanish ecclesiastical authorities followed the pope in declaring that baptized converts were entitled to all the privileges of the Christian community. But the Sentencia-Estatuto represented powerful forces which could not easily be suppressed. The state of civil war then reigning in Castile made the crown all too willing to win friends by conciliation, and in 1450 the pope was asked by King Juan II to suspend his excommunication of those practising racialism. A year later, on 13 August 1451, the king formally gave his approval to the Sentencia-Estatuto. This meant a victory for the Old Christian party – a victory repeated once more when, on 16 June 1468, in the year after the Toledo riots of 1467, King Henry IV confirmed in office in the city all holders of posts formerly held by conversos. The same king on 14 July of the same year conceded to the city of Ciudad Real the privilege of excluding conversos from all municipal office.[26]

In each case the conflict was purely local, reflecting faction rivalries. There had been virtually no agitation since the great riots of 1391, and little outside central Castile. In other cities where conversos were powerful, such as Burgos and Ávila, there were no riots. No immediate danger to the peace of the realm existed. The fact, however, that two Castilian cities tried to exclude conversos from public office was ominous. So was the fact that Old Christian oligarchies deliberately used antisemitic feeling to arouse the populace against their enemies. Some clergy were also worried about the effect on the unity of the Christian body. It was after some deliberation, therefore, that in about 1468 the archbishop of Toledo, Alonso Carrillo, condemned the existence in Toledo of guilds organized on racial lines, some of them excluding conversos and others excluding Old Christians. The archbishop stated:

> Divisions bring great scandal and schism and divide the seamless garment of Christ who, as the Good Shepherd, gave us a command to love one another in unity and obedience to Holy Mother Church, under one Pontiff and Vicar of Christ, under one baptism, formed under the law into one body, so that whether Jew, Greek or Gentile we are regenerated by baptism and made into new men. From which it is obvious how culpable are those who, forgetting the purity of the law of the gospel, create different lineages, some calling themselves Old Christians and others calling themselves New Christians or conversos ... What is evil is that in the city of Toledo, as in the other cities, towns and places of our see, there are many guilds and brotherhoods of which some under pretence of piety do not receive conversos and others do not receive Old Christians ...[27]

The archbishop therefore ordered the dissolution of the said guilds and forbade any similar racial associations under pain of excommunication. His good intentions bore no fruit. The split between conversos and Old Christians had grown too wide for one prelate alone to heal. By constant propaganda and petty persecution the mood of the populace had been whipped into one of fury against the conversos.

Of the thousands of Jews who in the course of the preceding century had been forced by persecution and pressure to accept baptism, few could have embraced Catholicism sincerely. Over time, however, the converts settled into their new religion without problems. When the great controversies broke out in Toledo, half a century after the 1391 riots, not a single Christian writer doubted that the New Christians were for the most part orthodox in belief and intention. Claims to the contrary were made at the height of the civic troubles, but never substantiated.

For a quarter of a century after the Sentencia-Estatuto, controversy died down and little evidence emerged of heresy among the conversos. The issue raised its head again in the next round of anti-converso struggles. The triggers to conflict were never exclusively religious. Disturbances were also aggravated, during the later years of the fifteenth century, by more frequent economic difficulties. In 1463 a converso in Andalusia commented that 'here, thank God, there are disturbances but not directed against us'.[28] There were problems, however, in other parts of Spain, and in 1467 anti-converso riots occurred in Toledo and Ciudad Real. In Seville the aristocracy kept the trouble-makers under control, and (reported an official) 'the conversos were unharmed'.[29] Burgos, which also suffered, had been having tension for a decade. The worst incidents came in 1473, with anti-converso riots and massacres in several towns of Andalusia, notably Córdoba.[30] In Jaén that year one of the victims was the converso Constable of Castile, Miguel Lucas de Iranzo, cut down at the high altar of the cathedral as he attempted to defend the conversos. These events demonstrated the very serious political situation in the south of the peninsula, and how readily the finger was being pointed at New Christians. In many cases, it has been argued, it was the Old Christian oligarchies who were manipulating the situation against both conversos and Jews.[31]

It was the political events of those years, rather than any perceived heresy, that eventually brought an Inquisition into existence. The stage upon which the drama was played was central and southern Spain, roughly defined by the realms of Old and New Castile, and Andalusia. This area, still the effective frontier of the anti-Muslim Reconquest, was also that in which the majority of Spain's Jews lived. Home still to the precarious coexistence of three faiths, it was potentially the zone of greatest social conflict in the peninsula.

*

The ambiguous religion of conversos raised a crucial question. Were the conversos Jews? The issue was first broached seriously after the mass conversions of 1391. Those who remained in their Jewish faith wanted to know how to coexist with the converts. In the fifteenth century, long before the great expulsion, the rabbis in north Africa were frequently asked for their judgments on the matter. Their opinions, or *responsa*, were unequivocal. The conversos must be regarded not as unwilling converts (anusim) but as real and voluntary converts (meshumadim).[32] There was ample evidence to back up the judgments. In many parts of Spain the conversos continued living in some measure as Jews, but with the advantage now of enjoying rights accorded to Christians. In Mallorca, a rabbi commented, the authorities 'are lenient with the conversos and allow them to do as they will'.[33] The conversos here were virtually practising Jews, from the Christian point of view. Enjoying official tolerance, they remained as Christians. And it was their voluntary Christianity which marked them out in Jewish eyes as renegades, meshumadim.

The spate of conversions throughout Spain during the fifteenth century intensified the controversy. Easy-going Jews who converted for convenience became, naturally, easy-going Christians. In an anti-Jewish polemic of the 1480s, the *Alborayco*,[34] the author described the conversos as being neither practising Jews nor practising Christians. Being neither one thing nor the other, they were known in some places as *alboraycos*, after the fabled animal of Mohammed which was neither horse nor mule (*al-buraq*). Antisemitic writers at the time of the Inquisition were, for their part, unanimous that conversos were secret Jews and must be purified ruthlessly.

Many modern writers, in no way antisemitic, have consistently identified the conversos as Jews. An influential school in modern Jewish historiography has likewise ironically insisted that the Inquisition was right, and that all conversos were aspiring Jews. Yitzhak Baer states uncompromisingly that 'the conversos and Jews were one people, united by destiny'.[35] 'Every converso', writes another historian, 'did his best to fulfil Mosaic precepts, and one should regard as sincere the aim they *all* set themselves: to live as Jews'.[36] The main evidence used by those who call in doubt the Christianity of the conversos, is the documentation of the Holy Office, a huge mass of often unsolicited and damning testimony to the errors of thousands of conversos. If this view is accepted, not only does it appear to justify the establishment of the Inquisition but it also contradicts the testimony of many conversos of the late fifteenth century.

The true religious status of the conversos before 1492 is therefore a question of primary importance.[37] There are three principal groups of witnesses: the Jews, the conversos themselves, and the enemies of the conversos.

Among the Jews there appear to have been no doubts about the Christianity of the conversos. The opinions of religious leaders, cited above, are unequivocal. Jews and conversos might come together for family and social reunions, but always with the consciousness that they belonged to different streams of belief and practice. The most convincing testimony of all can be found after the founding of the Inquisition. The failure of Jews, in those years, to make any significant move to help conversos, shows that they were conscious of the gap between them.

The converso apologists of 1449, anxious to defend themselves against their critics, insisted on their own unquestionable Christianity. Fernán Díaz insisted that if there were any judaizers in Toledo they could be counted on the fingers of two hands. He pointed out that even the term 'converts' was meaningless: 'how can one call *conversos* those who are children and grandchildren of Christians, were born in Christianity and know nothing about Judaism or its rites?'[38] Later converso leaders, more realistically, were willing to admit the existence of religious confusion. The chronicler and royal secretary Hernando del Pulgar, himself a prominent converso, vouched for the existence of judaizers among the New Christians of Toledo. But he also pinpointed a cause: no attempts had ever been made to deal with the problem by missionary preaching rather than persecution. Despised by Old Christians for their race, scorned by the Jews for their apostasy, the conversos lived in a social atmosphere they had never willingly chosen. Many of them lived close to the Jewish quarter, to which they still felt a cultural affinity. They retained traditional characteristics in dress and food that were difficult to shake off. Several had vivid memories of the persecutions that in the 1440s and then in the 1470s had forced them to abandon their original culture. A Jewish doctor in Soria in 1491 recalled an old converso who 'told him, weeping, how much he repented having turned Christian'. Speaking of another converso, the doctor said that 'he believed in neither the Christian nor the Jewish faith'.[39]

Pulgar reports that within the same converso household some members might be sincere Christians and others active Jews. His experience was that many 'lived neither in one law nor the other', retaining key Jewish customs while practising formal Christianity. None of this altered the essentially Christian culture of most conversos. The syncretic nature of much of their religious practice left their faith unaffected. Like the Malabar and Chinese Christians of later centuries, who combined aspects of hereditary culture with their faith, they were believing Christians and proud of it. The converso family of the bishop of Segovia, Diego Arias Dávila (1436–97), is a case in point. His still-Jewish sister lived in the household. Members of the family attended weddings in the Jewish quarter, and occasionally gave gifts to the synagogue.[40]

Those among the Christians who criticized the conversos were their enemies. From the anti-Jewish propaganda of the 1440s to the polemics of half a century later, their anti-converso theme was constant. All conversos, went the refrain, are secret Jews. All of them are a threat to our society and our religion. It was alleged that they continued to practise the Jewish rites both secretly and openly, presenting the authorities with a large minority of pseudo-Christians who had neither respect nor love for their new faith.

Was there in reality a 'converso danger'? Were thousands of converso Christians all over Spain secretly observing Jewish practice? There is, as we shall see, good reason to doubt it.[41]

Writing several years later, when so much blood had been spilt that it would have been intolerable to deny the justice of what had happened, the anti-Jewish chronicler Bernáldez declared unhesitatingly that the conversos were secret heretics. Throughout the provinces of the south, according to the author of the *Alborayco*, of all the conversos 'hardly any are true Christians, as is well known in all Spain'.[42] Written a decade after the birth of the Inquisition, it was a clear case of *post hoc ergo propter hoc*. By contrast, ten years previously the hard evidence for the claim would have been difficult to find. Prosecutions of judaizers in the bishops' courts were to be counted on the fingers of one hand. What, in any case, did 'judaizing' imply? Even when the inquisitors started their work, they had no clear view of the offence. The basic ignorance of Jewish law shown by the inquisitors meant that by default they accused people of offences which were cultural rather than religious. When in 1484 Inés de Belmonte admitted that she had habitually observed Saturday as a day of rest, she was condemned as a heretic, apostate and observer of the Jewish law, even though no evidence existed that she subscribed to any Jewish beliefs.[43] With time, the inquisitors defined the offence more clearly; but in doing so they were in effect bringing a crime into existence. People were consequently accused for what they were supposed to have done, rather than for what they really did. 'I know very well of others who have erred much more than I', complained a woman of Cuenca in 1489 who felt that her offence was negligible.[44]

There was another important aspect to the problem. New Christians who shared day-to-day doubts and unbeliefs were treated as heretics, whereas the very same doubts could be found everywhere among the non-semitic Christian population. Popular scepticism about an after-life persisted among Spain's population. 'There is only birth and death, nothing more', 'you'll not see me do badly in this life nor will you see me suffer in the next',[45] were affirmations, however, that in the mouth of conversos seemed to the inquisitors in the 1480s to be particularly suspicious. Blasphemies against Christ, the Virgin and the mass were (as the inquisitors knew very well) commonplace among Old Christians.[46] Yet in the anti-converso trials they carried a mortally heavy assumption of guilt. For a converso to say: 'I swear to God it's all a joke, from the pope to the cope'; or to suggest that 'I can't swallow the words of the holy gospels'[47] invited denunciation, even though they were sentiments that could be found anywhere in the Old Christian countryside. It was thanks in part to her advocate arguing that 'to say such things does not necessarily imply unbelief in the faith', that Catalina de Zamora, who had insulted the Virgin publicly, was in 1484 acquitted of judaizing.[48] Ignorant witnesses contributed to the confusion of criteria: in 1492 not knowing the creed, or eating meat in Lent, were seen as signs of Judaism.[49] Anyone who did not conform to the rest of the community was looked upon as a 'Jew'. Manuel Rodríguez, alchemist of Soria in the 1470s, treated official religion with disdain but was described by the parish priest as 'among the most learned men in the world in just about everything'. Common repute consequently (according to the testimony of an official) held him to be a 'Jew'.[50]

We may conclude that there was not, in the late 1470s, any proven or significant judaizing movement among the conversos. Nor is there any evidence to explain why such a movement should arise in the late fifteenth century.

However, even if there was little active judaizing, those who influenced crown policy thought they *perceived* it. They observed what certainly existed in many households: vestigial Jewish practices in matters of family habits and cuisine, residual Jewish culture in vocabulary, kinship links between Jews and conversos. These remnants were identifiably Jewish. They were not, however – and on this all those arrested by the Inquisition were agreed – evidence of judaizing. The 'converso danger', it can be argued on this evidence, was invented to justify spoliation of conversos. The harvest of heretics reaped by the early Inquisition owed its success to deliberate falsification or to the completely indiscriminate way in which residual Jewish customs were interpreted as being heretical. Though it can certainly be identified in the period after the forced conversions of 1492, there was no systematic 'converso religion' in the 1480s to justify the creation of an Inquisition.[51] Much of the evidence for judaizing was thin, if not false. In 1484 in Ciudad Real five witnesses were used by the prosecution against a converso. Four of them testified to events they claimed to remember from twelve, thirty-five and forty years before.[52] One may reasonably doubt whether the accused was an active judaizer.

Logically, conversos never ceased to protest that false witness and greed were the driving forces of the Inquisition. Wherever possible, they attempted to clamp down on the voices alleging that there was heresy. In Aragon in 1484 the authorities, favourably disposed to the conversos, claimed that there was no heresy anywhere in the realm. In Segovia in 1485 a group of conversos went 'threatening anyone who said anything about there being heretics in this city'.[53] 'Most of those burnt by the Inquisition', a converso of Aranda said in 1501, 'were burnt because of false witness'. 'There's no reason for them to come here', another said, with reference to the inquisitors, 'there are no heretics to burn'. 'Very many of those arrested and burnt by the reverend fathers were arrested and burnt only because of their property'. 'Of all those burnt in Aranda', a resident stated in 1502, 'not one was a heretic'.[54] The outright denial that there was any heresy was not necessarily an attempt to cover up by those who were guilty. The claim may have been, and shows every sign of having been, true.

The differing opinions among scholars in our day are testimony to the highly confusing nature of converso culture. The most plausible view of the matter is probably that held by very many at the time, namely that all were practising Christians, but that some were sympathetic to Judaism. Simply to be of Jewish origin did not mean that one shared Jewish beliefs. The Consellers (city councillors) of Barcelona expressed this opinion forcefully to their new inquisitor in 1486: 'We do not believe that all the conversos are heretics, or that to be a converso makes one a heretic'.[55] A prosecution witness in Toledo in 1483, by contrast, expressed a view that was more congenial to the inquisitors: 'all the conversos of this city were Jews'.[56] The 'all', commonplace in antisemitic polemic of the time and in writers like Andrés Bernáldez, was the big lie that justified the Inquisition.[57]

A factor that undoubtedly contributed to tension, over and above anti-converso feeling, was the conversos' own sense of a separate identity.[58] Already a powerful minority by the mid-fifteenth century, conversos were secure of their social position and proud to be both Christian and of Jewish descent. They did not, as is sometimes thought, attempt to disguise their origins. They were, as many of their own writers affirmed clearly, a *nation*. They had their own identity, and took pride in it. Andrés Bernáldez reported that 'they entertained the arrogant claim that there was no better people in the world than they'. Alonso de Palencia reported complaints by Old Christians that the conversos acted 'as a nation apart, and nowhere would they agree to act together with the Old Christians; indeed, as though they were a people of totally opposed ideas, they openly and brazenly favoured whatever was contrary to the Old Christians, as could be seen by the bitter fruit sown throughout the cities of the realm'. Implicit in the converso attitude was the claim that they were even *better* than Old Christians, because together with Christian faith they combined direct descent from the lineage (*linaje*) of Christ. It was said that Alonso de Cartagena when he recited the Hail Mary used to end with the words, 'Holy Mary, Mother of God and my blood-relative, pray for us'. Converso nobles were considered to be even better than Old Christian nobles, because they were of Jewish origin. 'Is there another nation so noble [as the Jews]?' asked Diego de Valera, quoting the Bible directly.

Converso separateness had a certain logic. The large number of converts after 1391 could not be easily fitted into existing social structures. In Barcelona and Valencia in the 1390s they were given their own churches, in each case a former synagogue. They also set up their own converso confraternities.[59] In the crown of Aragon they called themselves proudly 'Christians of Israel'.[60] They had their own social life and intermarried among themselves. Palencia observed that they were 'puffed-up, insolent and arrogant'; Bernáldez criticized their 'haughty ostentation of great wealth and pride'.[61]

These converso attitudes were probably created by self-defensiveness rather than arrogance. But they contributed to the wall of distrust between Old and New Christians. In particular, the idea of a converso *nation*, which rooted itself irrevocably in the mind of Jewish Christians, made them appear as a separate, alien and enemy entity. This had fateful consequences.

*

The Inquisition was not unknown in Spain. Since 1232 papal commissions for inquisitors had been issued in the crown of Aragon, as part of the campaign against Catharism then being conducted in Languedoc.[62] This was the period when the Church for the first time began to take a serious view of heresy. Catalans such as the Dominicans Ramon Penyafort in the thirteenth and Nicolau Eimeric in the fourteenth century were active in the tribunal. They gave it a distinct anti-Jewish tendency though it did not actually prosecute Jews.

By the fifteenth century, the papal Inquisition in the Aragonese territories had lapsed into virtual inactivity. Only a handful of trials took place at the end of the century.[63] Castile, on the other hand, had never known the existence of an Inquisition. The bishops and their Church courts had so far sufficed to deal with the punishment of heretics. The unusual nature of the converso question, however, led to demands for a special 'inquisition' well before the reign of Ferdinand and Isabella. In 1461 a group of Franciscans led by Alonso de Espina approached the general of the Jeronimite order with a view to 'setting up in this realm an inquisition into heretics such as they have in France'.[64] The general, Alonso de Oropesa, supported the move warmly, and Henry IV appealed to Rome for an Inquisition to be set up.[65] Nothing more was heard of the proposal. Another attempt was made by Oropesa some time later, in 1465. But it was an inopportune moment, for Henry IV was faced by a serious rebellion that very year. Riots against the conversos broke out shortly after, notably in Toledo in 1467 and Segovia in 1473.

Meanwhile, the discovery (and immediate burning) at Llerena in September 1467 of two conversos for practising Judaism seemed to confirm the religious insincerity of New Christians. Preachers made the most of such cases. Among them was Alonso de Hojeda, a Dominican prior of Seville, who devoted all his energies to making the crown aware of the reality of the danger from Jews and false converts.[66] In 1474 Isabella succeeded her brother Henry on the throne. Hojeda's opportunity came when the queen visited Seville in July 1477 and stayed until October 1478. Historians are unanimous in citing Hojeda's preaching as one of the immediate influences on the queen in her final decision about the conversos. Soon after Isabella's departure from Seville, Hojeda claimed to have uncovered evidence of a secret meeting of judaizing conversos in the city. With this in hand he went to demand the institution of measures against the heretics.

The evidence seems to have impressed the government, which asked for information on the situation in Seville. The report, supported by the authority of Pedro González de Mendoza, archbishop of Seville, and that of Tomás de Torquemada, prior of a Dominican friary in Segovia, suggested that not only in Seville but throughout Andalusia and Castile the conversos were practising Jewish rites in secret. Accepting this testimony, Ferdinand and Isabella consented to introduce the machinery of an Inquisition into Castile, and sent a request to Rome for the bull of institution.

The controversy over the conversos broke out at a time when the monarchs were fully occupied in the pacification of a realm laid waste by the turmoil of civil war. They were threatened on all sides by continuing conflicts at local level, threats by dissident nobles and clergy, and a breakdown of law and order everywhere. With no civil service or permanent army at their command, they were unable to control events in the way they might have wished, and were obliged to make compromises with the political elites that ran the country. From 1476 onwards they encouraged the creation of local police forces known as the Hermandad. At the same time they attempted, through the civil governors (*corregidores*), to enforce the peace, punish and execute criminals and thieves, and in general restore public confidence in the crown.[67] In the midst of these measures of 'pacification', which inevitably had a high cost in lives, they were drawn from 1482 onwards into a long and expensive war against the Muslim kingdom of Granada.

The converso problem, when brought to the queen's attention during her stay in Seville, may at the time have seemed a small matter of detail in the midst of her other commitments. The request for an Inquisition was, likewise, not unusual. Royal officials had for some time now been authorized to make general 'inquisitions' into crimes and offences, and it was part of the pacification policy to make 'inquisitions' into the activities of known or unknown delinquents.[68] When the crown sanctioned an inquisition into the activities of alleged judaizers, it was a more or less routine measure. In the event, it soon turned into something much more serious, because it implicated converso urban elites who till that date had supported the crown without question.

According to Hojeda and others, the converso problem was so grave that only the introduction of a full-time 'inquisition' would be adequate. Consequently, the bull which was finally issued by Pope Sixtus IV on 1 November 1478 provided for the appointment of two or three priests over forty years of age as inquisitors. Powers of appointment and dismissal were granted to the Spanish crown.[69] After this, no further steps were taken for two years. This long interlude would seem to contradict Hojeda's argument about the urgency of the converso danger. What seems a likely explanation is that the crown favoured a cautious period of leniency before going on to severe measures, and that this policy may have been influenced in part by the large number of conversos in prominent positions at court. Finally, Ferdinand grew convinced of the need. As he explained several years later: 'We could do no less, because we were told so many things about Andalusia'.[70] On 27 September 1480, at Medina del Campo commissions as inquisitors in accordance with the papal bull were issued to the Dominicans Juan de San Martín and Miguel de Morillo, with Juan Ruiz de Medina as their assessor or adviser. With these appointments the Spanish Inquisition came into definitive existence.

The new body had clearly been set up as the result of agitation against the New Christians. This fact alone does not suffice to answer some fundamental questions.

Of these, the most crucial is: on what evidence did the tribunal justify its existence? Historians have tended to accept without question the reason given by the Inquisition, namely that the conversos were judaizing. The fact is that apart from a handful of scattered cases there was no systematic evidence of judaizing. New Christian writers in mid-century had firmly denied such accusations. Zealots such as Espina could point only to unsubstantiated rumours and allegations. Nowhere in Spain, outside of the handful of cities in the south where political riots had taken place, was there pressure for an enquiry. The book of the *Alborayco*, written in these years, expressly claimed that, unlike the south of the country, there were virtually no heretics among conversos in northern Spain.[71] If the Inquisition claimed to have religious motives, those motives were difficult to justify by the evidence.

What did the monarchs hope to gain by its foundation? There is much to be said for the argument that the crown, in the person above all of Ferdinand, who was the guiding force in its establishment and who continued his efforts after the death of Isabella, wished to use it to consolidate his power. Further definition of Ferdinand's intentions is, however, difficult to arrive at and will long be the subject of dispute. The purity of his religious motives may be questioned. He and Isabella may have been zealous Catholics, but they were by no means anti-Jewish or even anti-converso. It may also be doubted whether Ferdinand thought that the work of the Inquisition would augment his revenues. Nor is it possible to document the view that Ferdinand was hoping to consolidate his power by directing opposition against the converso elite in Spain.[72]

Was there a long-term strategy, or was the tribunal intended to be purely local and temporary? Neither the crown nor the early supporters of the Inquisition looked, around 1480, much further than the frontiers of Andalusia. The immediate purpose was to ensure religious orthodoxy there. For the first five years of its existence the tribunal in Castile limited its activity only to the south, particularly to the sees of Seville and Córdoba. It was the area where the social conflicts of the preceding century had concentrated. There was, as yet, no thought of a nation-wide Inquisition.

By mid-October 1480, operations had begun in Seville. In Andalusia, as in the rest of Castile, these had been years of political conflict. The appearance of the inquisitors was made possible because Isabella's supporters in the civil wars imposed their authority on the local elite. The opposition, many of them conversos and supporters of rebel nobles, were pushed out. This background affected events in Seville. One of the city councillors there was the converso Diego de Susán – father to Susanna, famous as the *fermosa fembra* (the 'beautiful maiden') – who was connected with a group of merchants and political figures opposed to Isabella's supporters.[73] A subsequent local chronicler put together a largely fictitious narrative in which Susán was presented as the centre of a plot to stage a rising against the Inquisition. According to this account, he called a meeting of Seville dignitaries and of

> many other rich and powerful men from the towns of Utrera and Carmona. These said to one another, 'What do you think of them acting thus against us? Are we not the most propertied members of this city, and well loved by the people? Let us collect men together ...' And thus between them they allotted the raising of arms, men, money and other necessities. 'And if they come to take us, we, together with armed men and the people will rise up and slay them and so be revenged on our enemies'.[74]

The narrative goes on to say that the rising might well have succeeded but for the *fermosa fembra* who, anxious about the possible fate of her Old Christian lover, betrayed the plot to the authorities. All those implicated were arrested and the occasion was made the excuse for detaining the richest and most powerful conversos of Seville. According to Bernáldez:

> A few days after this they burnt three of the richest leaders of the city, namely Diego de Susán, who was said to be worth ten million maravedis

and was a chief rabbi, and who apparently died as a Christian; Manuel Sauli; and Bartolomé de Torralva. They also arrested Pedro Fernández Benadeba, who was one of the ringleaders and had in his house weapons to arm a hundred men, and Juan Fernández Abolafia, who had often been chief magistrate and was a great lawyer; and many other leading and very rich citizens, who were also burnt.[75]

When Susanna saw the result of her betrayal, she is said to have first retired to a convent, and then to have taken to the streets, remorse eating into her soul until she died in poverty and shame, her last wishes being that her skull should be placed over the door of her house as a warning and example to others. The whole story about the plot and betrayal was in reality a myth: Susán had died before 1479, the plot is undocumented, and there was no daughter Susanna.[76]

The first *auto de fe* of the Spanish Inquisition was celebrated on 6 February 1481, when six people were burnt at the stake and the sermon at the ceremony was preached by Fray Alonso de Hojeda. Hojeda's triumph was short-lived, for within a few days the plague which was just beginning to ravage Seville numbered him among its first victims.

There was as yet little, in the spring of 1481, to cause alarm among conversos. No more than a handful of people had been executed. Many, however, did not trust the motives or the mercy of the inquisitors. They may or may not have been judaizers; in any case, they preferred to absent themselves. Over the next few months throughout Andalusia, according to the chronicler Hernando del Pulgar, thousands of households took flight, women and children included:

> and since the absence of these people depopulated a large part of the country, the queen was informed that commerce was declining; but setting little importance on the decline in her revenue, and prizing highly the *limpieza* [purity] of her lands, she said that the essential thing was to cleanse the country of that sin of heresy, for she understood it to be in God's service and her own. And the representations which were made to her about this matter did not alter her decision.[77]

The scale of operations created an enormous amount of work. More inquisitors were obviously needed. Accordingly, a papal brief of 11 February 1482 appointed seven more, all Dominican friars. One of them was the prior of the friary of Santa Cruz in Segovia, Tomás de Torquemada. New tribunals were set up at Córdoba in 1482, and at Ciudad Real and

Jaén in 1483. The tribunal at Ciudad Real was only temporary, and was permanently transferred to Toledo in 1485. By 1492 the kingdom of Castile had tribunals at Ávila, Córdoba, Jaén, Medina del Campo, Segovia, Sigüenza, Toledo and Valladolid. Not all these had a permanent existence, and the southern tribunals were far more active than those in the north.

The story of a plot in Seville looks suspiciously like an attempt to find good reasons for a subsequent repression. Doubts may similarly be expressed about the plot that took place in Toledo, apparently planned for the feast of Corpus Christi 1485. The outcome, say the sources, followed the pattern of Seville, with betrayal, arrest and execution. All the relevant circumstances, however, suggest that the plot was spurious, an invented story embroidered upon by subsequent commentators.[78]

The machinery of the Inquisition was regulated in accordance with the needs of the administration. Isabella was at this time engaged in reforming the organs that controlled central government in Castile. When in 1480 at the Cortes of Toledo it was decided to reform the governing councils, it seemed natural to follow this up with a separate council for the increasingly important affairs of the Inquisition. A few years later, in 1488, this new council (known as the *Suprema* for short) came into existence.[79] It consisted initially of three ecclesiastical members, and a fourth member as president of the council, with the title of Inquisitor General. The first Inquisitor General was Fray Tomás de Torquemada. The problem now was whether the Castilian Inquisition should be extended to the kingdom of Aragon.

Resistance to the introduction of the Inquisition into Castile had been meagre and abortive. Popular opinion had been prepared for it and community rivalry welcomed it. The only serious setback to royal policy occurred on 29 January 1482 when Pope Sixtus IV, responding to protests from Spanish clergy about abuses committed by the inquisitors of Seville, revoked the powers granted by the bull of foundation and allowed the Seville inquisitors to continue only if subjected to their bishop. The appointment of seven new inquisitors on 11 February 1482, far from being a surrender by the pope to the king, was accompanied by firm gestures by the pontiff in favour of the conversos. Ferdinand in May 1482 protested bitterly to Rome, particularly since a further conflict had now arisen over the Inquisition of Aragon.

As part of his vigorous new policy, Ferdinand took steps in 1481 and 1482 to assert royal control over the appointment and payment of inquisitors in Aragon. His aim was to resurrect the old papal Inquisition but also to subject it to his own control so as to come into line with practice in Castile. In Aragon, therefore, the new Inquisition was simply a continuance of the old tribunal, with the difference that the crown now controlled appointments and salaries, so that the tribunal became effectively more dependent on Ferdinand than on the pope.

The first activities of this reformed tribunal, with its main centres in the cities of Barcelona, Saragossa and Valencia, were directed against the conversos, who took alarm at developments and prepared for mass emigration. But differences with the pope, supplemented no doubt by pressure on Rome from conversos, brought activities to a temporary stop. On 18 April 1482 Sixtus IV issued what the historian Henry Charles Lea calls 'the most extraordinary bull in the history of the Inquisition'. In this bull the pope protested

> that in Aragon, Valencia, Mallorca and Catalonia the Inquisition has for some time been moved not by zeal for the faith and the salvation of souls, but by lust for wealth, and that many true and faithful Christians, on the testimony of enemies, rivals, slaves and other lower and even less proper persons, have without any legitimate proof been thrust into secular prisons, tortured and condemned as relapsed heretics, deprived of their goods and property and handed over to the secular arm to be executed, to the peril of souls, setting a pernicious example, and causing disgust to many.[80]

Accordingly, in future all episcopal officers should act with the inquisitors; the names and testimony of accusers should be given to the accused, who should be allowed counsel; episcopal gaols should be the only ones used; and appeals should be allowed to Rome. The bull was extraordinary because, in Lea's words, 'for the first time heresy was declared to be, like any other crime, entitled to a fair trial and simple justice'.[81] Besides, there is little doubt that the pope welcomed the chance to assert once more his authority over an Inquisition that had once been papal and had now slipped entirely into the hands of the king of Aragon. So favourable was the bull to converso claims that their influence in obtaining it cannot be doubted. Ferdinand was outraged by the papal action and pretended to disbelieve in the authenticity of the bull on the grounds that no sensible pontiff would have issued such a document. On 13 May 1482 he wrote to the pope:

> Things have been told me, Holy Father which, if true, would seem to merit the greatest astonishment. It is said that Your Holiness has granted the

conversos a general pardon for all the errors and offences they have committed
. . . To these rumours, however, we have given no credence because they seem
to be things which would in no way have been conceded by Your Holiness,
who have a duty to the Inquisition. But if by chance concessions have been
made through the persistent and cunning persuasion of the said conversos,
I intend never to let them take effect. Take care therefore not to let the
matter go further, and to revoke any concessions and entrust us with the care
of this question.[82]

Before this resolution, Sixtus IV wavered, and in October announced
that he had suspended the bull. The way lay completely open to Ferdinand.
Papal cooperation was definitively secured by the bull of 17 October 1483,
which appointed Torquemada as Inquisitor General of Aragon, Valencia
and Catalonia, thus uniting the Inquisitions of the Spanish crown under a
single head. The new tribunal came directly under the control of the crown
and was the only institution whose authority ran in all the territories of
Spain, a fact of great importance for future occasions when the ruler of
Castile wished to interfere in other provinces where his sovereign authority
was limited. This was not the end of papal interference. The next half-
century or so witnessed several attempts by Rome to interfere in questions
of jurisdiction and to reform abuses that might give the Inquisition a bad
name. Besides this, the conversos in Spain never gave up their struggle to
modify the practices of the tribunal, which they rightly considered a threat
not just to judaizers, but to the whole body of New Christians. Because of
their representations to Rome, papal intervention was continued on their
behalf, leading to several minor quarrels between crown and papacy.

Within the crown of Aragon there was bitter opposition to the introduction of the Castilian tribunal. Though Castile and Aragon had been
joined by the marriage of the Catholic monarchs, they remained politically
separate and each kingdom preserved its individual administration and
liberties. In the eastern realms the *fueros* (laws) vested supreme authority
less in the king alone, as was the case in Castile, than in the king acting
together with the Cortes. When the latter was not in session its standing
committee, the Diputación of each realm, watched over the laws. The
resurrection of the old papal Inquisition posed a threat to the conversos
but was no innovation and aroused little criticism. It was a different matter
when Castilian inquisitors were appointed to realms where the fueros
stipulated that senior officials must be native-born. The converso elite
found that they had a constitutional argument to support their hostility.

In the kingdom of Aragon, converso families had long played a prominent role in politics and finance. Regardless of inevitable opposition, on 4
May 1484 Torquemada appointed the first two inquisitors for Aragon,
Gaspar Juglar and Pedro Arbués de Epila. According to Lea, the inquisitors
set to work immediately, holding autos de fe on 10 May and 3 June 1484.
These dates, however, are not only excessively early, they also sin against
the inquisitorial rule which allowed a term of grace, usually about a month,
to elapse before taking action against heretics. It is therefore more likely
that the autos in question were held in 1485. This activity of the new
tribunal deeply disturbed not only conversos but all those whose loyalty
was to the fueros of Aragon. As the chronicler of Aragon, Jerónimo de
Zurita, reported:

> Those newly converted from the Jewish race, and many other leaders and
> gentry, claimed that the procedure was against the liberties of the realm,
> because for this offence [of heresy] their goods were confiscated and they
> were not given the names of witnesses who testified against them.

As a result (continued Zurita) the conversos had all the kingdom on
their side, 'including persons of the highest consideration, among them
Old Christians and gentry'.[83]

When public opposition grew so great that there was a move to summon
the four estates of the realm, Ferdinand hastily sent a circular letter to the
chief nobles and deputies, justifying his position:

> There is no intention of infringing the fueros but rather of enforcing their
> observance. It is not to be imagined that vassals so Catholic as those of
> Aragon would have demanded, or that kings so Catholic would have granted,
> fueros and liberties adverse to the faith and favourable to heresy. If the old
> inquisitors had acted conscientiously in accordance with the canons there
> would have been no cause for bringing in the new ones, but they were
> without conscience and corrupted with bribes.
>
> If there are so few heretics as is now asserted, there should not be such
> dread of the Inquisition. It is not to be impeded in sequestrating and
> confiscating and other necessary acts, for be assured that no cause or interest,
> however great, shall be allowed to interfere with its proceeding in future as
> it is now doing.[84]

Whatever the motives, whether personal dread or constitutional opposition, resistance continued. The most remarkable case of resistance in the
whole of Spain occurred in 1484 at the city of Teruel, a hundred miles to

the south of Saragossa.[85] In that year the tribunal of Saragossa sent two inquisitors to the city to establish the tribunal, but the magistrates refused them permission to enter. The inquisitors thereupon withdrew to the neighbouring town of Cella, from which they issued an excommunication and interdict against the city and its magistrates. The clergy of Teruel promptly obtained papal letters releasing the city from these censures. The city wrote to the king protesting that 'they were coming to set up an Inquisition that will repeat the excesses committed in Castile'. The Inquisition then decreed in October 1484 that all the public offices in Teruel were confiscated to the crown and their present holders deprived of them. This was followed by an appeal to the king to carry out the decree. It was now the turn of the representatives of Aragon to protest to the king that 'this is a kingdom of Christians', that there were no heretics in the realm, and that heretics in any case should be approached 'with warnings and persuasion', not force.[86] Ferdinand replied with an order in February 1485 to all his officials in Aragon, asking them to raise arms and help the inquisitors. The response to this was not adequate, so Ferdinand also called on troops from the borders of Castile to help in the enterprise. Faced with such massive coercion the city was easily reduced to obedience. With its submission in the spring of 1485 the Inquisition seemed to have triumphed everywhere in Aragon. Teruel's resistance did not arise exclusively from the great influence exercised there by conversos. The city was head of the only region of Aragon with autonomous laws.[87] Both it and Saragossa had to be brought to heel if the new Holy Office were to survive.

Although the mediaeval Inquisition was moribund in Catalonia, the city of Barcelona had in 1461 received papal approval to have its own local inquisitor, Joan Comes. The Catalans therefore saw no need for a new tribunal. When the Cortes of the crown of Aragon met at Tarazona in April 1484, Catalonia refused to send deputies to approve the new Inquisition. In May Torquemada took the step of nominating two new inquisitors for Catalonia and at the same time revoked the commission held by Comes. The Catalans exploded into anger. The appointment of the new inquisitors, they wrote to Ferdinand, was 'against the liberties, constitutions and agreements solemnly sworn by Your Majesty'. In Barcelona both legal and Church authorities ruled that Comes was the only rightful inquisitor of the city.[88] In reply, Ferdinand affirmed that 'no cause nor interest, however great, will make us suspend the Inquisition'.

The conflict dragged on, and conversos began to emigrate in large numbers from the city. Fearing for the economic life of Barcelona, the Consellers complained to Ferdinand in December 1485 of the 'losses and disorder caused in this land by the Inquisition that Your Highness wishes to introduce ... The few remaining merchants have ceased to trade ... Foreign realms are growing rich and glorious through the depopulation of this country.' In May 1486, they warned Ferdinand that the city would be 'totally depopulated and ruined if the Inquisition were introduced'. The protests were in vain. In February 1486 Pope Innocent VIII found a way out of the dilemma by sacking all the existing papal inquisitors in the crown of Aragon and securing the simultaneous withdrawal of the Castilian nominees. The initiative was handed back to Torquemada, who appointed a new inquisitor for Catalonia, Alonso de Espina, a Dominican prior from Castile. Not until June 1487 did Espina succeed in entering the city, but his entry was boycotted by the Diputació and the Consellers. Ferdinand therefore warned the city 'to remember the example of Teruel, which was ruined because it did not obey the Inquisition'.[89] The Consellers protested in their turn that the inquisitors were acting 'against the laws, practice, customs and liberties of this city'. The Holy Office was now firmly implanted, but little fruit remained for it to pluck. Throughout 1488 it burnt only seven victims, and in 1489 only three. There was never any doubt as to whom the Inquisition was directed against. Of 1,199 people it tried in Catalonia between 1488 and 1505 – most in their absence since they had fled – all but eight were conversos.[90] Among the distinguished refugees was Antoni de Bardaxi, regent of the *Chancillería*, whose task it had been to give legal approval to the establishment of the Holy Office.

In Valencia, opposition was based similarly on the fueros. There were two existing inquisitors with papal commissions, the Dominicans Juan Cristóbal de Gualbes and Juan Orts, who from 1481 represented the revived mediaeval tribunal, but they seem to have done little. In March 1484 they were removed and Torquemada nominated, as representatives of the new Inquisition, the Aragonese Juan de Epila and the Valencian Martín Iñigo. Since the Cortes of Tarazona in 1484 had approved the new Inquisition, the nominee should have had no problems in Valencia. From July to October, however, the three estates of the Valencian Cortes kept up a stream of protests, asking 'not that the Inquisition be suspended but that it be in the hands of natives of this realm';[91] and detailing other requests, such as an end to secret testimony. Opposition crumbled before the obduracy of Ferdinand, who recalled that no protest had been made by the Valencians at Tarazona, and that the fueros must never be used to shield

heresy. Even after the inquisitors began work in November 1484, opposition continued and the king was obliged to alternate threats with arguments. 'If there are so few heretics in the realm', his representatives
commented acridly, 'one wonders why people should be afraid of the
Inquisition.'[92]

Converso opposition had by no means been destroyed. On the one hand it
was growing in strength with the passive support of Old Christians who
resented the introduction of the new tribunal into Aragon, and on the
other it was becoming more desperate because of the obvious failure of
resistance as shown by the example of Teruel. In the highest converso
circles the idea of the assassination of an inquisitor gained currency. It was
also supported by some Old Christians, and by conversos as eminent as
Gabriel Sánchez, treasurer of the king, and Sancho Paternoy, the royal
treasurer (*maestre racional*) in Aragon. The climax came on the night of
15/16 September 1485, as the inquisitor Pedro Arbués was kneeling in
prayer before the high altar of Saragossa cathedral. Beneath his gown the
inquisitor wore a coat of mail and on his head a steel cap, because of
warnings about threats against his life. On the night in question, eight
conspirators hired by conversos entered the cathedral by the chapter door
and stole up behind the inquisitor. After verifying that this was indeed
Arbués one of them stabbed him in the back with a stroke that went
through his neck and proved to be his death wound. As Arbués staggered
away, two of the others also inflicted wounds on him. The murderers made
their escape and the canons of the cathedral rushed in to find the inquisitor
dying. Arbués died twenty-four hours later, on 17 September.

The shock of this murder led to developments that the conversos should
certainly have foreseen.[93] When it was discovered that the assassins were
conversos the whole mood of the city of Saragossa, and with it that of
Aragon, changed. Arbués was declared to be a saint,[94] miracles were worked
with his blood, mobs roamed the streets in search of conversos, and a
national assembly voted to suspend the fueros while the search for the
assassins went on. In this atmosphere the inquisitors came into their own.
Autos of the reformed Inquisition were held on 28 December 1485, and
the murderers of Arbués expiated their crime in successive autos de fe
lasting from 30 June 1486 to 15 December the same year. One of them
had his hands cut off and nailed to the door of the Diputación, after which
he was dragged to the market-place, beheaded and quartered, and the
pieces of his body suspended in the streets of the city. Another committed

suicide in his cell the day before his ordeal, by breaking a glass lamp and swallowing the fragments; he too suffered the same punishment, which was inflicted on his dead body.

More than these initial measures was needed in order to uproot the whole conspiracy, which involved so many and such eminent people that individuals were being punished for it as late as 1492. The heads that now rolled came from the highest families in Aragon. Whether they were judaizers or not, members of the leading converso houses had connived (or so it was claimed) in the murder and were sooner or later destroyed by the Inquisition, which remained in full control of all the judicial measures taken. A study of the list of accused shows the constant appearance of the great names of Santa Fe, Santangel, Caballería, and Sánchez. Francisco de Sante Fe, son of the famous converso Jerónimo and a counsellor of the governor of Aragon, committed suicide by jumping from a tower and his remains were burnt in the auto of 15 December 1486. Sancho de Paternoy was tortured and imprisoned. A member of the Santangel family, Luis, who had been personally knighted by Juan II for his military prowess, was beheaded and burnt in the market-place of Saragossa on 8 August 1487; his more famous cousin Luis, whose money loans made possible the voyages of Columbus, was made to do penance in July 1491. Altogether, over fifteen members of the Santangel family were punished by the Inquisition before 1499; and between 1486 and 1503 fourteen members of the Sánchez family suffered a similar fate. This substantial sweep of conversos into the nets of the tribunal was effective in shaking the grip of New Christians on the Aragonese administration. Not for the first time, a cause triumphed through one useful martyrdom. For the conversos one murder, cheaply achieved at a total cost of 600 gold florins (which included the wages of the assassins), turned out to be an act of mass suicide that annihilated all opposition to the Inquisition for the next hundred years. The foolishness of the conspiracy can, with reason, call in doubt whether the conversos were really implicated.[95] But, in default of documentation to prove it, we may also doubt whether the murder was deliberately staged by the crown in order to smooth the way for the Inquisition.

Opportunely for Ferdinand, the crisis in Aragon coincided with his attempts to gain political control after the chaos of the civil wars. His constant emphasis on the need for the Inquisition was clear Realpolitik. The new tribunal became one of the instruments he used in order to assert his authority. But he was never in a position to, nor did he attempt to, increase his power substantially. Nor did he ever attempt to destroy the conversos as a political force.[96]

The king was wily enough to know that conversos in the crown of Aragon were a power network he could not trifle with. He had had their support from the beginning of his reign, and in return he gave his support to those not directly implicated in the troubles. Members of Luis de Santangel's family were accused of Judaism, but the king protected them. Gabriel Sánchez's case was particularly notable. Both his brother and his father-in-law were directly implicated in the Arbués murder. Accusations were made against both Sánchez and Alfonso de la Caballería. The king protected them firmly, and ordered the Inquisition to exempt them from its jurisdiction.[97]

In Mallorca, where the old Inquisition had already begun activities against judaizers in 1478, the new tribunal was introduced without incident in 1488 and began operations immediately. The inquisitors, Pedro Pérez de Munebrega and Sancho Marín, found enough work to keep them occupied in the hundreds of cases that filled the years 1488 to 1491.[98] Politically, the island was undisturbed, and no outbreaks against the tribunal occurred until a generation later under Charles V when a rising headed by the converso bishop of Elna in 1518 led to the temporary expulsion of the inquisitors from the city of Palma. The acceptance by Mallorcans of the activities of the tribunal is all the more unusual since conversos formed a considerable part of the population, thanks to the riots of 1391 in Palma, the preaching of Vincent Ferrer in 1413 and 1414, and the final forcible conversion of Jews there in 1435. The large number of conversos who were pardoned because they confessed voluntarily, or were condemned because they had fled, demonstrates that the inquisitors had managed to identify a problem.

The Spanish Inquisition was established everywhere in Spain several years before the final decision to expel the Jews. In those twelve terrible years, conversos and Jews alike suffered from the rising tide of antisemitism. While the latter were being harassed and then threatened with expulsion from dioceses in Aragon and Andalusia, the former were being purged of those who retained vestiges of their ancestral Judaism. Many conversos fled abroad without necessarily intending thereby to defect from the Catholic faith. Refugees feature prominently among those condemned in the early years. In the first two years of the tribunal at Ciudad Real fifty-two accused were burnt alive but 220 were condemned to death in their absence. In the Barcelona auto de fe of 10 June 1491, three persons were burnt alive but 139 were judged in their absence. In Mallorca the same process was repeated when at the auto of 11 May 1493 only three accused were burnt in person but there were forty-seven burnings of the effigies of absent fugitives.[99]

The figures indicate clearly who bore the brunt of the Inquisition: 99.3 per cent of those tried by the Barcelona tribunal between 1488 and 1505, and 91.6 per cent of those tried by that of Valencia between 1484 and 1530, were conversos of Jewish origin.[100] The tribunal, in other words, was not concerned with heresy in general. It was concerned with only one form of religious deviance: the apparently secret practice of Jewish rites.

Information about such practices was gleaned through the edict of grace,[101] which was a procedure modelled on that of the mediaeval Inquisition. The inquisitors would preach a sermon in the district they were visiting, recite a list of heresies, and invite those who wished to discharge their consciences to come forward and denounce themselves or others. If they came forward within the 'period of grace' – usually thirty to forty days – they would be absolved and 'reconciled' to the Church without suffering serious penalties. The benign terms encouraged self-denunciation. The edicts of grace, more than any other factor, served to convince the inquisitors that a heresy problem existed. Before that period, there had been only polemics and rumours. Now the confessions, as Andrés Bernáldez was later to argue, demonstrated that 'all of them were Jews'.

Hundreds of conversos, well aware that they had at some time been lax in observing the rules of their faith, came forward to admit their offences and be reconciled. In Seville the prisons were filled to overflowing with conversos waiting to be interrogated as a result of their voluntary confessions. In Mallorca 300 persons formed a procession during the first ceremony of contrition in 1488. The tribunal at Toledo initiated its career by reconciling an astonishing total of 2,400 repentant conversos during the year 1486.[102] This is no way implied (despite a common but mistaken assumption) that they were judaizers or had tendencies to Judaism. Fear alone was the spur. Faced by the activity of the inquisitors, who now identified as heresy what many converso Christians had accepted as normal practice within the framework of belief, they felt that it was safer to clear their record. There were very many others who did not trust the Inquisition and preferred flight. They wandered from one province to another, always one step ahead of the reverend fathers. The majority, it seems, preferred to take the risk. They confessed and put themselves in the hands of the inquisitors.

By its willingness to condone the confessions of those who came forward during periods of grace, the Inquisition was accepting that an offence had been committed but that no intended or hidden heresy was involved. Those who confessed and accepted the conditions of penitence were henceforward free of possible civil disabilities. This optimistic view was obviously not accepted by the conversos, who had been forced into a compromising position that, in the long run, brought them further miseries. 'One day when some others and I were talking about the Holy Inquisition', a resident of Sigüenza stated in 1492, 'they said that in Toledo very many had come forward to be reconciled, out of fear that false testimony would be made against them. And I said: Who is there who has not gone to be reconciled out of fear, even though he has done nothing?'[103] Some no doubt regretted bitterly that they had voluntarily joined the procession of penitents. 'Did you see me yesterday in the procession of the reconciled?', a woman from Cuenca asked a friend in 1492. She burst out weeping: 'and she wept a lot for having gone to be reconciled'. 'God must be really put out that the reverend fathers do these things, they are devils and are not acting justly'.[104] Such persons did not feel that they had strayed from the Catholic faith.

Between fear and humiliation, many conversos lived in constant dread. 'I was concerned because the Inquisition was coming', a tanner of Segovia said. 'I would rather see all the Muslims of Granada enter this city', a resident of Cuenca exclaimed in 1491, 'than the Holy Office of the Inquisition, which takes away life and honour'.[105]

Punishment by the Inquisition brought with it a number of civil disabilities.[106] In principle this situation could be avoided. From an early period many who admitted their faults during an edict of grace were allowed to wipe the slate clean by making a cash payment to the inquisitors. It was a welcome source of income to the Holy Office. 'Rehabilitation' by this means must have appeared to many conversos a worthwhile price to pay for security. A major advantage was that no confiscation of goods was exacted of those who confessed voluntarily.[107] Thousands were 'reconciled' to the Catholic faith, in Toledo alone some four thousand three hundred persons in 1486–7.[108] Though there is no evidence of how common it was to rehabilitate offenders, lists that survive from Toledo, Segovia, and several Andalusian towns, show that the inquisitors were quite happy to exact the cash payment from thousands of conversos. There was, of course, no proof that those who paid for 'rehabilitation' were in fact convinced judaizers. Moreover – and this was the sting in the tail of voluntary disclosure – it was a calculated risk whether the inquisitors would accept the repentance implied in confessions. Several were subsequently brought to trial for offences committed after their rehabilitation.[109]

The determination of the tribunal to strike hard at supposed heresy was unmistakable. Because documentation for the early years has not usually survived, it is difficult to arrive at reliable figures for the activity of the Inquisition. The period of most intense persecution of conversos was between 1480 and 1530. Hernando del Pulgar estimated that up to 1490 the Inquisition in Spain had burnt two thousand people and reconciled fifteen thousand others under the 'edicts of grace'.[110] His contemporary, Andrés Bernáldez, estimated that in the diocese of Seville alone between 1480 and 1488 the tribunal had burnt over seven hundred people and reconciled more than five thousand, without counting all those who were sentenced to imprisonment.[111] A later historian, the annalist Diego Ortiz de Zúñiga, claimed that in Seville between 1481 and 1524 over twenty thousand heretics had abjured their errors, and over a thousand obstinate heretics had been sent to the stake.[112]

There is little doubt that the figures are exaggerated. The total number of persons passing through the hands of the inquisitors, however, certainly ran into the thousands. The Toledo tribunals may have dealt with over eight thousand cases in the period 1481–1530.[113] The overwhelming majority of these were not in fact brought to trial; they were disciplined as a result of the edicts of grace, and had to undergo various penalties and penances, but escaped with their lives. Trial cases were very much fewer. In them, the penalty of death was pronounced for the most part against specific absent refugees. Effigies, which were burnt in their place, may form part of the total figures for executions given by early chroniclers. The direct penalty of death for heresy was in fact suffered by a very much smaller number than historians had thought. A recent carefully considered view is that in these years of the high tide of persecution, the tribunal of Saragossa had some one hundred and thirty executions in person,[114] that of Valencia possibly some two hundred and twenty-five,[115] that of Barcelona some thirty-four.[116]

In Castile the incidence of executions was probably higher. In the auto de fe at Ciudad Real on 23 February 1484, thirty people were burnt alive and forty in effigy; in the auto at Valladolid on 5 January 1492, thirty-two were burnt alive. The executions were, however, sporadic and concentrated only in the early years. In rounded terms, it is likely that over three-quarters of all those who perished under the Inquisition in the three centuries of its existence, did so in the first half-century. Lack of documentation, however, makes it impossible to arrive at totally reliable figures.[117] One good estimate, based on documentation of the autos de fe, is that 250 people were burnt in person in the Toledo tribunal between 1485 and 1501.[118] Since this tribunal and that of Seville and Jaén were among the few in Castile to have had an intense level of activity, it would not be improbable to suggest a figure five times higher, around one thousand persons, as a rough total for those executed in the tribunals of Castile in the early period. Taking into account all the tribunals of Spain up to about 1530, it is unlikely that more than two thousand people were executed for heresy by the Inquisition.[119]

The final death toll may have been smaller than historians once believed, but the overall impact was certainly devastating for the cultural minorities most directly affected. The reign of terror had an inevitable consequence. Conversos ceased to come forward to admit their errors. Instead, they were forced to take refuge in the very beliefs and practices that they and their parents had turned their backs on. Active Judaism, which existed among some conversos, seems to have been caused primarily by the awakening of their consciousness under persecution. Under pressure, they reverted to the faith of their ancestors. A Jewish lady living in Sigüenza was surprised in 1488 to encounter a man whom she had known previously in Valladolid as a Christian. He now professed to be a Jew, and was begging for charity among the Jews. 'What are you doing over here?' she asked him. 'The Inquisition is around and will burn you'. He answered: 'I want to go to Portugal'.[120] After no doubt equivocating for many years, he had made his decision and was going to risk all for it.

Since conversos occupied a significant place in administration, the professions and trade, diminishing numbers through persecution and emigration must have had a considerable impact on areas of Spain where they had been numerous. In Barcelona, according to the Consellers in 1485, the refugees 'have transferred to other realms all the money and goods they have in this city'.[121] In 1510 the few conversos who remained there claimed that they had once been a flourishing group of 'over six hundred families, of whom over two hundred were merchants', and that they now numbered only fifty-seven families, close to ruin.[122] In Valencia, we know the professions of 736 conversos tried by the Inquisition: 34 per cent were in commerce and 43 per cent were artisans, principally in textiles.[123] The conversos of Spain were in no way the cream of the population, but their ruin could not fail to cause concern to the civic authorities. This, indeed, together with defence of local independence, was among the main causes of non-converso resistance to the Inquisition in Teruel. The persecution of the conversos was far more damaging to the economy than the later and more spectacular expulsion of the Jews. The latter, because of their marginal status, had played a smaller role in key sectors of public life and controlled fewer economic resources.

The wish to eliminate the conversos from public life was, it has been argued, the main reason for the establishment of the Inquisition, and religion was never a genuine motive. In the process, the tribunal and the crown would get rich on the proceeds from confiscations.[124] The argument is plausible, particularly if we deny that there was any widespread judaizing movement among conversos. But, as we shall see, other issues were also involved, making it difficult to accept anti-converso greed as the only motive. Moreover, Ferdinand, who always continued to employ conversos in his service, vigorously denied any hostility to them. 'We have always had these people, like any others, in our service', he declared in 1507, 'and they have served us well. My intention always has been and still is that the good among them be rewarded and the bad punished, though charitably and not harshly'.[125]

The founding of the Inquisition has often been cited as evidence that the Catholic monarchs desired to impose uniformity of religion on Spain. The expulsion of the Jews would seem to confirm it. The monarchs, as fervent Catholics, certainly wished the nation to be united in faith. But there is no evidence at all of a deliberate policy to impose uniformity. Throughout the first decade of the Inquisition's career, Ferdinand and Isabella did not cease to protect their Jews while simultaneously trying to eliminate judaizing among the conversos. Even after the expulsion of the Jews, the Mudéjars remained in full enjoyment of their freedom of religion – in Castile for another decade, in Aragon for another thirty years. The ruthless drive against 'heresy', far from aiming at unification, was no more than the culmination of a long period of social and political pressure directed against the conversos.

When official chroniclers of those years, most of them sympathetic to the Holy Office, came to give an account of events, they slipped all too easily into a standard version of what had happened. All those who had fled from the Inquisition were considered, by implication, guilty. All those who had come forward for rehabilitation were, equally, written off as guilty; their confessions were there as evidence. It went without saying that all those found guilty and condemned, were deemed by the chroniclers to have been rightly judged. The Jewishness of the conversos became accepted as historical fact.

Yet the trial documents of the Holy Office itself give little cause to accept such a verdict. Many accused undoubtedly had pro-Jewish tendencies, for they had lived their lives in an ambivalent Christian-Jewish environment. But very rarely did the Inquisition manage to identify conversos who had consistent Jewish beliefs and practices. The majority seem to have been dragged before the court on the basis of neighbours' gossip, personal malice, communal prejudice and simple hearsay. According to a Jewish chronicler, conversos testified against conversos who would not pay them off.[126] The prosecution papers are full of the type of evidence that normal courts would have thrown out.[127] Some of the practices denounced to the inquisitors, moreover, by no means implied Judaism. Was it only Jews who turned their heads to the wall when they died?[128] The Inquisition had no problem in accepting as reliable the testimony of witnesses who knew nothing of an accused's present religious life but could testify that twenty or thirty years ago they had seen him change his sheets on a Friday or nod his head as though praying in the Jewish manner. Sancho de Ciudad, a leading citizen of Ciudad Real, was accused of practising Judaism on the basis of events allegedly remembered by witnesses from ten, twenty and nearly thirty years before.[129] Juan de Chinchilla, tailor of Ciudad Real, made the mistake in 1483 of owning up to Jewish practices after the expiry of the edict of grace. All those who worked with him testified that he appeared to be a practising Catholic. The only witnesses against him spoke of things they claimed to have seen sixteen and twenty years before. On their evidence he was burnt at the stake.[130] In Soria in 1490 the inquisitors accepted the word of a witness who had seen an official say Jewish prayers 'twenty years ago', and that of another who had seen certain objects in a house 'over thirty years ago'.[131] An elderly woman in the same city remembered another saying something 'fifty years ago'.[132] Very rarely indeed could witnesses say they had seen firm evidence of Jewish practices in the previous month or even year. In most cases, the prosecution in these years relied either on voluntary confessions or on fragments of hearsay evidence dredged out from long-range memory. When María González was brought before the inquisitors at Ciudad Real in 1511, the only firm evidence against her was her own confession during an edict of grace in 1483. 'Since then', her defence attorney argued (and there was no evidence to the contrary), 'she has lived as a Catholic'. However, her husband had been burnt as a heretic at that time, and in subsequent years she never ceased to maintain that 'they burnt him on false witness' and that 'he went to heaven like a martyr'.[133] On this flimsy evidence she too was sent to the stake.

When Juan González Pintado, a former secretary to the king and now city councillor of Ciudad Real, was tried by the Inquisition in 1484 for judaizing, the only detailed testimony against him dated from thirty-five years before.[134] By contrast, many witnesses testified that he was at that moment an excellent believing Christian. In such cases, other motives for the prosecution may be suspected. González, indeed, had been implicated in a rebellion twenty years before,[135] and echoes from that event may have now prejudiced his case.

If the idea that conversos were secret Jews is to be sustained principally by the evidence dug up by the Inquisition during the 1480s, there can be no doubt of the verdict. Very little convincing proof of Jewish belief or practice among the conversos can be found in the trials. There is no need to question the sincerity of the inquisitors, or to imagine that they maliciously fabricated evidence. It is true that, in the beginning at least, they were not trained lawyers, nor did they have a very clear idea of Jewish religious practice. But they themselves were instruments of a judicial system in which social pressures and prejudices, expressed through unsupported oral testimony, were given virtually unquestioned validity. Those convicted of judaizing fall into three main categories. First, there were those condemned on the evidence of members of the same family. Where this happened, the charges usually appear plausible, though personal quarrels were evidently involved. Second, there were those condemned in their absence. Here the automatic presumption of guilt, the lack of any defence, and the fact that property of the accused was confiscated, tend to make the evidence unacceptable. Third, there were those condemned on the hearsay of often malicious neighbours, most of whom had to reach back in their memory between ten and fifty years in order to find incriminating evidence. The inevitable conflict between various testimonies can be seen in the trial of Catalina de Zamora in Ciudad Real in 1484. She was accused by a number of witnesses of being a convinced and practising Jew, and thoroughly hostile to the Inquisition (which she evidently was). An equally convincing group of witnesses swore that she was a good Catholic, and that the prosecution witnesses were 'vulgar women of low intelligence'.[136] The inquisitors threw the charges out, but imposed a punishment on her for having blasphemed against the Virgin.

In short, the trial papers leave no doubt that some conversos were addicted to Jewish practices and culture (like the converso of Soria who in the 1440s insisted on going into the synagogue and praying beside the Jews until one day they got fed up with him and threw him out into the street despite his loud protests).[137] But there is no systematic evidence that conversos as a group were secret Jews. Nor is it possible to build on this fragile evidence any picture of a converso consciousness whose principal feature was the secret practice of Judaism.[138] In the perception of contemporary Jews who witnessed the persecution of the conversos, 'only a few of them died as Jews, and of these most were women'.[139] This testimony was repeated so often at the time by Jews that it cannot be called in question. Isaac Abravanel stressed four times in his writings that the charges made against the conversos were false. Deeply concerned for the fate of his own people, he would hardly have written off the conversos had he felt they were of the same faith. 'The people will always call them "Jews"', he wrote about the conversos, 'and brand them as Israelites and falsely accuse them of judaizing in secret, a crime for which they pay with death by fire'.[140] Another contemporary Jewish scholar, Isaac Arama, was no less explicit. 'The Gentiles', he wrote, 'will always revile them, plot against them and falsely accuse them in matters of faith; they will always suspect them as judaizers, especially in our time, when the smoke of the autos de fe has risen towards the sky in all the realms of Spain'.[141]

This picture changed radically with the expulsion of 1492. To the large number of Jews who converted that year, was soon added the very many who returned from exile and accepted baptism. Among both converts and returnees, few were happy with the situation. 'If it were not for the debts owed to me', said a man who came back from Portugal in 1494, 'I would neither turn Christian nor return from Portugal'. 'This is the real captivity', another (reported in 1502) is said to have commented some years before, 'when we were Jews we were lords, now we are slaves'.[142] From 1492, accordingly, a real problem of judaizing arose. These judaizers had lived all their lives as Jews and refused now to forgo their birthright.

The major qualitative change that took place in converso culture after 1492 has never been adequately analysed.[143] The new converts were decidedly not a part of the old 'converso nation' of Christians. Whereas the older generation had been fundamentally Christian, the new converts were still consciously Jewish and yearned for their former culture.[144] 'I repent of having become a Christian', a resident of Medinaceli claimed in 1504. 'We were well off in the Jewish faith', another stated in Sigüenza. The expulsion had taken place because they were not good Jews, said a man in Almazán:

'if evil has befallen us we deserve it, for we did not observe the ceremonies nor the other things that we had to do, and so the expulsion came upon us'. The opinion reflects that of a later Jewish chronicler who took the moralistic view that 'the exile which appears so terrible to the eye will be the cause of our salvation'.[145] Speaking of a refugee who had gone to Portugal, another in Almazán in 1501 stated that 'if I were now in that country I would not turn Christian'. 'When we were Jews we never wanted for anything, and now we go in want of everything', was the stated view of a new convert in 1505. 'We were better off then and had much more than we now have.'

This attitude, evidently, continued to give the inquisitors much work to do. It is significant that in the 1480s their main hope of obtaining evidence had been through the edicts of grace and the spontaneous confessions of conversos. After the 1490s those edicts were no longer needed. The large number of accumulated testimonies was sufficient material from which to work. Moreover, the inquisitors could now count on the help of those conversos who, in revenge for denunciations made by Jews at that time, turned the tables on the ex-Jews and proffered evidence against them.

4

A CONTINUING OPPOSITION

In this land they bear ill will to the Inquisition and would destroy it if they could.
Inquisitors of Catalonia, 1618[1]

Throughout the history of the Inquisition, commentators agreed on the impressive support given to it by the people. Foreign visitors to the peninsula were appalled by the mass participation of the public in autos de fe. Subsequent defenders of the tribunal felt that they could in part justify the Inquisition by the evidence of its roots in the authentic faith of Spaniards.[2] Opponents of the tribunal were equally impressed. Even the great Llorente, the first modern historian of the tribunal, was staggered by the lack of evidence for any opposition to it in Spain. As he declared in 1811 in a discourse read to the Royal Academy of History, meeting in Madrid at the height of the Peninsular War:

> If in investigating what a nation thought about a certain institution we were to be guided solely by the testimony of public writers, there is no doubt that the Spanish people had as much love as hate for the Inquisition . . . You will find hardly a book printed in Spain from the time of Charles the Fifth to our own days in which the Inquisition is not cited with praise.[3]

The apparent support given by the people to the Inquisition has inevitably created problems of interpretation. Partisans of the Holy Office have maintained that its popularity was based on its unswerving sense of justice, and that it responded to a profound religious need. Critics, by contrast, have presented it as a tyranny imposed by the state upon the free consciences of Spaniards. Both extremes of opinion can probably be supported by contemporary evidence, but neither is wholly plausible. The primitive state bureaucracies of fifteenth-century Castile and Aragon were ill equipped to impose a tyranny on the mass of the people and in reality never attempted to do so. If the Inquisition acquired a broad base of support, on the other hand, we need to examine why this came about.

Its support among the masses arose out of the bitter social struggles of the late fifteenth century, and it represented the interests of the vast majority of the population – the Old Christians – against those of a small converso minority. But though such support always remained the basis of the Inquisition's power, it was seldom more than passive; the Holy Office, as we shall see, was accepted but never loved.

There can be little doubt of the strong opposition to its introduction. The Aragonese had never fully activated their mediaeval Inquisition and were in no mood to accept another. The Castilians were in an even more sensitive position: never in all their history had they institutionalized the persecution of heresy. It had traditionally been a tolerant, open society, with no sectarian movements of the type that had arisen in England, France and Germany. Judaizers had occasionally been condemned by episcopal courts prior to the establishment of the Inquisition, but in accord with existing law.[4] How, then, did Spaniards come to accept a tribunal that was not only alien to their own traditions[5] but which from the first diverged from traditional principles of justice? The most eloquent testimony to the initial mood of revulsion comes from the pen of the sixteenth-century Jesuit Juan de Mariana. According to him, inquisitorial procedure

> at its inception appeared very oppressive to Spaniards. What caused the most surprise was that children paid for the crimes of their parents, and that accusers were not named or made known, nor confronted by the accused, nor was there publication of witnesses: all of which was contrary to the practice followed of old in other tribunals. Besides this, it appeared an innovation that sins of that sort should be punished by death. And what was most serious was that because of these secret investigations they were deprived of the liberty to listen and talk freely, since in all the cities, towns and villages there were persons placed to give information of what went on. This was considered by some to be the most wretched slavery and equal to death.[6]

Despite the strong language in which it is phrased, this opinion was not apparently shared by Mariana, who also presents as 'better and more correct' a contrary view in favour of the Inquisition. Significantly, he nowhere gives the impression that the critical view was held only by conversos. The specific points quoted, on innovations in judicial procedure, the death sentence for judaizing, and the practice of spying, were indeed questions that Old Christians raised in Castilian and Aragonese Cortes over the next few years. Fully aware of the novelty of inquisitorial practice, Mariana admitted that the new harsh measures were a deviation from the normal charitable procedure of the Church; but, he says, it was held 'that at times the ancient customs of the Church should be changed in conformity with the needs of the times'.

'The needs of the times': it is the clue to the survival of the Inquisition. While urban factions in Toledo, Ciudad Real and other cities were struggling to dislodge conversos from power, in the 1480s Ferdinand and Isabella, fresh from the civil wars and the constitutional settlement achieved at the Cortes of Toledo (1480), were beginning a military crusade against the Muslims of Granada. In 1486 they sought blessing for their cause at the shrine of St James in Compostela. Crisis times required crisis measures: the message was implicit in every major directive issued by Ferdinand in these years, and helps to explain the unusual cooperation he obtained throughout Spain. It may also help to explain the totally uncompromising firmness with which he insisted that the Inquisition be accepted everywhere, regardless of consequences. We have his remarkable statement to the Consellers of Barcelona in 1486, that

> before we decided on introducing this Inquisition into any of the cities of our realms, we carefully considered and looked at all the harm and ill that could follow from it and that could affect our taxes and revenue. But because our firm intention and concern is to prefer the service of God to our own, we wish the Inquisition to be established regardless, putting all other interests aside.[7]

The deliberate stimulation of a feeling of crisis (aggravated by alleged converso plots, by the murder of Arbués, by the episode of the La Guardia infant), and the universal response to the great twelve-year-long crusade against Granada, pressurized public authorities to conform and stilled the protests of individuals. Because the Inquisition was a crisis instrument, it may be that Ferdinand never intended it to be permanent (no steps, for example, were taken to give it a regular income). This certainly was the feeling of the Toledo writer who commented in 1538 that 'if the Catholic monarchs were still alive, they would have reformed it twenty years ago, given the change in conditions'.[8] The unprecedented activities of the Holy Office were deemed to be acceptable only as an emergency measure, until the crisis had passed.

Critics remained uneasy that harsh penalties should be imposed on those who had never been properly Christianized. Were judaizers wholly to blame? Had they ever been catechized after their forced baptism? And were the penalties not extreme? Mariana testifies to a great deal of dissent in Spain:

At the time there were differing opinions. Some felt that those who sinned in this way should not suffer the death penalty: but apart from this they admitted that it was just to inflict any other kind of punishment. Among others sharing this opinion, was Hernando del Pulgar, a person of acute and elegant genius.[9]

We may conjecture that Pulgar's view was widely held in higher circles. The Diputados of Aragon, as we have seen, protested to Ferdinand that correction should be by example and not by violence. Many Spaniards were indeed appalled at the tide of bloodshed. 'We are all aghast', the Consellers of Barcelona informed Ferdinand bluntly in 1484, 'at the news we receive of the executions and proceedings that they say are taking place in Castile.'[10] Pulgar was no less horrified. Denouncing the resort to coercion at a time when evangelization had not been tried, the royal secretary informed the archbishop of Seville that thousands of young conversos in Andalusia

> had never been out of their homes or heard and learned any other doctrine but that which they had seen their parents practise at home. To burn all these would be not only cruel but difficult to carry out.
>
> I do not say this, my lord, in favour of the evildoers, but to find a solution, which it seems to me would be to put in that province outstanding persons who by their exemplary life and teaching of doctrine would convert some and bring back others. Of course [the inquisitors] Diego de Merlo and doctor Medina are good men; but I know very well that they will not produce such good Christians with their fire as the bishops Pablo [de Santa Maria] and Alonso [de Cartagena] did with water.[11]

While agreeing that heresy should be repressed, Pulgar objected to capital punishment. His principal authority for this position was Saint Augustine, who had advocated the use of force but not the death penalty against the Donatist heretics of north Africa in the fifth century.

His contemporary Juan de Lucena, a noted humanist and servant of the crown, entered, like Pulgar, into public controversy over the methods of the Inquisition. At one time royal emissary to Rome and then a member of the royal council, Lucena was apparently a converso and, according to his adversary Canon Alonso Ortiz of Toledo, not only 'attempted with his sophistries to defend the conversos' but also 'insisted to the king and queen that there should be no Inquisition'. Lucena claimed, says Ortiz, that Jews 'baptized through fear did not receive the sacrament properly, and should therefore be treated not as heretics but as infidels', and that 'conversos ought to be convinced with reasons and inducements, not with coercion and punishments'.[12]

Further evidence of opposition to the persecution of Jews and conversos comes from an official of the Holy Office itself. The inquisitor Luis de Páramo (as we have observed) wrote that many learned Spaniards, both before and after 1492, thought the expulsion wrong in principle, as well as harmful to the Church, for two main reasons: firstly, because those who had been baptized by force had not received the sacrament properly and therefore remained essentially pagan;[13] secondly, because the expulsion was an implicit invitation to annihilate the Jews, which would be contrary to Scripture. The first reason was clearly of paramount importance, for if Jews had been forced into conversion their baptism was invalid and the Inquisition had no jurisdiction over them. The standard reply to this argument was simple. The mere fact that the Jews had *chosen* baptism as an alternative to death or exile meant that they had exercised the right of free choice: there was therefore no compulsion, and the sacrament was valid.

Throughout the subsequent period, criticisms were made of the treatment of conversos. Fray José de Sigüenza, sixteenth-century historian of the Jeronimite order, lamented that there had been no other prelates in Spain like Hernando de Talavera, archbishop of Granada and confessor to queen Isabella. In his treatment of New Christians, says Fray José, Talavera

> would not allow anyone to harm them in word or deed, or burden them with new taxes and impositions, for he detested the evil custom prevalent in Spain of treating members of the sects worse after their conversion than before it ... so that many refused to accept a Faith in whose believers they saw so little charity and so much arrogance.
>
> And if [continues Fray José] there had been more prelates who walked in this path, there would not have been so many lost souls stubborn in the sects of Moses and Mohammed within Spain, nor so many heretics in other nations.[14]

Talavera's position was stated most clearly in his *Católica impugnación*, a sharp attack that he directed against a 'heretical leaflet' issued in 1480 by a pro-Jewish converso of Seville. Deflating the pretensions of the Jews and conversos to be a specially gifted nation ('the Greeks were much more so, and the Romans, and even the Arabs'), Talavera supported the traditional death penalty for heresy. On the other hand, he attacked the antisemitism to which conversos were subjected, stating firmly that reason rather than persecution was the way of bringing them back to the fold: 'Heresies need to be corrected not only with punishments and lashes, but even more with Catholic reasoning'.[15] It was the policy he later adopted towards the Moriscos of Granada. His tract, possibly because of its controversial nature, was placed on the Index of Prohibited Books in 1559. The Inquisition subsequently decided merely to remove some phrases from it, but never got round to doing this.[16]

In the early years of the Inquisition, opposition was invariably promoted by conversos. Unable to secure support in Spain they turned to Rome. A bull issued by Sixtus IV on 2 August 1483, and almost certainly obtained by converso money, ordered greater leniency to be exercised in the tribunal of Seville and revoked all appeal cases to Rome. Only eleven days later, however, the pope withdrew the bull, after pressure from the Spanish rulers. Sixtus IV died in 1484, to be succeeded by Innocent VIII, a pontiff who followed his policy of intervening in favour of the conversos while taking care not to anger the Catholic monarchs. The bulls issued by Innocent on 11 February and 15 July 1485, asking for more mercy and leniency and for greater use of the practice of secret reconciliation, are typical of the efforts made by the Holy See to avoid lasting infamy falling on the tribunal's victims. Yet even if we see the hand of the conversos in all these attempts to mitigate the worst aspects of Inquisitorial procedure, it is impossible to maintain that conversos alone constituted the opposition.

Hostility to the practice of *sanbenitos*, for example, was shared by Old and New Christian alike. These penitential garments were ordered to be worn in public by the condemned, causing them public humiliation and bringing ill-fame to the towns where they lived. It was this that Mariana singled out as being 'very oppressive to Spaniards'. In Andalusia, according to Bernáldez, people were allowed to cease wearing them 'so that the disrepute of the territory should not grow'.[17] Another grievance was spying, which would have been objected to in any community and, as we shall see, aroused appropriate reactions. Prior to 1492 the Jews themselves were asked to spy on conversos. At Toledo in 1485 the inquisitors collected the rabbis and made them swear to anathematize in their synagogues those Jews who did not denounce judaizers.[18] In practice, ex-Jews rather than Jews appear to have been the active delators: in Ciudad Real in 1483–5 a former Jew, Fernán Falcón, was the chief witness used against most of those arrested for judaizing.[19]

Although conversos in Castile were notoriously hostile to the new tribunal, we hear little of opposition by Old Christians during the first two decades of the Inquisition's existence. Yet this was, as we have seen, by far the most bloody period of its history. Thousands of Christians of Jewish origin had been executed, ruined or driven into exile in a campaign without precedent in Spanish or European history, and through all this few Old Christians had bestirred themselves to raise their voices in protest. Only when the officers of the tribunal in Castile began to extend their activities to non-conversos did the murmurs of discontent become audible.

In 1499 the inquisitor of Córdoba was replaced after being found guilty of fraud and extortion. His successor, appointed in September that year, was Diego Rodríguez Lucero. Within a short time Lucero began his own bizarre career of extortion, arresting leading citizens on trifling or false pretexts in order to seize their property in confiscations. Prominent members of Old Christian families soon became ensnared in Lucero's net, and an atmosphere of terror gripped the community. That, at any rate, was the picture presented by those who opposed the inquisitor. Lucero himself had a different story. He had, he said, unearthed in the area a dangerous pro-Jewish millennarian movement.[20] There is, in effect, evidence that such a movement had arisen among groups of conversos in the region. Large numbers were arrested and persuaded to confess. In 1500, states a report made to the royal council, 130 people were 'relaxed' in two autos de fe.[21] After protests were made the council sent a commission of enquiry that interviewed many of those arrested. The commissioners seem to have been convinced by the voluntary confessions of some prisoners, and gave their support to Lucero, who was left free to continue his activities. An annalist of Córdoba reports that

> to gain credit as a zealous minister of the faith and to gain higher dignities, he began to treat the accused in prison with extreme rigour, forcing them to declare their accomplices, which resulted in the denunciation of so great a number of people, both conversos and Old Christians, that the city was scandalized and almost burst into rioting.[22]

Converso witnesses testified that they had been forced to teach Jewish prayers to Old Christian prisoners so that Lucero could accuse the latter of judaizing. A report from the cathedral chapter and city council in December 1506 accused Lucero of 'killing and robbing and defaming any and everybody'. An independent enquiry by the Córdoba authorities in November concluded that Lucero's evidence against his victims was 'all fabricated'; that Fray Diego de Deza, archbishop of Seville and Inquisitor

General, had failed to respond to petitions against the inquisitor; that 400 innocent prisoners were currently in the cells; and that Lucero had deliberately burnt as many of his victims as possible (120 were burnt alive in one auto in December 1504; twenty-seven in another in May 1505) to stop them complaining to the new king of Castile, Philip the Fair. The king opportunely in June 1506 suspended another holocaust, this time of 160 persons, that Lucero was preparing.[23]

The inquisitor's enquiries also led him to find evidence of the millennarian movement among members of the household of the eighty-year-old Jeronimite archbishop of Granada, Hernando de Talavera. Accusing Talavera of having a 'synagogue' in his palace, Lucero arrested the archbishop and all his household (which included his sister, two nieces and their daughters, and the servants). Both relatives and servants were tortured and duly produced denunciations against Talavera. The papacy opportunely intervened, the archbishop was acquitted of all charges in April 1507, and he and his family were set free.[24] It came too late to benefit the old man. Walking barefoot and bareheaded through the streets of Granada in the procession on Ascension Day, 13 May, he was seized by a violent fever which the following day ended his life. On his deathbed he denounced 'Lucero and his accomplices' for 'trying to wipe out the conversos'; 'which', he continued, 'is clearly against the Holy Catholic Faith, which requires that there be no distinction between Jew and Greek'.[25] Talavera's care for his flock had left him no time to care for himself. He died in perfect poverty; his household, for which he had not provided, had to resort to the charity of the bishop of Málaga.

On 16 July the same year Gonzalo de Ayora, captain general and chronicler, wrote a letter of protest to the king's secretary Miguel Almazán.

> The government had failed to exercise effective control over its ministers. As for the Inquisition, the method adopted was to place so much confidence in the archbishop of Seville and in Lucero . . . that they were able to defame the whole kingdom, to destroy, without God or justice, a great part of it, slaying and robbing and violating maids and wives to the great dishonour of the Christian religion.
>
> The damages which the wicked officials of the Inquisition have wrought in my land are so many and so great that no reasonable person on hearing of them would not grieve.[26]

The redress so urgently demanded began with the resignation of Deza under pressure, and the appointment on 5 June 1507 of Francisco Jiménez de Cisneros, cardinal archbishop of Toledo, as Inquisitor General. In May 1508 the Suprema eventually voted to arrest Lucero, who was taken in chains to Burgos, while his victims in the prison of Córdoba were all released. The ex-inquisitor received no punishment for his crimes, but was allowed to retire to Seville, where he died in peace.

At the same time as the troubles in Córdoba, complaints were raised in Llerena (Extremadura) against the activities of the new inquisitor, a man named Bravo, who had for a time been an assistant of Lucero in Córdoba. So many wealthy prisoners were thrown into the cells by Bravo, despite the protests of one of his colleagues, that the relatives of the condemned finally gathered enough courage to petition the crown:

> We the relatives and friends of the prisoners in the cells of the Inquisition of Llerena kiss the royal hands of Your Highness and testify that the inquisi-tors of that province, together with their officials, have persecuted and persecute both the prisoners and ourselves with great hatred and enmity, and have carried out many irregularities in the procedure of imprisonment and trial, and have maltreated not only the said prisoners but their wives and children and property.[27]

There is no record of any censure of Bravo's policy, and it appears likely that he was allowed to pursue his career unchecked. Lucero's influence also seems to have haunted the tribunal at Jaén, where a professional 'witness' who had formerly served the inquisitor now extended his activities. The man's name was Diego de Algeciras, and for a reasonable pittance he was ready to perjure himself in testifying to the judaizing activities of any number of conversos. Thanks to his assistance, the richest conversos of the city were soon in gaol on suspicion of heresy. Those who still remained free petitioned the crown to restore jurisdiction over heresy to the bishop of Jaén, whose mercy they trusted more than the abuses of the officials of the Inquisition.[28]

Most abuses probably originated not with the inquisitors themselves but with their subordinate officials. Among the more notorious cases was the notary at Jaén, who locked a young girl of fifteen in a room, stripped her naked, and whipped her until she agreed to testify against her mother.[29] A deposition drawn up by witnesses at Toledo and dated 26 September 1487 asserts that the receiver of confiscated goods in that tribunal, Juan de Uria, had defrauded sums amounting to 1.5 million maravedis (4,000 ducats), enough to set himself up in comfort.[30] There were opportunities for lining one's pockets even at the bottom of the ladder. In 1588, the inquisitor from Madrid who carried out the inspection of the tribunal at Córdoba reported that both the doorkeeper and the messenger of the tribunal were criminals and profiteers, and that this was well known throughout the city, although apparently not to the inquisitors of Córdoba.[31]

In the crown of Aragon, too, Old Christians who had condoned the persecution of conversos now began after the death of Queen Isabella to rally to the defence of fueros. Meeting together at Monzón in 1510, the representatives of Aragon, Catalonia and Valencia raised the question of reform in jurisdiction. No further steps were taken until their next meeting at Monzón in 1512, when a comprehensive list of reforms was drawn up. To this list Ferdinand added his signature, thus agreeing to the first of the many *concordias* made between the Inquisition and the individual provinces of Spain. Among other things, the concordia of 1512 stipulated that the number of familiars in the kingdom should be limited; that the Inquisition should not be exempt from local taxes; that officials of the tribunal who committed crimes should be tried by a secular court; that in cases of confiscation, property which had formerly belonged to the condemned should not be included in the confiscation; and that trade with conversos should not be prohibited, since this depressed commerce. Moreover, the tribunal was not to exercise jurisdiction over usury, bigamy, blasphemy and witchcraft unless heresy were involved. The fact that pressure had to be put on the king through the Cortes proves how serious were some of the objections raised in Aragon against inquisitorial procedure. Yet the demands made in 1512 are relatively mild when compared with some of those made at a later date.

At the death of Ferdinand on 23 January 1516 the crown passed to his grandson Charles, who was in Flanders at the time. Since the death of Isabella on 26 November 1504 Ferdinand had been king of Aragon only, and Castile had been under the rule of their daughter Juana (the Mad), widow since 1506 of Philip the Fair of Austria. The death of Ferdinand would normally have meant the acceptance of Juana as queen, but her mental dislocation made her obviously unfitted to rule, so that her son Charles was everywhere accepted as rightful sovereign.

While awaiting the arrival of Charles in Spain, Cisneros maintained control of the Inquisition. In his will the Catholic King had called upon his successor to preserve the Inquisition. Charles had every intention of doing this. But the new reign aroused hopes of reform, particularly in converso hearts, and Cisneros was greatly alarmed by a rumour that Charles intended to allow the publication of the names of witnesses in inquisitorial trials. In a letter which the now ageing cardinal wrote to Charles, apparently in March 1517, he asserted that the Inquisition was so perfect a tribunal 'that there will never be any need for reform and it would be sinful to introduce changes'.[32] The publication of witnesses' names would lead inevitably to their murder, as had happened recently in Talavera de la Reina when an accused converso, on learning the name of his denouncer, went out to waylay him and assassinated him. Cisneros was not, however, unalterably opposed to reforms, as his own life and career had demonstrated. During his tenure of the post of Inquisitor General, he had taken care to dismiss the more notorious inquisitors, including the secretary of the Suprema. He wrote to Charles in December 1576 advising him that the royal secretary Calcena and others should have nothing further to do with the Inquisition, in view of their excesses. Lea's very fair verdict is that 'we may feel assured that he showed no mercy to those who sought to coin into money the blood of the conversos'.[33]

Whatever Cisneros' views may have been, many contemporaries thought that some reform in the judicial procedure of the Inquisition was essential, even if they did not question the tribunal's existence. The arrival of the seventeen-year-old king from Flanders set off a train of requests and demands which constituted the last chapter in the struggle to subject the Inquisition to the rule of law. When Charles, after his arrival in Spain in September 1517, held the first Cortes of his reign at Valladolid in February 1518, the deputies petitioned 'that Your Highness provide that the office of the Holy Inquisition proceed in such a way as to maintain justice, and that the wicked be punished and the innocent not suffer'.

They asked moreover that the forms of law be observed, and that inquisitors be chosen from reputable and learned men. The main result of this was the series of instructions for the Inquisition drawn up principally on the initiative of Jean le Sauvage, chancellor of the king, a man who was accused of being in the pay of the conversos. The preamble to these proposed instructions claims that

> accused people have not been able to defend themselves fully, many innocent
> and guiltless have suffered death, harm, oppression, injury and infamy ...
> and many of our vassals have absented themselves from these realms: and (as
> events have shown) in general these our realms have received and receive

great ill and harm: and have been and are notorious for this throughout the world.

The proposed reforms, therefore, included provisions that prisoners placed in open, public prisons be able to receive visitors, be assigned counsel, be presented with an accusation on arrest, and given the names of witnesses. In addition, goods of the accused could not be taken and sold before a verdict, nor could the salaries of inquisitors be payable out of confiscations. Prisoners should be allowed recourse to mass and the sacraments while awaiting trial, and care should be taken not to let those condemned to perpetual prison die of hunger. If torture were used, it should be in moderation, and there should be no 'new inventions of torture as have been used until now'.[34] Each of these clauses points to the existence of evils which the new pragmatic was supposed to remedy.

Had the instructions ever been approved, a totally different tribunal would have come into existence. The burden of secrecy would have been completely lifted, and opportunity for abuses largely removed. Happily for those who supported the Inquisition, the new Inquisitor General appointed by Charles on the death of Cisneros was his own tutor the Dutch Cardinal Adrian of Utrecht, bishop of Tortosa, who firmly opposed any innovation. Shortly after this, early in July 1518, Sauvage died. With him collapsed any hope of fundamental alterations in the structure of the Inquisition. Adrian, who as a Netherlander appears not to have had any close knowledge of Spanish problems, even reversed some of the reforms of Cisneros, by reappointing Calcena to a post of authority as secretary to the Suprema.

Meanwhile Charles had gone to Aragon, where he accepted the allegiance of the kingdom in the Cortes which opened at Saragossa in May 1518. Surprisingly, when the Cortes offered to advance him a large sum of money in exchange for agreement to a list of thirty-one articles which were substantially the same as those drawn up by Sauvage, the king agreed. It soon became clear that he had no intention of observing the agreement, for a subsequent message to the Spanish ambassador in Rome asked him to secure from the pope revocation of the articles and a dispensation from his oath to observe them. However, the Cortes had already taken the step of having Charles's signature to the articles authenticated by Juan Prat, the notary of the Cortes. All the relevant papers were then sent to Rome in the hands of Diego de las Casas, a converso from Seville. After the dissolution of the Cortes in January 1519, the Inquisition stepped in to arrest Prat on the charge of having falsified the articles drawn up at the Cortes. The accusation was obviously false, but both ecclesiastical and secular authorities in Castile acted as though it were true. The new chancellor, Mercurino Gattinara, urgently drew up papers which he sent to Rome in April, claiming that these were genuine and that the official copy was a forgery. By now a serious constitutional quarrel had arisen inside Aragon, and the deputies and nobility of the realm, meeting in conference in May, sent a request to Charles for the release of Prat, threatening not to grant any money until their demands were met. They summoned the Cortes and refused to disperse until justice had been done.

At this stage Pope Leo X intervened in favour of the Aragonese. In July 1519 he issued three briefs, one to Charles, one to the Inquisitor General and one to the tribunal of Saragossa, reducing the powers of the Inquisition to the bounds of ordinary canon law and revoking all special privileges granted by his predecessor. Charles and his officials refused to allow the publication of the brief in Spain, and sent a firm protest to Rome. The pope now shifted his position and suspended the briefs without revoking them. At this time the Aragonese immediately discontinued payment of any grants to the crown. Finally, in December 1520 the pope confirmed the concordia of 1518, but in terms which did not specify whether it was Prat's or Gattinara's version that was the correct one. A compromise was eventually reached in 1521, when Cardinal Adrian accepted the Aragonese version for the time being, and released Prat. The victory of the Aragonese was an unsubstantial one. The Inquisition at no time afterwards admitted the validity of the concordias of 1512 and 1518, so that the struggles of these years were after all in vain.

At the Castilian Cortes of La Coruña in 1520, the requests made at Valladolid for a reform in the procedure of the Inquisition were repeated, but to no avail. Later that same year, while Charles was away in Flanders, another plan for reform was presented to him. This and subsequent proposals fell through. On his return to Spain, a Cortes was held at Valladolid in 1523. Again the old suggestions for reform were brought up, fortified by a request that the salaries of inquisitors should be paid by the crown and not be drawn from confiscations. Failure was again the result. In 1525 the Cortes which met at Toledo complained of abuses committed by both inquisitors and familiars, but they achieved nothing beyond a promise that wrongs would be righted if they really existed. In 1526 in Granada the king was presented with a memorial demonstrating the evils of the secret procedure of the Inquisition, and asking for prisoners to be kept in public gaols instead of the secret cells.[35] To this there is no recorded reply. Almost annually such requests had been presented to the crown, and as regularly refused. Quite obviously a persistent stream of opposition was in continuous existence, dedicated not so much to the suppression of the Inquisition as to the cure of abuses. Against a stubborn Charles, however, no impact could be made. In April 1520 the king observed to a correspondent that 'in the Cortes of Aragon and Catalonia the Holy Office has been criticized and attacked by some people who do not care much for its preservation'.[36] The reference to Aragon should not divert us from the fact that, as we have seen, criticism had been raised just as frequently in the realm of Castile. Throughout Spain, the organs of constitutional government became the last channels of protest available to opponents of the Holy Office.

From 1519 to 1521 the energies of the peninsula were occupied in the famous revolt of the Comuneros, a confusing and complex struggle waged partly by town oligarchies against the royal authorities who had the support of the nobility, and partly by rival factions against each other in some of the great cities. Inevitably some conversos, with their known activity in many municipalities, could be found on the rebel side. Among the leading Comuneros were a Coronel in Segovia, a Zapata in Toledo, and a Tovar in Valladolid. Rumour, seasoned in part with malice, tended to exaggerate their role. The Constable of Castile informed Charles V in 1521 that the 'root cause of the uprising in these realms has been the conversos'; and after the rebel defeat at Villalar on 23 April 1521, according to the emperor's jester, 'many dead were found without foreskins'.[37] A generation later the archbishop of Toledo, Siliceo, could claim that 'it is common knowledge in Spain that the Comunidades were incited by descendants of Jews'. In practice there seems to have been no significant identification of the converso cause with that of the Comuneros, and many known conversos fought on the royalist side. It is certain that some rebels hoped to modify or abolish the Inquisition: the Admiral of Castile claimed early in 1521 that 'the Comuneros say there will be no Inquisition', and hostility to the tribunal is recorded in various parts of the realm. But the Junta that headed the Comunidad was scrupulously careful to cause no offence to the Holy Office, and not a single reference to the Inquisition occurs among the demands made to the government.[38] The tribunal survived this critical period with its functions intact. In Valencia, where a parallel revolt of *Germanías* ('brotherhoods') was taking place, its functions were reinforced by the compulsory mass baptisms carried out on the Mudéjares by the rebels.

In the years after the Comunidades, objections to the activities of the Inquisition continued to be made in both Castile and Aragon. A typical example is the memorial drawn up on 5 August 1533 and read to Charles at the Aragonese Cortes in Monzón.[39] The sixteen articles included complaints that 'some inquisitors of the Holy Office, in the voice and name of the Inquisition, have arrested and imprisoned people for private offences in no way touching the Holy Office'; that inquisitors were taking part in secular business; that they had extended their jurisdiction illegitimately by prosecuting cases of sodomy, usury and bigamy – questions which had nothing to do with heresy; that the inquisitors of Aragon, Catalonia and Valencia had an excessive number of familiars, whose identity was kept concealed, thus provoking numerous abuses. As for the Moriscos, said the protest, addressing itself to the Inquisitor General, 'Your Reverence knows well the way in which they were "converted", and the little or no teaching or instruction in our Holy Catholic faith which has been given them, and the lack of churches in the places where they live. Yet despite this lack of teaching and instruction, they are being proceeded against as heretics.' Worse still, the Inquisition was illegitimately seizing the land they had confiscated from the Moorish converts. To all these complaints Alonso Manrique, the Inquisitor General, gave a firm, negative reply. The protests were shelved.

Complaints along these lines were to play an important part in future controversies over the Inquisition. Inquisitorial jurisdiction in moral matters, for instance, was considered then, as later, a wrongful extension of its powers. But sweeping appeals like the protest of 1533 were growing fewer as the position of the Holy Office became stronger. Not only did the existence of the Inquisition become wholly unquestioned, but toleration of its attendant abuses became more widespread and pronounced. As papal and royal favour confirmed it in its position as one of the key institutions of the realm, it survived all opposition and criticism.

By the mid-sixteenth century the tribunal was constitutionally invulnerable. In part this had happened because of the implicit support of the Old Christian majority, who had tolerated two decades of blood-letting directed against the conversos because it suited their own interests and who, too late, attempted to restrain the Inquisition when it appeared to be working against them. By then, in the new social atmosphere created by the European Reformation, the Holy Office had become essential to the maintenance of the established religion. In part, also, the Inquisition survived because of the unswerving support of the crown, which could ill afford to lose so useful an institution. Like Ferdinand before him, Charles V was wholly dedicated to it, and introduced a similar tribunal into the Netherlands in 1520. When the Aragonese disputes over Juan Prat occurred in 1518, Charles informed the Cortes: 'you can be sure that we would rather agree to lose part of our realms and states than permit anything to be done therein against the honour of God and against the authority of the Holy Office'.[40] During the Comunidades, Charles exhorted his viceroys in Spain to resist any attack on the Inquisition.[41] In subsequent years, therefore, the monarchy had at its disposal a unique institution upon which it could call in case of need. This continued to have repercussions in the crown of Aragon, where the activities of the tribunal were always regarded as unconstitutional.

The somewhat simplified picture of popular 'support' for the Inquisition evidently needs to be modified. Support is easiest to identify in the realms of Castile, where the tribunal in its early period came into conflict with no interest group except the converso elite. Moreover, unlike the institutions of the Church, the tribunal levied no taxes on the people. There was consequently no pressing reason for popular hostility. The Inquisition merged itself into existing power structures, and gained the collaboration of local elites, who were happy to accept honorary posts (as 'familiars') in the tribunal.

Outside Castile, the degree of support became much more tenuous. Converso elites continued to be potent enemies of the Inquisition, particularly in Aragon. But more than anything else it was the question of legal privileges that blighted the attempt to collaborate with non-Castilians. In Italy, Aragon and Catalonia, 'local elites never lost their jealousy of its special privileges'.[42] There was also a wide variety of other reasons that condemned the inquisitors to unpopularity. They were resented by local clergy, they were foreigners, they could not speak the language. 'We are hated as officials of the Holy Office, especially in this town', the inquisitor of Navarre wrote in 1547.[43] He happened to be in a gloomy mood. Moreover, in that mountainous frontier the Inquisition, even by the late sixteenth century, was a novelty that the population, most of whom spoke no Spanish, refused to accept. In 1574 an Inquisition official narrowly escaped lynching by the people of the Vall d'Arán in the Catalan Pyrenees. He reported back that 'in that land they will not on any account permit the Holy Office to enter'.[44] In Catalonia the tribunal was never fully accepted. 'In this province', the inquisitors complained in 1618, 'they bear ill-will to the tribunal of the Holy Office and would destroy it if they could'.[45] The hostility did not impede Catalans collaborating with the tribunal against some conversos in the early years of the tribunal, and against French immigrants later.

For three centuries more, the Inquisition would continue to be a standard feature of the Spanish landscape. Just as it had been bitterly opposed by the conversos, so in time it would also earn the profound hatred of other minorities. Its anti-Morisco activity arguably earned it some popularity among Christians. The chief victims at its autos in the crown of Aragon were 'nearly always', it has been pointed out, 'people for whom the general public had little sympathy'.[46] In Aragon and Valencia the victims were Moriscos, in Catalonia they were French immigrants. Despite this victimisation of minorities, the Inquisition found it difficult to earn genuine popular support in the eastern realms of the peninsula. The rest of the Spanish population gradually came to accept it, but in a spirit that can hardly be described as enthusiastic.

In perspective, the Inquisition cannot be seen as the imposition of a sinister tyranny on an unwilling people. Brought into being by a particular social situation, it was impelled and inspired by a decisively Old Christian ideology, and controlled by men whose outlook reflected the mentality of the mass of Castilians. Outside Castile, support for it was grudging. Outside Spain, the opposition was total.

Within Golden Age Spain, little evidence exists of objections to its existence from intellectuals or ordinary people. It fulfilled a role – as guardian against heresy, as keeper of public morality, as arbiter between factions, as tribunal for small causes – that no other institution fulfilled. Moreover, over long periods of time and substantial areas of the country, it quite simply did nothing.[47] After its explosive entry into the course of Spain's history, it slipped surreptitiously into the stream of daily life. Its impact and duration was to be much longer than anyone could have imagined at the beginning.

EXCLUDING THE REFORMATION

We live in such difficult times that it is dangerous either to speak or be silent.

Juan Luis Vives to Erasmus, 1534[1]

In the early dawn of the European Reformation many intellectuals in Spain were foremost in their support for change. At the 1520 Diet of Worms, when Luther had to defend himself publicly, 'everybody, especially the Spaniards, went to see him', admitted the humanist Juan de Vergara. 'At the beginning everybody agreed with him', Vergara went on, 'and even those who now write against him confess that at the beginning they were in favour of him'.[2]

Spaniards of that generation were excited at the new horizons opened up by Renaissance scholarship. Scholars who went to Italy, such as Antonio de Nebrija who returned from there to take up a chair at Salamanca in 1505, were in the vanguard of the drive to promote learning. From Italy Peter Martyr of Anghiera came in 1488 to educate the young nobles of Spain, preceded four years before by Lucio Marineo Siculo, who joined the ranks of the professors at Salamanca. A key figure in the advancement of learning was Cisneros, archbishop of Toledo from 1495 and Inquisitor General from 1507. He founded the university of Alcalá, which became the centre of humanist studies in Spain. Its first chancellor, Pedro de Lerma, had studied at Paris. Nebrija was, as Erasmus wrote to the Valencian humanist Luis Vives in 1521, its 'principal ornament'. Among its professors were the converso brothers Juan and Francisco de Vergara. The latter was described by Lucio Marineo Siculo as the greatest classical scholar in Spain. One of the key tasks that Cisneros set the professors of the university was the production of a critical edition of the Bible which would remain a classic of contemporary scholarship. The great Polyglot Bible that resulted from this enterprise consisted of six volumes, with the Hebrew, Chaldean and Greek originals of the Bible printed in columns parallel to the Latin Vulgate. The Complutensian (from Compluto, the Latin name for Alcalá) Polyglot was finally published in 1522.

The accession of Charles I of Spain to the Imperial title (as Charles V of Germany) in 1519 also generated enthusiasm among scholars in the peninsula. It seemed as though Spain was about to participate in a great European enterprise. From Charles's own homeland, the Netherlands, the influence of Erasmus began to penetrate the open frontiers of Spain. In 1516 the name of Erasmus was first traced by a Spanish pen, and in 1517 Cisneros unsuccessfully invited him to come to Spain. By 1524 a number of intellectuals in the peninsula had rallied to the doctrines of Erasmus, to whom Vives wrote in June 1524, 'our Spaniards are also interesting themselves in your works'. The wit and satire directed by Erasmus against ecclesiastical abuses, and particularly against lax standards in the mendicant orders, found a ready hearing in a country where the highest Church officials had themselves led the movement in favour of reform. The presence of prominent intellectuals and literary men in the entourage of Charles V ensured protection for the new ideas at court. Finally, the two principal prelates in the Church – the archbishop of Toledo, Alonso de Fonseca, successor to Cisneros, and Alonso Manrique, the Inquisitor General – were enthusiastic Erasmians. The success of Erasmus was confirmed with the translation of his *Enchiridion*, undertaken in 1524 by Alonso Fernández, archdeacon of Alcor. Published towards the end of 1526, it was greeted by widespread enthusiasm. The translator wrote to Erasmus in 1527:

> At the emperor's court, in the cities, in the churches, in the convents, even in the inns and on the highways, everyone has the *Enchiridion* of Erasmus in Spanish. It used to be read in Latin by a minority of Latinists, and even these did not fully understand it. Now it is read in Spanish by people of every sort, and those who had formerly never heard of Erasmus have learned of his existence through this single book.[3]

The publisher of the *Enchiridion*, Miguel de Eguía, was printer to the university of Alcalá and brought out about a hundred books of humanist orientation. Erasmus, by far the best seller, was informed in 1526 that 'though the printers have produced many thousands of copies, they cannot satisfy the multitude of buyers'. There were many personal contacts between friends of the humanist who came to Spain and Spaniards who went north to see him. Among the latter the most significant was young Juan de Vergara, who left the peninsula with the emperor in 1520 and spent two years with Erasmus in the Netherlands. On his return, starry-eyed, he wrote to Vives: 'The admiration felt for Erasmus by all Spaniards is astonishing.' This was not quite true. Many Spanish scholars were critical of the northerner's methods of exegesis. Others were uneasy at similarities between Erasmus and Luther. Some of the mendicant orders in particular were smarting under the satirical attacks of Erasmus, and pressed for a debate on his 'heresies'. A conference presided over by Manrique, and including some thirty voting representatives of the orders, eventually met at Valladolid in the summer of 1527.[4] The deliberations were inconclusive, with half the representatives coming out in favour of the Dutchman. The failure of the attack appeared as a victory for the humanists. On 13 December Charles V himself wrote to Erasmus, asking him not to worry over controversy in Spain:

> as though, so long as we are here, one could make a decision contrary to Erasmus, whose Christian piety is well known to us ... Take courage and be assured that we shall always hold your honour and repute in the greatest esteem.[5]

The triumphs of Spanish humanism were, inevitably, exaggerated by contemporaries. No more than a fraction of the elite (notable among them the grandee Mendoza family[6]) were active patrons of the arts, and only a small number of clergy and scholars were devoted to classical studies. Few lasting advances were made in education or literacy, and the popular tradition in literature (represented for example by the *Celestina* of 1499) was still predominant. The learned aspects of humanism always took second place to the influence of scholastic theology.[7] The new learning and Erasmianism were largely phenomena of the emperor's court. Beyond its confines, even among the nobles and elite, Latin was virtually a dead tongue, studied but never spoken.[8] The Florentine ambassador Guicciardini in 1512 made an observation that other foreigners were to echo throughout the century. The Spaniards, he said, 'are not interested in letters, and one finds very little knowledge either among the nobility or in other classes, and few people know Latin'. Regular contact with the Netherlands and Italy had by the early 1500s introduced some literate Spaniards to the art and spirituality of the North and the literature of the Renaissance. The impact was significant but small. The study of Greek never caught on. When some years later in 1561 Cardinal Mendoza y Bobadilla of Burgos was asked to suggest scholars with knowledge of Greek who might suitably represent Spain at the Council of Trent, he could name only four people in the whole country.[9]

The opening of intellectual horizons in Spain was soon threatened from within by the growth of illuminism and the discovery of Protestants, and from without by the limitations imposed throughout Europe on free thought by political events.

The spiritual and devotional movements in Castile in the late fifteenth century were warmly patronized by Cisneros, and produced a literature of which the most outstanding example was the *Spiritual ABC* (1527) of the Franciscan friar Francisco de Osuna. Adepts of the Franciscan school believed in a mystical method known as *recogimiento*, the 'gathering up' of the soul to God. Those who practised it were *recogidos*. Out of this mystical school there grew up a version (condemned by the general chapter of the Franciscans in 1524) emphasizing the passive union of the soul with God. The method was known as *dejamiento* (abandonment), and adepts were called *dejados* or *alumbrados* (illuminists). Mystical movements and the search for a purer interior religion were common coin in Europe at this time. In Spain there was powerful patronage of mystics by the great nobility. One alumbrado group was patronized by the Mendoza Duke of Infantado in his palace at Guadalajara. It consisted of the *beata* Isabel de la Cruz, Pedro Ruiz de Alcaraz, and María de Cazalla and her Franciscan brother Juan, auxiliary bishop of Ávila. Alcaraz was also connected with another group at Escalona, patronized by the Marquis of Villena. Meanwhile a parallel group of mystics emerged in Valladolid. The chief influence here was the beata Francisca Hernández, whose fame as a holy woman attracted into her circle Bernardino Tovar, a brother of Juan de Vergara, and the Franciscan preacher Francisco Ortiz.

In 1519 Isabel de la Cruz was denounced to the Inquisition by a servant-girl of the Mendozas. There had been fusses before about other beatas – the beata of Piedrahita (1512) was a famous example – and little may have come of this denunciation. But investigations happened to coincide with alarm over Lutheranism in Germany. The inquisitors quickly realized that elements of heresy were involved. One by one, in a slow and patient enquiry that stretched over several years, the illuminist leaders were detained on the orders of Inquisitor General Manrique. Isabel and Alcaraz were arrested in April 1524. On 23 September 1525 Manrique issued an 'edict on the alumbrados', a list of forty-eight propositions which gives a valuable summary of their doctrine and leaves little doubt that their beliefs were indeed heretical.[10] Isabel and Alcaraz were sentenced to appear in an auto de fe at Toledo on 22 July 1529. The attention of the inquisitors now shifted to Valladolid, where Francisca Hernández had gathered around her a group of adepts who practised recogimiento in opposition to the method of the Guadalajara mystics. Her most devoted admirer was the well-known preacher Francisco Ortiz,[11] and she lived for a while with the rich Cazalla family, relatives of María de Cazalla. Her fame spread: great lords and clergy visited her, and Erasmians such as Eguía and Tovar frequented the house. Her imperious character brooked no rivalry, however, and she quarrelled first with the Cazallas, then with the Erasmians. When she was arrested by the Inquisition in March 1529, the indignant Francisco Ortiz went into his pulpit and denounced the Inquisition for its 'public and open' sin in detaining her, but was himself immediately arrested and sentenced to reclusion in a monastery.

In August 1529 Manrique fell into disfavour and was confined to his see of Seville. At the same time the protecting hand of the emperor was withdrawn: Charles left in July for Italy and took with him some of the most influential Erasmians. This made it possible for the traditionalists, who had been biding their time after the defeat at Valladolid, to take the offensive.

One of the first prosecutions for Erasmian ideas was that of Diego de Uceda, chamberlain to a high official in the Order of Calatrava. A deeply religious Catholic, Uceda was also an Erasmian who shared the Dutchman's scepticism about superstitions and miracles. Journeying in February 1528 from Burgos to his native city of Córdoba, he fell in with a travelling companion to whom he talked too earnestly and freely about religion, particularly about Luther. He was denounced to the Inquisition by his companion, arrested, tortured, and sentenced despite all the evidence that he was blameless in his religious beliefs and practices. He finally abjured his 'errors' at the Toledo auto de fe of 22 July 1529.[12]

The mingling of mystical, Erasmian and heretical influences made the late 1520s a unique period of both freedom and tension. The inquisitors sought Lutheran ideas everywhere, and located them in the views of some of the alumbrados. More significant for them, perhaps, was the fact that nearly every person implicated in the groups of these years was a converso: Isabel, Alcaraz, Hernández, Ortiz, Tovar, the Cazallas. It was as though conversos were seeking to reject formal Catholicism by interiorizing their religion. The tendency had a long history among them. Completely at home neither in Judaism nor in Christianity, many of them at all social levels had demonstrated signs of scepticism, unease and Nicodemism. As far back as the reign of King Juan II of Castile (d. 1454), there had been the reputed case of the converso Alfonso Fernández Samuel, who in his will had requested that when laid out in his coffin, he should have the cross placed at his feet, the Koran at his breast, and the Torah, 'his life and light', at his head.[13] In the early years of the Inquisition, considerable evidence came to light not simply of judaizing but also of messianism on one hand and irreligious scepticism on the other. Many conversos, indeed, were ironically condemned for beliefs that orthodox Judaism would have regarded as heretical, such as denying the immortality of the soul.[14] Spiritual dissent among the conversos did not, therefore, necessarily imply any drift towards Judaism. There was nothing remotely Jewish about the beliefs of the alumbrados: the root influence was Franciscan spirituality, the environment was the comfortable patronage afforded by Old Christian nobility.[15]

From the moment she was detained, Hernández attempted to save her skin by incriminating all those against whom she bore a grudge. Tovar had persisted in following her despite the warnings of Vergara. It was no doubt knowledge of Juan de Vergara's hostility that moved Hernández, at her trial in 1530, to denounce him as a Lutheran, a claim that was supported by other disciples of hers. Tovar was already in prison. He was followed there by his brother in June 1530. Finally in April 1532 María de Cazalla was imprisoned and tortured and accused of the various heresies of Lutheranism, illuminism and Erasmianism.[16] Her trial dragged on until December 1534, when she was fined and ordered not to associate again with illuminists. Her brother the bishop had opportunely died in 1530. The Inquisition had not yet finished with their family, however, for from them sprang the circle of Protestants that alarmed Valladolid two decades later. Although the circle had closed round the mystics, they emerged comparatively unscathed.[17] Hernández was by 1532 living in freedom in Medina del Campo; Isabel and Alcaraz, condemned to 'perpetual' prison, were released after a few years;[18] María de Cazalla was fined and had to express her repentance.

The attack on the alumbrados, though of short duration and with few serious casualties, had consequences of lasting importance. This can be seen clearly in the case of the famous preacher Juan de Avila. Active in the mission field in Andalusia in the late 1520s, Avila was denounced as an alumbrado and spent nearly a year (1532–3) in the cells of the Inquisition. He used his idle hours to think out the shape of a book of spiritual guidance, the *Audi, Filia*, which was not in fact presented for publication until 1556. An innocent victim of the alumbrado scare in the 1530s (Avila was a converso), in the 1550s he fell foul not only of the Protestant scare but also of an Inquisitor General, Valdés, who was suspicious of all mystical writings ('works of contemplation for artisans' wives' was how he saw them, according to Luis de Granada). Valdés banned the book in his 1559 Index, and Avila in despair burnt a large number of his manuscripts.[19] Though the *Audi, Filia* circulated in manuscript for several years, it was not until after its author's death in 1569 that the Inquisition allowed it to be published again, at Toledo in 1574. A whole generation of spirituality – we shall come across the case of Luis de Granada – fell under suspicion because of the supposed danger from illuminism.

The most direct threat, however, seemed to come from Lutheranism. An Old Christian, the Basque priest Juan López de Celaín, who had links with the alumbrados of Guadalajara, was arrested in 1528 and burnt as a 'Lutheran' in Granada in July 1530.[20] Lutheranism was also one of the allegations made against Juan de Vergara.[21] Secretary to Cisneros and later to his successor as archbishop of Toledo, Alonso de Fonseca, Vergara was one of the foremost classical scholars in Spain. He had collaborated in the Polyglot Bible, had held the chair of philosophy at Alcalá, and had proposed offering the chair of rhetoric there to Vives. Arrested in 1530, tried and imprisoned, Vergara was obliged to abjure his errors in an auto at Toledo on 21 December 1535, and to pay a heavy fine of 1,500 ducats. After this he was confined to a monastery, from which he emerged in 1537. Like others who completed their allotted penance, he was able to resume his old position in society. We encounter him once more in 1547 at the centre of the great controversy in Toledo over the proposed statutes to exclude conversos from office in the cathedral. He died, still honoured, in Alcalá in May 1566.[22]

Alonso de Virués, a Benedictine and preacher to Charles V, was the first of several eminent preachers to the emperor to be accused of heresy, presumably because of contracts that he, like Vergara, had made abroad. Arrested in 1533 and confined in prison by the Inquisition of Seville for four long years, he pleaded in vain that Erasmus had never been condemned as unorthodox. Finally in 1537 he was made to abjure his errors, condemned to confinement in a monastery for two years, and banned from preaching for another year. Charles V made strenuous efforts to save Virués, and in May 1538 obtained from the pope a bull annulling the sentence. Virués was restored to favour and appointed in 1542 as bishop of the Canary Islands, where he died in 1545.

Another outstanding case, sometimes connected with the origins of Protestantism in Spain, was Juan de Valdés, also of the university of Alcalá, who in the fateful year 1529 published his theological study *Dialogue of Christian Doctrine*, which was closely based on some of Luther's early writings. It was immediately attacked by the Inquisition despite the testimony of Vergara and others. The controversy over the book took so dangerous a turn that in 1530 Valdés fled to Italy, just in time to avoid the trial that was opened against him. His treatise was thereafter distinguished by its appearance in every Index of prohibited books issued by the Inquisition.[23] In 1533 Mateo Pascual, former rector of the Colegio Mayor of San Ildefonso at Alcalá University, and at the time vicar general of the see of Saragossa, fell under suspicion for his links with Juan de Valdés. He was detained for a while in the Inquisition of Toledo, then released to return to Saragossa. Some years later he left Aragon and went to live in Rome, where he died in 1553.[24]

A further casualty of the alumbrado trials was the printer to Alcalá University, Miguel de Eguía, denounced by Francisca Hernández for Lutheranism. He was imprisoned in 1531 and spent over two years in the cells of the Inquisition at Valladolid,[25] but was released at the end of 1533 and was fully absolved. Less fortunate was Pedro de Lerma. Former chancellor of Alcalá University, former dean of the theological faculty at the Sorbonne, canon of Burgos cathedral, he fell under the influence of Erasmus and publicized it in his sermons. He was denounced to the Inquisition, imprisoned, and finally in 1537 was made to abjure publicly, in the towns where he preached, eleven propositions he was accused of having taught. In shame and resentment the old man shook the dust of Spain off his feet and fled to Paris where he resumed his position as a dean of the faculty, dying there in August 1541. According to his nephew Francisco de Enzinas (famous in the history of European Protestantism as Dryander), people in Lerma's home city of Burgos were so afraid of the possible consequences of this event that those who had sent their sons to study abroad recalled them at once.[26] Such a reaction shows an awareness among some Spaniards of the problems involved. Erasmianism and the new humanism were being identified with the German heresy, and for many the only protection was dissociation.

In December 1533 Rodrigo Manrique, son of the Inquisitor General, wrote from Paris to Juan Luis Vives, on the subject of Vergara's imprisonment:

> You are right. Our country is a land of pride and envy; you may add: of barbarism. For now it is clear that down there one cannot possess any culture

without being suspected of heresy, error and Judaism. Thus silence has been imposed on the learned. As for those who take refuge in erudition, they have been filled, as you say, with great terror ... At Alcalá they are trying to uproot the study of Greek completely.[27]

Erasmus's links with his friends in Spain were affected by the reaction. His last surviving letter to that country is dated December 1533. Three years later he died, still highly respected in the Catholic world, so much so that in 1535 the pope had offered him a cardinal's hat. In Spain his cause (as we shall see) survived, but was restricted to a few learned circles. His works remained on sale to the Spanish public for much of the century. But the tide now turned against him.

The decline of interest in Erasmianism, and the suspicions directed against liberal humanism, seemed to be justified by the apparent links between Erasmus and the growing Protestant menace. In our time, Bataillon has shown how the Protestant stream which sprang from illuminism between 1535 and 1555 adapted Erasmianism to its own purposes and moved towards the Lutheran doctrine of 'justification by faith alone' without ever formally rejecting Catholic dogma.[28] Many leading humanists, such as Juan de Valdés, were Erasmians whose defections from orthodoxy were so significant as to give cause for the belief that they were crypto-Protestants. Vigilance against radical Erasmianism was therefore strengthened.

The Lutheran threat, however, took a long time to develop. In 1520 Luther had probably not been heard of in Spain. Lutheran books were first sent to the peninsula, with what result we do not know, by Luther's publisher Froben in 1519. The first Spaniards to come into contact with his teachings were those who accompanied the emperor to Germany. Some of them, seeing in him only a reformer, were favourable to his ideas.

However, a full generation went by and Lutheranism failed to take root in Spain. There was, in those years, no atmosphere of restriction or repression. Before 1558 possibly less than fifty cases of alleged Lutheranism among Spaniards came to the notice of the inquisitors.[29] In most of them, it is difficult to identify specifically Protestant beliefs.

There was some curiosity about the heresies that Luther was propounding, but little sign of any active interest. What explanation can we offer for this astonishing inability of Protestant ideas to penetrate the peninsula? With its unreformed Church, backward clergy and mediaeval religion, Spain was surely ripe for conquest by the Reformation. In one major respect, however, the country was peculiarly unfertile ground. Unlike England, France and Germany, Spain had not since the early Middle Ages experienced a single significant popular heresy. All its ideological struggles since the Reconquest had been directed against the minority religions, Judaism and Islam. There were consequently no native heresies (like Wycliffism in England) on which the German ideas could build. Moreover, Spain was the only European country to possess a national institution dedicated to the elimination of heresy. By its vigilance and by coordinating its efforts throughout the peninsula, the Inquisition may have checked the seeds of heresy before they could be sown. In the 1540s, possibly the only Spanish intellectuals to come directly into contact with Lutheranism were those in foreign universities (at Louvain, for example, where Philip II was shocked by the views of some of the Spaniards in 1558; or in France, where Miguel Servet was educated); those accompanying the emperor's court in Germany; and those who, with the opening of the Council of Trent (1546), were obliged to read Lutheran books in order to combat the errors in them. Among the labouring classes, Spaniards occasionally came into touch with immigrant workers from France or the Netherlands who had direct experience of the new beliefs. Ideas transmitted at this level, however, were confused, distorted, and unlikely to strike root anywhere.

The area most vulnerable to the penetration of foreign ideas was Seville, centre of international commerce. In 1552 the Inquisition there seized some four hundred and fifty Bibles printed abroad.[30] As archbishop of Seville, Manrique had encouraged the appointment of scholars from Alcalá to be canons and preachers in the cathedral. But times were changing, both in Spain as a whole and in Seville. In 1546 the city obtained a new archbishop who was also made Inquisitor General, Fernando de Valdés, a ruthless careerist who saw heresy everywhere.[31] One of the cathedral preachers, Juan Gil, commonly known as Egidio, was nominated by Charles V in 1549 as bishop of Tortosa. The appointment was quashed when Egidio was accused of heresy and in 1552 made to retract ten propositions. 'In truth', commented a member of the disciplinary committee, Domingo de Soto, 'apart from this lapse he is a very good man, and his election [as bishop] was a good decision'.[32] Egidio died in peace at the end of 1555.[33] In 1556 Valdés objected to the appointment as cathedral preacher of Constantino Ponce de la Fuente, an Alcalá humanist and converso who had been chaplain to Charles V in Germany. His writings were examined for heresy; arrested by the Inquisition, he died in its cells two years later.

Neither Egidio nor Constantino can be considered Lutherans. They were humanists who believed in a strongly spiritual religious life and none of their views appears to have been explicitly heretical.[34]

There were, certainly, Protestant sympathizers in Seville. International trade links brought together in the city a broad range of people and opinions that could not fail to influence some Spaniards. Heretical books were imported in quantity. The Spanish 'Protestants' in Seville probably totalled around one hundred and twenty persons, including the prior and members of the Jeronimite monastery of San Isidro, together with several nuns from the Jeronimite convent of Santa Paula. The group managed to exist in security until the 1550s, when some monks from San Isidro opportunely fled. The exiles included Cipriano de Valera, Casiodoro de Reina,[35] Juan Pérez de Pineda and Antonio del Corro, who played little part in Spanish history but were glories of the European Reformation.

Meanwhile, in northern Castile, another circle of Protestant sympathizers had come into existence.[36] The founder was an Italian, Carlos de Seso, who had turned to Protestantism after reading Juan de Valdés, and who from 1554 had been corregidor (civil governor) of Toro. His missionary zeal soon converted an influential and distinguished circle centred on Valladolid and numbering some fifty-five persons, most of noble status and some with converso origins. The most eminent of the converts was Dr Agustín Cazalla, who had been to Germany as chaplain to Charles V and had also accompanied Prince Philip there. Cazalla was influenced by his brother Pedro – parish priest of Pedrosa, near Valladolid – and with him the whole Cazalla family, led by their mother Leonor de Vivero,[37] fell into heresy. Their beliefs were no simple extension of the illuminist or Erasmian attitudes of the previous generation. In their clear rejection of most Catholic dogma the Valladolid heretics were true Protestants. They also included scions of impeccably Old Christian nobility. A leading member of the group, Fray Domingo de Rojas, son of the Marquis of Poza, recruited young Anna Enríquez, daughter of the Marquesa of Alañices. He told her 'that there were only two sacraments, baptism and communion; that in communion Christ did not have the part attributed to him; and that the worst of all things was to say mass, since Christ had already been sacrificed once and for all'.[38]

The Seville group was exposed in 1557, when Juan Ponce de León, eldest son of the Count of Bailén, was arrested together with others for introducing books from Geneva. His chief accomplice was Julián Hernández, who had spent a considerable time in the Reformed churches of

Paris, Scotland and Frankfurt, and who specialized in smuggling Protestant literature into his native country.[39] The Inquisition collected information and in 1558 made a wave of arrests, including the whole Cazalla family in April and Constantino in August. A merciless repression was set in train by Fernando de Valdés, who was concerned to exaggerate the menace in order to regain the favour he had recently lost with the court in Spain.

Commenting on the high social origins of many of the accused, Valdés told Charles V that 'much greater harm can follow if one treats them with the leniency that the Holy Office has shown towards Jewish and Muslim conversos, who generally have been of lowly origin'. The emperor did not need to be alerted. The sudden emergence in Spain's two principal cities of a contagion from which everyone felt the country had been free, sent shock waves through the nation.[40] Charles, in retirement at his villa beside the monastery of Yuste in Extremadura, saw to his horror the rise within Spain of the very menace that had split Germany apart. For him there could be only one response: ruthless repression. His historic letter of 25 May 1558 to his daughter Juana, regent in Spain during Philip II's absence in the Netherlands, appealed to her to follow the tough policy that he himself had used against heresy in Flanders.

I am very satisfied with what you say you have written to the king, informing him of what is happening about the people imprisoned as Lutherans, more of whom are being daily discovered. But believe me, my daughter, this business has caused and still causes me more anxiety and pain than I can express, for while the king and I were abroad these realms remained in perfect peace, free from this calamity. But now that I have returned here to rest and recuperate and serve Our Lord, this great outrage and treachery, implicating such notable persons, occurs in my presence and in yours. You know that because of this I suffered and went through great trials and expenses in Germany, and lost so much of my good health. Were it not for the conviction I have that you and the members of your councils will find a radical cure to this unfortunate situation, punishing the guilty thoroughly to prevent them spreading, I do not know whether I could restrain myself leaving here to settle the matter. Since this affair is more important for the service of Our Lord and the good and preservation of these realms than any other, and since it is only in its beginnings, with such small forces that they can be easily put down, it is necessary to place the greatest stress and weight on a quick remedy and exemplary punishment. I do not know whether it will be enough in these cases to follow the usual practice, by which according to common law all those who beg for mercy and have their confession accepted are pardoned with a light penance if it is a first offence. Such people, if set free, are at liberty to commit the same offence, particularly if they are educated persons.

One can imagine the evil consequences, for it is clear that they cannot act without armed organization and leaders, and so it must be seen whether they can be proceeded against as creators of sedition, upheaval, riots and disturbance in the state. They would then be guilty of rebellion and could not expect any mercy. In this connection I cannot omit to mention what was and is the custom in Flanders. I wanted to introduce an Inquisition to punish the heresies that some people had caught from neighbouring Germany and England and even France. Everyone opposed this on the grounds that there were no Jews among them. Finally an order was issued declaring that all people of whatever state and condition who came under certain specified categories were to be *ipso facto* burnt and their goods confiscated. Necessity obliged me to act in this way. I do not know what the king my son has done since then, but I think that the same reason will have made him continue as I did, because I advised and begged him to be very severe in dealing with these people.

Believe me, my daughter, if so great an evil is not suppressed and remedied without distinction of persons from the very beginning, I cannot promise that the king or anyone else will be in a position to do it afterwards.[41]

This letter really marks the turning point in Spain. From now on, thanks to the fears of Charles and the policy laid down for Inquisitor General Valdés, heterodoxy was treated as a threat to the state and the religious establishment. Writing to the pope on 9 September the same year, Valdés affirmed that 'these errors and heresies of Luther and his brood which have begun to be preached and sown in Spain, threaten sedition and riot'.[42]

Sedition and riot, armed organization and leaders – how far from the dreams of Cazalla and Constantino! Yet once again well-meaning men were prey to the tensions gripping Europe, and the result was a series of autos de fe that burnt out Protestantism in Spain. The first significant auto was held at Valladolid on Trinity Sunday, 21 May 1559, in the presence of the regent Juana and her court. Of the thirty accused, fourteen were burnt, including Cazalla and his brother and sister. The only one to die unrepentant was Francisco Herrero, from Toro. All the rest died repentant after professing conversion, among them Agustín Cazalla, who blessed the Holy Office and wept aloud for his sins. The next auto at Valladolid was held on

8 October in the presence of Philip, who had now returned to Spain and for whom an impressive ceremony was mounted. Of the thirty accused, twenty-six were considered Protestants, and of these, twelve (including four nuns) were burnt at the stake. Carlos de Seso was the showpiece. The inquisitors had for days attempted to make him recant and, in fear for his life, he had shown every sign of repentance. But when at last he realized that he was to be executed regardless, he made a full and moving statement of belief: 'in Jesus Christ alone do I hope, him alone I trust and adore, and placing my unworthy hand in his sacred side I go through the virtue of his blood to enjoy the promises that he has made to his chosen'.[43] He and one other accused were burnt alive as impenitents. 'How could you allow this to happen?', he is said to have called out to the king during the auto. 'If my own son were as wicked as you', Philip is said to have replied indignantly, 'I myself would carry the wood with which to burn him!' The exchange, not documented in any reliable source, was probably apocryphal.

It was now the turn of Seville, where sympathy for Constantino and hostility to the actions of the Inquisition were widespread. A Jesuit reported in 1559 of the former that 'he was and still is highly esteemed', and that 'there are a great many of these murmurings [against the Inquisition]'.[44] The first great auto there was held on Sunday, 24 September 1559.[45] Of the seventy-six accused present, nineteen were burnt as Lutherans, one of them in effigy only.[46] This was followed by the auto held on Sunday, 22 December 1560.[47] Of the total of fifty-four accused on this occasion, fourteen were burnt in person and three in effigy; in all, forty of the accused were Protestants. Egidio and Constantino were two of those burnt in effigy, while those actually burnt included two English sailors, William Brook and Nicholas Burton, and a native of Seville, Leonor Gómez, together with her three young daughters. This auto de fe was followed by one two years later, on 26 April 1562, and by another on 28 October. The whole of that year saw eighty-eight cases of Protestantism punished; of these, eighteen were burnt in person, among them the prior of San Isidro and four of his priests.

With these burnings native Protestantism was almost totally extinguished in Spain. For contemporaries in 1559, it was the start to an emergency without precedent in Spanish history. That very August the primate of the Spanish Church, Archbishop Carranza of Toledo, was arrested by the Inquisition on charges arising in part out of allegations made by Cazalla and Seso. Threatened, as it seemed, by the incursions of heresy, the inquisitors stretched their resources to check the contagion wherever it might appear. In Toledo in September 1559 placards were found posted up on houses and in the cathedral itself, attacking the Catholic Church as 'not the Church of Jesus Christ but the Church of the devil and of Antichrist his son, the Antichrist pope'.[48] The culprit, apprehended in 1560 and burnt, was a priest, Sebastian Martínez. At the same time, in Seville pamphlets circulated attacking 'these thieves of inquisitors, who rob publicly and who burnt the bones of Egidio and of Constantino out of jealousy'. The leaflets also asked the public to 'pray to God for his true Church to be strong and constant in the truth and bear with the persecution from the synagogue of Satan' (that is, the Inquisition).[49]

The great autos de fe up to 1562 served to remind the population of the gravity of the crisis and taught them to try to identify Lutherans in their midst. As a consequence the tribunals of the Inquisition in the 1560s devoted themselves to a hunt for Lutheran heresy, and drew into their net scores of Spaniards who in an unguarded moment had made statements praising Luther or attacking the clergy. In Cuenca, for instance, no sooner had one resident heard the news from Valladolid than he zealously denounced one of his neighbours to the Inquisition for reading a certain book of whose contents he – being illiterate – knew nothing. In those same weeks the archbishop of Tarragona (Fernando de Loazes, who had some years before been inquisitor in Barcelona) stopped over in Cuenca on his way to his diocese. He was asked about the Carranza case, and replied: 'If the archbishop was a heretic, we are all heretics'. He too was denounced to the Inquisition. In both cases, the inquisitors sensibly took no action.[50]

These years helped the old and ailing Inquisitor General Valdés to save his career for a while longer. He attempted to convince Philip II that a major crisis was in the making, and that only the Inquisition could resolve it. In May 1558 he wrote informing Philip, then in Brussels, of Lutheran books in Salamanca and many other places, of problems with the Moriscos, of the discovery of judaizers in Murcia, and of the Lutherans in Valladolid and Seville.[51] The Murcia cases, in which a large number of people were executed on very flimsy evidence,[52] was in fact a local phenomenon of passing importance. The Protestant cases were serious enough, on the other hand, to encourage Valdés to ask, virtually, that the country be put into the hands of the Inquisition.[53] He suggested that new tribunals be set up immediately in Galicia, Asturias and the Basque country; that a second tribunal be set up in Valladolid; that special vigilantes be set up everywhere; that no book should in future be printed without the permission of the Inquisition; that no books should be sold without prior examination by the inquisitors; and so on. Fortunately, the new king took no notice of these suggestions.

The Protestant scare was in any case never as grave as Valdés made out. After the anti-Lutheran repression of these months, the Inquisition was in reality over the hump. From the 1560s Judaism was no longer an issue, and the Reformation no longer a threat. Autos de fe were wound down. When held they were more showy and ceremonious, in the manner of the great autos of 1559, to make up for the lack of penitents.[54] In perspective, the Protestant crisis in Spain, often presented as a singularly bloody period of repression, seems almost humane when compared with the ferocity of religious persecution in other countries. In all Spain probably just over a hundred persons were condemned to death by the Inquisition between 1559 and 1566.[55] The English authorities under Queen Mary had executed nearly three times as many heretics as died in Spain in the years just after 1559, the French under Henry II at least twice as many. In the Netherlands ten times as many had died. In all three countries, very many more died for religious reasons in the years that followed. 'The healthiest of all is Spain', Philip II observed with some justice to the Inquisitor General.[56]

Protestantism never developed into a real threat in Spain. Several cases, from all over the peninsula, are known to us because they appear in the records of the Inquisition. Three men appeared on suspicion in an auto in Saragossa on 17 May 1560. In an auto of 20 November 1562 two were burnt alive for Protestantism.[57] The total number of Spaniards accused of 'Lutheranism' (as the inquisitors insisted on labelling all varieties of Reformation belief) in the last decades of the century totalled about two hundred. Most of them were in no sense Protestants. The majority of these cases demonstrated in reality the ignorance of the inquisitors rather than any real Lutheran threat. They recall the equally indiscriminate persecution that the tribunal had directed against conversos a half-century before. Irreligious sentiments, drunken mockery, anticlerical expressions, were all captiously classified by the inquisitors (or by those who denounced the cases) as 'Lutheran'. Disrespect to church images, and eating meat on forbidden days, were taken as signs of heresy. A hapless uneducated woman of Toledo who claimed in 1568 that 'all those who die go straight to heaven', was accused of the heresy of denying the existence of purgatory.[58] It is clear that in such cases, of which there were very many, the agents of the Holy Office were reacting to unofficial beliefs among the people rather than to any infiltration of heresy.

There were of course a few convinced heretics to be found – among them the nobleman Gaspar de Centelles, burnt in Valencia in 1564,[59] and Fray Cristóbal de Morales, burnt in Granada in 1571 – but fewer than a dozen Spaniards were burnt alive for Lutheranism in the later part of the century outside the cases tried at Valladolid and Seville. Others – like the slightly crazy Friar Pedro de Orellana,[60] who spent twenty-eight years in the prisons of the Holy Office – were arrested for offences that included suspicion of 'Lutheranism', but had no identifiable Lutheran beliefs.

Much of the potential Spanish Reformation had emigrated abroad. Since the mid-sixteenth century Spaniards sympathetic to the Reformation could be found dotted around intellectual groups in western Europe. Rather than refugees, they were part of the well-worn tradition of wandering scholars. True emigration commenced with the discovery of the Protestant cells in Seville and Valladolid. A small stream of refugees made their way into the Reformation communities abroad.

Many in Spain were alarmed by the trend. In some cases, there were fears of the dishonour that could be brought on families by heresy. This provoked at least one murder, that of Juan Díaz in Germany (referred to below in Chapter Eleven). The government, for its part, tried to repatriate Spaniards who fell under suspicion. Philip II was convinced by his officials that it would be a useful policy. In 1560 his ambassador in London, Quadra, reported that several Spanish Protestants were turning up in that city. 'They arrive every day with their wives and children and it is said that many more are expected'.[61] Philip's father had in the 1540s condoned the occasional seizure outside Spain of Castilians who became active Protestants. They were packed off home and made to face the music there. The intention was not, as a subsequent ambassador of Philip in England explained, to eliminate them but to keep an eye on them and hope that others would take the hint and mend their ways.[62] Under Philip II, the selective kidnapping was carried out by two agents based in the Netherlands, one of them the army paymaster Alonso del Canto. They were sponsored by the king's secretary Francisco de Eraso. With the help of special funds, a little network was set up to spy on Spanish émigrés living in England, the Netherlands and Germany. Their most notable success was in persuading the famous humanist Furió Ceriol to return to Spain in 1563. In the process, they collected valuable information on Spanish Protestants abroad.[63] Canto in the spring of 1564 was able to inform Madrid of the preparation by Juan Pérez de Pineda of a new version of the Bible in Spanish.[64]

The real brunt of the attack on so-called 'Lutheranism' was borne by foreign visitors, such as traders and sailors, and by foreigners resident in Spain. The heresy scare intensified xenophobia among many sections of the population. It made Spain, at least for a while, unsafe for foreigners. The Holy Office had been active against them from as early as the 1530s. Spain's extensive trade with northern Europe made contact with outsiders inevitable, especially in the ports. The first Protestant foreigner to be burnt by the Inquisition was young John Tack, an Englishman of Flemish origin, burnt in Bilbao in May 1539.[65] Up until 1560, nine other foreigners were arrested and 'reconciled' by the inquisitors on this coastline.

In the Toledo area in the 1560s French and Flemish residents were those principally accused of heresy.[66] Some had accompanied Philip II back from Flanders or had come with the new queen, Elizabeth Valois, from France. The 1560s were the only decade in which Flemings figured in any number.[67] More usually, those accused were French. In Barcelona the inquisitor in 1560 felt it opportune to hold an auto de fe 'so that people are on their guard against foreigners'.[68] Foreigners indeed constituted the bulk of prosecutions in these years, especially in frontier tribunals.[69] In Barcelona between 1552 and 1578 there were fifty-one alleged Lutherans burnt in person or in effigy, but all were foreign. Nearly all the cases arising at Valencia from 1554 to 1598 involved foreigners, eight of whom were burnt in person or in effigy. In the tribunal of Calahorra (later transferred to Logroño), though there were as many as sixty-eight cases of suspected Lutheranism in 1540–99, the majority (82 per cent) were foreigners. 'All the people punished in this Inquisition are poor foreigners', the tribunal reported in 1565.[70] In northern Spain, as a result of the proximity of the Calvinist areas of France, Frenchmen were singled out for suspicion. Between 1560 and 1600, the Inquisition in the provinces of the crown of Aragon and in Navarre executed some eighty Frenchmen as presumed heretics, burnt another hundred in effigy, and sent some three hundred and eighty to the galleys.[71]

The victimization of non-Spaniards by the Inquisition brings into focus its xenophobic and racialist tendencies. As it had pointed the finger once at conversos and Moriscos (see Chapter Ten), so it now pointed the finger at all foreigners, regardless of religion. The attitude, even when practised in the crown of Aragon, must be attributed mainly to the Castilian inquisitors. In the 1560s the Consellers of Barcelona reminded the inquisitors that they were unwise to pick on French people indiscriminately, since they must know that the greater part of Frenchmen were Catholic. But the inquisitors, sticking by an ideological attitude that endured into the first half of the twentieth century, persisted in describing all nations outside Spain as '*tierras de herejes*' (heretical countries).[72]

The Castilian inquisitors looked with special suspicion on the Basques and Catalans. In 1567 the local inquisitor, who happened to be visiting San Sebastián, commented that 'the natives of this town have too much contact with the French, with whom they link up through marriage; and they always speak their language [i.e. French], rather than their own or Spanish'.[73] In Catalonia, the inquisitors were continuously suspicious of the religion of the Catalans, but failed all the same to find any heresy in the province. 'Their Christianity is such', an inquisitor reported in 1569, 'that it is cause for wonder, living as they do next to and among heretics and dealing with them every day'.[74] There was, in effect, an open frontier between France and Catalonia. The bookshops of Barcelona were full of books printed in France. Possibly one-tenth of the population of Barcelona and one-third of that of Perpignan, Catalonia's two main cities, were French. Despite this unimpeded contact between the two nations, Catalans made not the slightest move towards embracing heresy. In default of victims among the Catalans, the Inquisition sought them among the French.

The failure of the Protestant cause in the Mediterranean inevitably raises the question of why no Reformation occurred in Spain. Efficiency of repression is not the answer. Repression was more efficient and more brutal in other countries, notably the Netherlands, yet persecution there did not check the Reformation. Philip II was convinced that *timely* repression and continuous vigilance were the key. 'Had there been no Inquisition', he affirmed in 1569, 'there would be many more heretics, and the country would be much afflicted, as are those where there is no Inquisition as in Spain'.[75] The king may have believed it, but it was not true.

Nor is it possible to maintain that Spain was sealed off from contact with heresy. The outdated image of an iron curtain of the Inquisition descending on the country and cutting it off from the rest of the world, has no relation to reality. Precisely in the 1550s and 1560s, very many Spaniards were travelling abroad. More Spaniards than ever before published (as we shall see) their books in foreign parts. Tens of thousands, mainly Castilians, served overseas in the army, where they rubbed shoulders with people of other faiths. The land frontier in the Pyrenees was occasionally watched, because of the danger of military intervention by French

Protestant nobles and by bandits, but it could never be closed. Throughout the late sixteenth century, Spaniards drifted at will over the frontier. Some went to trade, some to be educated, some because they wished to join the Calvinists in Geneva. At the same time, many foreigners, principally artisans, came to Spain. It was a handful of these who, through carelessness on their part, fell into the hands of the Inquisition.

The difficulty in controlling the Pyrenees frontier, Spain's chief overland link with the world outside, comes through in the anxious correspondence of the ambassador to France in the 1560s, Francés de Álava. In 1564 and 1565 he sent reports to the king about booksellers from Saragossa, Medina del Campo and Alcalá who had come to Lyon and Toulouse to purchase books on law and philosophy for taking home.[76] In one of the cases, he said, the bookseller had links with Geneva. This importation of foreign books, we may observe, was carried out in open contravention of the laws of Castile. Álava also confirmed that 'many books, catechisms and psalters in Basque' had passed through Toulouse to Spain.[77] Basque was his own native language, so he knew of what he spoke. Books in Catalan, he reported, had also been taken into Catalonia, and other heretical books had gone to Pamplona.[78] In those same weeks the archbishop of Bordeaux forwarded a report on a citizen of Burgos who 'had taken four or five loads of heretical books in Spanish and in Latin through the mountains of Jaca'.[79] Despite the open frontier, heresy failed to penetrate at all. The Reformation remained, for Spaniards, a phenomenon that did not affect them.

6

THE IMPACT ON LITERATURE AND SCIENCE

The times are such that one should think carefully before writing books.

Antonio de Araoz, SJ, September 1559[1]

Almost from the beginning the Inquisition took an interest in aspects of literature. When Hebrew books and the Talmud were found in the possession of conversos, they were seized and destroyed. The inquisitors also seem from an early period to have frowned on magic and astrology. There is a reference, probably from the late 1480s, to the burning of a large quantity of such books found in the university of Salamanca. The diffusion of the printing-press in Europe at the end of the fifteenth century made authorities in both Church and state aware of the need to oversee book output.

In Castile controls by the government over printing dated back to Ferdinand and Isabella. On 8 July 1502 they issued a pragmatic by which licences were made obligatory for the printing of books inside the realm as well as for the introduction of foreign books. Licences could be granted only by the presidents of the Chancillerías (high courts) of Valladolid and Granada, and by the prelates of Toledo, Seville, Granada, Burgos and Salamanca.[2] Publishing was in its infancy, and the law had little effect. In the rest of Spain printing remained free of government control.

The intervention of the state in pre-publication censorship was new. The Lateran Council in 1515 and in particular the Council of Trent in 1564, granted bishops in Europe a general power to license books for printing. But printing was still a novelty, printed books were few, and controls in the early years of the century were lax. The coming of the Reformation by contrast unleashed a flood of controversial literature, which authorities everywhere attempted to curb. In England the government produced licensing laws in 1538, and in the 1540s various Italian authorities passed similar edicts. Spain came late into the field of censorship.

The Inquisition was given no formal powers to license books, though between 1520 and 1550 it informally managed to issue a few permits to print.[3] After the 1550s it limited itself exclusively to post-publication censorship. Since there were no existing guides to heretical books, the tribunal had to rely at first on foreign direction. It was a papal order that provoked the first ban on Lutheran books in Spain, issued by Cardinal Adrian of Utrecht in April 1521 in his capacity as Inquisitor General. Thereafter prohibitions of individual books were notified through letters (*cartas accordadas*) sent to the tribunals, and from 1540 regular lists of banned works were issued by the Holy Office. When feasible, a catalogue of prohibited works, the famous Index, was issued.

In the 1530s and 1540s the Inquisition attempted to stop the entry of heretical literature into the peninsula. As the only Spanish tribunal with authority over all Spain, it was able to act in areas (such as seaports) where state officials could not. The government took no direct initiative over controlling literature until the shock discovery of Protestants in 1558. That event stung the regent Juana into action. On 7 September 1558 she issued a radical decree of control. The law banned the introduction into Castile of all books printed in other realms in Spanish, obliged printers to seek licences from the council of Castile (which in 1554 had been granted control over such permits), and laid down a strict procedure for the operation of censorship. Contravention of any of these points would be punished by death and confiscation. At the same time the Inquisition was allowed to issue licences when printing for its own purpose. According to the new rules, manuscripts were to be checked and censored both before and after publication, and all booksellers were to keep by them a copy of the Index of prohibited books. So wide-ranging was the decree of 1558 that it remained theoretically in force until the end of the ancien regime.[4]

Philip was in Brussels, from which he wrote approving all the measures taken by his sister. Heresy was spreading through European universities. As a consequence, just before returning to Spain, the king banned his Netherlands subjects from studying in France. When he arrived in the peninsula in 1559, he issued an order on 22 November to all subjects of the crown of Castile studying or teaching abroad to return within four months. An exception was made for those studying at particular named colleges at Bologna, Rome, Naples and Coimbra. No Castilians were in future to be allowed abroad to study except at these.

The censorship law of 1558 and the ban on studying abroad were harsh measures because they had no precedent. They have always been considered, mistakenly, as virtually converting Spain into a police state in the area of literature. There were in reality several weaknesses in the legislation.

First of all, the biggest loophole in both measures was that they only affected Castilians. Philip was able to issue his decrees through the council of Castile; in the other realms by contrast he would have had to summon the Cortes, which he did not do. The entire eastern half of the peninsula, and the whole length of the Pyrenees, were consequently exempt from control. Any author who had difficulties getting a licence to publish in Madrid could therefore simply go to a printer in one of the other non-Castilian peninsular realms and publish there. In Catalonia, the king complained in 1568, 'the printers publish many new books without having our licence'.[5] Not until the later years of the reign did the crown manage to claim some degree of control over licensing in the crown of Aragon: in Catalonia from 1573, in Valencia from the 1580s, in Aragon from as late as 1592.[6] Even in Castile the 1558 law exempted most ecclesiastical books (which constituted the most important part of regular book production), and Inquisition publications, from the need to obtain state control.[7] Over a large part of Spain, consequently, the 1558 law had no force. In these areas, printing normally had to be licensed by the local bishop.

Second, the control of imports was operative in Castile alone. The 7 September law regulated the import of books *only* 'into these realms' (Castile and León). The other realms, namely 'Aragon, Valencia, Catalonia and Navarre', were excluded.[8] Books coming *from* them to Castile were subject to control, but there was no legislation to restrain books coming to them from outside. The bookshops of Barcelona imported freely books published abroad in Spanish and other languages.[9] Outside Castile, as a consequence, the government was obliged to rely on the Inquisition in its attempts to oversee the book import trade.

Third, the printing controls had to contend with the reality that Spain relied heavily on foreign imports for its access to literature.[10] When the tutor of the future Philip II went book-shopping for the prince in Salamanca in the 1540s, most of the books he bought were printed abroad. Imported volumes on humanities (including the complete works of Erasmus), literature, science and art featured in the list.[11] Effective application of the law governing imports was not possible, because bookshops in Spain depended for their living on supplies from abroad. Foreign presses continued to dominate the printing of religious works not only in Bibles but also in mass-books and works of devotion.[12] The flow of literature never stopped, as the case of Barcelona shows. No attempt was ever made by the Inquisition to interfere with trade in this city. Ten years after the decrees of 1558–9, booksellers continued to rely for their income on the uninterrupted import of foreign books, many of which went on to Castile. 'The books that enter through this frontier are very numerous', the inquisitors reported from Catalonia in 1569, 'and even if there were many inquisitors we would not be enough to deal with so many volumes'.[13]

Fourth, the biggest problem with the legislation of 1558–9 was that, true to form, many Spaniards simply ignored it. The printer of a new book normally preferred to apply for the licence issued by the council of Castile, because it carried with it a 'privilege' or exclusive right to publish and sell. Reprints on the other hand did not require a new licence. Printers and authors therefore felt free to bring out 'reprints', even if important changes had been introduced into the text.[14] But many authors tried successfully to avoid the censorship process, which could involve interminable delays. They published without permission, or (more frequently) published abroad, in Italy or in France. In the 1540s, most books by Spaniards were published outside Spain, notably in Antwerp, Paris, Lyon and Venice.[15] Despite the apparently restrictive nature of the 1558 law, Spanish writers continued throughout the latter half of the century to publish as much abroad as they did at home. It was a freedom enjoyed, ironically, by no other European country.[16] The works published abroad were, of course, imported into Spain. No intention of heresy arose. In the late sixteenth century at least sixty leading Spanish writers published their works abroad, in Lyon in France, rather than in Spain.[17] The fact was that the quality of presses outside Spain was much better, and controls less onerous.[18] As a consequence, the penalties laid down by the 1558 law often remained a virtual dead letter. Enjoying the ability to publish with impunity in the realms of Aragon, Italy, France or the Netherlands, Spaniards could boast that they had more freedom of literature than their neighbours. In Valencia at a later period, some forty per cent of publications had no licence or permission of any sort.[19] Despite all the unlicensed publishing, not a single author or printer in Spain – other than those condemned as Protestants – is known to have suffered the death penalty. By contrast, in England and France the risk of punishment was real.

Throughout Europe, the Reformation crisis generated hopes but also fears. It was the beginning, both in Spain and outside it, of an epoch of caution. 'Before that time', a Dominican said of the year 1558, 'Spain was wholly untouched by these errors'. 'There was no need at that time to be suspicious of anyone', an abbot observed of the previous decades.[20]

Among humanists and university men, the old ideal of an international republic of letters began to break down. When there had been one sole faith in Europe, scholars travelled freely across frontiers. Now they tended to remain within national boundaries. Institutions began to give classes in the local language rather than in Latin. Spanish students were probably the least affected by the process, since they had seldom gone to foreign colleges. The ones they most frequented, in Bologna and Rome, were precisely those still permitted to them. In addition, they could of course attend any of the colleges in the king's dominions, such as the Netherlands. In practice, difficulties of distance, financing and language, were tending to rule these out. Active contacts continued for a while only with French universities. The spread of heresy there, and Spanish restrictions, reduced these to a minimum. Of 228 Spanish scientific authors from the early sixteenth century, some eleven per cent had been professors in foreign universities and twenty-five per cent had studied abroad; after 1560 the proportion was negligible. Montpellier, famous for its medical studies, turned Calvinist during the 1560s. Between 1503 and 1550, 310 Spaniards (mostly Aragonese) studied there; up to 1565 fourteen more registered; after 1573 no further Spaniards feature in the official lists.[21]

The frontiers, however, were never closed, least of all with France. Only Castilians, as we have seen, were bound by the new restrictions. In 1565 the Spanish ambassador in France reported that there were twenty Aragonese and Catalan students at the university of Toulouse, and he knew of two Catalans studying medicine at Montpellier.[22] In the 1560s Navarrese with Protestant sympathies emigrated freely to France. Not until 1568 was the ban extended to Spaniards living in the eastern part of the peninsula.[23] However, as late as 1585 a frontier guard at Irún could report 'having seen pass through some Spaniards on foot, others on horseback on excursion (though he does not know how many nor from where they came); and that there have also passed through the frontier-post Italians, Flemings, and Burgundians; and many Portuguese on foot and on horse with their wives, children and clothing'.[24] Students crossed over to study in France. The secretary of the Inquisition in Logroño reported the case in 1584 of 'a Dr León, a medical doctor, who said he was a citizen of Valladolid, with two sons whom he said he was taking to study in Bordeaux. When asked why he was taking his sons to Bordeaux, where there was little security in matters of religion, and when there were so many good universities in Spain, he replied that if he did not find conditions suitable in Bordeaux he would take them to Paris'.[25] Nothing was done to impede the doctor, who left his sons in Bordeaux and returned tranquilly to Valladolid. Several other scholars continued to study in France, but the Spanish government turned a blind eye. The new controls, despite their limited efficacy, may have curbed movement across frontiers. But they had little perceptible impact on intellectual life.

Systematic guides to forbidden literature were first issued in the form of an 'index' by the university of Paris in 1542. The university of Louvain began to issue indexes in 1546, and in Italy various indexes were published in the 1540s.[26]

The first printed Index to be used in Spain, issued by Inquisitor General Valdés in September 1551, was no more than a reprint of one compiled by the university of Louvain in 1550, with a special appendix devoted to Spanish books. Steps were taken to have the Index distributed by the tribunals.[27] Each tribunal was allowed to modify its local version, so we know of at least five indexes issued in 1551–2, by the tribunals of Toledo, Valladolid, Valencia, Granada and Seville.[28] The works of sixteen authors, mainly the leaders of the Reformation, were condemned in their entirety; but for the rest the Inquisition was content to ban some sixty-one works individually, and lay down regulations about Bibles, books in Hebrew and Arabic, and works printed without authorization.

During those years a large number of unlicensed Bibles and New Testaments was entering the peninsula, many with translations or comments that did not coincide with orthodox views. The Inquisition began steps to censor the editions, and meanwhile ordered its tribunals in May 1552 to collect up any available copies. The results were astonishing. In Seville alone, the inquisitors rounded up 450 volumes.[29] In Saragossa the tribunal confiscated 218 unlicensed Bibles, most of them published in Lyon.[30] At least twenty unlicensed Bibles were identified in Valencia. Many could be found in Salamanca. Faced by an extensive distribution of unapproved volumes, Valdés issued in 1554 a general censure of Bibles and New Testaments, identifying for correction sixty-five editions of the Scriptures issued in Lyon, Antwerp, Paris and other places.[31]

All the steps taken till the middle of the century were in response to an indirect threat from the Reformation. Heresy was still something distant; even the infiltration of Bibles could (it was felt)[32] be handled without problems. The discovery of Protestants and the emergency laws of 1558 changed the situation radically. The Inquisition, entrusted with some of the censorship regulations, was ordered to put together an Index as quickly as possible.

The task was undertaken by Fernando de Valdés. In little less than a year, and consulting with very few experts other than his fellow Dominican and friend Melchor Cano,[33] Valdés managed to draw up a substantial Index of Prohibited Books, published in the summer of 1559. Books were divided into sections according to language, and forbidden if they fell into the following categories: all books by heresiarchs; all religious books written by those condemned by the Inquisition; all books on Jews and Moors with an anti-Catholic bias; all heretical translations of the Bible; all vernacular translations of the Bible, even by Catholics; all devotional works in the vernacular; all controversial works between Catholics and heretics; all books on magic; all verse using Scriptural quotations 'profanely'; all books printed since 1515 without details of author and publisher; all anti-Catholic books; all pictures and figures disrespectful to religion.

The approximately seven hundred books listed as forbidden were in no way a carefully considered response to the problem of Reformation heresy, or an attempt to ban books that Spaniards might actually possess. Valdés and his friends for the most part simply stuck together, in a scissors and paste operation, prohibitions decreed in other countries. Seventy per cent of the entries[34] were drawn directly from the previous Index of 1551, from the Indices of Louvain (1550) and Portugal (1551), and from other Indices, notably of Paris and Venice. The biggest category of prohibited books, those in Latin, representing nearly two-thirds of the 700 items, were almost all (with seven exceptions) published in foreign countries.

These details are highly significant. They demonstrate that the weight of the Index was directed to keeping *out* of Spain books that had for the most part never entered the country. The prohibition of fifty-four items in Dutch, a language unknown in Spain, could hardly be interpreted otherwise. Evidently, many foreign editions were circulating within Spain, for booksellers relied heavily on book imports. But the true interest and significance of the Index for Spaniards at the time was less in its shadow-boxing with books that they had neither seen nor read, than in those few books that they were able to read in their own language.

Three categories of books in Spanish stand out for their condemnation in the Index. First, there was the question of Erasmus. Philip II when young had been a devotee of the humanist, and on his trip to the Netherlands in 1548 he had made a special visit to his birthplace, Rotterdam.[35] The controversies of the Reformation epoch, however, undermined Erasmus's standing. The Index of 1551 included his *Colloquies*. While some were debating whether to condemn Erasmus more fully, the Roman Inquisition under Paul IV came out in 1559 with a general condemnation of all his works. The Jesuits protested strongly against this measure, among the most vociferous being the Dutchman Peter Canisius. Diego Laínez for his part said openly that the papal Index was something 'which restricted many spirits and pleased few, particularly outside Italy'.[36] The Jesuits were no friends of Erasmus, but they felt that sweeping bans were unhelpful. The Spanish Index of 1559 listed fourteen works in Spanish by Erasmus, including the *Enchiridion*. From this time his name fell into disfavour. The Spanish Index of 1612 banned completely all his works in Spanish, and classified the author in the category of *auctores damnati*.

Erasmus remained (despite a common but mistaken opinion to the contrary) for more than a generation a respected name.[37] His works were cited by leading authors both religious and secular, and in Barcelona they remained openly on sale. Even his forbidden books were kept in private collections and highly treasured. His influence remained in the stream of thought that stretched as far as Cervantes. Intemperate defences of him (Francisco Sánchez, 'El Brocense', in 1595 declared in a lecture, 'Whoever speaks ill of Erasmus is either a friar or an ass!')[38] might invite recrimination. But in the end, as with most thinkers, he quite simply ceased to be the fashion.

The second notable feature of the Index was its attention to literary works. In 1551 it had banned only a handful of Castilian works. By contrast, nineteen works of a literary character were now banned. Among the authors affected by prohibition of one or more items were Gil Vicente, Hernando de Talavera, Bartolomé Torres Naharro, Juan del Encina, and Jorge Montemayor.[39] The *Lazarillo de Tormes* was banned and also the *Cancionero General*.

The third and most notable aspect of the Index was its campaign against vernacular works of piety. Valdés and his advisers were vividly aware of the recent spiritualizing movements that had produced the alumbrados. They also suspected links between those movements and the Protestants. As a consequence they came down heavily on some of the best known spiritual writers of the generation. The most prominent casualties were Juan de Avila's *Audi, Filia*,[40] Luis de Granada's *Book of Prayer* and Francisco Borja's *Works of a Christian*.

Granada's *Book of Prayer*, first published in 1554, became so popular in Spain that it went through twenty-three editions up to the time it was put on the Index (principally at the instance of Melchor Cano, who had been among the first to smell heresy in the *Catechism* of the archbishop of Toledo). It was in vain that Fray Luis tried to get the ban rescinded. Finding no help in Spain, he succeeded in getting the *Book* approved by the Council of Trent and the pope. Such approval was not enough for the inquisitors, and it was only when he accepted 'corrections' in his text that the book was allowed to circulate freely.[41]

The ban on Borja also emanated from Cano, an open enemy of the Jesuits. Because it was an international order, many in Spain were suspicious of the Company of Jesus. A Jesuit from Valladolid reported the opinion among some 'that the Theatines (which is what they call us here in this Babel) have been the source of Luther's errors'. Valdés's Index fell like a thunderclap on the Company. Borja, Duke of Gandía and former viceroy of Catalonia, was the most distinguished recruit ever to join the society in Spain. The ban on his work threatened to bring disrepute not only upon him but upon all the Jesuits. Fearing that he was about to be arrested by the Inquisition, he left Spain for Rome in the spring of 1560 and never again returned to his homeland.[42] This was not the end of the travails of the Jesuits. The 1559 Index prohibited devotional works in the vernacular even if they were not printed (at that time many books used to circulate in manuscript form). The worried rector of the Jesuit college in Seville went to the inquisitors to ask if the ban applied also to Loyola's *Spiritual Exercises*, which was used by the novices in manuscript translation and not published in Castilian until 1615. To his horror he was told that the prohibition did apply. He went back to the college, collected all the copies of the *Exercises*, handed them to the Inquisition, then took to his bed in grief and mortification.[43] Seville was the scene also of another casualty of the drive against spiritualist piety. A much respected Dominican friar, Domingo de Valtanás, aged seventy-three at the time, was arrested in 1561 on very vague charges probably associated with illuminism, and confined to a monastery where he died shortly after.[44]

The Index of 1559 has often been taken to represent the beginning of an epoch of repression in Spanish culture. It would probably be more correct to see it as the *only* repressive Index prior to the eighteenth century. It was the first but also the only pre-1700 Index to attack notable works of Castilian poetry and literature, all of them antedating the mid-sixteenth century. None of the authors concerned had a serious brush with the Inquisition on account of the work affected. Thereafter, no Index before the age of the Enlightenment went any further in attacks on Spanish literature. Rather than opening a repressive phase, the 1559 Index seems to have been, on one hand, an ill-thought-out attempt to control some aspects of creativity; and on the other, a hostile response to aspects of native spirituality.

Censorship encouraged a practice which later became common: the burning of books. Book-burning was, of course, a traditional device used by Christians against their enemies. The emperor Constantine used it against Arian works. In 1248 the clergy in Paris burned fourteen cartloads of Jewish books. The mediaeval Inquisition followed suit, and in the sixteenth century it was a common practice in Italy and France. Torquemada in his day had organized a book-burning in his monastery in Salamanca. Jewish sacred books were the object of a bonfire in Toledo in May 1490 when 'many books by the said heretics were burnt publicly in the square'.[45] A royal decree of October 1501 ordered Arabic books to be burnt in Granada, and a huge bonfire was held under the auspices of Cisneros. From March 1552 the Inquisition ordered that heretical books be burnt publicly.[46] Some twenty-seven books were ordered to be burnt at a ceremony in Valladolid in January 1558.[47] In mid-century the Spaniards probably resorted to burning because it seemed the simplest way to get rid of offending material. Very many works perished. 'On seven or eight occasions we have burnt mountains of books here in our college', a Jesuit working for the Barcelona Holy Office reported in 1559.[48] In 1561 an official in Seville asked what should be done with the numerous books he had rounded up. There were many books of hours, he said, which could be easily corrected. 'Burn them', the Inquisition replied. And what of the Bibles? 'Burn them'. And the books of medicine, many with superstitious material? 'Burn them'.[49] This drastic solution was not always applied. Subsequently, when the tribunal had elaborated its new system of expurgation rather than condemnation, books were kept in store and not normally destroyed.

The 1559 Index had set out to identify suspicious books and prohibit them outright. Subsequent Indices started from a completely different perspective. The next Index was not issued for a quarter of a century, and in the interim the Inquisition proceeded by cartas acordadas, issuing some forty-three orders affecting a total of fifty books.[50] The single most important influence on Catholic thinking about censorship at this period was the Index of Prohibited Books issued by the Council of Trent in 1564. Its premises were accepted as authoritative by all the theologians and inquisitors who helped to prepare the next Spanish Index. Meanwhile Philip II had arranged for the Tridentine Index to be published in Flanders in 1570, and sponsored the preparation there by Benito Arias Montano, the distinguished Hebraist, of a special 'expurgatory' Index (1571). Montano's Index was novel because it adopted the practice of excising offending passages from otherwise orthodox books, which thereby escaped blanket prohibition. Philip II felt that there were lessons to be learnt from the method of censorship adopted in Flanders, for he informed the Duke of Alba at the end of 1569 that Montano's draft index 'will be a model for making one like it here, and to this effect a copy has been given to those of the Inquisition'.[51]

The Indices of 1564 and 1571 played a fundamental part in the elabo-ration of Spain's new Index, first discussed at a committee meeting in Salamanca in the latter year. Very little progress was made, possibly in part because of profound disagreements among the professors of Salamanca, some of whom (as we shall see) were in 1572 arrested by the Inquisition as a result of intrigues within the professorial body. Only after the end of this affair, in 1578, were the plans to prepare an Index resumed.[52] Juan de Mariana devoted considerable time to helping the compilers: 'I worked on it as much as anybody, and for a long time had four secretaries together helping me'.[53] The Index which emerged consisted of two volumes – one of prohibited books (1583), the other of expurgated (1584) – issued by the Inquisitor General Gaspar de Quiroga. There was an impressive increase in items compared with the previous Index. Valdés had prohibited some seven hundred items; the 1583 Index included 2315, three times as many.[54] Of these, 74 per cent were in Latin, 8.5 per cent in Castilian and 17.5 per cent in other languages.

The scope of the 1583 Index was, in appearance, staggering. By its sheer size it drew into its ambit the whole of the European intellectual world, both past and present. Editions of classical authors and of fathers of the Church, the collected works of Peter Abelard and of Rabelais, selected works by William of Ockham, Savonarola, Jean Bodin, Machiavelli, Juan Luis Vives, Marsiglio of Padua, Ariosto, Dante and Thomas More (whose *Utopia* was banned until expurgated, although the Index conceded that he was *vir alius pius et catholicus*) were among the casualties. At first glance it would appear that the Inquisition was declaring war against the whole of European culture.

In reality the Quiroga Index was much less aggressive than appears. For the most part it simply took over existing condemnations in the Catholic world. It integrated almost wholesale the previous Index of 1559, the Tridentine Index of 1564, the Antwerp Index of 1570, and items from other sources.[55] The result was a big increase in titles, but as far as peninsular items were concerned there was very little change. About forty further books were added to those in the Valdés list. Some were uncorrected editions of works that were otherwise now permitted, such as the *Lazarillo* and the *Audi, Filia*. In general, none of the new prohibitions was readily identifiable as a work of creative literature. Though it is possible, then, to criticize the Valdés Index for the harm it may have done to elements of Spanish literature, the Quiroga Index did virtually nothing to affect the literary or reading habits of Spaniards. The overwhelming bulk of books it prohibited was unknown to Spaniards, had never entered Spain, and was in languages that Spaniards could not read. The 215 books prohibited in Dutch and German, for example, featured in the Index simply because the Quiroga compilers copied the Antwerp Index wholesale. It is consequently misleading to regard the 1583 Index as directly repressive. It affected only in part the daily reality of readers, students or booksellers. More directly relevant may have been the expurgations listed in the 1584 Index.[56] Authors and printers may have been irritated by these, but they were hardly a blow to creativity.

Among the influences behind the Quiroga Index were Montano, Mariana, and other intellectuals. All were zealous upholders of the Counter Reformation who saw in the machinery of censorship a golden opportunity not to repress freedom of learning but actively to *form* the culture of the society in which they lived. The vast borrowing of prohibitions from the Tridentine Index was their gesture to papal authority, but of more direct interest to them than the obvious struggle against heresy was the problem of educating Spaniards. A contemporary of theirs, the Toledo humanist and poet Alvar Gómez de Castro, left a memoir on principles of censorship.[57] He divided harmful works into two categories: those in Latin and those in the vernacular. Harmful books in the first category might be kept by instructed persons, but should not be used in schools. Of those in the second category, some such as Boccaccio should be carefully expurgated. As for Spanish books in the second category, some are books of romance and chivalry, and 'since they are without imagination or learning and it is a waste of time to read them, it is better to prohibit them, except for the first four books of Amadis'. Others in this class are books on love, of which some, such as the *Celestina*, are serious and good, while others are of such poor quality that they should be banned. Also in this class are works of poetry, again including both good and bad; the bad should be expurgated or eliminated. The interesting criterion employed was obviously that of literary merit.

Mariana conceded in 1579 that otherwise excellent books by Borja and others should continue to be banned because of 'the evil times', and was even firmer than Gómez de Castro in his views on the educative role of books.[58] He recommended that the Spanish Index should include the Tridentine rule banning 'absolutely those books that narrate or teach lascivious and obscene things' (his advice was not followed). Mariana also urged that 'in particular one should ban such books both in Latin and in Castilian, to wit *Celestina, Diana de Montemayor*, and books of chivalry, even if it were only to force people to read good books and genuine histories'. His full list of unworthy literature also included select works by Virgil, Ovid, Catullus, Propertius and other classical authors. Not all these suggestions were adopted by the compilers of the 1583 Index.

The inquisitors very seldom went looking for books to censor. They already had long lists to guide them, and further items were brought to their attention by zealous members of the public. They had to rely heavily on expert *calificadores* (censors), usually theologians from the religious orders. In the earlier period these tended to be mostly Dominicans;[59] by the seventeenth century many were Franciscans and Jesuits.[60] The system, if it can be called such, was (like all censorship systems) haphazard. Completely arbitrary decisions were made, and censors frequently contradicted each other. Judgments were made that had nothing to do with religion. The resulting confusion can be seen in the case of Bodin's *Republic*, a Spanish translation of which suffered so many different criticisms in 1594 from the censors that it was decided to ban it totally.[61] Fortunately, subsequent inquisitors reversed the decision and let the book through after expurgations. The example demonstrates that there was seldom any identifiable 'inquisitorial' censorship. The inquisitors and their censors simply put into effect the ideas prevailing among those who controlled the system. The fact that prominent intellectuals like Juan de Mariana and Melchor Cano were employed as censors did not affect – or improve – the criteria applied.

The Spanish Index was controlled only by the Spanish authorities and had no connection with that of Rome, where in the sixteenth century the authorities began to draw up their own list of prohibited books. While Spain often had on its list works which Rome had prohibited, there was no rule that one Index should follow the lead of the other, and several authors were astonished to find that Spain had forbidden books of theirs which circulated freely in Italy. Alternatively, Rome would ban books which circulated freely in Spain.[62] There was one other important difference between the two. The Roman Index was exclusively a prohibitory one: that is, it banned books without regard to the number of errors in them, and without specifying whether a book could be published if it were expurgated. The Spanish Index, on the other hand, both expurgated and prohibited books, so that some works could circulate if the relevant passages cited in the Index were excised. In this respect the Spanish system was more liberal. When the Indices clashed, reasons were invariably political, as in the case of the Italian Cardinal Baronio, who some years later, in 1594, complained that although the pope had sanctioned his writings there were moves to put him on the Spanish Index. Baronio was certainly not in favour in Spain, but the relevant work by him was banned only by the state and not by the Inquisition.[63]

The Indices of the seventeenth century were those of 1612 (with an appendix in 1614), 1632 and 1640. A prominent part in their compilation was played by the Jesuit Juan de Pineda, aided among others by Francisco Peña, the editor of Eimeric. Over twenty years after Quiroga's Index, the Suprema in 1605 began preparation of a new one.[64] It took seven years to draw up. The Index of 1612, issued under Inquisitor General Sandoval y Rojas, departed from previous practice. Instead of publishing separate volumes for prohibited and expurgated books, as was done in 1583–4, the cardinal published both together in an *Index librorum prohibitorum et expurgatorum*. The volume departed in another way from previous practice. Instead of dividing the material simply into Latin and vernacular books, it now divided the material into three classes. Into the first went authors who were completely prohibited; into the second went books that were prohibited, even if their authors were not; and into the third went books not bearing the names of their authors. For example, all heresiarchs would go into the first class, whereas Dante's *De Monarchia* would go into the second. Even this classification, however, was not strictly adhered to. Though Erasmus fell into the first class, and all his works without exception were banned in Spanish translation, several of his Latin works which were clearly beyond suspicion were permitted.

The Index of 1632 was issued by Inquisitor General Zapata, and that of 1640 by Inquisitor General Antonio de Sotomayor. Similar to the 1612 compilation in scope and content, Sotomayor's Index offered a general survey of the intellectual advances of the seventeenth century, and complemented the efforts of the Quiroga Index to oversee aspects of European thought. It is not surprising to find Francis Bacon and other major writers condemned in the first class as heretics. Like the Quiroga Index, that of 1640 had little impact on native literature, apart from the surprising appearance of Mariana, who had to endure expurgations in seven of his works as well as in his *De mutatione monetae* (on the coinage) and his *Treatise on death and immortality*; and the well-known case of Cervantes, who lost by expurgation a sentence in book two, chapter thirty-six, of his *Don Quixote*, concerning works of charity. Despite its coincidence with the early period of the Scientific Revolution, moreover, the 1640 Index was tolerant towards some aspects of science. Johannes Kepler and Tycho Brahe, as heretics, were classified as *auctores damnati* and therefore appeared in the first class; but virtually all their works were permitted in Spain after very minor expurgations. Some were allowed without any expurgation, but with the proviso that a note on the book should state that it was by a condemned author. Into this category fell Kepler's *Astronomia nova* of 1609, his *Epitome Astronomiae Copernicanae* of 1618, and his *Chilias logarithmorum* published at Marburg in 1624.

With these Indices ended the first great period in the censorship of the Inquisition. The great compilations of 1583 and 1640 were not by their nature repressive weapons, and served more to dissuade Spaniards from reading foreign authors whom none but a few could have read anyway. The real weight of censorship in the country operated, it must be stressed, outside the scope of the Indices: in the various systems of control at the disposal of both state and Inquisition, and in the *formative* restrictions that the Counter Reformation introduced into Spain.

Any evaluation of the role of the Indices also needs to take into account the practical question of whether they were put into effect. We may consider the situation in Catalonia. Twelve copies of the Quiroga Index arrived in Barcelona in October 1584. They were at once redistributed, a copy being sent to each bishop in Catalonia. The bishop was asked to collaborate with the *comisarios* (local clergy who helped the Inquisition) of that area. The comisario in his turn had to communicate the contents of his single copy to the leading persons of his district, and to the main booksellers. The booksellers for their part refused to buy copies of the Index 'because they say they are very expensive'. In this instance, it appears that a single copy of the Index had to serve for an entire bishopric. If the example is typical, it would appear that in many parts of Spain the Index remained unknown. 'There must be a great many books that are not corrected', the inquisitors of Barcelona mused in 1586, when they commented on the lack of available copies of the Index. Certainly, its availability was an excuse given by some booksellers in the city in 1593, when they were accused of selling prohibited books.[65]

The first concern of the Inquisition in matters of book control was over the entry of foreign books. The successful activities of Julián Hernández, who perished in the auto at Seville in December 1560, were a fraction of the effort made by Protestants to bring books into the country. In 1556 Margaret of Parma, Philip II's regent in the Netherlands, informed the Spanish council of state that heretics 'intend to send to Spain through Seville thirty thousand books of Calvin, and I hear that Marcus Pérez, who is here in Antwerp, is charged with this task'.[66] Seaports were inevitably the centre of inquisitorial scrutiny, and foreign sailors were vulnerable to arrest if they happened to be carrying Protestant devotional literature. Diplomats abroad sent back regular information on any unusual activity by printers or traders. The Inquisition began to claim the right to be the first to visit foreign ships when they entered territorial waters. This provoked continuous conflicts with local officials: in Bilbao the corregidor was ordered by the crown to give precedence to the Inquisition; in the Canaries the diocesan vicars were similarly told to give way.[67] From the beginning of the Protestant scare, the inquisitors were aware that a rigid control of book imports had to be exercised. By early 1521 Lutheran books, translated into Spanish by conversos in Antwerp, were entering Spain via the Flanders trade route. The first ban on them was issued by Cardinal Adrian of Utrecht, regent of Spain and Inquisitor General, on 7 April 1521. In view of the Comunero revolt a few months before, the political no less than the religious implications of Luther were taken seriously. Books continued to arrive at all the major ports in the peninsula, but the Inquisition was vigilant: a vessel seized at Pasajes had its hold full of books 'of writings by Luther and his followers'. In Burgos Bernardino Tovar was able to purchase Lutheran books imported from Flanders. By 1524, it was reported from the court, 'there is so much awareness of Luther that nothing else is talked about'.[68]

The flow of books was impossible to stop completely, since Spain depended on imports for much of its literature. 'From one hour to the next', the Inquisition commented in 1532, 'books keep arriving from Germany'. Its officials were ordered to keep a watch at seaports. Special attention was paid to the Basque coast. In 1553, for perhaps the first time,[69] detailed instructions were issued to inquisitors about how to carry out visits to foreign ships in Spanish ports. But few heretical books were ever found. The real victims of vigilance were booksellers. From 1559, when a shipment of 3,000 books, destined for Alcalá, was seized on a French vessel in San Sebastián,[70] booksellers in Spain had to put up with wholesale embargoes of their precious imports. In general, the shipments were neither confiscated nor censored. They were simply delayed until the bureaucracy had decided that no illegal imports were taking place. In 1564 the Inquisition ordered its officials in Bilbao and San Sebastián to send on to booksellers in Medina 245 bales of books imported from Lyon. Three years later the books were still in the ports. Embargoes apart, books continued to enter freely. 'Every day', the inquisitors of Catalonia reported in 1572, 'books enter both for Spain and for other parts'.[71]

Although commercial cargo was the usual hiding-place for illegal books, the ever-zealous Inquisition insisted in 1581 that 'the packages and the beds of the sailors' should also be examined.[72] The searching of ships was always subject to diplomatic agreements. The peace treaty between England and Spain in 1604, for example, gave English ships protection, and in 1605 inquisitors in the ports were ordered not to visit English or Scottish vessels.[73]

In general, the operation to control book imports was riddled with inefficiency. The inquisitors of Barcelona in 1569, unable to process the great number of books entering, reported that 'to entrust the work to friars and experts is not enough to keep people happy, and annoys the booksellers'. They therefore proposed 'a commission of two persons to look at the books, paid by the booksellers, whose suggestion it is'.[74] Orders were sent out periodically by the Suprema for books to be seized; but, the council complained in 1606, 'it is reported that many of the books ordered to be picked up are not being collected'.[75] Inevitably, some condemned books filtered into the country. In Barcelona in 1569 the bookshops were still selling 'many forbidden books'.[76] The continuing entry of books is demonstrated by the case in Madrid of Joseph Antonio de Salas, knight of the Order of Calatrava, whose library was offered for sale to the public on his death in 1651. It was then found that among the 2,424 volumes in the collection, to quote the censor, 'there were many books prohibited or unexpurgated or worthy of examination, either because they were by heretical authors or were newly published abroad by unknown writers'.[77] There were 250 prohibited works in the library – a proportion of one in ten – confirming that foreign books were smuggled regularly and often successfully into Spain, despite the death penalty attached to the offence.

The second major control was at the point of contact between a book and its potential reader. Libraries and bookshops were at intervals visited and checked. Bishops were encouraged to inspect all libraries in their dioceses, and at Salamanca University a score of the staff went carefully through the library to weed out any dangerous books. As early as 1536 Thomas de Villanueva was employed by the Inquisitor General to visit bookshops in Valencia. A lightning check in 1566 in Seville is described thus by an inquisitor: 'at a fixed hour, nine in the morning, all the bookshops of Seville were occupied by familiars of the Holy Office, so that they could not warn each other nor hide nor take out any books, and later we came and made all the shops close and are visiting them one by one'.[78] In reality, such visits were few and far between. They also took place only in big towns where there was an inquisitorial presence. And even there, as the inquisitors of Barcelona admitted in 1569, the bookshops 'have not been visited for many years'.[79] Bookshops, moreover, pleaded ignorance if found with books that needed censoring. In Barcelona in 1593, as we have seen, they said that no copies of the Index were available, and they were consequently unable to monitor forbidden items.[80] On this occasion, some booksellers were fined. It is the only recorded case of any action being taken against bookshops in that city.

The task of censorship obviously took many years. Total prohibition was in principle easier. In Barcelona in 1560 the inquisitors appointed a Jesuit to be their censor. With the Index by his side, he advised worried librarians of religious houses 'what books they can keep and which they have to tear up and burn'.[81] Expurgation, on the other hand, was more onerous. One censor reported to the Inquisition that to expurgate a private library in Madrid worth 18,000 ducats he had laboured eight hours daily for four months.[82] Benito Arias Montano, whose task was to check the entire library of the Escorial, inevitably took a little longer. One way or the other, both authors and booksellers always found reason to complain.[83] A few privileged readers were conceded exemption from the system. Up to the 1540s it had been common for the Inquisition to allow individuals special licences to read or keep prohibited books, usually for purposes of study (how, for instance, could one refute Luther without first reading him?). After 1559 all such licences were suspended, and not until the 1580s were exceptions made.

The greatest damage of all, in any system of censorship, was suffered by the book itself. Some books probably disappeared altogether, and not exclusively through the fault of the inquisitors. A report drawn up for them at the end of the sixteenth century says that:

> many, to avoid taking their books to the inquisitors, burn not only those prohibited and to be expurgated but even those that are approved and harmless, or else get rid of them or sell them for a pittance. In this way an infinite number are neither examined nor corrected, but are eventually lost to nobody's advantage, for their owners suffer great losses and, what is more important, a great many good books disappear.[84]

Clumsy expurgators of books tore out pages, or cut them up carelessly, or defaced them horribly by inking out passages and pictures. To avoid this sort of mistreatment, book-owners preferred to have their property examined by a cultured expurgator, such as the Jesuit father Gubern in Barcelona in 1559. There, apparently, 'no one shows resentment even though he scores through the rare and precious books they have'.[85] An even more preferable alternative, adopted by many book-owners, bookshops and institutions, was to get hold of a copy of the Index and carry out the expurgations without letting anybody else handle the books.[86]

Literature collected during searches was, from the end of the sixteenth century, not burnt but sent to the nearest tribunal for further judgment. There it remained until disposed of. Thus in December 1634 the tribunal of Saragossa had in its keeping 116 copies of the Bible, fifty-five copies of various works by Erasmus and eighty-three volumes of the works of Francisco de Quevedo.[87] Later generations sometimes preferred to store the prohibited books. The Escorial was used regularly for this purpose. In 1585 the prior reported that its library possessed 'many prohibited books sent at different times by His Majesty, and kept there by licence from Don Gaspar de Quiroga'. Half a century later the practice was still being carried on, for in 1639 the Escorial possessed a total of 932 prohibited books.[88] Laudable as this may appear, it was not practised everywhere, with the result that some works condemned by the Inquisition may have been wiped out of existence. In the early seventeenth century there was a plan, supported by both inquisitors and booksellers, to set up a central store of banned books; but 'none of those in favour of setting it up wished to take on the task of doing it',[89] so nothing was done.

There were always strong differences of opinion over the criteria to be adopted in censorship. Everyone agreed on the need for control, but they disagreed on the methods. No one, even in that day, was so sanguine as to believe that the inquisitors knew best. A Salamanca professor, Francisco Sancho, was one of those who in the 1550s tried to advise the Suprema;[90] and there were many others who did likewise. It was a Spaniard resident in Rome, Bartolomé de Valverde, chaplain to Philip II, who in 1584 protested to Cardinal Sirleto, the then director of the Roman Index, over the poor quality of his censors, 'condemning works they have never handled . . . [they are] usually nonentities who know not a word either of Greek or of Hebrew, and lack either judgment or capacity. They are paid nothing for reading innumerable books, and therefore to discharge themselves from a task little to their taste, they take the way out which confers on them an air of learning, and suppress the books.'

Malicious and ignorant inquisitors were not a rarity, and none put his personal ambition to greater use than Inquisitor General Fernando de Valdés, who undermined the career of Juan de Vergara and destroyed that of Bartolomé de Carranza. In general, however, the involvement of the Inquisition in cultural matters was governed less by the personality or inadequacy of the inquisitors than by the social climate. In literature, no less than in religious matter, prosecutions were set in motion largely by denunciations made by private individuals, so that the Inquisition, although prosecutor, was seldom the initiator. This can be seen in the brush that Ignatius Loyola, founder of the Jesuits, had with the Inquisition, when current suspicions of conversos and illuminists caused him to be denounced because of his religious practices while a student at Alcalá in 1527.[91] The change in the cultural climate in 1558 had a crucial influence on the Inquisition, which hardened its attitudes rapidly under Valdés. Ideas which might in other times have been tolerated were now discouraged. The idea of a vernacular Bible was one of the great casualties of those years, in a country that had been active in Biblical scholarship.

Much of the conflict was very simply over language. How could one distinguish between orthodox and unorthodox piety if both used the same language? How could one grasp the real meaning of a religious text? Dissenting from the tendentious interpretation put on Carranza's writings by Melchor Cano, his fellow Dominican Juan de la Peña argued that 'it is impossible to avoid all the methods of expression used by heretics, unless we learn our speech all over again'. Yet the inquisitors were, of course, right to suspect – as in the case of the alumbrados and even more of Juan de Valdés – that heterodoxy was sheltering behind pious language. This did not stop many from criticizing the 1559 Index. In September that year, a Jesuit wrote:

The faint-hearted have reacted by becoming more faint-hearted and those dedicated to virtue are in dismay, seeing that the Inquisitor General has published an edict forbidding almost all the books in Spanish that have been used up to now by those who try to serve God; and we are in times when women are told to stick to their beads and not bother about other devotions.[92]

Some of the most bitter intellectual conflicts of the period originated not in the Inquisition but among university professors. Personal malice and partisan interest were, then as now, potent forces. The drive against Erasmus in the university of Valencia in the 1520s took the form of a personal campaign promoted by the rector, Juan Celaya. As a result, classical studies were seriously prejudiced by the refusal of a chair to the humanist Pedro Juan Oliver.[93]

Apart from rivalry between persons and between religious orders, university men had a long-standing dispute between 'grammarians' (literary scholars) and theologians. The dispute was already active in the first decades of the Inquisition. In 1504 the Inquisitor General Diego de Deza confiscated the papers of the humanist Nebrija. Nebrija had dared to maintain that as a philologist he was no less capable than a theologian like Deza, of determining the texts of Holy Scripture. Subsequently Nebrija was able to rely on the full protection of Cisneros. In an *Apologia* ten years later, he accused Deza of seizing his writings 'not to examine them or condemn them, but to stop me writing. That good prelate wanted to wipe out all traces of the two languages on which our religion depends [Hebrew and Greek].' The humanist commented indignantly on the injury to scholarship:

> Must I reject as false what appears to me in every way as clear, true and evident as light and truth itself? What does this sort of slavery mean? What unjust domination when one is prevented from saying what one thinks, although to do so involves no slight or insult to religion![94]

Perhaps the most notorious conflict between intellectuals and the Inquisition originated in the malicious denunciations of some of his colleagues made by a professor at the university of Salamanca, León de Castro. In December 1571 Castro and a Dominican colleague, Bartolomé de Medina, laid before the Inquisition at Valladolid some accusations against three professors at the university of Salamanca. The three in question were Luis de León, of the Order of St Augustine, Gaspar de Grajal and Martín Martínez de Cantalapiedra. The denunciations said that they had taken heretical liberties with their study of Scripture and theology. Fray Luis de León in particular bore the brunt of the attack. Famous as a theologian and celebrated now as one of Spain's finest poets, at the age of thirty-four he was elected to a chair at Salamanca. He thereby aroused the hostility of his rivals, who slandered him because of his converso descent and accused him of uttering dangerous theological propositions. It was said that he had questioned the accuracy of the Vulgate translation of the Bible; had preferred the Hebrew text to the Latin; had translated the Song of Songs as a profane love song instead of a divine canticle; and had held that scholastic theology harmed the study of Scripture. Grajal was arrested on similar charges on 22 March 1572. Five days later Luis de León and Martínez de Cantalapiedra were taken into custody. Blind belief in the justice of their cause and in the benevolence of the Holy Office cheered the prisoners, but they were soon disillusioned. For Fray Luis de León it was to be the beginning of an imprisonment that lasted four years, eight months and nineteen days. Cut off completely from the outside world in the tribunal at Valladolid, he had one consolation, which was the permission he received to read and write in his cell, out of which emerged his classic devotional treatise *The Names of Christ*. From the first he was aware of a campaign against himself. On 18 April 1572 he wrote from his cell:

> I have great suspicions that false testimony has been laid against me, for I know that in the last two years people have said and still say many things about me that are transparent lies, and I know that I have many enemies.

He awaited justice, yet none was forthcoming, nor was there any promise of an early trial. His constant appeals were of no avail. A year later, on 7 March 1573, he was writing to the inquisitors:

> It is now a year since I have been in this prison, and in all this time you have not deigned to publish the names of witnesses in my case, nor have I been given any opportunity of a full defence.

He was finally sentenced to a reprimand which involved retraction of the several propositions he was said to have held. In prison he had suffered despair, fever and humiliation. Release from the cells came in mid-December 1576. Weary but undefeated, he greeted his freedom with characteristic restraint:

> Aqui la envidia y mentira
> Me tuvieron encerrado.

dichoso el humilde estado
del sabio que se retira
y de aqueste mundo malvado,
y con pobre mesa y casa,
en el campo deleitoso,
con solo Dios se compasa,
y a solas su vida pasa
ni envidiado ni envidioso.

(Here envy and lies held me in prison. Happy the humble state of the scholar who retires from this malicious world and there in the pleasant countryside, with modest table and dwelling, governs his life with God alone, and passes his days all by himself, neither envied nor envying.)

Restored once more to his rostrum at the university, he is said to have begun his first lecture with the words, 'As I was saying last time . . .' But for his enemies this was not the last time. In 1582 he was summoned to a second trial for having uttered rash propositions. The Inquisitor General, Gaspar de Quiroga, intervened on his behalf and in 1584 he escaped with a warning to avoid controversial issues in future.[95]

Less fortunate than Fray Luis de León were his other colleagues at the university. In the cells of the Inquisition Gaspar de Grajal's health gave way, and he died before judgment could be passed on him. A colleague from the university of Osuna, Alonso Gudiel, who was professor of Scripture there, was also arrested in the same month on the basis of Castro's accusations. Before his case had been dealt with he also died in prison, in April 1573. The only one to outlast his treatment was Martínez de Cantalapiedra, who had been professor of Hebrew at Salamanca and whose whole life had been dedicated to the study of Holy Scripture. His term of imprisonment in a Valladolid cell exceeded even that of Luis de León. It lasted for over five years, from March 1572 to May 1577, and despite his constant appeals for a quick decision there was no hurry to bring him to trial. Eventually he was freed but never regained his academic post. 'I have laboured to interpret scripture before the whole world', he told the inquisitors in 1577, 'but my only reward has been the destruction of my life, my honour, my health and my possessions'.[96] The bitter lesson he drew from this was that 'it is better to walk carefully and be prudent' (*sapere ad sobrietatem*).

The work of León de Castro was not yet over. The Hebrew scholar and humanist Benito Arias Montano had spent several years collaborating with Netherlandish scholars on the preparation, patronized by Philip II, of a new Polyglot Bible, which was printed and issued in Antwerp in 1571 in eight volumes.[97] Provisional approval was secured from Rome in 1572 and 1576. There was, however, considerable criticism of the project in Spain. In 1575, writing from Rome, Montano complained of

> a great rumour which a certain León de Castro of Salamanca has raised in that university, to criticize and discredit the greatest work of letters that has ever been published in the world, the Royal Bible which His Majesty has for the benefit of Christendom ordered to be printed in Antwerp under my direction.

León de Castro was not the only critic. There were others, wrote Montano in 1579, 'men of letters who seek to find and note some error in my writings, making extraordinary efforts to do so'.[98] The conflict was primarily one between scholars, and the criticisms then made of the Polyglot are now seen to have been in part justified, but the danger was that the Holy Office might be brought into the quarrel.

Although the storm passed, Montano was the object of further, and this time indirect, attacks. In 1592 he was instrumental in bringing about a profound change in the spiritual life of José de Sigüenza, Jeronimite historian and monk of the Escorial, where Montano was librarian. Montano, it has been suggested, had heterodox views on religion which he had picked up in the Netherlands and may have communicated to Sigüenza. No evidence for this thesis has been found, but it is undeniable that Montano had an enormous influence on Sigüenza. In 1592 some of Sigüenza's malicious colleagues, motivated in part by hostility to Montano's Hebraic studies, denounced Sigüenza to the Inquisition. It was a brief three-month trial, and Sigüenza was completely exonerated.[99]

Another famous man of letters to fall foul of the Holy Office was Francisco Sánchez, 'El Brocense', professor of grammar at Salamanca. He was denounced in 1584 on charges of loose and presumptuous opinions on theological matters, and summoned before the tribunal of Valladolid. Although the tribunal voted for his arrest and the sequestration of his goods, the Suprema altered the sentence to one of grave reprimand only. El Brocense's turbulent and intemperate mind was not put off by this narrow escape, and he returned to the battle, disputing theology with theologians (once again it was a case of conflict between theologians and grammarians) and expressing contempt for Aquinas and the Dominicans. In 1593, at the age of eighty, this excitable old man found himself in trouble once more. Reports of his speeches were relayed to the tribunal of

Valladolid, and in 1596 the Inquisition began proceedings. No action was taken until 1600, when he was put under house arrest and his papers sequestrated. Among the charges raised against him was that 'he always subjects his understanding to obedience to the faith; but that in matters that are not of faith he has no wish to subject his understanding'.[100] In ill health and humiliated by his treatment, Sánchez died at the beginning of December 1600. Because of the scandal hanging over his name, he was denied funeral honours by the university of Salamanca.

These were virtually the only intellectuals to be denounced to the Inquisition. Their cases were provoked not by the Inquisition but by rivalry between theologians and grammarians at one university, Salamanca. It is notable that three of the victims – Luis de León, Gaspar de Grajal and Alonso Gudiel – were of converso origin; witnesses claimed that Martínez de Cantalapiedra was also one. The importance of the prosecutions lay less in the small number of victims than in the repercussions felt by others. When Luis de León heard of the arrest of his colleague Grajal he wrote indignantly to a friend in Granada, 'This fate of the master has scandalized everyone and given just cause for keeping silent out of fear'. On another occasion, Fray Luis informs us, he had been lecturing about the fraternal correction of heretics when

> those students who were furthest from the rostrum signalled that I should speak louder, because my voice was hoarse and they could not hear well. Whereupon I said, 'I am hoarse, and it's better to speak low like this so that the inquisitors don't hear us.' I don't know if this offended anyone.[101]

The prosecutions inspired a strong reaction in the Jesuit historian Juan de Mariana. In a famous passage, he said that the case

> caused anxiety to many until they should know the outcome. There was dissatisfaction that persons illustrious for their learning and reputation had to defend themselves in prison from so serious a threat to their fame and good name. It was a sad state when virtuous men, because of their great achievements, had to undergo hostility, accusations and injuries from those who should have been their defenders ... The case in question depressed the spirits of many who observed the plight of another, seeing how much affliction threatened those who spoke freely what they thought. In this way, many passed over to the other camp, or trimmed their sails to the wind. What else was there to do? The greatest of follies is to exert oneself in vain, and to weary oneself without winning anything but hatred. Those who

agreed with current ideas did so with even greater eagerness, and entertained opinions that were approved of and were the least dangerous, without any great concern for the truth.[102]

The cases of the 1580s help us to set in perspective the view that the Inquisition set out to crush intellectuals. It was perhaps inevitable that there should be clashes between independent-minded thinkers and a body with pretensions to control literature. But conflicts were surprisingly few. In part this was because writers seem to have steered clear of the inquisitors. In part also it was because the inquisitors dealt sensibly with most cases. One prosecution was that of the Seville writer Juan de Mal Lara. From 1561 to 1562 he was imprisoned by the Seville Inquisition, not for any errors but for allegedly writing defamatory verses.[103] The incident had no ill effect on his career.

Conflicts between different approaches to learning or to spirituality inevitably continued. Where they could, protagonists would bring in the Inquisition on their side, using where possible (as in Salamanca) antisemitic insinuations. A learned and conservative Dominican at Salamanca in 1571 complained that 'in this university there is great play about novelty and little about the antiquity of our religion and faith'.[104] The Inquisition, to its own lasting ill fame, tended to operate in favour of the conservatives. The inquisitorial prosecutor of El Brocense alleged that he was 'a rash, insolent heretic, temerarious and stubborn like all grammarians and Erasmians'.[105] Independent investigation was criticized because it might lead to error. Why search out a dangerous new truth if the old one were safer? This was the dilemma faced by the humanist Pedro Juan Núñez when he wrote to Jerónimo de Zurita in 1556 that the inquisitors did not wish people to study humanities

> because of the dangers present in them, for when a humanist corrects an error in Cicero he has to correct the same error in Scripture. This and other similar problems drive me insane, and often take away from me any wish to carry on.[106]

The reaction against humanism was common to much of the post-Reformation world, and was by no means uniquely a consequence of inquisitorial prejudice. In the same way the reaction against unorthodox spirituality was common to much of Counter-Reformation Europe, and the Inquisition was no innovator in this respect. The continued suspicion of illuminism and of certain types of popular religion explains the difficulties that St Teresa of Ávila had to suffer. On one occasion, she remarks in her *Life*,

> people came to me in great alarm, saying that these were difficult times, that some charge might be raised against me, and that I might have to appear before the inquisitors. But this merely amused me and made me laugh. I never had any fear on that score.

The optimism she showed at this time was not repeated later. In 1575 her *Life* fell under suspicion and was examined by the Inquisition, which decided not to license it for publication until after her death (1582). In 1576 denunciations were made to the tribunal of Seville against her and her reformed Carmelites, but the Inquisition did not press the matter. She was seriously worried, but told one of her preoccupied advisers, Father Gracián, 'Father, would that we could all be burnt for Christ', and on another occasion, 'Father, the Holy Inquisition, sent by God to protect his faith, is hardly likely to harm someone who has such faith as I'.[107] After her death further denunciations were made against her in 1589–91 by Alonso de la Fuente, a friar with an obsession about illuminists, but the Inquisition ignored him.

The continuing history of the later alumbrados, with which the incident of St Teresa is closely related, revolves around the denunciations made by Alonso de la Fuente from 1573 onwards against groups of adepts in Extremadura and later in Andalusia. Undoubtedly crazed, with a burning hatred of Jews and of Jesuits, Fray Alonso de la Fuente was perceptive enough to be able to identify the new illuminism and its leaders, most of whom were clergy. At a big auto de fe in Llerena on 14 June 1579, twenty alumbrados were among the sixty penitents. The group had strange beliefs, rejecting the Church and Christ and centring their devotion on 'God'. Their leader, Hernando Alvarez, 'said that Jesus Christ was good for nothing except to be a gipsy'. The alumbrados of Andalusia were subsequently disciplined at an auto held at Córdoba on 21 January 1590.[108]

An important undercurrent in the academic disputes of the time was, we have seen, the suspicion directed against writers of Jewish origin. The identification of creativity with conversos became, in the hands of the twentieth-century scholar Américo Castro, a tool of literary analysis.[109] A key part in this analysis was concerned with the impact of the Inquisition on conversos and, by implication, on Spanish literature.

Castro argued in several brilliant essays that the semitic background of

Spain, as expressed through the careers of thinkers and writers of Jewish origin, contributed to the formation of an intense converso (or neo-Jewish) consciousness. This consciousness supposedly suffered under, but was also stimulated by, constant persecution at the hands of the machinery of the Holy Office. Some followers of the Castro thesis, using racial origins as a tool of literary analysis, have offered a vision of peninsular history in which the crucial element is the 'converso'.[110] The suffering converso (a concept that inculpates the Inquisition) is seen as the key to Spain's genius. The most notable attempt to use the interpretation has been in studies of the *Celestina*, on the premiss that its author, Fernando de Rojas, was a converso.[111] Claims have also been made – so far without evidence – to suggest that many other notable personages such as Hernando de Talavera, Benito Arias Montano and Bartolomé de las Casas were of converso origin.[112]

A crucial distinction should probably be made between, on one hand, the existence of antisemitic sentiment in Spanish society and, on the other hand, the persecution of individual writers as conversos. Thanks to generations of polemic and prejudice, antisemitism was commonplace in Golden Age Spain. It could be found anywhere, in popular conduct and attitudes, in universities and in the government. Inquisitors, like others, often shared an antisemitic viewpoint and brought it to bear in their work. In their experience, heresy had nearly always (in the case of judaizers, alumbrados, some Lutherans) been associated with people of Jewish origin.

There are several examples of the way in which converso blood could, in the antisemitic society of Spain's Golden Age, have serious consequences. The most outstanding is the case of the humanist Juan Luis Vives, who spent his entire career outside Spain. Born in Valencia of converso parents who continued to practise their Jewish religion in secret, Vives was sent by his father to study abroad in Paris at the age of sixteen in 1509, a year after the death of his mother in an epidemic. His life and career were thereafter based in the Netherlands. After Nebrija's death in 1522 Vives was invited to occupy his chair at Alcalá, but refused. Family circumstances combined to make Vives a permanent exile from his homeland. In 1520 his father was arrested by the Inquisition as a judaizer and burnt alive in 1524. Four years later his long-dead mother was also prosecuted and her bones disinterred and burnt.[113]

To argue from individual cases like that of Vives, however, that converso thought in Spain represented an undercurrent of dissidence and also produced a confrontation between the Inquisition on one side and creativity on the other, is difficult to substantiate. The example of Vives possibly demonstrates, if anything, the reverse. Clergy in Spain maintained a conspiracy of silence over his origins, and he was always held in the highest respect by the establishment in Spain; not until the twentieth century was it possible for researchers to discover his origins. The same occurred with St Teresa of Ávila. She was notoriously of converso stock. Her grandfather was penanced by the Inquisition in 1485 for allegedly judaizing. Yet the fact was never cited against her nor did it affect her career.

Public figures continued to have problems if their converso origins clashed with antisemitic prejudices. But, as in the case of St Teresa, there was no systematic pressure. A case in point is that of Diego Pérez de Valdivia, apostle of the Counter Reformation in Catalonia in the 1580s.[114] Of converso origin, he spent several months in the cells of the Inquisition of Córdoba, where he was accused of asserting that conversos were better people than non-conversos, and that 'it is a sin to observe the rules of limpieza'. The incident was quietly buried by all concerned. Pérez spent his subsequent life in Barcelona where, with the support of bishops, Inquisition and clergy he pursued a prominent career as religious writer, reformer and preacher.

There are two distinct opinions about the impact of the Inquisition on literature. One, strongly supported by traditionalists, denies any negative influence. Menéndez y Pelayo asserted that 'never was there more written in Spain, or better written, than in the two golden centuries of the Inquisition'.[115] The other, reflected in many modern studies of literature, claims that Spaniards virtually ceased to write and think. 'It would seem superfluous to insist', argued Lea, 'that a system of severe repression of thought by all the instrumentalities of Inquisition and state, is an ample explanation of the decadence of Spanish learning and literature.'[116] For the English Catholic historian, Lord Acton, the injury inflicted on literature by the Inquisition was 'the most obvious and conspicuous fact of modern history'.[117] Américo Castro put the argument succinctly. For him, 'not to think or learn or read' became habitual for Spaniards faced by 'the sadism and lust for plunder of those of the Holy Office'.[118]

The available evidence does not support either of these extreme views. Both assume that the censorship system functioned effectively in Spain; one view claims it worked for the better (purging heresy), the other that it worked for the worse (suppressing creativity). In reality, neither the Index nor the censorship system produced an adequate machinery of control.

The Index was, for several reasons, less significant than is often thought.

First, most of the books banned in it were never even remotely in reach of the Spanish reader and had never been available in the peninsula. In order to compile their lists, the inquisitors (as we have seen) copied out foreign prohibitions (notably that of Louvain) or the items on offer at the famous book fairs of Frankfurt.[119] The Indexes are a very good guide to what the inquisitors would have liked to prohibit,[120] but since Spaniards had no access to most of the books the effective impact on their reading was minimal. Second, the Index was large, expensive, in short supply and inevitably both imperfect and out of date. It was consequently difficult to enforce. In Barcelona, banned books continued to be on sale years after appearing in the Index.[121] Third, the Index faced sharp criticism from booksellers and from those who felt that its criteria were faulty. Finally, the bulk of creative and scientific literature available to Spaniards never appeared in the Index. The romances of chivalry which made up the staple reading of ordinary Spaniards at home and the campfire reading of venturers on the American frontier – between 1501 and 1650 a total of 267 editions of chivalric novels were issued, two-thirds of them in the early sixteenth century[122] – were never proscribed, though often attacked. The vast riches of scholarship opened up by the imperial experience during the Inquisition's great period, were never affected: the histories of Herrera, Oviedo, Díaz and Gómara, the natural history of Sahagún, the treatises on mathematics, botany, metallurgy and shipbuilding that flourished under Philip II, never came within the ambit of the inquisitors. Long after the measures of 1558–9 Spain continued to profit from a world experience vaster than that of any other European nation. Its contribution to navigation, geography, natural history and aspects of medicine was highly valued in Europe, leading to some 1,226 editions of Spanish works of the period 1475–1600 being published abroad prior to 1800.[123]

The overall impact of systems of literary censorship is difficult to judge. Though it is widely believed that Spanish literature suffered at the hands of the Inquisition, there are good reasons to question the belief. Most western countries had a comparable system of control, yet none appears to have suffered significantly.[124] Moreover, prohibited books had a negligible readership in the peninsula. The works most in demand by the public were, as in other Catholic countries, religious and devotional works, and textbooks (such as Latin grammars) for use in schools. Few of these appeared on the Index. Those who really wished to obtain banned books of special interest – in astrology, medicine, scholarship – faced few obstacles. They brought books in personally, or through commercial channels, or asked friends abroad to send them.[125] Total freedom of movement between the peninsula and France and Italy guaranteed an unimpeded circulation of people, books and – at one remove – ideas. Finally, no evidence has ever emerged that the book controls eliminated promising new life among intellectuals, or prejudiced existing schools of thought. Up to the mid-sixteenth century, the Inquisition played no significant part in the literary world, prosecuted no notable writer, and interfered substantially only with some texts of Renaissance theatre.[126] Not until the onset of the Reformation, and many years after censorship was being practised in England and France, did the Holy Office attempt to operate a system of cultural control.

The Inquisition's overseeing of literature, in short, looked imposing in theory but was unimpressive in practice. A glance at the content of the later Indices reveals that they had a limited, even petty role. Góngora had minor problems with the censor in 1627;[127] in 1632, one line by Cervantes was excised from *Don Quixote*;[128] the expurgations of Francisco de Osuna and Antonio de Guevara in the Index of 1612 are trivial; that of Florián de Ocampo in 1632 ridiculous.[129] Many creative writers had brushes with the Inquisition, but the total effect of these incidents appears to have been so slight that no convincing conclusion can be drawn. Lope de Vega appeared on the Index, but a century after his death.

Some experts in literature maintain that even if there was little quantifiable damage to literary creativity, there was hidden damage. Writers, they argue, exercised self-censorship; and if they published, they did so in a 'coded' language where words meant something different from what they appeared to mean. The approach is an intriguing way of analysing literary texts, but has no historical evidence to support it.

The fact is that book control and censorship were systematically evaded in all countries where practised. In both Italy[130] and France[131] the attempts at control were both 'futile' and 'inefficient'. The evidence for Spain is similar.[132] There are no convincing grounds for believing that the Spanish Inquisition was unique in Europe in its efficiency at imposing control,[133] or that Spaniards were subjected to a regime of 'thought control' which 'fossilized academic culture' for three hundred years.[134] Moreover, the book trade continued to function for a long time without disruption, as we know from the evidence of Barcelona. At a later date, when authors tended to publish in the vernacular rather than in Latin, the nature of the trade changed; but if there was an 'almost total rift from the book culture of Europe'[135] the Holy Office was hardly the culprit. If ordinary Spaniards did not read foreign authors it was for the very same reason that prevails today: the books were not available in Spanish, or were too specialized for their tastes.

The impact on science was largely indirect. Spaniards in the early modern period had possibly the least dedication to science, measured by the university affiliation of scientists,[136] of any nation in western Europe. Those who took learning seriously went to Italy. Thanks to access to Italian and foreign scholarship, scientific enquiry did not collapse. Technology filtered into the country: foreign treatises were translated, engineers were imported by the state. Foreign technicians – all of them Catholic – came to the peninsula with their expertise. The Inquisition, for its part, did not normally interfere.

Scientific books written by Catholics tended to circulate freely, though the works of Paracelsus and a few others were disapproved of.[137] The 1583 Quiroga Index had a negligible impact on the accessibility of scientific works, and Galileo was never put on the list of forbidden books. The most direct attacks mounted by the Inquisition were against selected works in the area of astrology and alchemy, sciences that were deemed to carry overtones of superstition.[138]

If there was, then, an imbalance between scientific progress in the peninsula and in the rest of Europe during and after the Renaissance, the Inquisition was not perceptibly responsible. The range of books it prohibited, of course, may well have dissuaded a few readers. Arguably, this would not have had serious consequences for learning during the sixteenth century. By the late seventeenth century, on the other hand, it was clear that English and Dutch intellectuals had become the pioneers in science and medicine. They were Protestants, and their books automatically fell within the scope of inquisitorial bans. Logically, Spanish intellectuals from the mid-seventeenth century began to look on the Holy Office as the great obstacle to learning. The complaint of the young physician Juan de Cabriada in 1687 echoed the outlook of his generation: 'how sad and shameful it is that, like savages, we have to be the last to receive the innovations and knowledge that the rest of Europe already has'.[139] Those who could read French managed to import scientific and philosophical works privately. Descartes was being read in Oviedo, Hobbes in Seville. During the eighteenth century, however, intellectuals in the peninsula faced an uphill struggle against the attempts of the Inquisition to block the spread of the new learning.

*

At no time was the peninsula cut off from the outside world by the decrees of 1558–9, or by any subsequent legislation.[140] Under Habsburg rule the armies of Spain dominated Europe, its ships traversed the Atlantic and Pacific, and its language was the master tongue from central Europe to the Philippines. Tens of thousands of Spaniards went abroad every year, mainly to serve in the armed forces. Cultural and commercial contact with all parts of western Europe, especially the Netherlands and Italy, continued absolutely without interruption. It is consequently both implausible and untrue to suggest that Spain (and with it Portugal) was denied contact with the outside world.

The image of a nation sunk in inertia and superstition because of the Inquisition was part of the mythology created around the tribunal. Scholars continue still to suggest that Spaniards 'had to guard their speech carefully'.[141] These views must be set against the reality that, like other European states, Spain had active political institutions at all levels. Free discussion of political affairs was tolerated, and public controversy occurred on a scale paralleled in few other countries. Unpalatable aspects of national life – antisemitism, intolerance to Moriscos and their eventual expulsion, oppression of peasants, high taxes – were nowhere so hotly debated as among Spaniards themselves. The historian Antonio de Herrera affirmed that such free discussion was essential, for otherwise 'the reputation of Spain would fall rapidly, for foreign and enemy nations would say that small credence could be placed in the words of her rulers, since their subjects were not allowed to speak freely'.[142] In the seventeenth century the *arbitristas* continued the tradition of controversy, and the diplomat Saavedra Fajardo commented approvingly that 'grumbling is proof that there is liberty in the state; in a tyranny it is not permitted'.

The freedom in Spain was a positive side of the picture. The negative side was the unquestionably isolated state of peninsular culture. Spain remained during the early modern period on the fringe of the major currents in western European philosophy, science and creative art. In the great age of empire, Philip II had to rely for technological expertise on Italians, Belgians and Germans.[143] Spanish printing was probably the worst in western Europe.[144] The Grand Tour, by which Western nobles hoped to polish up their experience and education, never saw fit to include Spain in its itinerary. The Castilian elite, with a few prominent exceptions, was criticized at the time by Italian and German diplomats for its lack of cultural sophistication.[145] Though the Inquisition had little responsibility for the situation, many observers felt that the tribunal incarnated in some sense the backward aspects of peninsular society. This Black Legend, as we shall see, contributed powerfully to mould the enduring image of the Holy Office.

7

STRUCTURE AND POLITICS

In the days of the blessed memory of Philip II, the Inquisition experienced great felicity.

Inquisitors of Catalonia, 1623[1]

From its inception, the Inquisition was meant by Ferdinand and Isabella to be under their control and not, like the mediaeval tribunal, under that of the pope. Sixtus IV was surprisingly cooperative. His bull of institution of 1 November 1478 gave the Catholic monarchs power not only over appointments but also, tacitly, over confiscations. The inquisitors were to have the jurisdiction over heretics normally held by bishops, but were not given any jurisdiction over bishops themselves. Subsequently the pope saw his error in granting independence to a tribunal of this sort, and stated his protest in a brief of 29 January 1482. At the same time he refused to allow Ferdinand to extend his control over the old Inquisition in Aragon.

Further conflict ensued with the bull issued by Sixtus on 18 April, denouncing abuses in the procedure of the Inquisition. Ferdinand held firm to his policy despite opposition in Rome and Aragon. His victory was confirmed by the bull which on 17 October 1483 appointed Torquemada as chief inquisitor of the kingdom of Aragon. Earlier that year Torquemada had also received a bull of appointment as Inquisitor General of Castile. He was now the only individual in the peninsula whose writ extended over all Spain, since even the crowns of Castile and Aragon were only personally and not politically united.

The Inquisition was in every way an instrument of royal policy, and remained politically subject to the crown. 'Although you and the others enjoy the title of inquisitor', Ferdinand reminded his inquisitors of Aragon firmly in 1486, 'it is I and the queen who have appointed you, and without our support you can do very little'.[2] But royal control did not make it exclusively a secular tribunal. Any authority and jurisdiction exercised by the inquisitors came directly or indirectly from Rome, without which the tribunal would have ceased to exist. Bulls of appointment, canonical regulations, spheres of jurisdiction – all had to have the prior approval of Rome. The Inquisition was consequently also an ecclesiastical tribunal for which the Church of Rome assumed ultimate responsibility.

The central organization of the new tribunal was in 1488 vested in a council (Consejo de la Suprema y General Inquisicion).[3] This joined the other administrative councils whose existence had been confirmed at the Cortes of Toledo in 1480. Although Torquemada was the first Inquisitor General, the main inspirer of the Inquisition may have been Cardinal Mendoza, archbishop of Seville and later of Toledo. It was this prelate, famous as a patron of Columbus, who is said to have put in motion the negotiations with Rome leading to the establishment of the tribunal. Yet above him towers the shadow of Torquemada. The austere Dominican friar, prior of the friary of Santa Cruz at Segovia, left his indelible mark on the tribunal, and in 1484 Sixtus IV praised him for having 'directed your zeal to those matters which contribute to the praise of God and the benefit of the orthodox faith'.[4] Though of distant converso origin himself, Torquemada was the first to introduce a statute of limpieza into a Dominican house, his own foundation at Ávila dedicated to St Thomas Aquinas.

The importance of Torquemada suggests that the Dominicans were controlling the new Inquisition as they had controlled the mediaeval one. In fact, though all the early appointments were of Dominicans, and they continued to play an important role, only a minority of inquisitors came from the order. In Valencia there were only six Dominicans among the fifty-two for whom details are available over the period 1482–1609.[5] A special privilege was obtained on 16 December 1618 when Philip III, at the request of the Duke of Lerma, created a permanent place in the Suprema for a member of the order, to be occupied in the first place by the then Inquisitor General, Aliaga.[6] By the late seventeenth century, Jesuits had become influential in the Inquisition.

Although the Inquisitor General may seem to have been a powerful individual, in practice his commission was often limited in authority, and renewable only after papal approval. Moreover, the pope could grant equivalent powers to other clerics in Spain, as in 1491 when a second Inquisitor General of Castile and Aragon was appointed for a brief time, and in 1494 when four bishops in Spain were promoted to this post at the same time that Torquemada held it. This plural headship of the tribunal continued to exist for political reasons. When Torquemada died in 1498 he was succeeded by Diego de Deza, who in 1505 became archbishop of Seville.

It was not until 1504 that Deza became sole head of the Inquisition, because the bishops appointed under Torquemada continued to hold office up to that date. The death of Queen Isabella on 26 November 1504 led to a temporary separation of the kingdom of Castile and Aragon, because of Ferdinand's quarrels with his son-in-law, Philip I of Castile. As a result, Ferdinand asked the pope to appoint a separate Inquisitor for Aragon. This occurred in June 1507 when Cisneros was appointed to Castile and the bishop of Vic, Juan Enguera, to Aragon. The two posts remained separate until the death of Cisneros in 1518, when Charles V appointed Cardinal Adrian of Utrecht, bishop of Tortosa and since 1516 Inquisitor General of Aragon, as Inquisitor for Castile as well. After this the tribunal remained under one head alone.

The Spanish Inquisition was based essentially on the mediaeval one. It is a crucial fact that may easily be overlooked because of the wholly different conditions under which each tribunal came into existence. There was in reality no other precedent from which to work, and the Spanish inquisitors followed down to the last detail – in all aspects of arrest, trial, procedure, confiscations, recruitment of personnel – the regulations that had been in use in thirteenth-century Languedoc and Aragon. As late as the reign of Philip II, the classic Aragonese manual of Eimeric could be accepted as a standard guide by its Spanish commentator, Francisco Peña.[7] There is no reason, therefore, to suggest that the Inquisition in the peninsula was peculiarly Spanish. Apart from some obvious differences, such as the transfer in Spain of authority over heresy from bishops to inquisitors, the Inquisition in the peninsula was simply an adaptation to Spanish conditions of the mediaeval French tribunal.

The first rules drawn up were those agreed upon in a meeting at Seville on 29 November 1484. Under Torquemada these were amplified in 1485, 1488 and 1498. His successor Diego de Deza added some articles in 1500. All these regulations were later known under the collective title of *Instrucciones Antiguas*. They were unsystematic, had to be regularly modified, and led to variations of practice between different tribunals. An organized, bureaucratic Inquisition emerged only with the issue in 1561 of the Instructions of Fernando de Valdés, in eighty-one clauses. These set out to achieve a centralized organization, firm control by the Suprema and financial stability for the tribunals. A product of the crisis years after 1558, the Valdés Instructions gave the Holy Office a reputation for rigidity.[8] Subsequent modifications were collected and printed by Gaspar Isidro de Argüello at Madrid in 1627 and 1630 (*Instrucciones del Santo Oficio de la Inquisición, sumariamente, antiguas y nuevas*). This was followed by the comprehensive *Compilación de las Instrucciones* published at Madrid in 1667 by the Inquisitor General.[9]

The council of the Inquisition (sometimes known for short as the Suprema) was presided over by the Inquisitor General. All authority exercised by inquisitors was at one time held to be by direct delegation from the pope, but later this was modified to the opinion that it was the Inquisitor General himself who delegated the papal powers. Though he might be nominated by the crown, only the pope could appoint him. Growth of the Inquisitor General's power was modified by the increasing authority of the Suprema. The relationship between Suprema and Inquisitor General was never satisfactorily settled because they usually acted in concert and did not dispute supremacy. But there were several occasions when the council attempted to take an independent line. In the early years of Philip IV, conflicts between the council and its chairman were persistent. But the Inquisitor General of the time, Cardinal Zapata, angrily told his councillors not to interfere in what did not concern them. 'There was a dead silence', a secretary recorded, 'and none of the members of the council said a word'.[10]

In the early seventeenth century the Suprema consisted of about six members, who usually met every morning and also three afternoons a week. The afternoon sessions, normally on legal business, were attended by two members of the council of Castile. Correspondence was divided between two secretariats, one for 'Aragon'[11] and one for Castile. Members of the Suprema were appointed by the king alone, and the Suprema usually issued orders without any need to have the vote of the Inquisitor General. When divisions arose in the council a decision was taken by majority vote, in which the vote of the Inquisitor General counted no more than that of another. This did not affect his unique authority. Inquisitors General, such as Antonio de Sotomayor in 1643,[12] continued to insist unequivocally on their exclusive right to exercise the powers conferred by the pope.

The substantial autonomy of the Inquisitor General, however, was confined to matters of ecclesiastical jurisdiction. In political matters, the authority of the crown could always prevail. One outstanding case, that of Fray Froilán Díaz, brought out clearly the extent to which the crown could decide the relative roles of the Inquisitor General and the Suprema.

Froilán Díaz, a Dominican who had been confessor since 1698 to the king, Charles II (1665–1700), was arrested in 1700 after various palace intrigues on the charge of having helped to cast a spell over the hapless king, known in Spanish history as 'El Hechizado', the bewitched. The prosecution was at the instance of the German queen and her friend Balthasar de Mendoza, bishop of Segovia, who in 1699 had been appointed Inquisitor General. Díaz, an ex-officio member of the Suprema, was imprisoned while an investigation was made by five theologians. They found that there was no basis for charges against him. Accordingly, in June 1700 all the members of the council except Mendoza voted for his acquittal. Mendoza refused to accept the findings and ordered the arrest of the other members of the Suprema until they assented to the arrest of Díaz. At the same time he ordered the tribunal of Murcia to bring Díaz to trial. This the inquisitors did – and acquitted him. Mendoza thereupon ordered a retrial and kept Díaz in prison. Opposition to the actions of the Inquisitor General was by now universal. There was consequently wide support for the new French king, Philip V, when he discovered that Mendoza was politically opposed to the Bourbon dynasty and confined him to his see of Segovia. Mendoza now made the mistake of appealing to Rome, an act unprecedented in the whole history of the Spanish Inquisition. The crown immediately stepped in to prevent any interference from Rome, and finally in 1704 Díaz was rehabilitated and reinstated in the Suprema, whilst Mendoza was replaced as Inquisitor General in March 1705.[13]

The case proved to be the last important one in which the Inquisitor General attempted to assert his supremacy. Thereafter the preoccupation of the tribunal with administrative routine and censorship, rather than great matters of state, involved fewer opportunities for personal initiative, and authority came more and more to reside in the Suprema and the machinery it controlled. More obscure prelates were also chosen as Inquisitor General, a significant example being the choice of the bishop of Ceuta to succeed Mendoza in 1705.

The growth of the Suprema's authority led to greater centralization, a process hastened in the seventeenth century as the volume of heretics, and therefore of business, diminished in the provincial tribunals. In the early days, as the case of Lucero showed, local autonomy could be carried to scandalous extremes. At first, cases were referred by provincial tribunals to the Suprema only if agreement could not be reached, or if the council summoned a case before it. In 1550, when it was felt that the Barcelona tribunal was showing excessive severity in suppressing a witch-craze in

Catalonia, all sentences passed by it were required to be confirmed by the Suprema. The Barcelona inquisitors do not seem to have accepted interference from the centre, for the Inquisitor General in 1566 was obliged to examine their records and to denounce the irregularities and cruelties in the tribunal. From this time onwards greater attention was paid by the Suprema to the procedure and sentences of local tribunals. These were required after 1632 to send in monthly reports of their activities. By the mid-seventeenth century all sentences were required to be submitted to the Suprema before being carried out. With this, the machinery of the Inquisition reached its most complete stage of centralization. In the eighteenth century business became so rare that the tribunals became mere appendages of the Suprema, which initiated all prosecutions.

The tribunals of the Inquisition in their early days were itinerant. Inquisitions were set up wherever there seemed to be a need and political conditions permitted. In 1486, for example, a special inquisition was sanctioned by Torquemada, to act solely within the Jeronimite order. It seems to have functioned for about five years. Even when inquisitors had a fixed base, they moved around for their duties. The Barcelona inquisitors, for example, celebrated autos de fe in Girona and Tarragona. In the first years of the Inquisition the following tribunals were established:[14] 1482, in Seville, Córdoba, Valencia and Saragossa; 1483, in Jaén and Cuidad Real (moved to Toledo 1485); 1484, in Barcelona and Teruel; 1485, in Toledo, Llerena and Medina del Campo (moved to Salamanca 1488); 1486, in Segovia and Lleida; 1488, in Salamanca, Murcia, Alcaraz, Mallorca and Valladolid (moved to Palencia 1493); 1489, in Burgos, Cuenca and Osma; 1490, in Ávila; 1491, in Calahorra, Sigüenza and Jérez; 1492, in León. This proliferation of tribunals became uneconomic once the number of prosecutions decreased. In 1503, therefore, the five tribunals of León, Burgos, Salamanca, Ávila and Segovia were suppressed and merged into the single vast tribunal of Valladolid. By 1507 there were only seven tribunals in Spain where in 1495 there had been sixteen.

Several changes occurred in the sixteenth century, including the establishment of the tribunal at Granada in 1526. After two unsuccessful attempts, an Inquisition was finally set up in Galicia in 1574. The permanent tribunals of Spain, with dates of first establishment, were:[15]

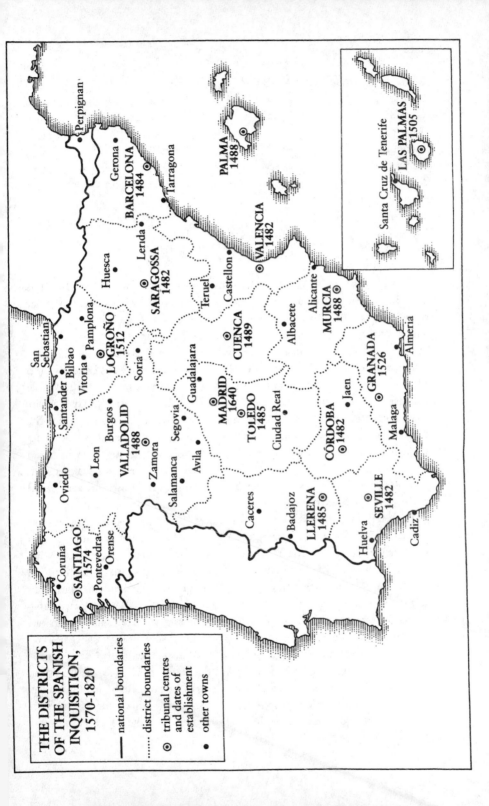

THE DISTRICTS
OF THE SPANISH
INQUISITION,
1570–1820

—— national boundaries

········· district boundaries

◎ tribunal centres
and dates of
establishment

• other towns

LAS PALMAS
1505

Santa Cruz de Tenerife

Perpignan

Gerona

BARCELONA
1484

Tarragona

PALMA
1488

Lerida

Huesca

SARAGOSSA
1482

Pamplona

Teruel

Castellon

VALENCIA
1482

San
Sebastian

Vitoria

Bilbao

LOGROÑO
1512

Soria

Alicante

MURCIA
1488

Santander

Guadalajara

Albacete

Oviedo

Leon

Burgos

VALLADOLID
1488

Zamora

Segovia

MADRID
1640

TOLEDO
1485

CUENCA
1489

GRANADA
1526

Almeria

Salamanca

Avila

Ciudad Real

CÓRDOBA
1482

Jaen

Malaga

Coruña

SANTIAGO
1574

Pontevedra

Orense

Caceres

Badajoz

LLERENA
1485

SEVILLE
1482

Huelva

Cadiz

Crown of Castile

Seville	1482	Cuenca	1489
Córdoba	1482	Las Palmas	1505
Toledo	1485	Logroño	1512
Llerena	1485	Granada	1526
Valladolid	1488	Santiago	1574
Murcia	1488	Madrid	1640

Crown of Aragon

Saragossa	1482	Barcelona	1484
Valencia	1482	Mallorca	1488

The location of the districts is shown in the map on page 143. It is evidence of the remarkable indifference of the Inquisition to other secular or ecclesiastical authority that its districts often crossed political frontiers. The territory of Orihuela in Valencia, for example, was put under the tribunal of Murcía; Teruel in Aragon was put under the tribunal of Valencia; Calahorra in Castile was put under the Navarrese tribunal of Logroño; and Lleida in Catalonia fell under the control of the tribunal of Aragon. The Inquisition was able to do this because its authority, unlike that of the crown, covered the whole of Spain regardless of frontiers. Portugal, for the period 1580–1640 when it came under the Spanish crown, at first kept its Inquisition entirely independent. In 1586, however, Philip II nominated the Cardinal Archduke Albert of Austria, who was governor of Portugal, as head of the Portuguese Inquisition, so bringing the Portuguese tribunal more into touch with Spain.

Each tribunal, according to Torquemada's Instructions of 1498, was to consist of two inquisitors ('a jurist and a theologian, or two jurists'), an assessor (calificador), a constable (alguacil), and a prosecutor (fiscal), with any other necessary subordinates. The number of personnel grew rapidly. By the end of the sixteenth century the major tribunals of the peninsula had three inquisitors each.[16] Contrary to the image – still widely current – of inquisitors as small-minded clerics and theologians fanatically dedicated to the extirpation of heresy, in the sixteenth and seventeenth centuries the inquisitors were an elite bureaucracy.[17] Because the Holy Office was a court, its administrators had to be trained lawyers: Diego de Simancas thought that 'it is more useful to have jurists rather than theologians as inquisitors'. Theological problems were normally left to the assessors to sort out. By the same token, inquisitors did not have to be clergy and could be laymen. All this shows that the inquisitors were in principle a bureaucracy not of the Church but of the state. They received their training in the same institutions that contributed personnel to the councils of state, corregidorships and high courts.

This conclusion is confirmed by what we know of the origins and careers of the inquisitors. An analysis of fifty-seven inquisitors of Toledo, from the period 1482–1598,[18] shows that all but two had degrees and doctorates based on the study of law at university, and that nearly half had been trained in the exclusive Colegios Mayores. Philip III in 1608 stipulated that all inquisitors must be *letrados*, or jurists. Making use of this legal background, many went on to serve in the high courts of the realm. For these, service in the Inquisition was merely a stepping-stone to a further career. In practice, of course, the bureaucracy of state and Church over-lapped, so that although some inquisitors were laymen it was more useful to be in holy orders. Moreover, the ecclesiastical character of inquisitors was underlined by their dependence on canonries for income and by the subsequent promotion of many to bishoprics.

The sparsity of tribunals, and their limited personnel, made it essential to seek additional help from members of the public. This was achieved through familiars and comisarios.

The familiar was a common feature of the mediaeval Inquisition and was continued in the Spanish one. Essentially he was a lay servant of the Holy Office, ready at all times to perform duties in the service of the tribunal. In return he was allowed to bear arms to protect the inquisitors, and enjoyed a number of privileges in common with the other officials. To become a familiar was normally an honour, and the Inquisition in its peak days could boast of a high proportion of nobles and titled persons among its familiars. By the beginning of the sixteenth century the familiars were banded together in a brotherhood (*hermandad*) known as the Congregation of St Peter Martyr, modelled directly on the associations founded by the mediaeval Inquisition after the murder of an inquisitor, Peter Martyr, in Italy in 1252. Comisarios were normally local parish priests who acted for the Inquisition on special occasions and also supplied it with information. They were brought into existence from the 1560s.

Familiars acquired notoriety in fact and in legend for acting as informers, but this was never their real purpose. Neither familiars nor comisarios were meant to be spies. The records of the Inquisition show clearly that the majority of denunciations were made not by them but by ordinary people – neighbours, acquaintances – in response to appeals made in the edicts of faith or simply as a result of personal conflicts.

Since familiars were usually laymen[19] it was inevitable that jurisdiction over them in cases of crime should be claimed by the secular courts. Conflicts arose regularly over this, and it was only in 1518 that Charles V decreed that the cognizance by secular courts of criminal cases concerning familiars and other officials and servants of the Inquisition was contrary to its privileges. After this ruling the tribunal did not hesitate to protect even the humblest of employees from the justice of the civil courts, a position that led to further friction and quarrels.

One solution to which the Inquisition agreed was a voluntary limitation on the number of familiars. The concordia of Castile in 1553 was devoted largely to defining the number of familiars and the jurisdiction of the civil courts. In all serious crimes secular justice was to hold good and the Inquisition was limited to the cognizance of petty offences only. Although this concordia remained in force until the end of the Inquisition, it was only partly successful. Disputes continued as before, and neither the secular nor the inquisitorial courts were concerned to observe it. In the fuero provinces the concession of new concordias became more frequent because they were even less observed than in Castile. Although Valencia received a concordia in 1554 by which the number of familiars was reduced and jurisdiction defined, it was found necessary in 1568 to issue a new one reinforcing the clauses of the earlier concordia and adding new rules. Philip II, in a note to the Inquisitor General in 1574, admitted that he had personal experience of the problems: 'we all know that in the past there have been very great irregularities, and I can assure you that I saw it in Valencia with my own eyes'.[20] Reforms were not effective, to judge by a report of the council of Aragon on 21 July 1632 which claimed that no peace or safety could be expected in Valencia unless there was a reform in the selection of familiars, since nearly all the crimes committed involved familiars who were sure to escape with impunity, relying as they did on the intervention of their protectors the inquisitors.[21]

In Aragon the struggle was even more pronounced because of the great pride taken in their constitutional liberties by the aristocracy of the realm. Here the question of familiars was not resolved by the concordia of 1568, which was the same as that issued in Valencia the same year. It was only after 1646, when the Cortes of Aragon had passed measures which restricted the jurisdiction of the Inquisition, that some satisfaction was gained by the secular tribunals of the realm.

In Catalonia conflicts over familiars were nominally settled by a concordia made at the Cortes of Monzón in August 1512, but the Inquisition never really accepted this. Then in 1553 the Cortes ruled that no official exercising civil jurisdiction in Catalonia could be a familiar. Further disputes ended in the Inquisition proposing a concordia in 1568. This was violently opposed by the Catalans. The viceroy reported that 'all the courts, the Consellers, the Diputats and other judicial officers are determined to lay down their lives' rather than accept it. Small wonder that the Barcelona inquisitors reported that 'they will not be content until they have driven the Inquisition from this realm'.[22] Finally in 1585 it was agreed by the Inquisition at Monzón that in Catalonia 'familiars and officials of the Holy Office cannot be admitted to office in the courts or in public administration'. It was a unique concession.

The endless story of disputes over the numbers of familiars and problems over jurisdiction, has tended to overshadow the history of the familiars themselves. By creating a network of them within each tribunal district, the Inquisition was able to attach to its interests a possibly influential section of the local population. Because the number appointed was often excessive, concordias between state and Inquisition in both Castile and Aragon attempted to set ceiling figures. The Castile concordia of 1553 suggested 805 familiars for Toledo, 554 for Granada and 1,009 for Galicia.[23] In reality the number of familiars might vary widely. In Galicia in 1611 there were a total of 388 familiars and 100 comisarios for the whole province (a ratio of one per 241 households in the population), but these officials were distributed through less than six per cent of the towns and villages – evidence of a very low level of contact between Inquisition and people.[24] In Valencia, by contrast, in 1567 there were as many as 1,638 familiars (a ratio of one for every 42 households).[25] Midway between them was the tribunal of Barcelona, which in 1600 had 815, or one per 110 households.[26]

The social standing of familiars was of paramount importance to the Inquisition, which attempted to recruit from the highest circles and the purest blood. In Galicia the policy seems to have succeeded in the trading areas, for the twenty-five familiars in Santiago were the wealthiest merchants in the city; but inland it was difficult to find suitable candidates. As a rule, people were happy to accept the post if it protected them from secular jurisdiction and gave them privileges of freedom from some types of taxation. In both Andalusia and Valencia gentry were a small but significant portion of familiars.[27] In the predominantly rural society of those times, however, most familiars were inevitably peasant farmers (labradores).

Virtually all familiars in Catalonia, for example, were farmers, with merchants as a significant proportion only in the ports.[28] Thanks to the accord of 1585, in Catalonia no public officials could become familiars, so the post was neither prized nor respected. In 1632 the Inquisition was complaining that it had only five familiars in Barcelona, and all of lowly status.[29]

Although the network of familiars established a presence for the Inquisition, it did little else. It did not act as a form of social control. In Catalonia only about half the parishes in 1600 had familiars; in Valencia there were few in the Morisco towns where they were most needed; and in Galicia only a tiny fraction of towns had them. Nor is it likely that a single familiar in a rural community would have risked his life to become a professional informer. In some areas familiars were openly discriminated against, if we may believe the inquisitors of Llerena, complaining in 1597 of 'the injuries which the corregidores, legal officials and town councils commit against the familiars of this Holy Office simply because they are familiars. The fact is that a man can live in his village for twenty or thirty years without the officials doing anything to injure him, but as soon as he becomes a familiar they move against him, especially if there are conversos in the town council.'[30] The steady decline in the number of familiars in Spain suggests that the post, even with its privileges, was never much sought after. Between 1611 and 1641 in Galicia the number of familiars fell by 44 per cent; where previously they had existed in 226 villages, now they were to be found in only 108.[31] The evidence suggests that the Inquisition never built up an organizational apparatus of social control, and that its impact on the daily lives of most Spaniards was infrequent and marginal.

The Inquisition had to pick its familiars from available material, and the same applied to comisarios. Chosen mainly from the rural clergy, comisarios helped with paperwork and with religious aspects of the Holy Office.[32] They also frequently passed on denunciations to the regional inquisitors. Without their essential help, the inquisitors would have been wholly unable to carry out their role in the Spanish countryside. In some areas, depending on the duties they had to carry out, comisarios were men of education.[33] In others, they fell far short of the required standard. In 1553 the bishop of Pamplona complained that those in his diocese were 'idiots', and had elected to become comisarios only in order to escape from his jurisdiction.[34]

The most surprising aspect of the administration of the Holy Office was its often inadequate financing.[35] Even though it was a government department, it was left to fend for itself. In this it mirrored the model of the mediaeval Inquisition, which never received a fixed source of revenue. The Spanish tribunal was from the first financed out of the proceeds of its own activities. Confiscations were, in the early period, far and away the most important source.

Confiscation of property was the standard punishment prescribed by canon law for heresy. Ferdinand stated in 1485 that confiscations imposed in Spain were by order of the pope, so it would seem that the Church controlled the process. In fact, at the beginning it was the secular authorities who carried out confiscations. Only later did the inquisitors take over control. There were normally two stages to the exercise. At the first stage, upon the arrest of a suspect, his goods and income were 'sequestrated'. This could have terrible consequences and was much dreaded. The sequestrations were used to pay the costs of the prisoner in gaol. If he were there long enough the money might all be used up, thereby driving his dependants into poverty. In effect therefore, a sequestration might amount to confiscation. Confiscation proper, which occurred only at the second stage, resulted from a judicial verdict and was a regular penalty for major crimes.

The principal victims of confiscations were the richer conversos, whose wealth must have stirred many an orthodox spirit. As Hernando del Pulgar wrote sardonically of the citizens of Toledo during a time of civil disturbances: 'What great inquisitors of the faith they must be, to be finding heresies in the property of the peasants of the town of Fuensalida, which they rob and burn!'[36] The initial seizures carried out by the Inquisition were substantial. The alleged plot of conversos against the Inquisition in Seville in 1481 was followed by confiscation of the property not only of the fabled Susán but of 'many others, very prominent and very rich', to quote Bernáldez. In the words of a later chronicler of Seville, 'what was noticeable was the great number of prosecutions against moneyed men'.[37] In the years after this, great and wealthy converso families were ruined by even the slightest taint of heresy, for 'reconciliation' meant that all the culprit's property was confiscated and none of it was allowed to pass to his descendants, so that widows and children were often left without any provision.

Not surprisingly, many ordinary Spaniards came to the conclusion that the Inquisition was devised simply to rob people. 'They were burnt only for the money they had', a resident of Cuenca averred. 'They burn only the well-off, because they have property; the others they leave alone', said another. In 1504 an accused stated that 'only the rich were burnt by the

Inquisition, not the poor'.[38] When a woman in Aranda de Duero in 1501 expressed alarm about the announced coming of the inquisitors to those parts, a man retorted: 'Don't be afraid of being burnt, they're only after the money'.[39] In 1484 after a city councillor of Ciudad Real, the converso Juan González Pintado, was burnt for heresy, Catalina de Zamora was accused of asserting that 'this Inquisition that the fathers are carrying out is as much for taking property from the conversos as for defending the faith'.[40] 'It is the goods', she said on another occasion, 'that are the heretics'. This saying appears to have passed into common usage in Spain. The city authorities of Barcelona, protesting in 1509 against the technique of confiscations, complained that 'goods are not heretics'.[41] In addition to the profits made at Seville, the Inquisition found confiscations could be profitable elsewhere. During its brief year-long stay in the small town of Guadalupe in 1485, enough money was raised from confiscations by the tribunal to pay almost entirely for the building of a royal residence costing 7,286 ducats.[42]

In most of the cases we have on record, the money from confiscated property seems to have been largely disposed of by the Inquisition. It will probably never be clear what proportion of money went to the crown and what to the tribunal. Whatever King Ferdinand's expectations may have been,[43] no available documentation supports the idea of the crown raking in profits. In 1524 a treasurer informed Charles V that his predecessor had received 10,000,000 ducats from the conversos, but the figure is both unverified and implausible.[44]

From time to time confiscations might be substantial. In 1592 in Granada an inquisitor admitted that of the fifty-odd women he had arrested 'many or most were rich'.[45] In later periods there were bonanzas. In 1676, towards the end of the last great and fruitful campaign of the Inquisition against the Portuguese judaizers resident in Spain, the Suprema claimed that it had obtained from the royal treasury confiscations amounting to 772,748 ducats and 884,979 pesos. These sums are extremely large for the period, and suggest that the crown was receiving a high proportion of confiscations. Yet if we look at the value of property confiscated on Mallorca after the alleged converso conspiracy of 1678 had been discovered, we find that the totals come to well over 2,500,000 ducats,[46] certainly the biggest single sum gathered in by the Inquisition in all the three centuries of its existence. Of this vast sum, however, it seems that the crown received under five per cent.

Invariably judicial disputes arose over property that had been seized.

Debts of victims had to be paid, the expenses of officials and of court cases had to be met. The crown could claim a third, as had apparently occurred under Ferdinand and Isabella. Some of the money was invested in *censos* and houses by the inquisitors. In the city of Lleida in 1487, the confiscations from converso property were assigned to the city council, a religious order, a hospital, and to various other needs, so that the Inquisition did not manage to control all the revenue available.[47] By a thousand different routes the money trickled out of the hands of the inquisitors. When the reason was not mismanagement, it was the sheer dishonesty of minor officials. Whatever the income from confiscations at any time, it is safe to assume that the tribunals did not grow appreciably wealthier, or at least did not keep up their temporary wealth for long periods.

After confiscations, there were three important sources of flexible revenue. These were 'fines', which could be levied at any rate desired and were often used simply to raise money to cover expenses; and 'penances' (*penitencias*), which were more formal and were usually decreed at a solemn occasion such as an auto de fe. Both fines and penances could, of course, be realized out of sequestrated property. Finally, there was the category of 'dispensations' or 'commutations', when a punishment decreed by the Inquisition was commuted to a cash payment. Many with money were only too willing to pay for relief from the public shame of having to wear a sanbenito or penitential garment. Others managed to escape service in the galleys by paying for dispensations. Together, these apparently small sources of income produced respectable sums, though never enough to substantiate the view that the Inquisition was founded solely to rob the conversos. Between 1493 and 1495 the various tribunals handed to the council of the Inquisition some seventeen million maravedis (about forty-five thousand ducats) for fines.[48] In 1497 the royal treasurer acknowledged receipt from the Toledo Inquisition of 6.5 million maravedis (about seventeen thousand ducats) realized from dispensations.[49] In general, it is likely that these various sources of income never came to more than two per cent of government treasury receipts in any year.[50] The crown was not in the business for profits. It does not alter the fact that many families probably faced misery as a result of the fines.

Why, during this phase of comparatively high income, was no provision made for a secure financial base? This may have been in part, as mentioned above, because the Spanish Inquisition was modelled on the mediaeval, which had no secure funds either. But we must also take into account the fact that the early Inquisition in Spain was an itinerant tribunal, created for an emergency and with no long-term plans, as the various Instructions of Torquemada show clearly. The Catholic monarchs may well have thought of it as being no more permanent than that other useful organization of theirs, the Hermandad.

There were certainly no financial problems in the first years. After Isabella's death in 1504, however, there was a sharp drop in confiscation income. 'It is reported that the costs of the Inquisition exceed its income', an official noted.[51] The treasury of the Inquisition received in 1509 one-tenth of what it was receiving in 1498.[52] Over the next generation, with the disappearance of the great persecution of conversos, income plummeted. The crown had to decide what to do about this situation. Because the Inquisition was strictly a royal tribunal, revenue from confiscations and fines went in the first instance to the crown, which then paid out for the salaries and expenses of the inquisitors. Under the Catholic monarchs the Holy Office was totally subject to the crown for finance. As late as 1540 the Suprema reported that orders for salaries of inquisitors in the crown of Aragon were always signed by the king and not by the Inquisitor General.[53]

The crown, however, helped itself to considerable inquisitorial income and very soon it had to find extra money for salaries. Ferdinand therefore turned to the Church. In 1488 the pope granted him the right to appoint inquisitors to one prebend (when vacant) in each cathedral or collegiate church. The king made ten presentations that year. His state expenditure had, however, endangered the financial position of the Inquisition, and under the absentee Charles V the Suprema slowly began to take control away from the crown. In the 1540s royal control was virtually nominal, and by the 1550s the Suprema was withholding details of confiscations from the king.[54] It was at this period that the Inquisition obtained its next secure source of revenue.

Already, in 1501, the pope had granted to all the tribunals of Spain the income from specified canonries and prebends, but for several reasons this had never fully taken effect. The government was still wrestling with the problem half a century later. In 1547 Prince Philip informed his father that he was discussing with Inquisitor General Valdés and Francisco de los Cobos 'a memorandum they have drawn up on their ideas for the reform and supply of the salaries of the Inquisition'. The emperor, he added, 'knows better than anybody how important it is to maintain the Inquisition in these realms, and how great an advantage it would be if they had secure salaries'.[55] Impressed by the struggles of the Inquisition against heresy within Spain, the pope in 1559 generously repeated the terms of the grant of 1501. The concession was a response to efforts which Valdés and Philip II had been making for several years. From now on, aided by the income from ecclesiastical offices and from various financial agreements made with the Moriscos in the 1570s, the Inquisition became less dependent on the crown for survival. It also ceased to rely on confiscations. The canonries and investments (censos) provided a more enduring income.

The evolution from deficit to relative stability can be seen in the case of the tribunal of Llerena. In the early sixteenth century, with profitable income from judaizers now virtually a thing of the past, most tribunals faced severe problems. The dangers of this situation were certainly in the mind of the anonymous converso of Toledo who in 1538 directed a memorial to Charles V: 'Your Majesty should above all provide that the expenses of the Holy Office do not come from the property of the condemned, because it is a repugnant thing if inquisitors cannot eat unless they burn [recia cosa es que si no queman no comen]'.[56] Unfortunately, this is exactly what the inquisitors of Llerena were forced to do. With no revenue coming in, they were obliged to go out and look for it. 'We must look out', one inquisitor commented, 'for a solution to maintain the said tribunal in the future'. In 1550 the salaries of officials, amounting to 523,000 maravedis (1,395 ducats), could not be met by income from current fines, which brought in only 375,000 maravedis (1,000 ducats).[57] In July 1554 the inquisitor Dr Ramírez informed the Suprema that 'this Inquisition cannot subsist without going on a visitation every year'. As remedies he proposed that one of the two posts of inquisitor be suppressed; that the post of receiver be dropped and the work given to the notary; that confiscations be looked after directly by the remaining inquisitor; and that further visitations be made to the diocese of Badajoz, which was promisingly full of suspicious people, so that 'with a bit of care there will be no lack of business whereby God our Lord will be served and the Holy Office be able to sustain itself'. By July 1572, with the new system of canonries, all this had changed. Two canonries, in Badajoz and Ciudad Rodrigo, now brought in 680,000 maravedis a year (1,813 ducats), and extensive confiscations from the wealthy family of Lorenzo Angelo in Badajoz raised income in 1572 to nearly two million maravedis (5,000 ducats).[58]

For the next two centuries confiscations and canonries remained the chief direct sources of finance for each tribunal. Two canonries, in Málaga and Antequera, provided the tribunal of Granada with 12.8 per cent of its income in 1573;[59] three canonries, in Córdoba, Jaén and Ubeda, together provided 40 per cent of the income of the tribunal of Córdoba in 1578;[60] and four canonries – in Badajoz, Plasencia, Coria and Ciudad Rodrigo – provided 37.1 per cent of that of the tribunal of Llerena in 1611.[61] Without the regular annual income from these Church offices, the Inquisition would have gone bankrupt.

By their nature, confiscations and sequestrations could never bring in a reliable income. The vast majority of all those accused by the Inquisition were people of humble means, and the inquisitors would need to have had a regular annual turnover of hundreds of prisoners in order to get anything like a substantial revenue. Windfalls like the great persecution of Chuetas in Mallorca in the 1680s were exceptional. The normal picture was of tribunals trying desperately to find income for the costs of administration, prosecution, maintenance of prisoners, and the increasingly expensive autos de fe. The documentation is full of complaints by local inquisitors that they cannot provide either for themselves or for their prisoners. The regular state of deficit in the tribunals can be seen by the statements of income and expenses available for the years 1618, 1671–78, and 1705.[62] Income in Granada in 1618, for example, was 3 per cent more than costs, but in 1671 expenses were 3 per cent more and in 1705 they were 27 per cent more than income.

The figures leave no doubt that the Inquisition was in a parlous financial state. The continuous accounts of income and expenditure of the tribunal of Córdoba show us a persistent history of debt over three centuries: in 1578 expenses exceeded income by 14.6 per cent; in 1642 by 26.8 per cent; in 1661 by 33.8 per cent; and in 1726 by 11.2 per cent.[63]

Why were the tribunals in constant debt? Quite apart from insufficient income, and the difficulties caused by the highest inflation rate in Europe, the problems of the Inquisition can be explained simply by the fact that bureaucracy was absorbing an enormous proportion of income. In 1498 Torquemada had suggested that each tribunal have two inquisitors and a small number of officials. By the late sixteenth century this concept of a modest establishment had disappeared for ever. Córdoba in 1578 had twenty-six officials, Llerena in 1598 had thirty;[64] the number in each case included three inquisitors. In Córdoba salaries consumed 75.6 per cent of income. In addition to this, each tribunal had to send a proportion of income to the Suprema, which had its own heavy expenses. The sum contributed by Córdoba to the Suprema in 1578 represented nearly a fifth of its costs. At this period the salaries of the Suprema bureaucracy were impressively high.[65] The Council spent 5.8 million maravedis (15,500 ducats) a year on wages (the Inquisitor General got 1.5 million and each inquisitor over 700,000), compared with an average total wage bill for each of the bigger provincial tribunals of just under one and a quarter million (3,200 ducats). Local tribunals also had to finance special expenses such as the autos de fe. In 1655, at a time when its normal annual income was around three and a half million maravedis, Córdoba put on an auto which cost over two millions.[66]

This brings us to the most crucial source of inquisitorial income: censos, or investment income. We know that the Inquisition never became a great property-owning institution, and that the estates owned at the end of the eighteenth century were of modest value only. The tribunal of Seville, for example, owned a total of twenty-five rented dwellings and two small estates in 1799.[67] The Holy Office had never lacked the opportunity to become rich, but several factors hindered it doing so. Sequestrations and confiscations did not always produce their full values. Against them had to be set the cost of maintaining prisoners, the debts already owed by those arrested and the claims of innocent dependent relatives. For example, when in 1760 a royal official in Santander was arrested, his sequestrated property was valued at 350,972 reales (32,000 ducats), but of this 36.6 per cent went to payment of his debts, 31.7 per cent to his heirs, and only the remaining 31.7 per cent to the Inquisition.[68] The example is not necessarily typical: in all too many cases the Inquisition refused to pay creditors or family, and kept confiscated property for itself. From the beginning, moreover, the crown had decided that the tribunal required cash rather than an accumulation of property. Confiscations were therefore put up for sale in the open market, and the cash obtained was invested, 'as ordered by the Catholic king' (the reference, to the late King Ferdinand, was made in 1519).[69] Many tribunals were very lax in buying censos, and in 1579 the Suprema had to insist that as soon as one censo was paid off the cash must be reinvested in another. The need to have a steady income – one quite independent of the unreliable and irregular income from confiscations – was undoubtedly the main reason why by the sixteenth century most tribunals were investing heavily in censos. After the turmoil of the Morisco expulsions, we find the Valencia tribunal in 1630 with 45,500 ducats invested in censos at 5 per cent, yielding an annual income of 2,275 ducats.

Censos, in short, became the regular cash source of the Inquisition. In 1573 no less than 74 per cent, and in 1576 80 per cent, of the income of the Granada tribunal came from censos and house rents;[70] in 1611, 63.3

per cent of the income of Llerena came from censos.[71] Everywhere the tribunals began to rely on investment income for survival. In the tribunals in Morisco territory the Inquisition was excessively vulnerable because most of the censos were on land worked by the Moriscos. Events such as the Alpujarra risings or the Morisco expulsion after 1609 (see Chapter 10) were therefore disastrous, not simply because of the loss of the special payments made by the racial minorities but because most of the cash income, in censos and rents, came from Moriscos.

The Inquisition, in financial terms, became a sort of bank through which money from various sectors of society – conversos, Moriscos, financiers – was channelled. Since the inquisitors needed a regular flow rather than future benefits, censos were a fair business risk and preferable to any other economic activity (they brought in 7 per cent in the late sixteenth century, arguably a higher rate of return than most other investments). Thus the Holy Office joined other ranks of society whom González de Cellorigo was later (in 1600) to condemn for their devotion to the quick profit from censos, 'the plague and ruin of Spain'.

Inevitably, individual inquisitors saw no reason why they should not also profit. Lea cites the cases of the Suprema president who was banished in 1642 for malversation of funds, and the inquisitor who died in 1643 allegedly leaving 40,000 ducats in gold and silver.[72] One may well suspect that some tribunals were richer than their financial statements suggested. Take, for instance, the tribunal of Toledo, which on paper had a permanent deficit. If this were really true, how does one explain the interesting case-history of the accountant of the Inquisition there, the priest Juan de Castrejana, who was born in poverty but who managed before his death in 1681 to buy up lands in his home town, endow a chapel and a hospital, lend money to his town council, buy investments in Madrid, set up a silk-manufacturing company and lend money to the silk merchants of Madrid?[73]

In the late seventeenth century there were some positive economic signs despite a decline in personnel. The oft-criticized familiars had all but disappeared. In 1748 their numbers had been reduced to less than a fifth of those permitted. In Galicia and in Aragon, 98 per cent of towns had no familiar.[74] Cases of heresy also declined. The only aspect that improved, from the Inquisition's point of view, was finance. At the end of the seventeenth century and in the early eighteenth, numerous tribunals were faced once again by a lucrative spate of confiscations. This happened most notably in Granada, in Murcia and – most impressively of all – in Mallorca. In the course of the eighteenth century, with the almost total disappearance of prosecutions, revenue from fines and confiscations obviously slumped. By contrast, the fixed investments (censos), in an expanding agrarian economy, now yielded splendid returns. The tribunal of Murcia may serve as example. In 1792 its income was 38.6 million maravedis (103,000 ducats). Because it had few or no cases to deal with, costs absorbed only 40 per cent of this, leaving a nice favourable balance of 60 per cent.[75]

Though the Inquisition led a relatively tranquil existence among the people of Spain, its political life was always stormy. Quarrels of jurisdiction plagued its entire career; it had serious disputes with the papacy, the bishops, and virtually every other authority in the state.

Its conflicts with Rome usually concerned jurisdiction, but occasionally issues of principle might transform a question of jurisdiction into something much greater. The Inquisition derived its authority from the pope and was consequently governed by papal regulations. Complaints against the tribunal could be best dealt with if taken directly to the fount of authority, the pope. The conversos in the fifteenth century did their best both in Castile and in Aragon to obtain papal decrees to modify the rigour of the Holy Office. This was a legitimate procedure, since the constitution of the tribunal allowed appeals to Rome. Rome was eager to maintain its rights, not only to preserve control over the tribunal but also to protect possible sources of revenue, for the conversos paid liberally for any bulls granted by the pope. But the Spanish monarchs, supported by the inquisitors, refused to take cognizance of papal letters that contradicted the verdict of their courts. Ferdinand's famous letter to Sixtus IV in May 1482 illustrates the firmness of the Spanish attitude. The vacillation of Rome before Spanish claims, and the contradictory policies followed by successive popes, made it possible in the end for inquisitors to have things their own way. As early as 2 August 1483 Sixtus IV granted to the conversos a bull which revoked to Rome all cases of appeal, but only eleven days later he suspended this, claiming he had been misled. When his successor Innocent VIII tried to pursue a similar policy of issuing papal letters to appellants from Spain, Ferdinand stepped in and on 15 December 1484 issued a pragmatic decreeing death and confiscation for anyone making use of papal letters without royal permission.[76]

Ferdinand's next decree of 31 August 1509 renewed the penalties of the 1484 decree. Under Charles V the papacy became more cautious. Clement VII in 1524 and 1525 renewed the permission that had regularly (in 1483, 1486, 1502, 1507, 1518 and 1523) been granted to the Inquisitor General to exercise appellate jurisdiction in place of the pope and to hear appeals that would normally have been directed to the Holy See. This did not mean that Rome had given up the right to hear appeals, and when papal letters again began to be issued Charles V in 1537 reinforced the decree of 1509.

Although Rome did occasionally refer appeals back to Spain,[77] the Inquisition was more usually employed rejecting the claims made by holders of papal letters. This situation continued throughout the seventeenth century. But the Inquisition was not unduly concerned by difficulties with Rome, and even before the end of the sixteenth century we find the secretary of the Suprema asserting complacently that the Holy See had abandoned its claim to ultimate jurisdiction over cases tried by the tribunal. Under Philip V the new Bourbon dynasty tolerated no interference by Rome, and so continued the tradition of Philip II. Hostility under Philip V was aggravated by the international situation and by the pope's support for the Archduke Charles, Habsburg pretender to the throne of Spain. In 1705 papal decrees were forbidden in Spain and all appeals to Rome prohibited. This assertion of 'regalism' was supported by most of the bishops and also by the advocate-general Melchor de Macanaz in a famous memorandum of 1713. With the advent of the Bourbons and their new extension of power over the western Mediterranean, in both Spain and Italy, a declining papacy had little opportunity to assert its old jurisdictional claims.

Before the birth of the papal Inquisition in the thirteenth century, bishops had the principal jurisdiction over heretics. This episcopal power was not continued in the Spanish Inquisition, which claimed and maintained exclusive authority over all cases of heresy. Bishops still in theory retained their rights of jurisdiction, but in practice they seldom or never put the claim into effect. In January 1584 the Suprema informed the bishop of Tortosa that the popes had given the Inquisition exclusive jurisdiction over heresy and had prohibited cognizance by others. This claim was obviously false since in 1595 the pope, Clement VIII, informed the archbishop of Granada that the authority of inquisitors in cases of heresy did not exclude episcopal jurisdiction.[78] These opposing pretensions led to frequent and serious quarrels between bishops and tribunals that were never satisfactorily settled.

Most of the religious orders were subject immediately to the papacy by their constitution, and were therefore generally free from episcopal jurisdiction. Since, however, the powers of the Inquisition derived from the papacy, the tribunals made every effort to bring the friars under their control in matters of faith. Political rivalry entered into this question, because the Dominican order had won for itself a special position not only in the mediaeval Inquisition but also in the Spanish. Hostility between Dominicans and Franciscans led to the latter obtaining bulls from Rome to protect their privileges. Under Charles V the opposition crumbled. In 1525 the emperor obtained two briefs from the pope subjecting all friars in Spain to the Inquisition and its officers. This did not last long, for in 1534 the pope restored to the Franciscans and other orders all the privileges they had previously enjoyed. The struggle went on intermittently over the following decades until the papal briefs of 1592 and 1606 decided entirely in favour of the Inquisition.

We have seen that the Society of Jesus, although founded and controlled by Spaniards, encountered suspicion in sixteenth-century Spain. Siliceo, the archbishop of Toledo, was hostile; and the famous Dominican Melchor Cano led a vigorous campaign in which he denounced the *Spiritual Exercises* of Ignatius as heretical. Cano and Siliceo were only part of a wider campaign to discredit the Jesuit order.[79] One of the liberties questioned by the Inquisition was the Jesuit privilege of not having to denounce heretics to anyone but their own superior in the order. When in 1585 it was learned that the fathers of the Jesuit college at Monterrey in Galicia had been concealing the heresies of some of their number instead of denouncing them to the Holy Office, the latter acted immediately by arresting the provincial of Castile and two fathers from Monterrey. The Inquisition did not succeed in punishing its victims because the case was revoked to Rome in 1587, but the affair clinched its victory over the religious orders.

Only one class of people, the bishops, remained beyond inquisitorial jurisdiction. Bishops could be tried only by Rome, a rule that had been upheld in the mediaeval Inquisition. In Spain the issue was of some importance, because of the high proportion of bishops who had converso blood. Among the earliest of those singled out for attack by the Inquisition was Bishop Juan Arias Dávila of Segovia, who took over the see in 1461. He had refused to allow the Holy Office into his diocese, and on being accused by the tribunal was summoned to Rome in 1490, in his eightieth year.[80] Even more distinguished was Pedro de Aranda, bishop of Calahorra and in 1482 president of the council of Castile. He was summoned to Rome in 1493 and died there in disgrace in 1500. One of the most eminent bishops to suffer patent injustice was Hernando de Talavera, whose case we have already noted. But the most famous example of a clash between inquisitorial and episcopal authority, in a case that also involved royal and papal privileges, was that of Bartolomé de Carranza, archbishop of Toledo.

Bartolomé de Carranza y Miranda was born in 1503 in Navarre, of poor but *hidalgo* parents.[81] At the age of twelve he entered the university of Alcalá, and at seventeen joined the Dominican order. He was sent to study at Valladolid where his intellectual gifts soon won him a chair in theology. In his early thirties he went to Rome to win his doctorate in the same subject, and returned to Spain famous. For a while he acted as a censor to the Inquisition, but refused all offers of promotion. In 1542 he refused the wealthy see of Cuzco in South America, and likewise rejected the post of royal confessor in 1548, and that of bishop of the Canaries in 1550. He was twice sent to the sessions of the Council of Trent as a Spanish representative, in 1545 and 1551. He returned to Spain in 1553 and in the following year accompanied Prince Philip on his journey to England to marry Mary Tudor. There he distinguished himself by the zeal with which he crushed heretics and purified the universities of Oxford and Cambridge, winning for himself the title of the Black Friar. In May 1557, Archbishop Siliceo of Toledo died. Philip immediately decided to give the post to Carranza, who refused the honour as he had refused all others. The king was adamant. Eventually Carranza said that he would accept only if ordered to do so. In this way he became the holder of the most important see in the Catholic world after Rome. Carranza was a parvenu in the ecclesiastical circles of Spain. His claims to Toledo were less than those of other distinguished prelates in Spain, notably Inquisitor General Valdés. Like Siliceo, he was a man of humble origins thrown into a rigidly aristocratic milieu. He had been nominated to the see while abroad, without any effort by Philip to consult his Spanish advisers. Intellectually he was far inferior to his brother Dominican, Melchor Cano, a brilliant theologian who had always been Carranza's bitterest rival in the order. The new archbishop obviously had enemies. Only the weapon of attack was lacking. This was supplied by Carranza himself in his *Commentaries on the Christian Catechism* which he published in 1558 at Antwerp.

The *Commentaries* were considered thoroughly orthodox in doctrine. The Council of Trent examined and approved the work, and numerous other distinguished theologians in Spain agreed with this. But it appears that Carranza was a careless theologian. Phrases in his work were seized upon by hostile critics, notably Cano, and were denounced as heresy. The archbishop of Granada called the *Commentaries* 'reliable, trustworthy, pious and

Catholic'; the bishop of Almería said the book 'contained no heresy and much excellent doctrine'. Yet Melchor Cano asserted that the work 'contains many propositions which are scandalous, rash and ill-sounding, others which savour of heresy, others which are erroneous, and even some which are heretical'. Led by Valdés, the Inquisition accepted Cano's opinion. Small wonder that Pope Pius V claimed that 'the theologians of Spain want to make him a heretic although he is not one!' If there were no actual heresies in Carranza why was he looked upon with suspicion by his enemies? Personal enmity loomed large. Both Valdés and Cano detested Carranza. Other mortal enemies were Pedro de Castro, bishop of Cuenca, who had entertained hopes of the see of Toledo; and his brother Rodrigo. Both these men, sons of the Count of Lemos, were aristocrats who resented the rise of men of humble birth to positions of influence. They were to play a key part in the eventual arrest and imprisonment of the archbishop.

What ruined Carranza was the Protestant crisis in Spain, which occurred at precisely the time of his elevation to the see of Toledo. Interrogation of Carlos de Seso and Pedro Cazalla resulted in detailed denunciations of the archbishop. On one occasion he was said to have told them he believed as they did; on another he was reported as saying, 'As for me, I don't believe in purgatory.' He was said to have used Lutheran terminology when preaching in London. The Inquisitor General carefully took note of all these testimonies. Still the Holy Office did not act against Carranza, for as a bishop he was answerable only to Rome. Valdés made urgent representations to Rome, and in January 1559 Pope Paul IV sent letters empowering the Inquisition to act against bishops for a limited period of two years, but both the prisoner and the case were to be referred to Rome. Valdés received the brief on 8 April 1559. On 6 May the fiscal of the Inquisition drew up an indictment calling for the arrest of Carranza 'for having preached, written and dogmatized many heresies of Luther'. After much pressure Philip II gave his sanction on 26 June. On 6 August Carranza, expecting the blow to fall any day, was summoned to Valladolid by the government.

Fearing the import of the summons, Carranza set out but delayed the progress of his journey. On 16 August he was met by a Dominican colleague and friend from Alcalá who warned him that the Inquisition was seeking to arrest him. Shaken by this, the archbishop continued his journey until four days later he reached the safety of Torrelaguna, just north of Madrid, where he met his friend Fray Pedro de Soto, who had come from Valladolid to warn him. But already it was too late. Carranza did not know that four days before his arrival the officials of the Inquisition had taken up their residence in Torrelaguna and were awaiting his coming. He reached the little town on Sunday, 20 August. Very early in the morning of Tuesday, 22 August, the inquisitor Diego Ramírez and Rodrigo de Castro (who was a member of the Suprema), together with about ten armed familiars, made their way up to Carranza's bedroom and demanded, 'Open to the Holy Office!' The intruders were let in, and an official addressed the archbishop, 'Your Honour, I have been ordered to arrest Your Reverence in the name of the Holy Office.' Carranza said quietly, 'Do you have sufficient warrant for this?' The official then read the order signed by the Suprema.

Carranza protested, 'Do the inquisitors not know that they cannot be my judges, since by my dignity and consecration I am subject immediately to the pope and to no other?' This was the moment for the trump card to be played. Ramírez said, 'Your Reverence will be fully satisfied on that account', and showed him the papal brief. All that day the archbishop was kept under house arrest and in the evening a curfew was imposed on the town. No one was to venture into the streets after 9 p.m. and nobody was to look out of the windows. In the silence and darkness of midnight the inquisitors and their prey were spirited out of Torrelaguna. In the early hours of 28 August Carranza was escorted into Valladolid, and allotted as his prison a couple of rooms in a private house in the city.[82] Here he was kept under house arrest for over seven years.

During the whole of his confinement he was not allowed any recourse to the sacraments. In human terms, the tragic story of the archbishop was just beginning; but politically the story was at an end. From now on Carranza ceased to matter as a human being and became a mere pawn in the struggle for jurisdiction between Rome and the Inquisition. He no longer counted in a controversy where the real issues had become the ambitions of individuals and the pretensions of ecclesiastical tribunals. The historian Marañón observes that in this atmosphere of villainy there was at least one just man – Dr Martín de Azpilcueta, known as Doctor Navarro – who accepted a commission from Philip II to go and protect the interests of the archbishop at his eventual trial in Rome.

In the prolonged negotiations between Rome and the Spanish authorities, the papacy was concerned to claim its rights over Carranza and thereby to vindicate its unique control over bishops. Philip II saw the papal claim as interference in Spanish affairs and refused to allow the Inquisition to surrender its prisoner. Pope Pius IV in 1565 sent a special legation to negotiate in Madrid. Among its member were three prelates who later became popes as Gregory XIII, Urban VII and Sixtus V. They failed to make the mission a success. As one of them wrote back to Rome:

> Nobody dares to speak in favour of Carranza for fear of the Inquisition. No Spaniard would dare to absolve the archbishop, even if he were believed innocent, because this would mean opposing the Inquisition. The authority of the latter would not allow it to admit that it had imprisoned Carranza unjustly. The most ardent defenders of justice here consider that it is better for an innocent man to be condemned than for the Inquisition to suffer disgrace.[83]

With the accession of Pius V to the papal throne in 1566, a solution came into sight. From his prison cell Carranza managed to smuggle a message out to Rome in the form of a paper bearing in his handwriting the words, 'Lord, if it be thou, bid me come to thee upon the waters' (Matthew XIV, 28). This was exactly what Pius intended to do. In July 1566 he managed to reach an agreement with the Spanish authorities to send Carranza and all relevant documentation to Rome. The ageing archbishop reached Rome and was placed in honourable confinement in the castle of Sant' Angelo. This second detention lasted nine years. Pius V died in 1572 without having decided the case. His successor Gregory XIII finally issued sentence in April 1576. The verdict was a compromise, made no doubt in order to placate Spain. The *Commentaries* were condemned and prohibited and Carranza was obliged to abjure a list of 'errors', after which he was told to retire to a monastery in Orvieto. Meanwhile the papacy was to administer the vacant and wealthy see of Toledo. The sentence was only in part satisfactory to Philip and to the Inquisition, whose authority would have suffered by an acquittal. It satisfied Rome, which had vindicated its sole authority over bishops; and, in a sense, it may have satisfied Carranza, who was not accused of any heresy despite the prohibition of his *Commentaries*, which was to remain in all the editions of the Spanish Index except the last one in 1790. Justice had been replaced by political compromise. Everything had been taken into consideration except the frail old man who, eighteen days after the papal verdict had been read over him, contracted an illness from which he died at 3 a.m. on 2 May 1576.

From the beginning, the tribunal was closely allied with and dependent on the crown, with the result that later historians came to regard it as a secular tribunal more than an ecclesiastical one. This argument was adopted especially by Catholic apologists who hoped to disembarrass the Church of an unattractive chapter in ecclesiastical history. There is a *prima facie* case for the argument. The Suprema was a government council, not a Church one. The crown had absolute powers of appointment and dismissal of inquisitors, power which Ferdinand employed whenever he felt it necessary. In questions of administration, although decisions were in practice left to inquisitors, the king was kept carefully informed. A letter from Ferdinand to Torquemada, dated 22 July 1486, even shows the king laying down regulations for detailed and minor points such as the salaries of doorkeepers in the Inquisition. For any other question, he tells Torquemada, 'see to it yourself and do as you think fit'.[84] Royal control over the Inquisition is demonstrated by the fact that pleas for redress and reform by the Cortes in the early sixteenth century were all addressed to the crown. Most important of all, the tribunal was financially dependent on the crown.

However, as we have seen, the Inquisition was also an ecclesiastical tribunal. The papacy recognised the juridical existence of the Inquisition, but not apparently of its council the Suprema, which was a state body.[85] Much ink has been spent on trying to define the nature of inquisitorial authority. The truth is that the Inquisition itself always claimed dual jurisdiction. Problems inevitably arose when it came to defining the frontier between the two types of authority. Though the question of jurisdiction over familiars, for example, had repeatedly been agreed upon through concordias, there continued to be constant quarrels between civil courts and the Inquisition. As late as the seventeenth century an official of the Inquisition, discussing 'whether the jurisdiction that the Holy Office exercises over its lay officers and familiars is ecclesiastical or secular', came arbitrarily to the conclusion that 'this jurisdiction is ecclesiastical'.[86] In other words, secular courts could not try familiars. On the other hand, the Inquisition itself claimed the right to try laymen for non-ecclesiastical offences and for injuries done to its officers. At one and the same time, then, the Inquisition claimed to be exempt from secular authority but also demanded to be able to exercise secular authority. It also claimed precedence over both Church and state in public events. This was one of the most common causes of conflict. The inquisitors argued that because they represented both pope and king they were entitled to precedence over all other authorities, including bishops and viceroys. As a result, Church and city authorities would often refuse to attend autos de fe (the Chancillería of Valladolid refused to attend the great auto of May 1559 for this reason), and in Barcelona the Consellers as a rule never went to autos.

The problem of jurisdiction arose out of the peculiar dual nature of inquisitorial power. To confirm its claim of exclusive authority over its own officials, the tribunal always took refuge in the papal bulls it had been granted. Neither the crown nor the Church courts, it argued, could go against these privileges. When critics pointed out that this limited the Inquisition to being a papal and ecclesiastical tribunal, inquisitors were quick to retort that, on the contrary, the Holy Office was also a secular tribunal, exercising power delegated by the crown. Indeed, the crown always supported this pretension. On 18 August 1501 King Ferdinand issued a decree prohibiting one of his own corregidors from 'issuing a declaration saying that the Inquisition is of a different jurisdiction, because in fact it is all ours'. And on 9 December 1503 at Ocaña, Queen Isabella confirmed the dual jurisdiction of the Holy Office, saying that 'the one jurisdiction aids and complements the other, so that justice may be done in the service of God'.[87] Armed with these powers, the inquisitors were, of course, free to arrest royal officials in the name of royal authority, even when royal courts ruled against. In the sixteenth century they arrested the corregidor of Murcia for disrespect, the Diputats of Perpignan for insults and the vicar general of Saragossa for arresting a comisario. They made the entire city council of Tarragona together with the dean and chapter of the cathedral attend mass as penitents with candles in their hands, to atone for not letting the inquisitors into their city when fleeing from a plague in Barcelona.[88]

Conflicts between the Inquisition and secular authorities were at their most acute in the fuero realms of the crown of Aragon. The undoubted hostility of the Inquisition to the fueros was put plainly in a statement of 1565: 'there is no point in saying that [the actions of the Inquisition] are against the fueros and laws of the realm, since *the Holy Office is not subject to the fueros when these are out of step with the law*'.[89] In practice the inquisitors were careful not to overstep the limits of prudence, yet nothing could efface from the minds of officials in the crown of Aragon the feeling that the Inquisition was an alien institution.

In Catalan-speaking areas, the question of language was crucial. In Catalonia, though Catalan was used in all early trials, after the 1560s it was decided that 'since Catalans normally understand our language, depositions should be made in the Castilian language and all trials held in private should be written in it'.[90] The rule was also applied in Valencia. The change, as noted below (p. 188), prejudiced the reliability of evidence used in trials. It also confirmed the alien character of the institution. In

1600 the Diputats of Catalonia observed that 'ever since foreigners [they meant Castilians] took over the Inquisition, there have been many cases of injustice'.[91]

In Valencia and Aragon, conflicts with the Inquisition centred on familiars and Moriscos. In both matters the nobility contested inquisitorial jurisdiction. In Aragon the Cortes of Monzón in 1564 claimed that 'the inquisitors publish edicts on whatever they please and against everybody, on matters outside their jurisdiction, and against all the rules and laws of this kingdom. For many years now they have begun arresting many people who have not been nor are heretics, some for having quarrelled with servants of their familiars, others for debts and petty causes.'[92] By 1566 the Diputados of Aragon were demanding that 'the inquisitors should not be able to issue edicts without the approval of the bishop'. By 1591, during the Antonio Pérez troubles (discussed below), the rebels were demanding 'that there should be no Inquisition in Aragon, or if there is one the inquisitors and their ministers should not be Castilians'.

Catalonia, of all the realms, was notoriously the most hostile to the Inquisition. In 1566 the Diputats of Perpignan arrested and imprisoned the officials of the Inquisition after a dispute. The Diputat Mossén Caldes de Santa Fe led the prisoners through the city, the Inquisition later complained, 'to the sound of trumpets, and held celebrations and banquets as though he had gained a triumph and done something heroic'. The quarrel extended to Barcelona in 1568 when the Catalans refused to accept the concordia of that year. The viceroy reported in 1569 that 'they are all determined to sacrifice their lives, family and property' rather than give in to the Inquisition.[93] Continuous conflicts were blamed directly on the Inquisition by the council of Aragon in Madrid. 'The said inquisitors', the members of the council stated in 1587, 'are those who normally give rise to the quarrels that occur'.[94] The persistent opposition of the Catalans to the pretensions of the Inquisition was never in theory successful. On the other hand, though the inquisitors scored in every skirmish, they never won the war.[95] In Catalonia the Inquisition was always a despised institution enjoying little more than the passive support of the elite and people.

In Castile jurisdictional conflicts were no less serious than in the fuero provinces. Several times in the course of the seventeenth century the council of Castile urged the king to take action, notably in proceedings in 1620, 1622, and 1631. In 1639 the inquisitors were accused of 'enjoying the privilege of afflicting the soul with censure, life with adversity, and honour with exposure'.[96] It is significant that most of these protests occurred in the crisis years of the century, when the statutes of limpieza and other aspects of policy were called in question. Opposition to the Inquisition in Castile was normally led by representatives of royal authority; by, that is, high courts, corregidores and government councils in Madrid. Government ministers repeatedly criticized the role of the tribunal. During the 1591 troubles in Saragossa (touched on below), his own advisers in Madrid protested to Philip II that 'it is very important that the tribunal not meddle in matters that do not concern it directly'.[97] Philip's commander in Saragossa, Vargas, likewise insisted that 'to conserve its authority the Inquisition should not interfere in things that do not concern it'.[98] The virtually unanimous opposition of ministers to the Inquisition during those events is confirmed by a memorandum written by the next king's chief minister, the Duke of Lerma, in 1599. 'It is important to see', he wrote, 'that the Inquisition does not meddle in things that are not its concern, since one can see the harm it did in Saragossa over Antonio Pérez'.[99] This seems to confirm that the tribunal was often seen as an obstacle rather than an asset to royal power. The few occasions when the crown made use of inquisitorial officials, in order to check smuggling at the frontiers or the distribution of false coin, were marginal and temporary. Occasionally the crown might interfere in trials, but discreetly. A case in point is that of Felipe de Bardaxi, an Aragonese noble condemned *in absentia* for blasphemous swearing by the tribunal of Saragossa in 1563. He stayed in France, where he remained safely out of the hands of the inquisitors. In France he also helped the king by acting as an agent in negotiations with the Catholic nobles. Philip therefore prevailed on the Aragonese Inquisition to suspend its verdict confiscating his property.[100]

Endless clashes between the Inquisition and other Castilian courts reached a climax at the end of the seventeenth century.[101] The Chancillería of Granada, a supreme court of the realm, had been humiliated by the Inquisition in a dispute in 1623, but in 1682 was caught up in yet another typically petty case over a secretary of the Inquisition who had ordered the arrest of a noisy neighbour. This time the city council, the archbishop and the Chancillería combined against the Holy Office with such effectiveness that the crown ordered the banishment until further notice of the inquisitors. At the same time the council of Castile protested energetically against the abuses committed by the Inquisition. The final straw came in 1696, when the Diputació of Catalonia entered into conflict with the inquisitor of Barcelona, Bartolomé Sanz y Muñoz, and complained that 'the disorders in this tribunal arise in part because inquisitors are normally foreigners, from another province, who have no understanding of the temperament of our people'.[102] Sanz was deported from Catalonia by royal order. As an immediate result, the government in Madrid set up a special committee consisting of two members from each of the six leading councils. On 12 May 1696 this body issued a damning report on the abuses of jurisdiction committed by the tribunal:

> There is no vassal free of its power whom it does not treat as an immediate subordinate, subjecting him to its mandates, censures, fines and prisons; no casual offence or light incivility to its servants which it does not avenge and punish as a crime against religion; not satisfied with exempting the persons and property of its officials from all public taxes and contributions, it even wishes to claim the immunity of not having criminals arrested in its houses; in the style of its letters it uses and affects ways to decrease respect for the royal judges and even respect for the authority of superior magistrates.[103]

It then went on to prove that precedent fully favoured complete royal authority over the Inquisition in all matters not pertaining to faith. Although the report was not acted upon, the attitude of Philip V in the subsequent reign made it clear that he wished to subject the tribunal more closely to royal control, and 'regalism' came to be the official policy of the state with regard to the Inquisition.

Can we conclude from its role in politics that the Inquisition served the interests of royal absolutism?[104] The notion rests on a confusion of ideas.

Because the Inquisition had a political role, it inevitably became involved in many political affairs. Its authority very conveniently extended over all the Spanish realms, and the crown happily made use of it when no other methods of coercion were available. But it would be difficult to demonstrate that royal power was strengthened in any way. Ferdinand the Catholic certainly used the Inquisition as a political lever. Behind virtually every move of his concerning the Inquisition, political motives can be discerned.[105] In 1507 he was pursuing the famous son of Pope Alexander VI, Cesare Borgia, into Navarre. Failing to secure his victim by any other means, Ferdinand persuaded the Inquisition to initiate proceedings against him for blasphemy, atheism and materialism. But death in battle cheated both the Holy Office and the King of Aragon of their prey. Later, in the case of Antonio Pérez, the crown made a similar use of the tribunal; though government ministers were (we have seen) firm that the Inquisition should not interfere. Never, in any of these cases, did the crown attempt to increase its own authority. In consequence, it is difficult to claim that the Holy Office served 'absolutism', a concept that existed neither in theory nor in practice in pre-Bourbon Spain. The Inquisition was certainly useful in some specific matters; but it normally restricted its activity to its own sphere, and did not give up its ecclesiastical role for a purely political one.[106] Though it was periodically involved in political intrigues, there is little evidence that its religious character was used for political purposes. The prominent case of Jerónimo de Villanueva, who enjoyed power and influence under Olivares and fell soon after his master, was based on legitimate charges arising out of the illuminism of the nuns of the convent of San Placido.[107]

In the sixteenth century the Venetian ambassadors, who were both biased and badly informed, claimed that Philip II was using the tribunal to extend his power. The papal nuncios had the same story. 'The king and his ministers', Nuncio Castagna reported in 1567 over the disputes with the Catalans, 'cannot exercise any control over them save through the Inquisition, so they refuse to listen to them at all and instead try to give the greatest possible authority to the Inquisition'.[108] These claims by Italian diplomats, though frequently accepted by scholars,[109] were wholly untrue.

In a few moments of national crisis the Holy Office certainly played a role, but only a marginal one. When the revolution of 1640 broke out in Catalonia, for example, it was the Inquisitor General himself who suggested that his tribunal should begin proceedings against the rebels. The Catalans drove out the Castilian Inquisition and in September 1643 re-established the old papal one. This was suppressed when Barcelona fell in 1652, and the Castilian tribunal was reintroduced in August 1653. During the war of the Spanish Succession from 1702 to 1714, when the provinces of Aragon broke away from Castilian tutelage, it was the Inquisition that threatened censures against those guilty of treasonable opinions. An inquisitorial edict of 1706 ordered penitents to denounce confessors who told them in the confessional that Philip V was not the rightful king of Spain.[110] These measures were in the realm of threat rather than action.

The tribunal rarely took any action that was nakedly political, and it would consequently be mistaken to regard it as an instrument of state. Philip II is said to have claimed on one occasion that 'twenty clerics of the Inquisition keep my realms in peace'.[111] The king never said it. The claim, moreover, has no meaning. There was no possible ground on which the tribunal could maintain that it had helped to keep the people of Spain subservient to the crown.

Although inquisitors habitually clashed with every other jurisdiction, both Church and secular, political conflict arose out of the way in which power was exercised in old-regime Europe, rather than out of any tendency on their part to quarrel. At town level the inquisitors found that local elites were their main protagonists. In the countryside, their biggest problem was always the authority of the local nobility. In the realm of Aragon they clashed repeatedly with the lords over familiars and over the question of Morisco vassals. In the mid-1550s the Inquisition in Aragon tried to press for the disarming of Moriscos, who had frequently used violence against its officers. The Aragonese lords tenaciously defended the Moriscos, provoking major incidents with the inquisitors. On both sides, the famous fueros were cited. The lords claimed that the fueros were threatened; the Inquisition claimed the fueros were an obstacle to good government. 'If your Majesty does not bare your teeth to them', the inquisitors of Saragossa wrote to the government in 1560, 'you will have great trouble with them'.[112] Trouble-makers tried to make use of this conflict of authority by passing from one jurisdiction to the other. In Aragon a noble in 1581 claimed that some of his vassals 'try to become familiars in order to avoid punishment by my officials'. In the same years other Aragonese vassals, reported the inquisitors, 'want to become familiars to be free of the jurisdiction of the count of Ribagorza and his officials'.[113]

Perhaps the first great case in which the crown used the Inquisition as a political instrument was that of Antonio Pérez. In 1571 Pérez became secretary of state to Philip II. Two years later his patron and Philip's chief minister, Ruy Gómez, Prince of Eboli, died. Pérez thereby obtained one of the most powerful posts in the monarchy and also inherited leadership of the court faction formerly led by Ruy Gómez. A contemporary observed that Pérez 'climbed so high that His Majesty would not do anything save what the said Antonio Pérez marked out for him. Whenever His Majesty even went out in his coach, Antonio Pérez went with him. When the pope, my lord Don Juan of Austria, or other lords required anything of the king, they had recourse to Antonio Pérez and by his means obtained what they solicited of His Majesty.' Another said, 'Great men worshipped him, ministers admitted his superiority, the king loved him.'[114] Philip confided matters of state to this brilliant young man of reputed converso origin whose success enabled him to live as a great lord and whose charm led him into a close and still-mysterious liaison with the Princess of Eboli, the beautiful one-eyed widow of Ruy Gómez.[115]

Ambition eventually led to Pérez's ruin. At the centre of the monarchy he held the king's secrets and controlled the money offered by pretendants to favours. His long hand stretched as far as Flanders, where at that moment the king's half-brother, Don Juan of Austria, was acting both as governor and as pacifier of rebellion. Pérez distrusted the implications of Don Juan's policies and disagreed with the attitude of Don Juan's secretary Juan de Escobedo. He began to influence Philip surreptitiously against them.

Suspicious of the way his plans for Flanders were being blocked by Madrid, Don Juan sent Escobedo to Spain in 1577 to make enquiries. When he arrived at court it became clear to Escobedo that Pérez had been playing a double game with his master and with the king. He began to look around for evidence to condemn the royal secretary. But Pérez had already managed to convince Philip that Escobedo was the malign influence in the affairs of Flanders. This would, in his mind, make it easier to get rid of Escobedo. He tried using poison, but this failed. Then on the night of Easter Monday, 31 March 1578, hired assassins came up to Escobedo as he rode with a few friends through the narrow, dark streets of Madrid, and ran him through the body.

Popular rumour quickly pointed to Pérez as the assassin. Escobedo's family, aided by Pérez's rival in the secretariat of state, Mateo Vázquez, demanded justice for the murdered man. Philip refused to believe in Pérez's guilt, but at the same time he initiated an investigation. It was over a year before any measures were taken. Then in July 1579 the king ordered the arrest of La Eboli and Pérez. Pérez's friend Gaspar de Quiroga, archbishop of Toledo and Inquisitor General, 'did not hesitate to face public opinion by showing an ostentatious liking for Pérez and his group. On the day after the imprisonment of Pérez and La Eboli, when all Madrid singled them out as responsible for the crime, Don Gaspar visited Antonio's wife and children, and offered money to them, as also to the princess's children.'[116]

Not until June 1584 were the charges against Pérez drawn up by the prosecutor. He was accused of selling posts, receiving bribes and betraying state secrets. The Escobedo affair was left aside as though it were irrelevant. The investigation that followed led to Pérez being sentenced to two years' imprisonment and an enormous fine. He continued to be treated leniently, principally because he had in his possession state papers that (he said) incriminated the king. His refusal to surrender them led to firmer treatment by the government, and in 1588 an accusation of murder was presented against him. After two years of rigorous imprisonment, in February 1590 he was put to the torture and ordered to state his reason for murdering Escobedo. His statement under torture produced a confession of responsibility for Escobedo's death, but did not directly implicate the king. All this time the Inquisitor General had continued to protect the secretary. He sent Pérez advice, guided the tactics of his defence, kept him informed of proceedings in the royal council, and knew of (and perhaps assisted in) plans to escape. Escape had now become necessary since all hope was lost after Pérez's confession. In April 1590, with the help of several highly placed friends, Pérez escaped from prison in Madrid and rode across country to the borders of Aragon.

There he was protected from the king's hand by the fueros. Once he had set foot in Aragon the crown of Castile was powerless to touch him. There was only one course open to Philip – to use the Inquisition to get at Pérez. And it was Quiroga, as Inquisitor General, who was forced to set in motion what Marañón calls the 'last and cruellest prosecution against his former friend'. Safe in Aragon, Pérez was lodged for his own security by the Aragonese authorities in the Justiciar's prison at Saragossa. From this vantage-point he began a campaign to win over Aragon to his cause. In Madrid, meanwhile, sentence of death was pronounced against him. Philip's recourse to the Inquisition encountered some difficulty at first, because it was necessary to find guilt of heresy before charges could be preferred. But the royal confessor, Father Chaves – who several years before had taken part in the prosecution of Carranza – now managed to find the necessary evidence in some of the more innocuous expletives used by Pérez. Of one sentence where Pérez wagered his word against God's nose, Chaves noted: 'this proposition is suspect of the Badian heresy which says that God is corporal and has human members'. Pérez's assumed intention to escape abroad from prison, in so far as it included a plan to escape across the Protestant state of Béarn, was presented as heresy because it implied consorting with heretics. Armed with these fabricated accusations, the Inquisition proceeded to move.

On 24 May 1591 the inquisitors in Saragossa had Pérez transferred from the Justiciar's prison to their own in the Aljafería, after the Justiciar had been induced to sign a warrant for the removal. By now, Pérez's propaganda against the king had made him a popular hero in Saragossa. No sooner had the news of Pérez's move been made known than a mob thronged the streets calling for his release and threatening the authorities. In the ensuing tumult the viceroy of Aragon, the Marquis of Almenara, received wounds from which he died a fortnight later. But Pérez was victoriously returned to the Justiciar's prison by the mob, who 'went all the way calling out, "Liberty!" And he cried out with them'.[117] The May riots were repeated on 24 September, when once again the Inquisition claimed jurisdiction over the prisoner and tried to remove him to the Aljafería. After this occasion, when the prisoner was set free by the rioters, the whole political situation changed. The Inquisition had failed in its immediate purpose and a viceroy had been murdered by rebels harbouring a fugitive. Philip therefore resorted to armed force. In October 1591 Castilian troops entered Aragon, subdued Saragossa and executed the Justiciar and other nobles.

Pérez fled abroad to Béarn, attempted an unsuccessful invasion of Spain in 1592 and then went into exile in France and England, still maintaining his campaign against Philip II. In his absence, in the spring of 1592 the Inquisition drew up a list of charges, accusing him of rebellion, heresy, blasphemy and homosexuality.[118] There was obviously no truth in the charge of heresy levelled by the Inquisition against Pérez. In 1607 Pope Paul V issued a brief absolving him from these accusations. In 1611, the year of Pérez's death in Paris, the papal nuncio there certified that he had lived and died a Catholic.

8

HOW IT OPERATED

We have gone into lands where no inquisitor has ever been.

The inquisitors of Catalonia, 1578[1]

The coming of the Inquisition to a town was, in principle, designed to cause fear. In his commentary on the fourteenth-century *Manual* of Eimeric, Francisco Peña in 1578 stated: 'we must remember that the main purpose of the trial and execution is not to save the soul of the accused but to achieve the public good and put fear into others'. The public activity of the Holy Office was thus based on a premiss, common to all policing systems, that fear was the most useful deterrent. When the inquisitors began operations in a district they would first present their credentials to the local Church and secular authorities, then announce a Sunday or feast day when residents would have to go to high mass, together with their children and servants, to hear the 'edict' read. At the end of the sermon or the creed, the inquisitor or his representative would hold a crucifix in front of the congregation and ask everybody to raise their right hand, cross themselves and repeat after him a solemn oath to support the Inquisition and its ministers. He would then proceed to read the edict.

In the early years this took the form of an 'edict of grace', modelled on those of the medieval Inquisition, which recited a list of heresies and invited those who wished to discharge their consciences to come forward and denounce themselves or others. If they came forward within the 'period of grace' – usually thirty to forty days – they would be reconciled to the Church without suffering serious penalties. The benign terms encouraged self-denunciation. In Mallorca the first edict to be published brought in 337 conversos who denounced themselves. In Seville the edict filled the prisons to overflowing. The scale of voluntary denunciation in Toledo was impressive: the number of penitents in the city alone in 1486 was 2,400.[2] After about 1500, edicts of grace against judaizers had served their purpose. They were replaced by 'edicts of faith', which omitted the period of grace and instead invited denunciation of those guilty of a detailed list of offences.

By contrast, when the drive against Moriscos was stepped up during the sixteenth century, edicts of grace were used once again, to elicit information from them. In 1568 an edict of grace in Valencia encouraged 2,689 Moriscos to denounce themselves.[3] In 1570 some of the Morisco vassals of the Duke of Medinaceli voluntarily asked for an edict of grace, so that they could, by their declarations, dissociate themselves from the more radical pro-Muslim attitudes of refugees from Granada.[4] On this evidence, edicts of grace were for the inquisitors a means of obtaining information, and for the cultural minorities a mechanism to regularize their position as painlessly as possible.

In the earlier period the heresies listed were principally Judaic or Islamic, but as time went on further offences were added. Even so, the edict of faith during the sixteenth century had no regular format, and each tribunal used the text that best suited its purposes. The Suprema seems to have adopted no official version. Not until around 1630 did it adopt an agreed text that was allowed into circulation.[5] This was an extremely lengthy and impressive document giving details of every conceivable offence, from Jewish and Muslim heresies to the errors of Lutherans and alumbrados, and so on to popular superstitions, moral offences and hostile attitudes to the Church and Inquisition. It must have taken well over half an hour to read from the pulpit. But it is highly unlikely that the congregation listened to it in 'fear and terror', as one historian claims.[6] Since virtually none of the offences could normally be found in Catholic communities, it is more likely that congregations were simply puzzled or bored. This was certainly the reason why inquisitors in Catalonia stopped reading out edicts after the 1580s.[7] Even when referring to judaizers, the edicts of the seventeenth century (as pointed out below in Chapter Thirteen) curiously mentioned practices that no longer existed and had no relevance to the current religious situation.

The fear set in train by the early Inquisition cannot be doubted. But fear of the tribunal was not the principal spur. The systems of justice prevailing at that time in Europe relied overwhelmingly on the collaboration of the community. And it was the testimony of the community – of, that is, neighbours, relatives, enemies – that the accused most dreaded. As we have had occasion to see, enmity and vengeance inspired much of the evidence offered to the Inquisition in its early years.

Fear of neighbours, rather than of the Inquisition, was on this premiss the first – and constant – concern of those denounced. We have ample evidence of it in the flight of conversos from Andalusia and Catalonia during the 1490s. An example is Manuel Rodríguez, a converso from Andalusia who was described by neighbours in Soria (where he found himself in 1490) as being 'pale and dead with fright'.[8] Fear of denunciation was not peculiar to the inquisitorial regime. It was a regular feature of the judicial system both in Spain and in other countries.[9] The prosecutors in all state tribunals relied heavily on informers, many of whom could claim the right to a proportion of the accused's property. It was a practice that on occasion aroused protests in the Cortes. Juan de Mariana, already cited above, reported the consternation among Spaniards when they found that 'they were deprived of the liberty to hear and talk freely, since in all the cities, towns and villages there were persons to give information of what went on. This was considered by some the most wretched slavery and equal to death.' The use of informers, common enough at the time, was nowhere resorted to so callously as in the period of anti-Jewish hysteria at the end of the fifteenth century, when within the community person was set against person on the accidental basis of blood origins. But denunciation, suspicion and hostility came of course from within the community itself. Sermons and public exhortations encouraged a moral obligation to denounce both oneself and others. We have seen that in 1485 the rabbis of Toledo were asked to tell Jews to report judaizers. The Jewish and converso communities were split apart by such pressures. A particularly striking example of how rock-solid resistance to persecution could suddenly crumble, leading to betrayal and terror, is supplied in the great Chueta tragedy in Mallorca in 1678.[10]

Even where antisemitism was not the driving force, the atmosphere of denunciation and recrimination would have been 'equal to death' for those caught up in it. Petty denunciations were the rule rather than the exception. The Inquisition became a useful weapon for paying off old scores. 'In Castile fifteen hundred people have been burnt through false witness',[11] a villager asserted in the 1480s. When the Lutheran crisis burst upon Seville in 1559–60, a stream of people turned up every day at Triana castle, the offices of the Inquisition, to report what they claimed to know. We have this information from the lips of one of the informants, who subsequently admitted that he had fabricated accusations out of malice.[12]

In 1530 Aldonça de Vargas in the Canary Islands was reported to the Inquisition for having smiled when she heard mention of the Virgin Mary. We can only imagine the motives of the person who denounced her. In 1635 Pedro Ginesta, a man over eighty years old and of French origin, was brought before the tribunal of Barcelona by an erstwhile comrade for having forgetfully eaten a meal of bacon and onions on a day of abstinence. 'The said prisoner', ran the indictment, 'being of a nation infected with heresy [i.e. France], *it is presumed* [our emphasis] that he has on many occasions eaten flesh on forbidden days, after the manner of the sect of Luther.'[13] Denunciations based on suspicion, therefore, led to accusations based on conjecture. This was the quality of thousands of pieces of information fed to the tribunal by malicious people living in the same community.

Some delations, of course, had nothing to do with heresy, as in the case of Alonso de Jaén, who was prosecuted in 1530 for urinating against the walls of a church; or in that of Gonzales Ruiz, who said to his opponent during a game of cards, 'Even with God as your partner you won't win this game.'[14] Both cases were self-denunciations, undoubtedly motivated by the fear that if one did not confess one would be denounced. For people in this frame of mind the edicts offered a welcome opportunity to unburden oneself of fear rather than of guilt. Two husbands accused themselves in 1581 of having asserted in conversation with their wives that fornication was no sin. The wives were summoned and confirmed the confessions. One possible motive for the action taken by the husbands was fear that their wives would denounce them.[15] Or they may simply have felt a compunction to confess the offence. By contrast, no such need was felt by Juan Batanero, priest and doctor of Alcazar de San Juan, who was said to have 'affirmed that simple fornication is no sin, and that he has papers with the arguments for this opinion, which he cannot reveal for fear of the Inquisition, but after his death they can be published'.[16]

The fear generated by the tribunal, in short, usually had its origins in social disharmony. The records of the Inquisition are full of instances where neighbours denounced neighbours, friends denounced friends, and members of the same family denounced each other. In the judaizing cases at Granada in the 1590s, the inquisitors had reason to be grateful to María Alvarez, 'who was the one who first revealed all that has been discovered about her mother and sisters and relatives'.[17] Many of these cases would have arisen through sheer malice or hatred. Vengeful witnesses had everything on their side: their hearsay evidence was usually unverifiable, their identity was always kept secret; and the costs of prosecution were borne not by them but by the tribunal.[18]

There were other cases, perhaps more significant and terrible, where fear of denunciation alone became the spur to confession and counter-denunciation. The 'term of grace' in the 1480s had an important clause which set the seal on all this. To denounce oneself as a heretic was not enough to be able to benefit from the terms of the edict. It was also necessary to denounce all those accomplices who shared the error or had led one into it. It was surely not entirely exaggeration for a converso writer of Toledo to claim in 1538 that

> preachers do not dare to preach, and those who preach do not dare to touch on contentious matters, for their lives and honour are in the mouths of two ignoramuses, and nobody in this life is without his policeman ... Bit by bit many rich people leave the country for foreign realms, in order not to live all their lives in fear and trembling every time an officer of the Inquisition enters their house; for continual fear is a worse death than a sudden demise.[19]

The travails of those of converso origin were, evidently, shared also by the Moriscos. The hatred of these for the Inquisition always included an element of fear. 'Out of fear', an inquisitor of Granada reported in 1568, some Moriscos who had previously refused to do so 'very quickly learned' the Castilian language. 'Out of fear', some women 'began to dress like Castilians'.[20]

There was, however, another face to this situation. In many Christian communities throughout Spain where internal discord was low and public solidarity high, fear of the Inquisition was virtually absent. Catalonia was an outstanding example of a community that held the Inquisition in contempt and despised its methods. In 1560 the inquisitors in Barcelona complained that the city authorities never came to autos de fe, and that in Catalonia as a whole the people, 'vaunting themselves as good Christians, all claim that the Inquisition is superfluous here and does nothing nor is there anything for it to do'. 'All the people of this land', they reported in 1627, 'both clergy and laymen, have always shown little sympathy for the Holy Office'.[21] A typical attitude was that of the parish priest of Taús (Urgell) who asserted in 1632 that 'he didn't recognise the Inquisition and didn't give a fig for it'.[22] Significantly, the Inquisition was unable to take any action against him, nor indeed was it ever able to impose its authority on the people of that diocese.

There were many other regions of Spain where a similar absence of fear prevailed. Because the information available to inquisitors came not from their own investigations but almost exclusively from members of the public, it was in effect the public that dictated the forms of inquisitorial justice. The judges were able to assert their own interpretations and prejudices, but the most substantive part of the matter, the evidence, was produced by witnesses. In a very real sense, the Inquisition was set in motion by ordinary people. And where they refused to cooperate the tribunal was impotent and incapable of inspiring fear.

In the first century of its existence the Inquisition went out to look for heretics rather than wait for them to be brought in. This was inevitable when tribunals were itinerant, but also continued when they were settled. The 1498 Instructions had laid down that 'the inquisitors go to all the towns that have not taken the oath of the general Inquisition'. In 1517 such visitations were once every four months, and by 1581 were required once a year. The purpose was to maintain an inquisitorial presence, though in practice, as we have seen from the case of Llerena, most of the effort was devoted to levying fines. In each town or village the inquisitors were to read the edict of faith and take testimonies. Minor offences could be dealt with on the spot by a single inquisitor, but graver ones required consultation.[23]

Visitations were invariably hated by the inquisitors.[24] Each visitation involved having to travel long periods through difficult countryside and sometimes through territory in private jurisdiction where the authorities were hostile. Perhaps the only consolation was that the inquisitor, accompanied by a secretary and a constable (alguacil), was undertaking real pastoral work. In his visitation of 1553 the inquisitor of Llerena went to twenty-five towns, and in that of 1554 to twenty-two; the former journey lasted six months and the latter four. In Galicia in 1569 and 1570 the visitations lasted eight months, but by the 1580s it was possible to cut the period down to three. In Toledo in 1541 and 1542 the period was ten months, but by the latter half of the century had been reduced to four. Journeys had to be made in good weather and not in harvest time: the months chosen were therefore normally between February and July.

The many months spent travelling show that visitations were a vital part of the inquisitorial presence, and could take up almost half the time of an inquisitor. Moreover, in visitation years the majority of those penanced might be out in the villages rather than in the tribunal's place of residence, so that few actual trials would take place. Between 1552 and 1559 the tribunal of Llerena sentenced an average of 122 persons a year on visitations, and managed to get about three hundred thousand maravedis (800 ducats) a year in fines. Against these gains were to be set the disadvantages that the offences punished were mostly petty; that the money raised was never sufficient even to cover salaries; that conflicts might arise between the inquisitor who stayed behind and the one who went visiting; and that business would pile up during absences (in 1590 the Llerena inquisitors refused pointedly to undertake a visitation, even though directed to do so by the Suprema, because of the urgent cases pending in the tribunal).[25] Not surprisingly, by the early seventeenth century visitations were practised in few of the tribunals, save for special areas such as the realm of Granada, where it was felt that vigilance over the Morisco population was needed.

In any case, visitations palpably failed to impose fear of the Inquisition on the Spanish people. The sheer impossibility of one inquisitor being able with any degree of frequency to visit the vast areas involved, meant that in practice visits were restricted to larger centres of population from which fines might more easily be raised. Add to this the infrequency of visitations after the early sixteenth century, and the fixing of tribunals in the cities, and we get a picture of a rural Spain that was largely out of touch with the Inquisition. 'This valley', a correspondent wrote in 1562 from the Vall d'Arán in the Catalan Pyrenees, 'does not know the Holy Inquisition.'[26] The Galician countryside and villages never saw the Holy Office.[27] This gulf between the Inquisition and much of rural Spain was, however, even greater than appears at first sight. Faced by the temerarious appearance in their midst of an outsider demanding to know their private sins and public errors, the rural communities responded with their own wall of silence.[28] Was the inquisitor of Barcelona in 1581, Dr Caldas, simply being naive when reporting after his visitation that he was surprised at how few denunciations there were?[29] It had been ten years since the last visitation to the archdiocese of Tarragona. Yet after four months visiting twenty-three towns (including very large ones such as Igualada, Cervera, Tarragona and Vilafranca), Dr Caldas obtained no more than fifty-three denunciations.

The very nature of the denunciations in these and other Catalan towns leads irresistibly to the conclusion that though villagers sometimes used the Inquisition to play off scores against each other, more commonly the rural communities solidly rejected the interference of the Inquisition. Five denunciations to Dr Caldas were against familiars; one involved alleged bestiality 'twelve years ago'; one was against a man for saying 'ten years ago' that simple fornication was no sin; one involved a woman having said thirty years before (she was now dead) that there was no heaven and hell. In town after town, in this and other visitations, there was silence. It is possible that the Catalans were different from other Spaniards. Year after year in the 1580s the Barcelona tribunal kept apologizing to the Suprema

The Virgin of the Catholic Monarchs, by an unknown painter. Kneeling behind Ferdinand is Torquemada, first Inquisitor General of Spain.

LEFT A penitent in *sanbenito*.

RIGHT A relapsed heretic due for the stake.

A seventeenth-century Dutch engraving of the procession to an *auto de fe*.

St Dominic presiding at an auto de fe, by Pedro Berruguete (c. 1490). The images are meant to emphasise the special role of the Dominican order (and its thirteenth-century founder) in the activity of the Inquisition.

Mercy and justice on the banner of the Inquisition.

Vexillum Inquisitionis Hispanæ.

A contemporary Dutch print depicting what the Valladolid *auto de fe* of May 1559 was imagined to have been like.

SPAANSCHE INQUISITIE.

An eighteenth-century print, by Bernard Picart, depicting an imagined scene of the burning of heretics, in Lisbon, after an *auto de fe*.

An imaginary scene of an inquisitorial torture chamber, based on an eighteenth-century engraving by Picart.

The great *auto de fe* of 1680, held in the Plaza Mayor at Madrid before King Charles II. Detail from the contemporary canvas by Francisco Rizi.

'Not everyone knows': a comment on the Inquisition by Goya.

'For opening his mouth in dissent': a penitent in *sanbenito*, sketched by Goya.

A masterpiece of satire: Goya's *Auto de fe*.

for the tiny number of prosecutions: 'it is not negligence on our part that there are no more cases' (1586); 'we have made every effort, so that it is not negligence that there are no more cases' (1588).[30] The inquisitors reported in 1623 that edicts of faith were now seldom read in Catalonia.

> They produce few denunciations, and this year we were almost resolved not to publish the edict in this city, because for the last four years not a single person has come to the tribunal in response to the edicts. And in 1621 we visited the regions of Girona and Perpignan, and even though it was ten years since the last visitation and both are large towns, there were only four or five denunciations, two of them trifling; and if we read the edicts every year the only fruit would be that people would lose their fear of and respect for the censures.[31]

In other communities, the number of cases that arose during visitations could be high. There were undoubtedly parts of Spain where old scores were paid off when the inquisitors came to call. The high figure of 240 denunciations in the diocese of Burgos in 1541[32] may possibly have reflected tensions between Old and New Christians. But in compact and stable communities, where there were few or no minority groups to victimize, the Inquisition was pushed aside as an irrelevance. In Morisco areas the people were willing to denounce themselves under the terms of edicts of grace, but when edicts of faith were proclaimed their community solidarity made them mute.

If the Holy Office welcomed denunciations, it often knew when to distinguish between the false and the true. In 1637 when Felipe Leonart, a needlemaker of French origin living in Tarragona, was unanimously denounced by his wife, son and daughter-in-law for Lutheranism, the tribunal very quickly realized that the charges had been made out of sheer malice, and suspended the trial after rejecting the accusations.[33] False-witness was, if we may believe the official figures, rare. In the tribunal of Toledo, there were apparently only eight cases of perjury detected in the 1,172 trials that took place between 1575 and 1610.[34] Anyone with the slightest experience of court testimony must reject such figures as absurd. The real level of perjury was obviously very much higher, but impossible to identify. Perjurers themselves were not treated with any severity commensurate with the ruin they brought upon their victims, though in some few cases they suffered burning, scourging and the galleys. More difficult to deal with were cases of pathological self-denouncers such as the French nun in a convent at Alcalá, Ursule de la Croix, who confessed to heresy and eating meat on Fridays. She was absolved, but confessed again to the offences. The second time she was reconciled and given a light penance. When she decided to denounce herself for the third time in 1594, however, she was obligingly sent to the stake.[35]

In the Spanish Inquisition, witnesses were given more advantages than in any secular court of justice, because their names were concealed. This provoked strong opposition, clearly expressed in the several Cortes held under Charles V, particularly that of Valladolid in February 1518. But the influence of Cisneros prevailed against allowing the publication of witnesses' names, and the practice remained unaltered. Concealment of names meant that when a charge was drawn up against a prisoner it had to be phrased in general terms, so that the accused could not identify witnesses and accusers.

The necessity for concealment, Cisneros had argued, was justified by cases in which witnesses had been murdered in order to prevent them testifying. But, as a memorial from the city of Granada put it in 1526, the system of secrecy was an open invitation to perjury and malicious testimony.[36] This objection might not have been valid but for the fact that all denunciations were taken seriously, and even if a man were later exonerated, the evil brought on him by a slight and secret accusation was immense. When, for example, Doctor Enrique Jorge Henriques, physician to the Duke of Alba, died in 1622, secret witnesses claimed that his body had been buried according to Jewish rites. The consequence was that all Henriques' family, relatives and household were thrown into prison and kept there for two years until their acquittal for lack of evidence.[37]

Judicially, the Inquisition was neither better nor worse than the secular courts. Secrecy was not, it seems, originally a part of the inquisitorial framework, and early records refer to public trials and a public prison rather than a private ('secret') one. But by the beginning of the sixteenth century secrecy became the general rule and was enforced in all the business of the tribunal. Even the various Instructions of the Inquisition, although set down in print, were for restricted circulation only and not for the public eye. This resulted logically in public ignorance of the methods and procedure of the Inquisition. In its earlier period it helped the tribunal by creating reverential fear in the minds of wrongdoers, but later on led to the rise of hostility based on a highly imaginative idea of how the tribunal worked. The Inquisition was therefore largely to blame for the unfounded slanders subsequently cast upon it. The natural outcome of this enforced ignorance is shown by the debates in the Cortes of Cádiz in 1813, on the projected decree to abolish the Inquisition. If the defenders of the tribunal relied on the argument of a mystical and mythical unity given to Spain by the Inquisition, its detractors relied almost completely on legendary misapprehensions about the entire structure and function of the institution.

The outside world may have been kept uninformed, but internally the flow of information was almost impeccable. The administrative and secretarial apparatus of the tribunal took care to set down on paper even the most trifling business. Thanks to this, the Spanish Inquisition is one of the few early modern institutions about whose organization and procedure an enormous amount of documentation is available. Like any judicial court, it needed paperwork in order to survive: the struggle to establish precedents and to keep written evidence of privileges forced officials to record everything.

Before an arrest took place, the evidence in the case was presented to a number of theologians who acted as consultants or assessors (calificadores) to determine whether the charges involved heresy. If they decided that there was sufficient proof, the prosecutor (fiscal) drew up a demand for the arrest of the accused, who was then taken into custody. Such at least were the rules. But in numerous cases arrest preceded the examination, so that all the preliminary safeguards against wrongful arrest were dispensed with. As a result, prisoners sat in inquisitorial gaols without any charge ever having been produced against them. This led the Cortes of Aragon in 1533 to protest against arrest for arbitrary reasons or on trifling charges. Zeal of officials and inquisitors alike often outran discretion. In the tribunal of Valladolid in 1699 several suspects (including a girl aged nine and a boy aged fourteen) had lain in prison for up to two years without any *calificación* having been made of the evidence against them.

Arrest was accompanied by immediate seizure of the goods held by the accused. An inventory was made of everything in the possession of the man or his family, and all this was held by officials of the Inquisition until the case had been decided. The inventories drawn up in this way are of great historical interest, since they allow us to see in minute detail exactly how the household of a sixteenth- or seventeenth-century family was run. Every item in the house, including pots and pans, spoons, rags and old clothes, was carefully noted down in the presence of a notary. In some cases these items were valued at the time of the inventory – an important measure because of the frequent need to sell the items to pay for the upkeep of a prisoner or his dependants. If a prisoner's case went unheard or undecided for years on end, the sequestration of his property involved real hardship for his dependants, deprived at one blow of their means of income and even of their own homes. For as long as the accused stayed in prison the costs of his upkeep were met out of his sequestrated property, which was as a rule sold piece by piece at public auction.

Initially no provision was made for relatives during sequestration and the government had to intervene to help. In July 1486 Ferdinand ordered the tribunal in Saragossa to support the needy children of an accused man, Juan Navarro, out of the latter's property while the case was being heard. Others were not so lucky. There were instances of a rich prisoner's children dying of hunger and of others begging in the streets. These evils were finally remedied in the Instructions of 1561, which allowed the support of dependants out of sequestrations. This concession, which until then had been in practice informally, came too late to save two generations of conversos from destruction of their property. Even after 1561, accused persons sometimes found little security for their property against dishonest officials, or against arbitrary arrest and lengthy trials.

The arrested person was usually spirited away into the prisons of the Inquisition, there to await trial. Normally each tribunal set aside a section of its building for the 'secret prison' ('secret' meant 'private', to distinguish it from 'public' prisons), meant particularly for the confinement of prisoners and not for temporary detainees awaiting trial. The Inquisition was usually fortunate in its choice of residences. In some of the largest cities of Spain it was allowed the use of fortified castles with ancient and reliable prison cells. The tribunal of Saragossa resided in the Aljafería, that of Seville in the Triana (in 1627 it moved to a site within the city), and that of Córdoba in the Alcázar.

In all these buildings the gaols were in a fairly good condition. This may explain why the secret prisons of the Inquisition were generally considered less harsh and more humane than either the royal prisons or ordinary ecclesiastical gaols. There is the case of a friar in Valladolid in 1629 who made some heretical statements simply in order to be transferred from the prison he was in to that of the Inquisition. On another occasion, in 1675, a priest confined in the episcopal prison pretended to be a judaizer in order to be transferred to the inquisitorial prison. In 1624, when the inquisitors of Barcelona had more prisoners than available cells, they refused to send the extra prisoners to the city prison, where 'there are over four hundred prisoners who are starving to death and every day they remove three or four dead'.[38] No better evidence could be cited for the superiority of inquisitorial gaols than that of Córdoba in 1820, when the prison authorities complained about the miserable and unhealthy state of the city prison and asked that the municipality should transfer its prisoners to the prison of the Inquisition, which was 'safe, clean and spacious. At present it has twenty-six cells, rooms which can hold two hundred prisoners at a time, a completely separate prison for women, and places for work.' On another occasion the authorities there reported that 'the building of the Inquisition is separate from the rest of the city, isolated and exposed on all sides to the winds, spacious, supplied abundantly with water, with sewers well distributed and planned to serve the prisoners, and with the separation and ventilation necessary to good health. It would be a prison well suited to preserve the health of prisoners.'[39]

By contrast, the tribunal of Llerena was housed in a building it described in 1567 as 'small, old, poor and shabby', with fifty-two cells, certainly not enough for the 130 prisoners it had that year.[40] The tribunal at Logroño in the sixteenth century had unhealthy premises that led directly, in times of epidemic, to the death of unfortunate prisoners. In the hot summer of 1584 more than twenty prisoners died in their cells.[41]

A more personal description of an inquisitorial prison is given by a prisoner who left an account of the cells of the tribunal at Lisbon in 1802. The picture resembles any Spanish inquisitorial prison:

The gaoler who for greater dignity has the name of Alcaide, addressed to me almost a little sermon, recommending me to behave in this respectable house with great propriety; stating also that I must not make any noise in my room, nor speak aloud, lest the other prisoners might happen to be in the neighbouring cells and hear me, with other instructions of a similar kind. He then took me to my cell, a small room twelve feet by eight, with a door to the passage; in this door were two iron grates, far from each other, and occupying the thickness of the wall, which was three feet, and outside of these grates there was besides a wooden door; in the upper part of this was an aperture that let into the cell a borrowed light from the passage, which passage received its light from the windows fronting a narrow yard, but having opposite, at a very short distance, very high walls; in this small room were a kind of wood frame without feet, whereon lay a straw mattress, which was to be my bed; a small water-pot; and another utensil for various purposes, which was only emptied every eight days, when I went to mass in the prisoners' private chapel. This was the only opportunity I had of taking fresh air during such a period, and they contrived several divisions in the chapel in such a manner that the prisoners could never see each other, or know how many were granted the favour of going to mass. The cell was arched above, and the floor was brick, the wall being formed of stone, and very thick. The place was consequently very cold in winter, and so damp that very frequently the grates were covered with drops of water like dew; and my clothes, during the winter, were in a state of perpetual moisture. Such was my abode for the period of nearly three years.[42]

The fact that the practice in its prisons could be humane should not be taken to mean that the Inquisition was benevolent. Efforts were made to see that the gaols were not dens of horror. Prisoners were fed regularly and adequately from their own purse on available food, particularly bread, meat and wine. In the cells in Madrid in 1676 prisoners were fed on bread, mutton, hake, sardines, soup, vegetables, lettuce, figs, oil, vinegar and wine.[43] Since the prisoners complained about this diet, the real quality of the items may be doubted. One fortunate prisoner in Toledo in 1709 managed to order for himself in addition regular supplies of oil, vinegar, ice, eggs, chocolate and bacon.[44] The expenses of all paupers were paid for by the tribunal itself: at Las Palmas the money spent on the pauper Catalina de Candelaria during her six-month stay in 1662 came to 54 reales (5 ducats). One of those who could afford to pay for themselves, Isabel Perdomo, had to pay 28 reales for her seven-week stay in the same prison in 1674.[45] Apart from food, prisoners in some tribunals were well cared for, this depending on their financial resources. One Juan de Abel of Granada was granted in his cell the use of 'a mattress, a quilt, two sheets, two pillows, a rug, a blanket' and other items.[46] Even paupers were given slippers, shirts and similar items. Besides this, some comforts were allowed, such as the use of writing paper – a concession exploited to the full by Luis de León, who spent his four years in prison at Valladolid composing his devotional treatise *The Names of Christ*.

There was, of course, another side to the picture. Prisoners were normally cut off from all contact with the world outside, and even within the prison were secluded from each other if possible. Inadequate cells often made overcrowding inevitable. In Granada in the 1570s, a period coinciding with the anti-Morisco repression, there were an average of four persons in each cell.[47] On finally leaving the gaol prisoners were obliged to take an oath not to reveal anything they had seen or experienced in the cells. Small wonder if this secrecy gave rise to the most blood-curdling legends about what went on inside. A rule of the Spanish and the Roman Inquisitions was that detainees were denied all access to mass and the sacraments. One of the most notable sufferers in this respect was Bartolomé de Carranza, whose trials must have been doubled by this heavy deprivation of spiritual comfort during his reclusion.

To balance the fortunate few who were treated reasonably there are records of the many who did not fare so well. John Hill, an English sailor captured in 1574 and imprisoned by the Las Palmas tribunal, complained of having to sleep on the floor with fleas, of lack of bread and water, and of being left all but naked.[48] These were standard complaints that could have been made of any other prison, secular or ecclesiastical. Other ordeals would include having to wear chains (not frequent in the Inquisition), and being left interminably in unlit and unheated cells. In addition the Inquisition used two instruments to punish awkward prisoners; one was the *mordaza* or gag, used to prevent prisoners talking or blaspheming; the other was the *pie de amigo*, an iron fork utilized to keep the head upright forcibly. In view of the general state of prisons in Europe down to relatively modern times, one may conclude with Lea 'that the secret prisons of the Inquisition were less intolerable places of abode than the episcopal and public gaols. The general policy respecting them was more humane and enlightened than that of other jurisdictions, whether in Spain or elsewhere.'[49]

The severities of prison life led to a regular death-rate which could be attributed not to torture (about which inquisitors were usually careful) but to disease and unhealthy conditions. As the Inquisitor General, Cardinal Adrian of Utrecht, observed in 1517, the prisons were meant for temporary detention only and not for punishment. Prisoners were seldom condemned to rot in the cells. They were there – some for lengthy periods – only as a preliminary to trial. Inquisitors usually took care to avoid cruelty, brutality and harsh treatment. This did not prevent tragedies. In 1699 a forty-year-old seamstress was confined in the cells at Valladolid on suspicion of judaizing. Confined with her were her four sons, aged thirteen to seventeen. Within six months the two youngest were taken to hospital, where they died.[50] It was a consequence of the practice, all too common, of throwing entire families, children included, into the cells. Madness and suicide were also regular consequences of imprisonment.

Interrogations were usually conducted in the presence of a secretary, who noted down questions and answers, and a notary. During the first half-century of the tribunal, when suspects came mainly from Andalusia and southern Spain, there were no language difficulties. As the inquisitors extended their activities, problems began to arise. Roughly one in four Spaniards during the sixteenth century did not habitually speak Spanish. If Moriscos were interrogated, a translator often had to be on hand. In Catalonia testimony might be taken in the native language but then transcribed in the only language understood by inquisitors, Spanish. The translated or transcribed text, *not* the original deposition, would then be used as the basis for prosecution. As may be imagined, the procedure opened the way to serious distortions of meaning and thus to very grave injustices. The Diputats of Catalonia in 1600 protested vigorously that all depositions made in French and Catalan were treated in this way.[51] The Inquisition blithely ignored such protests. From the 1560s all depositions had to be written in Spanish, even if dictated in another language.

The use of torture (inherited from the mediaeval Inquisition) was not considered as an end in itself. The Instructions of 1561 laid down no rules for its use but urged that its application should be according to 'the conscience and will of the appointed judges, following law, reason and good conscience. Inquisitors should take great care that the sentence of torture is justified and follows precedent.'[52] At a time when the use of torture was universal in European criminal courts, the Spanish Inquisition followed a policy of circumspection that makes it compare favourably with other institutions. Torture was used normally as a last resort and applied in only a minority of cases. Often the accused was merely placed in *conspectu tormentorum*, when the sight of the instruments of torture would provoke a confession.

Confessions gained under torture were never accepted as valid because they had obviously been obtained by pressure. It was therefore essential for the accused to ratify his confession the day after ordeal. If he refused to do this, a legal subterfuge was invoked. As the rules forbade anyone to be tortured more than once, the end of every torture session was treated as a suspension only, and refusal to ratify the confession would be met with a threat to 'continue' the torture. Besides being compelled to confess their own heresies, accused were often also tortured *in caput alienum*, to confess knowledge of the crimes of others.

In statistical terms, it would be correct to say that torture was used infrequently.[53] Though permitted by the Instructions of 1484, in the early years it seems to have been considered superfluous and was seldom used. Abundant testimony, from edicts of grace and from witnesses, was more than sufficient to keep the judicial process functioning. Out of more than four hundred conversos tried by the Inquisition at Ciudad Real in 1483–5, only two are known to have been tortured.[54] The incidence of torture in Valencia before 1530 was low. After the 1530s, however, things changed radically.[55] It was now a question of rooting out underground and unconfessed Judaism. Torture was therefore more frequently applied, though its use was limited only to cases of heresy. This meant that minor offences, which were the bulk of crimes tried by the Inquisition for a great part of its history, did not qualify for it. In the tribunal of Granada from 1573 to 1577, eighteen out of 256 accused were tortured, just over seven per cent. In Seville from 1606 to 1612, twenty-one out of 184 were tortured, just over eleven per cent.[56] By the mid-eighteenth century torture had virtually fallen out of use in the tribunal, and finally in 1816 the pope forbade it in any of the tribunals subject to the Holy See.

The statistical infrequency of torture has encouraged historians to downplay its importance. This ignores its very real impact at select periods on the group that most suffered from it: the alleged judaizers. It was applied rigorously after the early sixteenth century in cases of suspected Protestantism and Judaism. Lea estimates that in the Toledo tribunal between 1575 and 1610 about a third of those accused of heretical offences were tortured.[57] In the late seventeenth century at least three-quarters of all those accused in Spain of judaizing – several hundreds of people – were tortured.[58] In 1699 the inquisitors of Seville complained that they hardly had the time to carry out all the tortures required. Supporting evidence for the frequency of the punishment in this tribunal comes from the doctor who in 1702 claimed back-payment for his presence at 434 sessions of torture.[59]

Torture was employed exclusively to elicit information or a confession, and never used as a punishment. The scenes of sadism conjured up by popular writers on the Inquisition have little basis in reality, though the whole procedure was unpleasant enough to arouse periodic protests from Spaniards. Torturers used were normally the public executioners who worked for the secular courts. Those required to be present at the proceedings were the inquisitors themselves, a representative of the bishop, and a secretary to record everything faithfully. Physicians were usually available in case of emergency. On the evidence available, at no time were the inquisitors so sophisticated as to resort to psychological methods or brain-washing.[60] In the case of judaizers of the later period, however, the special care in tracking down family networks and in encouraging relatives

to denounce each other, may with some reason be considered as exceptionally cruel. It was a refinement of method never used for other offences.

The basic rule in torture was that the accused should suffer no danger
to life or limb. By Church law, ecclesiastical tribunals could not kill nor
could they shed blood. No distinctive tortures were used by the Inquisition.
Those most often employed were in common use in other secular and
ecclesiastical tribunals, and any complaints of novel tortures would certainly refer to rare exceptions. The three main ones were the *garrucha*, the
toca and the *potro*. The garrucha or pulley involved being hung by the
wrists from a pulley on the ceiling, with heavy weights attached to the
feet. The accused was raised slowly and then suddenly allowed to fall with
a jerk. The effect was to stretch and perhaps dislocate arms and legs. The
toca or water torture was more complicated. The accused was tied down
on a rack, his mouth was kept forcibly open and a toca or linen cloth was
put down his throat to conduct water poured slowly from a jar. The severity
of the torture varied with the number of jars of water used. The potro,
which was the most common after the sixteenth century, involved being
bound tightly on a rack by cords which were passed round the body and
limbs and were controlled by the executioner, who tightened them by
turns of the cords at the end. With each turn the cords bit into the body
and travelled round the flesh. In all these tortures it was the rule to strip
the accused first. Both men and women were divested of all their clothes
and left completely naked except for minimal garments to cover their
shame.[61]

There seems to have been no age limit for victims, nor was there any
limit on the torture. A victim would often have to undergo all three
tortures before he would confess. The less obdurate might need only one
torture. While the Inquisition did not usually subject very old and very
young people to torture, there are cases when tribunals apparently found
this necessary. Women aged between seventy and ninety years are on record
as having been put on the potro. In 1607 at Valencia a girl of thirteen was
subjected to torture, but she seems to have been mildly treated since she
overcame it without confession. Allowances for age might be made. In
1579 the inquisitors of Llerena informed the Suprema that 'all the clergy
arrested for being alumbrados have been tortured and they haven't confessed anything, though it must be said that since several of them are very
old and also ill and infirm from their long confinement, it has not been
possible to torture them with the required rigour'.[62] Those who had to
undergo the experience were often left in a sorry state. Many were left

with limbs irreparably broken, sometimes with both health and reason diminished; others died under torture.[63]

It was standard practice, which the Inquisition took over from secular courts,[64] to record all details of torture. A secretary noted every word and gesture during the proceedings, thus providing us with impressive if macabre evidence of the sufferings of the accused. Here are extracts from the official accounts of two tortures carried out in the sixteenth century. In the first is a woman accused in 1568 of not eating pork and of changing her linen on Saturdays.

> She was ordered to be placed on the *potro*. She said, 'Señores, why will you not tell me what I have to say? Señor, put me on the ground – have I not said that I did it all?' She was told to talk. She said 'I don't remember – take me away – I did what the witnesses say'. She was told to tell in detail what the witnesses said. She said, 'Señor, as I have told you, I do not know for certain. I have said that I did all that the witnesses say. Señores, release me, for I do not remember'. She was told to talk. She said, 'Señores, it does not help me to say that I did it and I have admitted that what I have done has brought me to this suffering – Señor, you know the truth – Señores, for God's sake have mercy on me. Oh Señor, take these things from my arms – Señor release me, they are killing me'. She was tied on the *potro* with the cords, she was admonished to tell the truth and the *garrotes* were ordered to be tightened. She said, 'Señor, do you not see how these people are killing me? I did it – for God's sake let me go!'[65]

Foreign heretics were submitted to the same procedure. Here is the case of Jacob Petersen from Dunkirk, a sailor aged twenty who was examined by the tribunal of the Canaries in November 1597. He was stripped and bound and given three turns of the cord.

> On being given these he said first, 'Oh God!' and then, 'There's no mercy': after the turns he was admonished, and he said, 'I don't know what to say, oh dear God!' Then three more turns of the cord were ordered to be given, and after two of them he said, 'Oh God, oh God, there's no mercy, oh God help me, help me!'[66]

After three more turns he confessed.

While these examples give us some insight into the agony of those who were tortured, it should be remembered that the procedure was often mild enough for very many to overcome it. A comparison with the cruelty and mutilation common in secular tribunals shows the Inquisition in a relatively favourable light. This in conjunction with the usually good level of prison conditions makes it clear that the tribunal had little interest in cruelty and often attempted to temper justice with mercy.

9

TRIAL AND PUNISHMENT

It makes one think that all this great machinery for the punishment of a few poor beggars, is more a wish for display on the part of the inquisitors than a real zeal for religion.

The French ambassador, Marquis de Villars, on the Madrid auto de fe of 1680[1]

Since the Inquisition normally arrested suspects only after the evidence against them seemed conclusive and had been approved by calificadores, the accused was naturally presumed guilty from the start and on him fell the onus of proving his own innocence. The sole task of the Inquisition was to obtain from its prisoner an admission of guilt and a penitential submission. If in the process of enquiry it was found that the evidence was false and the prisoner presumably innocent, he was immediately set free. The main task of the tribunal, however, was to act not as a court of justice but as a disciplinary body called into existence to meet a national emergency. In these circumstances, and considering the practice of the time, the courts of the Inquisition were adequate for their task. Apart from the much hated insistence on anonymity of witnesses, in broad terms they conformed to the principles (though not the methods) of the courts of Castile.

One of the peculiarities of inquisitorial procedure which brought hardship and suffering to many, was the refusal to divulge reasons for arrest, so that prisoners went for days and months without knowing why they were in the cells of the tribunal. Instead of accusing the prisoner, the inquisitors approached him and gave three warnings, over a period of weeks, to search his conscience, confess the truth and trust to the mercy of the tribunal. The third warning was accompanied by information that the prosecutor intended to present an accusation, and that it would be wisest to confess before the charges were laid. The effect of this enforced ignorance was to depress and break down a prisoner. If innocent, he remained bewildered about what to confess, or else confessed crimes the Inquisition was not accusing him of; if guilty, he was left to wonder how much of the truth the Inquisition really knew, and whether it was a trick to force him to confess.

When, after the three warnings, the prosecutor eventually read the articles of accusation, the accused was required to answer charges on the spot, with no time or advocate to help him present his defence. Any reply made in these circumstances could hardly fail to be incriminating. Only after this was permission given to enlist legal help for the defence.

One important concession made by the Spanish, but not by the mediaeval, Inquisition was that the accused could have the services of an advocate. This was written into the Instructions of 1484 and generally upheld, though later modifications to the rule sometimes rendered the use of a lawyer farcical. In the earlier years the accused could choose their lawyers freely, but the growing caution of the Holy Office later confined the choice to special lawyers nominated by the tribunal, so that by the mid-sixteenth century the prisoners' advocates or *abogados de los presos* were recognized as officials of the Inquisition, dependent upon and working with the inquisitors. This new class of lawyers was obviously distrusted by some prisoners, for in 1559 we have the case of a prisoner in Valencia telling his cell-mate that

> though the inquisitor might give him an advocate he would give him no one good but a fellow who would do only what the inquisitor wanted, and if by chance he asked for an advocate or solicitor not of the Inquisition, they would not serve, for if they went contrary to the inquisitor's wishes he would get up some charge of false belief or want of respect and cast them into prison.[2]

This does not mean that abogados de los presos did not do their duty conscientiously. But they were hindered by the restrictions of the tribunal and by the subtle and dangerous task of defending the prisoner while condemning his heresy. Some special cases exist where the accused were allowed counsel of their own choice: one such was Bartolomé de Carranza, who chose among others the distinguished canonist Martín de Azpilcueta to defend him.

When a prisoner was finally accused he was given a copy of the evidence against him in order to help him prepare a defence. This publication of the evidence was by no means as helpful as it might seem. In the first place, as we have seen, the names of all witnesses were suppressed. Even more important, all evidence that might help to identify witnesses was also suppressed. This meant that the prisoner was often deprived of details of the complete case against him. In this way the inquisitors were free to use as evidence information that had not been communicated to the accused. While this helped to protect witnesses against identification and recrimination, it sometimes crippled the defence. On this question the practice of the Suprema was not at first decided, but Valdés's instructions of 1561 finally stipulated that any evidence liable to betray a witness could be omitted, and that only published evidence was to be used in the case. This last regulation preserved the forms of justice.

The accused had several avenues of defence, short of proving the complete falsity of an accusation. He could call favourable witnesses, disable hostile witnesses by proving personal enmity, or object to his judges (this last was a process known as recusation). Several extenuating circumstances such as drunkenness, insanity, extreme youth, and so on, could also be pleaded. All these expedients were resorted to regularly, not always with equal success. In the great majority of trials before the Spanish Inquisition, the defence consisted solely in the resort to witnesses, since this was the only way to get at the unknown sources of evidence.

The problem caused by anonymous witnesses was a serious one. We have the case of Diego de Uceda,[3] who was accused in 1528 of Lutheranism on the basis of a chance talk with a stranger on the road from Burgos to Córdoba. The suppression of all details of time and place in the published evidence led Uceda to imagine that the accusation arose from a talk some nights later at Guadarrama, and all his energies were spent vainly on proving that this latter conversation had been innocuous, while the real evidence against him went uncontradicted. Uceda decided to call witnesses in his favour; he had to wait six months before they could all be traced, and even then their depositions did not help to contradict the evidence. The resort to favourable witnesses was thus an unreliable and lengthy procedure.

Greater success could be had by disabling hostile witnesses. Felipe Leonart, whose case we have already noted, had no difficulty in 1637 in proving that accusations by his family had been made out of malice. Similarly, Gaspar Torralba of the village of Vayona, near Chinchón, gave in his defence in 1531 a list of 152 persons as his mortal enemies; most of the thirty-five witnesses against him happened to be on the list, and he was consequently let off lightly.[4] Pedro Sánchez de Contreras was accused at Logroño of blasphemy in 1669, but because he happened to be a corregidor he had full material evidence on all his enemies, men whom he had prosecuted for various crimes. He therefore handed the tribunal an enormous dossier with the criminal records of all his potential accusers; the case was dropped.[5]

Recusation of judges called for considerable courage, and was therefore not resorted to except where the prisoner could prove their personal enmity. Carranza was one of the few who succeeded in having his judges changed for this reason, though in the event it was of little help to him. Attempts to escape trial by pleading insanity or a wide range of other extenuating circumstances (drunkenness, grief) were also often made. The Inquisition could go to great lengths to establish the truth, and some of its attitudes may even be described as enlightened (witchcraft, as we shall see, was treated as a form of insanity). Drunkenness was cited as an excuse in the case of Andrés González, aged twenty when accused by the tribunal of Toledo in 1678 of blaspheming and swearing that 'he cared not for God or the Virgin', 'he did not believe in God', 'he believed in Mohammed'. As the story of his life unfolded before the inquisitors, they heard of his mother who had died when he was ten, and of his father who had remarried with a woman who beat Andrés and forced him to leave home. He had wandered in search of work until he came to Toledo, where he married a girl and worked partly as an agricultural labourer, partly as a carpenter's assistant. They were poor, and lived in the house of his wife's sister, where his hostile in-laws drove him to drink, which was when he was heard to swear; 'and when I quarrelled with my wife, her cousin and his wife, her sister and her sister's husband, all used to turn on me and beat me till the blood came to my teeth'.[6] The Inquisition sympathized, but banished him from the area for three years.

There was no formal trial, in the sense of a single act carried out in a single room within a set period of time.[7] The trial was composed instead of a series of audiences at which the prosecution and defence made their respective submissions; and of a series of interrogations carried out by the inquisitors in the presence of a notary. When both prosecution and defence had completed their duties the case was held to be concluded, and the time arrived for sentence to be pronounced. For this it was necessary to form a *consulta de fe*, a body consisting of the inquisitors, one representative of the bishop, and officials qualified in theology or law, known as consultors. Together they voted on the case. In this way verdicts were seldom left to the arbitrary discretion of the inquisitors alone, but were monitored by legal experts from outside. In Barcelona, for example, nearly all verdicts were reached in the presence of the inquisitors together with two judges from the royal court, the Audiencia.[8]

According to the Valdés Instructions of 1561, if the inquisitors and the episcopal representative agreed, their vote prevailed even against a majority of consultors; but if they disagreed, the case was to be referred to the Suprema. By the eighteenth century, centralization under the Suprema meant that few if any important decisions were made by provincial tribunals, and consultas de fe ceased to exist because all sentences were passed by the Suprema alone.

Such was the basic procedure. But it was of course open to abuse at every stage. The most important drawback from the prisoner's point of view was the impossibility of adequate defence. His advocate's role was limited to drawing up articles of defence that were presented to the judges; beyond this no argument or cross-examination was allowed. It meant that in reality the inquisitors were both judge and jury, both prosecution and defence, and the prisoner's fate depended entirely on the mood and character of the inquisitors.

As a rule the tribunals tried to bring their prisoners to trial quickly, since it could often be costly keeping accused in the cells. But a few had to resign themselves to interminably long proceedings that were not always the fault of the Inquisition. The classic case is that of Carranza, but others suffered no less. The inquisitors of Llerena in 1590, overwhelmed by successive denunciations of alumbrados, judaizers and Moriscos, reported the urgency of 'attending to the trials of the prisoners in this Inquisition, of whom there are over sixty, and some of them have been in prison up to seven years and many up to four years, and every day they present complaints that their affairs are being delayed so long'. As if this were not enough, they were just receiving denunciations made by an aggrieved Morisco of Hornachos against the rest of the town, 'and he is giving so much information that we believe he will take several years to finish'.[9]

Other examples of delays include the case of Gabriel Escobar, a cleric in minor orders, who was arrested by the tribunal of Toledo in 1607 on a charge of illuminism, and died in prison in 1622 before his trial had finished. A Mexican priest, Joseph Brunón de Vertiz, who was arrested in 1649, died in prison in 1656 before his trial had even begun; he was eventually tried posthumously, condemned and burnt in effigy only in 1659.[10] These delays took a toll not only of the years and health of a prisoner but also of his sequestered property, which was retained all this time to pay for any expenses incurred.

*

Analysis of the punishments decreed by tribunals should ideally be based on reliable data. These do not exist. Nearly all the documentation on the first years of the Inquisition has disappeared. For subsequent years the records are incomplete. Despite all the defects and gaps, as a whole the available papers of the Inquisition constitute the fullest prosecution records to survive from any judicial tribunal of early modern times. Working from them, we see that the activity of the tribunal can be divided into five main phases: (1) the period of intense anti-converso persecution after 1480, to about 1530; (2) the relatively quiet early sixteenth century; (3) the great period of activity against Protestants and Moriscos, 1560–1614; (4) the seventeenth century, when most of those tried were neither of Jewish nor of Moorish origin; (5) the eighteenth century, when heresy was no longer a problem.

Some scholars have attempted to use the surviving records as a source for quantifying the impact of the Inquisition.[11] The method has helped us to obtain a broad vision of some aspects of its history, by indicating for example the periods in which Moriscos were most persecuted, or giving us an idea of the number of people sentenced for various offences. But as an exercise in statistics it is now seen to be wholly unreliable. The margin of error has been unacceptably high, sometimes between 50 and 100 per cent wrong.[12] The classification of offences has been unreliable and arbitrary. Important categories of offence did not appear at all in the analyses. The use of figures, in short, has been helpful only within certain limits. Above all, it is essential to remember that the available records are an index neither of offences nor of 'inquisitorial activity'.[13] More properly, they reflect only the response of the Inquisition to some cases referred to it by members of the public. Very many offences were not detected nor reported nor acted upon; and the inquisitors were active in many areas not referred to in the trial documents.

A recent careful breakdown of prosecutions has been offered for the tribunal of Toledo.[14] From a diagram of these (next page) we can get a rough perspective of the different categories (some of them discussed later in this book) prosecuted over the centuries of highest activity.

The outcome of a trial could take three main forms. Accused could be acquitted ('absolved' or 'suspended'); or punished by being penanced or reconciled; or burnt (in person or in effigy). Punishments usually combined both spiritual and corporal penalties. In the tribunal of Valencia, an estimate for 3,075 of the trials in 1566–1609 suggests that they concluded as

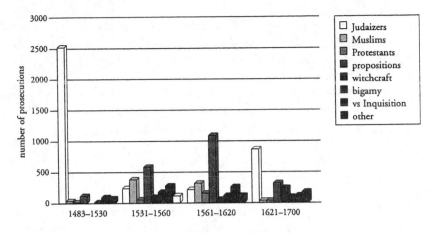

Prosecutions in the tribunal of Toledo, 1483–1700

follows: 44.2 per cent were penanced, 40.2 per cent reconciled, 2.5 per cent absolved, 9 per cent suspended, 2.1 per cent burnt in effigy, 2 per cent burnt in person.[15] In Galicia between 1560 and 1700, of 2,203 cases 18.5 per cent were absolved, 62.7 per cent penanced, 16.1 per cent reconciled, 1.9 per cent burnt in effigy, 0.7 per cent burnt in person.[16]

The number of acquittals were few, but an improvement on the mediaeval tribunal, which as a rule never acquitted. In its first cases in 1483–5 in Ciudad Real, the inquisitors acquitted several accused, among them the converso cobbler Diego López, accused of judaizing: 'we absolve him, declare him free and acquitted, and reaffirm his good reputation'.[17] Outright acquittal, however, meant admitting an error, so it was also common to suspend cases. Suspension was more to be feared than welcomed; it meant that the trial could at any time and under any provocation be renewed, and one remained thereafter technically under suspicion. From the sentence there was only a limited chance of appeal. In cases that ended in a public auto de fe, this was because the accused were not informed of their sentence until they were in the actual procession during the auto; by then it was too late to appeal. The delay in delivering a verdict would naturally heighten the suspense, fear and despair felt by prisoners. But when a man was sentenced to be executed he was always informed of his fate the night before the ceremony to give him time in which to prepare his soul for confession and repentance. Later in the history of the tribunal this information was given as much as three days in advance. In private autos there was much more opportunity to appeal after the sentence had been read out. In such cases the appeal always went to the Suprema, appeals to Rome not being encouraged.

To be penanced was the least of the punishments imposed. Those who did penance had to 'abjure' their offences spiritually: *de levi* for a lesser offence, *de vehementi* for a graver one. The penitent swore to avoid his sin in the future, and if he swore de vehementi, any relapse made him liable to severe punishment on the next occasion. Penitents were then condemned to physical penalties such as the sanbenito, fines, banishment or sometimes the galleys.

'Reconciliation' was in theory the return of a sinner to the bosom of the Church after due spiritual penance had been performed. In practice it was the most severe punishment the Inquisition could inflict, short of relaxation. All the penalties were heavier: in addition to the sanbenito, accused persons could be condemned to flogging and to long spells in prison or the galleys. In most cases confiscation of goods occurred, so that even if a prisoner escaped with a prison sentence of a few months, he came out an orthodox Catholic indeed but facing a life of beggary. An additional rule, frequently enforced, was that anyone backsliding after reconciliation was to be treated as a relapsed heretic and sent to the stake.

The sanbenito, a corrupt form of the words *saco bendito*, was a penitential garment used in the mediaeval Inquisition and taken over by the Spanish one. It was usually a yellow garment with one or two diagonal crosses imposed on it, and penitents were condemned to wear it as a mark of infamy for any period from a few months to life. Those who were to be relaxed at an auto de fe had to wear a black sanbenito on which were painted flames, demons and other decorative matter. Anyone condemned to wearing the ordinary sanbenito had to put it on whenever he went out of doors, a practice by no means popular in the first decades of the Inquisition. The order to wear a sanbenito for life should not be taken literally. It was invariably commuted to a much shorter period at the discretion of the inquisitor. The chief criticism levelled at the time against these garments was less over the deliberate shame they were meant to cast on their wearers, than over the policy of perpetuating infamy by hanging them up in the local church as a permanent record of the offence (see below, page 243).

The imprisonment decreed by the Inquisition could be either for a short term of months and years, or for life, the latter usually being classified as 'perpetual and irremissible'. Prison sentences, then as now, were not literally observed. By the seventeenth century 'perpetual' prison normally signified in practice a few months,[18] and rarely involved imprisonment for more than three years, if the prisoner was repentant. A 'lifetime' sentence was more commonly completed in ten years. Despite this the Inquisition continued to decree 'perpetual' sentences, probably because in canon law it was the custom to condemn heretics to life imprisonment. Incongruous sentences such as 'perpetual prison for one year' appear as a matter of course in inquisitorial decrees.

None of the sentences necessarily involved actual confinement in a prison. By the Instructions of 1488 inquisitors could at their discretion confine a man to his own house or to some other institution such as a monastery or hospital, with the result that very many 'prisoners' served their sentences in moderate comfort. The main reason for this surprising concession was that the tribunals often lacked prison space when their cells were already full, and had to make do with alternatives. Important prisoners, such as Carranza, normally underwent house-arrest rather than imprisonment. The prison cells also often had an open regime. In some tribunals, the prisoners were free to come and go, providing they observed basic rules.[19] In 1655 a report on the tribunal of Granada observed that prisoners were allowed out at all hours of the day without restriction; they wandered through the city and its suburbs and amused themselves at friends' houses, returning to their prison only at night; in this way they were given a comfortable lodging-house for which they paid no rent.[20]

The galleys were a punishment unknown to the mediaeval Inquisition, and were devised for the new one by Ferdinand, who thereby found a cheap source of labour without having to resort to open slavery. The punishment was, in the opinion of a recent scholar, perhaps the most feared (apart from the stake) of any operated by the Spanish Inquisition.[21] It began to be used more frequently from the mid-sixteenth century, to meet rising demand from royal ships. Offences such as bigamy and sodomy were normally punished with the galleys, but occasionally those condemned for heresy were sent there as well. The convicted were seldom sentenced to any period over five years, in contrast to secular tribunals which then and later condemned prisoners to the galleys for life.[22] The galleys constituted an economical form of punishment: tribunals were freed from the duty of maintaining penitents in their prisons, and the state was saved the need to hire rowers at some expense. After the uprising in Andalusia in 1569, the galleys became a frequent punishment for Moriscos.[23] The tribunals of the crown of Aragon were those that imposed the sentence most frequently, usually on Moriscos and foreign Protestants; in the late sixteenth century they sent about fifty men a year to the galleys.[24] By the mid-eighteenth century the Holy Office, like the state, ceased to use the galleys as a sentence.

A more common form of physical punishment was flogging. The use of the lash as chastisement was very old in Christian tradition. As a criminal punishment, however, it was very severe, carrying with it the stigma of degradation and shame. It could therefore be used only against those of low social status. In the Inquisition, the accused was usually condemned to be 'whipped through the streets', in which case (if male) he had to appear stripped to the waist, often mounted on an ass for greater shame, and was duly flogged through the streets with the specified number of strokes by the public executioner. During this journey, passers-by and children would show their scorn by hurling stones at the accused. Women were flogged in the same way as men. Nor was there any limit on age, cases on record showing that girls in their teens and women of seventy or eighty were subjected to the same treatment. It was the general rule to prescribe no more than two hundred lashes for the accused, and sentences of one hundred lashes were very common.

A convicted person might be sentenced to different punishments simultaneously. At the Granada auto on 30 May 1672 Alonso Ribero was sentenced to four years' banishment from the locality, six years in the galleys and a hundred strokes of the lash, for falsifying documents of the Inquisition; and Francisco de Alarcón to five years' banishment, five years in the galleys, two hundred strokes of the lash and a money fine, for blasphemy.[25] Other penalties in the canon need little explanation. Exile or banishment from the locality was a common sentence for bad influences. Confiscations were exacted whenever possible. Of the several unusual punishments which at one time or another made their appearance, it is worth noting the one dealt out in the Mexican Inquisition in December 1664 to a penitent who was smeared with honey, then covered with feathers and made to stand in the sun for four hours during an auto de fe.

The ultimate penalty was the stake. The execution of heretics was by the fifteenth century such a commonplace of Christendom that the Spanish Inquisition cannot be accused of any innovation in this respect. It had been the practice, hallowed by the mediaeval Inquisition, for Church courts to condemn a heretic and then hand him over, or 'relax' him, to the secular authorities. These were obliged to carry out the sentence of blood which the Holy Office was forbidden by law to carry out. In all this there was no pretence that the Inquisition was not the body directly and fully responsible for the deaths that occurred.

Two classes of people alone qualified for the stake – unrepentant heretics and relapsed heretics. The latter consisted of those who, after being pardoned a first time, had repeated the offence and were adjudged to have relapsed into heresy. Those who were sentenced to be 'relaxed' did not always die at the stake. They were normally given the choice between repenting before the auto de fe reached its climax, in which case they were 'mercifully' strangled when the flames were lit; or remaining unrepentant, in which case they were roasted alive. The vast majority of those who were 'relaxed' were in fact burnt in effigy only, either because they had died before the auto or because they had saved themselves by flight. In the early years of the Inquisition the large number of accused burnt in effigy testifies to the volume of refugees escaping from the tribunal.

The proportionately small number of executions is an effective argument against the legend of a bloodthirsty tribunal. Nothing, certainly, can efface the horror of the terrible first twenty or so years. Nor can occasional outbursts of savagery, such as overtook the Chuetas in the late seventeenth century, be minimized. But it is clear that for most of its existence the Inquisition was far from being a juggernaut of death either in intention or in capability. The figures given above for punishments in Valencia and Galicia suggest an execution rate of well under two per cent of the accused. It has been estimated that in nineteen of the tribunals, over the period 1540–1700, under two per cent of the accused were executed (i.e. 'relaxed' in person).[26] If this is anywhere near the truth, it would seem that during the sixteenth and seventeenth centuries fewer than three people a year were executed by the Inquisition in the whole of the Spanish monarchy from Sicily to Peru, certainly a lower rate than in any provincial court of justice in Spain or anywhere else in Europe. A comparison, indeed, of Spanish secular courts with the Inquisition can only be in favour of the latter. In 1573, for instance, the corregidor of Plasencia handed over to the Holy Office in Llerena a Morisco condemned by his jurisdiction to be hanged and quartered for allegedly smashing an image of the Virgin, but the Inquisition found the case unproven and set him free.[27] On a more continent-wide scale, one could compare death-rates of the Inquisition with those of other tribunals, but contexts are so different that no meaningful comparison is possible.

It must be remembered, of course, that although the death-rate was low it was also heavily weighted against people of Jewish and Muslim origin, in cases that involved 'heresy'. The executions probably made no impact on the population as a whole, but were a significant burden on conversos. The relative frequency of burnings in the earlier years diminished in the eighteenth century, and in the twenty-nine years of the reigns of Charles III and Charles IV only four people were burnt.[28]

Condemnation usually meant that the accused had to appear in an auto de fe. This ceremony was held either in private (*auto particular*) or in public (*auto público* or *auto general*); it is the latter that has become notorious as the auto de fe. The penalties decreed by the Inquisition were announced on these occasions.

The ceremony of an auto de fe has a literature all to itself.[29] Among the Spaniards it began its career as a religious act of penitence and justice, and ended it as a public festivity rather like bullfighting or fireworks. To foreigners it always remained a thing of impressive horror and fear. Their journals and letters written while on tour in Spain reveal both amazement and disgust at a practice that was unknown in the rest of Europe. The Fleming Jean Lhermite, who attended an auto de fe in the company of Philip II at Toledo in February 1591, went afterwards to see the executions and described the proceedings as 'a very sad spectacle, distressing to see'.[30] It was no doubt unpleasant to see clergy presiding over the killing of condemned persons, but in reality the public execution of criminals in other countries was not very different from an auto de fe, and more frequently outdid the auto in savagery.

Foreigners were also, like the French ambassador the Marquis of Villars, who attended the Madrid auto de fe of 1680, puzzled by the contrast between the often irreligious behaviour of Spaniards in their daily life, and the intensity of the auto ceremonial. The contrast is an important clue to the real significance of the auto.

It is one of the most surprising of all distortions of inquisitorial history that the auto has often been presented as typical of the Spanish mentality. The facts point in quite a different direction. Far from being a reflection of the religious inclinations of the community, the auto was the premeditated imposition of a ritual that had no roots whatever in the community. People flocked to see it because it was a strange phenomenon that did not form part of their normal faith, religion, and everyday existence. In the early history of the tribunal the public auto virtually did not exist; instead of elaborate ceremonial, there was little more than a simple religious rite to determine the penalties for arrested heretics. The ceremony was not even held necessarily on a holiday, proof that no role was assigned to participation by the public. It is significant that the only image available for the format of an auto in the early years is a wholly imaginary composite painting done at the end of the fifteenth century by Pedro Berruguete, showing St Dominic presiding over a session of the mediaeval tribunal.

In the mid-sixteenth century a new, ceremonial auto de fe was deliberately invented by Inquisitor General Fernando de Valdés and his associates, as a way of imposing the presence of the Inquisition. They may even have based themselves on the Berruguete painting.[31] The discovery of Protestant heretics in 1558, and the willingness of the crown to assist in their punishment, encouraged Valdés to draw up a set of rules for the staging of a flamboyant public ceremony that would reaffirm the power of the Inquisition and reinforce its presence. The first of the new style autos appears to have been that held in the presence of the court, in Valladolid in May 1559. Previous rulers of Spain, including Ferdinand and Isabella, had never attended the ceremony. Charles V, exceptionally, was present at an auto that the city of Valencia insisted on putting on when he visited it. Philip II had previously witnessed only one, a small affair in Toledo in 1550. The presence and patronage of the royal court at the Valladolid autos of 1559 immediately gave the ceremony a prestige it had not previously possessed.

The rules were enshrined for the first time in the inquisitorial Instructions of 1561,[32] and subsequently elaborated upon. It was now determined that autos be held on feast days, so as to ensure maximum public participation. All the leading officials and elite were expected to be present. The rules also laid special emphasis on the promotion of the Inquisition's own status, a fact that immediately led to conflicts with officials of both Church and state, who were asked to take oaths of loyalty to the Inquisition. A century later, when the incidence of heresy was trailing off, the ceremonial became even more elaborate, a true art-form of the Baroque. What is more, the tribunal took great care to distribute information sheets about these later autos, so as to assert its achievements.[33]

There is no doubt that autos were popular. They could hardly fail to be so in the 1560s, when their novelty obviously attracted (as was the intention) high levels of attendance. The novelty also attracted attention in Europe, where the first engravings of the ceremony appeared in the same decade.[34] Accounts, prints and paintings show us that most general autos had a maximum audience up to the last years of the seventeenth century. Far from being a typical component of inquisitorial procedure, however, the ceremonial auto had a relatively short lifespan. In Castile it had its heyday during the years of repression of Protestants, from 1559 to the 1570s.[35] In those same years, it was exported to the other tribunals of the monarchy. The first ceremonial auto to be held in Barcelona was staged in the public square of the Born in 1564, to celebrate a visit by Philip II to the city.[36] The first great auto to be held at Logroño was in 1570. The first at Palermo (Sicily) was in 1573, when 'for the first time' a special procession was held. After the 1570s, ceremonial autos were rare in Castile.[37] The famous and elaborate autos of the seventeenth century were few and far between. The most memorable of them all was held towards the end of the lifespan of the Habsburg dynasty, in 1680, and stood out by the mere fact of its rarity.

The auto in its heyday was an event without parallel in any other country. Visitors would throng in from outlying districts when it was announced that one would be held. The auto of 1610 at Logroño attracted, according to an official of the Inquisition, some thirty thousand people from France, Aragon, Navarre, the Basque country and Castile.[38] Since the town had a population of only around four thousand, the (evidently exaggerated) number of visitors would have created a memorable and historic impression.

The scene would invariably be set in the biggest square or public place available. The elaborate and impressive staging of the proceedings, depicted clearly in prints of the period, made for heavy expense and because of this public autos were not very frequent. Their frequency depended entirely on the discretion of individual tribunals and (since the proceedings were essentially a show) the availability of prisoners. When necessary, prisoners were brought from the very ends of the peninsula: for the great 1680 auto in Madrid condemned were brought from Galicia and Andalusia. When enough prisoners had accumulated to make the holding of an auto worthwhile, a date was fixed for the event and the inquisitors informed the authorities of the municipality and the cathedral. One calendar month before the auto a procession consisting of familiars and notaries of the Inquisition would march through the streets of the town proclaiming the date of the ceremony. In the intervening month, all the preparations would have to be made. Orders went out to carpenters and masons to prepare the scaffolding for the occasion, and furniture and decorations were made ready. The evening before the auto a special procession took place, known as the procession of the Green Cross, during which familiars and others carried the cross of the Holy Office to the site of the ceremony. All that night prayers and preparations would be made, then early next morning mass was celebrated, breakfast was given to all who were to appear in the auto (including the condemned) and a procession began which led directly to the square where the auto would be held.

There is available a contemporary account of the first auto de fe held at Toledo, on Sunday, 12 February 1486, during which over 700 judaizers were reconciled to the Church. At this early epoch ceremonial and ritual were notably absent. The inquisitors were occupied solely with the task of reconciling large numbers of heretics quickly and efficiently.

All the reconciled went in procession, to the number of 750 persons, including both men and women. They went in procession from the church of St Peter Martyr in the following way. The men were all together in a group, bareheaded and unshod, and since it was extremely cold they were told to wear soles under their feet which were otherwise bare; in their hands were unlit candles. The women were together in a group, their heads uncovered and their faces bare, unshod like the men and with candles. Among all these were many prominent men in high office. With the bitter cold and the dishonour and disgrace they suffered from the great number of spectators (since a great many people from outlying districts had come to see them), they went along howling loudly and weeping and tearing out their hair, no doubt more for the dishonour they were suffering than for any offence they had committed against God. Thus they went in tribulation through the streets along which the Corpus Christi procession goes, until they came to the cathedral. At the door of the church were two chaplains who made the sign of the cross on each one's forehead, saying, 'Receive the sign of the cross, which you denied and lost through being deceived.' Then they went into the church until they arrived at a scaffolding erected by the new gate, and on it were the father inquisitors. Nearby was another scaffolding on which stood an altar at which they said mass and delivered a sermon. After this a notary stood up and began to call each one by name, saying, 'Is X here?' The penitent raised his candle and said, 'Yes.' There in public they read all the things in which he had judaized. The same was done for the women. When this was over they were publicly allotted penance and ordered to go in procession for six Fridays, disciplining their body with scourges of hempcord, barebacked, unshod and bareheaded; and they were to fast for those six Fridays. It was also ordered that all the days of their life they were to hold no public office such as *alcalde, alguacil, regidor* or *jurado*, or be public scriveners or messengers, and that those who held these offices were to lose them. And that they were not to become moneychangers, shopkeepers, or grocers or hold any official post whatever. And they were not to wear silk or scarlet or coloured cloths or gold or silver or pearls or coral or any jewels. Nor could they stand as witnesses. And they were ordered that if they relapsed, that is if they fell into the same error again, and resorted to any of the forementioned things, they would be condemned to the fire. And when all this was over they went away at two o'clock in the afternoon.[39]

Two o'clock is the time of the midday meal in Spain. The inquisitors had therefore managed to get through 750 prisoners in one morning. This is a far cry from the dilatory pace, pomp and ritual of the post-1559 ceremonial autos, which went on well into the night and sometimes were continued the following day, as happened at Logroño in November 1610. The speed at Toledo in 1486 was probably a record, for after the 750 accused in February the tribunal managed to deal with 900 reconciliations on 2 April, 750 on 11 June, and 900 on 10 December, not to speak of two other autos on 16 and 17 August when twenty-seven people were burnt.

In striking contrast to the simplicity and efficiency of autos in the first years of the Inquisition, was the grandiose ceremony held on 30 June 1680 in the Plaza Mayor of Madrid in the presence of the king and his court. The scene was captured on an enormous canvas by the artist Francesco Rizzi, whose work now hangs in the Prado museum.[40]

A summarized version of the contemporary narrative of the auto was published in London in 1748 and goes as follows:

A Scaffold, fifty Feet in Length, was erected in the Square, which was raised to the same Height with the Balcony made for the King to sit in. At the End, and along the whole Breadth of the Scaffold, at the Right of the King's Balcony, an Amphitheatre was raised, to which they ascend by twenty-five or thirty Steps; and this was appointed for the Council of the Inquisition, and the other Councils of Spain. Above these Steps and under a Canopy, the Grand Inquisitor's Rostrum was placed so that he was raised much higher than the King's Balcony. At the Left of the Scaffold and Balcony, a second Amphitheatre was erected of the same Extent with the former, for the Criminals to stand in.

A month after Proclamation had been made of the Act of Faith, the Ceremony opened with a Procession [this procession took place on the eve, 29 June], which proceeded from St Mary's Church in the following order. The March was preceded by an Hundred Coal Merchants, all arm'd with Pikes and Muskets; these People furnishing the Wood with which the

Criminals are burnt. They were followed by Dominicans, before whom a white Cross was carried. Then came the Duke of Medina-Celi, carrying the Standard of the Inquisition. Afterwards was brought forwards a green Cross covered with black Crepe; which was followed by several Grandees and other Persons of Quality, who were Familiars of the Inquisition. The March was clos'd by Fifty Guards belonging to the Inquisition, clothed with black and white Garments and commanded by the Marquis of Povar, hereditary Protector of the Inquisition. The procession having marched in this Order before the Palace, proceeded afterwards to the Square, where the Standard and the Green Cross were placed on the Scaffold, where none but the Dominicans stayed, the rest being retired. These Friars spent Part of the Night in singing of Psalms, and several Masses were celebrated on the Altar from Daybreak to Six in the Morning. An Hour after, the King and Queen of Spain, the Queen-Mother, and all the Ladies of Quality, appeared in the Balconies.

At Eight O'clock the Procession began, in like Manner as the Day before, with the Company of Coal Merchants, who placed themselves on the Left of the King's Balcony, his Guards standing on his Right (the rest of the Balconies and Scaffolds being fill'd by the Embassadors, the Nobility and Gentry). Afterwards came thirty Men, carrying Images made in Pasteboard, as big as Life. Some of these represented those who were dead in Prison, whose Bones were also brought in Trunks, with Flames painted round them: and the rest of the Figures represented those who having escaped the Hands of the Inquisition were outlawed. These Figures were placed at one End of the Amphitheatre.

After these there came twelve Men and Women, with Ropes about their Necks and Torches in their Hands, with Pasteboard Caps three Feet high, on which their Crimes were written, or represented, in different Manners. These were followed by fifty others having Torches also in their Hands and cloathed with a yellow Sanbenito or Great Coat without Sleeves, with a large St. Andrew's Cross, of a red Colour, before and behind. These were Criminals who (this being the first Time of their prisonment) had repented of their Crimes; these are usually condemned either to some Years' Imprisonment or to wear the Sanbenito, which is looked upon to be the greatest Disgrace that can happen to a Family. Each of the Criminals were led by two Familiars of the Inquisition. Next came twenty more Criminals, of both Sexes, who had relapsed thrice into their former Errors and were condemn'd to the Flames. Those who had given some Tokens of Repentance were to be strangled before they were burnt; but for the rest, for having persisted obstinately in their

Errors, were to be burnt alive. These wore Linen Sanbenitos, having Devils and Flames painted on them, and Caps after the same Manner: Five or six among them who were more obstinate than the rest were gagged to prevent their uttering any blasphemous Tenets. Such as were condemned to die were surrounded, besides the two Familiars, with four or five Monks, who were preparing them for Death as they went along.

These Criminals passed, in the Order above mentioned, under the King's balcony; and after having walked round the scaffold were placed in the Amphitheatre that stood on the left, and each of them surrounded with the Familiars and Monks who attended them. Some of the Grandees, who were Familiars, seated themselves on two Benches which had been prepared for them at the lowest Part of the other Amphitheatre. The Officers of all the other Councils, and several other Persons of Distinction, both Secular and Regular, all of them on Horseback, with great Solemnity arrived afterwards and placed themselves on the Amphitheatre towards the Right hand, on both Sides the Rostrum in which the Grand Inquisitor was to seat himself. He himself came last of all, in a purple Habit, accompanied by the President of the Council of Castile, when, being seated in his Place, the President withdrew.

They then began to celebrate Mass . . .

About Twelve O'clock they began to read the Sentence of the condemned Criminals. That of the Criminals who died in Prison, or were outlawed, was first read. Their Figures in Pasteboard were carried up into a little Scaffold and put into small Cages made for that Purpose. They then went on to read the Sentences to each Criminal, who thereupon were put into the said Cages one by one in order for all Men to know them. The whole Ceremony lasted till Nine at Night: and when they had finished the Celebration of the Mass the King withdrew and the Criminals who had been condemn'd to be burnt were delivered over to the Secular Arm, and being mounted upon Asses were carried through the Gate called Foncaral, and at Midnight near this Place were all executed.[41]

In this auto de fe eleven people abjured their errors and fifty-six were reconciled, two of them in effigy because they had died in prison. There were fifty-three 'relaxations', of which nineteen were in person. The procedure at this auto represented the fully developed practice of the Inquisition. It can be seen that the burning of the condemned was not a part of the principal ceremony and took place instead at a subsidiary one, normally outside the city, where the pomp of the main procession was absent. The central features of the auto were the procession, the mass, the sermon at the mass and the reconciliation of sinners. It would be wrong to suppose, as is commonly done, that the burnings were the centrepiece. Burnings may have been a spectacular component of many autos but they were the least necessary part of the proceedings and scores of autos took place without a single faggot being set alight. The phrase auto de fe conjures up visions of flames and fanaticism in the mind of the average reader. A literal translation of the phrase would bring us nearer to the essential truth.

The burning of a judaizer is described in detail in a contemporary narrative by an inquisitor of the auto held at Logroño on 24 August 1719. We enter the picture at the stage where the accused is already on the stake and a lighted torch is passed before his face to warn him of what awaits him if he does not repent. Around the judaizer are numbers of religious who

pressed the accused with greater anxiety and zeal to convert himself. With perfect serenity he said, 'I will convert myself to the faith of Jesus Christ', words which he had not been heard to utter until then. This overjoyed all the religious who began to embrace him with tenderness and gave infinite thanks to God for having opened to them a door for his conversion. ... And as he was making his confession of faith a learned religious of the Franciscan Order asked, him, 'In what law do you die?' He turned and looked him in the eye and said, 'Father, I have already told you that I die in the faith of Jesus Christ'. This caused great pleasure and joy among all, and the Franciscan, who was kneeling down, arose and embraced the accused. All the others did the same with great satisfaction, giving thanks for the infinite goodness of God. ... At this moment the accused saw the executioner, who had put his head out from behind the stake, and asked him, 'Why did you call me a dog before?' The executioner replied, 'Because you denied the faith of Jesus Christ: but now that you have confessed, we are brothers, and if I have offended you by what I said, I beg your pardon on my knees.' The accused forgave him gladly, and the two embraced. ... And desirous that the soul which had given so many signs of conversion should not be lost, I went round casually behind the stake to where the executioner was, and gave him the order to strangle him immediately because it was very important not to delay. This he did with great expedition.

When it was certain that he was dead, the executioner was ordered to set fire at the four corners of the pyre to the brushwood and charcoal that had been piled up. He did this at once, and it began to burn on all sides, the flames rising swiftly up the platform and burning the wood and clothing. When the cords binding the accused had been burnt off he fell through the open trap-door into the pyre and his whole body was reduced to ashes.[42]

The ashes were scattered through the fields or on the river, and with this the heretic, whose conversion had brought him no temporal benefit, passed out of existence though not out of memory, for a sanbenito bearing his name would as a rule have been placed in the local church after his death. There was no age limit for those condemned to the stake: women in their eighties and boys in their teens were treated in the same way as any other heretics.

Because of the elaborate ceremony, formal autos tended to be costly. The auto held at Logroño on 18 October 1570 cost a total of 7,366 maravedis (20 ducats), most of which was spent not on the auto but on the feast of celebration held after it. The expenditure was criticized by the Suprema and the cost of an auto held the following year on 27 December 1571 was cut down to 1,548 maravedis.[43] These costs may be compared with those of a larger tribunal, Seville, which in 1600 calculated that each of its autos cost over three hundred ducats (112,500 maravedis).[44] Costs did not cease to rise in Seville: the auto there on 30 January 1624 cost 396,374 maravedis, and one on 29 March 1648 cost 811,588 maravedis.[45] Even these levels were surpassed by the tribunal of Córdoba, which spent 2,139,590 maravedis (5,700 ducats) on its auto of 3 May 1655.[46]

The popularity of public autos was in part a result of their comparative rarity. Uncommon in the early sixteenth century, after the Protestant scare of the mid-century they became infrequent once again, virtually once-in-a-lifetime events. Smaller tribunals, particularly those without conversos and Moriscos in their district, could seldom afford to have autos. This was regrettable, an inquisitor of Barcelona commented in 1560, because 'I certainly think autos necessary in order to induce fear both among foreigners who come here, and among the people of this country'. In Catalonia the Inquisition also had to put up with the fact that 'neither the viceroy nor the Consellers normally attend autos' – clearly a blow to its prestige.[47] By the early seventeenth century public autos were rare in Barcelona. 'This Inquisition', the inquisitors explained to the Suprema, 'is unique in Spain in that it does not celebrate autos with the same pomp and decency as in other Inquisitions, and this Inquisition is very poor, so that what used to be done in public autos is now more conveniently done in some church.'[48] Nevertheless, there were tribunals that held autos de fe frequently, because of particular local circumstances. We find, for example, the tribunal of Granada holding fifteen autos between 1549 and 1593, that of Murcia holding ten between 1557 and 1568, and that of Córdoba holding seven between 1693 and 1702.

Though autos were meant to impress they may also, by the end of the seventeenth century, have become on occasion less appealing to the public. This, at least, is the impression given by a visual representation of the Seville auto of 13 April 1660. The public here appear to have been largely indifferent to the twelve-hour ceremony that took place.[49] By the eighteenth century the lack of accused and the rising cost of public ceremonies meant that public autos gradually fell into disuse. The new Bourbon king, Philip V, was the first Spanish monarch to refuse to attend one, held in 1701 to celebrate his accession. Philip's reign saw the end of mass persecution in Spain. By the second half of the century only private autos were in use by the Inquisition. There is no need to attribute this to the growth of tolerance. The simple reason was that heretics had been purged out of existence, so depriving the tribunal of combustible material for its fires.

10

THE END OF MORISCO SPAIN

We were taken to the Inquisition where, for no more than following the truth, we were deprived of life, of property and of children.

A seventeenth-century Morisco exile in Tunis[1]

For a while in the Middle Ages, it seemed as if all Spain would go Muslim. Occupied by consecutive waves of invaders from north Africa, the peninsula remained in places under Muslim control for nearly seven centuries. Consequently, the peoples who thus entered Spanish history were no less a part of its structure than the Christian and Jewish population. They intermarried with them, and exchanged ideas and languages, so that the three religions developed side by side within the Spanish kingdoms.

The Reconquest changed all this. The Christian advance took Saragossa in 1118, Córdoba in 1236, Valencia in 1238 and Seville in 1248. Finally, after a long interval, a ten-year war ended with the fall of Granada in 1492. The end of the kingdom of al-Andalus meant that the Muslims (known among Spaniards as 'Moors') ceased to exist as a nation, and became no more than a minority within a Christian country. As subjects of a Christian king they were now, like the Muslims who had for centuries lived under Christian rule, known as 'Mudéjares'. The terms of the capitulation of Granada were generous to the vanquished and reflected mediaeval traditions of convivencia. The Mudéjares were guaranteed their customs, property, laws and religion. They kept their own officials, to be supervised, however, by Castilian governors. Those wishing to emigrate were allowed to do so. The reality of the settlement was somewhat different from these terms. Many of the elite found life under Christian rule intolerable and passed over into north Africa. Reorganization of the territory was entrusted to Iñigo López de Mendoza, second Count of Tendilla and later first Marquis of Mondéjar. Hernando de Talavera was appointed first archbishop, and encouraged conversions by means of charitable persuasion, respect for Mudéjar culture and the use of Arabic during religious services. Progress was slow, and in 1499 Cisneros asked Ferdinand and Isabella, who were then in Granada, for permission to pursue a more vigorous policy.

Mass baptisms now took place, and a mosque was converted into a church. These events provoked a revolt in December 1499 in the Albaicín, the Muslim quarter of Granada which was appeased only through the good offices of Tendilla and Talavera. There were further scattered revolts in other parts of the south, through most of 1500 and into the early weeks of 1501. They presented the government with a serious policy problem. Some, including Tendilla and Cisneros, favoured harsh measures. Cisneros's view was that by rebellion the Mudéjares had forfeited all rights granted by the terms of capitulation and they should be offered a clear choice between baptism or expulsion. His personal preference was 'that they be converted and enslaved, for as slaves they will be better Christians and the land will be pacified for ever'.[2] Ferdinand, by contrast, favoured moderation. 'If your horse trips up', he told his councillors, 'you don't seize your sword to kill him, instead you give him a smack on his flanks. So my view and that of the queen is that these Moors be baptized. And if they don't become Christians, their children and grandchildren will'.[3] It was an important indication of the widely different policy that the monarchs would adopt towards the Muslims in Castile and those in Aragon. In Granada and Castile, as Ferdinand saw it, circumstances made conversion inevitable. In Aragon, there was as yet no need for that approach.

Over the next few months the Mudéjares of Granada were systematically baptized; a few were allowed to emigrate. By 1501 it was officially assumed that the kingdom had become one of Christian Muslims – the Moriscos. They were granted legal equality with Christians, but were forbidden to carry arms and were subjected to pressure to abandon their culture. A huge bonfire of Arabic books, ordered by a royal decree of October 1501,[4] was held in Granada. It was the end of the capitulations and of Muslim al-Andalus. 'If the king of the conquest does not keep faith,' lamented a contemporary Arab leader and scholar, Yuce Venegas, at that time resident on his estates near Granada, 'what can we expect from his successors?'[5]

With Granada apparently converted, Isabella was not inclined to tolerate Muslims elsewhere in her realms. On 12 February 1502 all Mudéjares in Castile were offered the choice between baptism and exile. Virtually all of them, subjects of the crown since the Middle Ages, chose baptism, since emigration was rendered almost impossible by stringent conditions. With their conversion Islam vanished from Castilian territory, and continued to be tolerated only in the crown of Aragon. The different policy adopted in the two realms demonstrated that unity of religion was not an immediate priority of the crown.[6] By repeating a step that had already been taken against the Jews, Isabella abolished plurality of faiths in her dominions of Castile but also created within the body of Christian society the wholly new problem of the Moriscos.

From about 1511, various decrees attempted to make the new converts modify their cultural identity and abandon Muslim practices. These measures culminated in an assembly convoked by the authorities in Granada in 1526. At the meeting all the distinctive characteristics of Morisco civilization – the use of Arabic, their clothes, their jewellery, the ritual slaughter of animals, circumcision[7] – came under attack. A decree was passed encouraging intermarriage between old Christians and Moriscos. It was also decided to transfer the local tribunal of the Inquisition from Jaén to Granada.

In the crown of Aragon there was no comparable pressure on the Mudéjares. The principal reason for this was the great power of the landed nobility and the authority of the Cortes. On the estates of the nobles the Mudéjares formed a plentiful, cheap and productive source of labour, from which the expression arose, 'Mientras más Moros más ganancia' (more Muslims, more profit). Whether to placate his nobility or in pursuit of a moderate policy, Ferdinand repeatedly warned the inquisitors of Aragon not to persecute the Mudéjar population or resort to forced conversions. The Mudéjares therefore continued to lead an independent existence until the revolt of the Comuneros in 1520.

At the same time that the Comunidades of 1520 broke out in Castile, Valencia experienced disturbances of its own. Here the rebels, grouped into Germanías or brotherhoods, organized an urban revolution directed against the local aristocracy. Valencia had the second-largest Muslim population of any province in Spain. The Mudéjares were almost exclusively a rural community and were subjected to the big landowners of the realm. The Germanía leaders saw that the simplest way to destroy the power of the nobles in the countryside would be to free their vassals, and this they did by baptizing them. The years 1520–2 in Valencia thus witnessed the forcible baptism of thousands of Muslims. The defeat of the rebels by royal troops should in theory have allowed the Mudéjares to revert to Islam, since forced baptisms were universally regarded as invalid. But the authorities were not so eager to lose their new converts. The Inquisition in particular was concerned to hold the Mudéjares to the letter of their baptism. To the argument that the conversions had taken place under compulsion, the standard answer was once again given that to *choose* baptism as an alternative to death meant the exercise of free choice, which rendered the sacrament of baptism valid.[8] The Inquisition was therefore ordered to proceed on the assumption that all properly administered baptisms were valid.

It now seemed incongruous to tolerate Muslims elsewhere in the crown of Aragon. In November 1525 Charles V issued a decree ordering the conversion of all Mudéjares in Valencia by the end of the year, and of those elsewhere by the end of January 1526. From 1526 the Muslim religion no longer existed in Spain officially: all Mudéjares were now Moriscos. Writing to the pope in December that year, Charles V admitted that 'the conversion was not wholly voluntary among many of them, and since then they have not been instructed in our holy faith'. Considerable efforts were subsequently made to evangelize the new 'converts' in the regions of greatest concentration. Among the clergy leading the campaign was the distinguished humanist Antonio de Guevara, who laboured in Valencia and Granada.[9]

The situation of the Moriscos varied across the peninsula according to density of population. The highest concentration was in the kingdom of Granada, where Moriscos in the 1560s were some fifty-four per cent of the population; in areas such as the Alpujarra mountains they constituted the totality. In Valencia they formed a third of the population in the late sixteenth century, in Aragon about a fifth. In Catalonia Moriscos were a tiny group, and in Castile they were proportionately even less, perhaps a total of some twenty thousand in 1502,[10] scattered throughout the country in small urban groupings and living at peace with their Christian neighbours.

There were major differences between the Morisco communities. The Granadans, recently subjugated, included a flourishing upper class, preserved their religion and culture intact, and usually spoke Arabic (*algarabía*, the Christians called it). They were an integral Islamic civilization. The Valencians were largely a rural proletariat, but because they lived quite separately from the Christian population and were so numerous, they managed to preserve most of their customs, religion and language. Elsewhere in Spain, Arabic was almost unknown among the Moriscos. All spoke a form of Castilian. In Aragon, where Mudéjares had lived longest among Christians, the decline of Arabic produced the beginnings, in the sixteenth century, of a Morisco literature written in Spanish. Residual knowledge of Arabic, however, was sufficient to warrant the import of sacred texts from abroad.[11] Aragonese Moriscos, for the most part, lived and dressed like their Christian neighbours; they differed only in religion.[12]

Though deprived of access to Christian society by discrimination, the Moriscos were not uniformly poor. As a separate community, they had an economic life parallel to that of Christians. The majority worked the land. But in Aragon they also herded flocks of sheep and cattle for the market; in Saragossa they were carpenters, metalworkers, and clothworkers. They were active in the building industry, and produced swords and arms for sale. Some were traders, investing their profits in the land.[13] In towns wholly populated by Moriscos, such as Almonacid de la Sierra (in Aragon), the inhabitants logically produced their own liberal professions: a surgeon, a scrivener, a lawyer, a noble, in addition to lesser callings.[14]

To maintain their internal integrity, the Muslim leaders strengthened the social role of their community, the aljama. It was an institution that allowed them to preserve their autonomy and culture, but at the same time made it possible to cooperate on good terms with the authorities.[15] They spoke among themselves the version of Spanish known as *aljamía*.[16] When written down, in Arabic script, this produced a secret literature that the inquisitors were unable to read and that they normally categorized, when they discovered and confiscated writings, as 'Korans'.

Until the early years of the reign of Philip II the efforts of the Inquisition to keep Moriscos to their nominal Christianity were little more than a gesture. The largest numbers to be prosecuted were in the crown of Aragon, but they were only the tip of the iceberg of unbelief in Morisco Spain. There were two main reasons for the relative absence of prosecutions: the conviction of both Church and state that a proper programme of conversion should be undertaken, and the strong opposition of Christian seigneurs to any interference with their rights over their Morisco vassals. In Aragon, for instance, nearly seventy per cent of the Moriscos were under noble jurisdiction.[17] In January 1526 the leaders of the Valencian Moriscos succeeded in obtaining from the crown and the Inquisitor General Manrique a secret concordia or agreement that if they all submitted to baptism they would be free for forty years from any prosecution by the Holy Office, since it would be impossible for them to shed all their customs at once. In 1528 the concordia was made public, and in that same year the Cortes of Aragon, meeting at Monzón, asked Charles to prevent the Inquisition from prosecuting Moriscos until they had been instructed in the faith. Their request was timely, for the guarantee was no more lasting than the one granted to the Mudéjares of Granada. The Holy Office interpreted the concordia to mean that it could bring to trial those converts who had slipped back into Islamic practices.

In December of 1526, the year when the Inquisition was transferred from Jaén to Granada, regulations were reissued forbidding Granadan Moriscos to use the Arab language, Muslim clothes or Muslim names. Morisco money offered to Charles brought about the suspension of these rules. But the removal of one burden was balanced by the imposition of another in the form of the Inquisition, whose activity the Moriscos continued to try to curtail over the next generation. In Aragon, protests raised against the Inquisition in the Cortes of Monzón of 1533 included claims that the tribunal was seizing land confiscated from its victims, to the detriment of the feudal owners of the land. Similar complaints were raised in the Cortes of 1537 and 1542. In 1546 the pope intervened and agreed that for a minimum period of ten years the Inquisition should not confiscate any property from the Moriscos.

Only the year after this, however, we find the Cortes of Valencia stating that the tribunal was disregarding such injunctions. It was after great difficulty that finally in 1571 the Inquisition showed itself open to compromise. The resulting concordia was embodied in a decree of October 1571 by which, in return for an annual payment of 2,500 ducats to the Inquisition, the tribunal agreed not to confiscate or sequestrate the property of Moriscos on trial for heresy. Monetary fines could be levied, but with a limit of 10 ducats only. The agreement benefited all sides: the Inquisition, since it brought in a regular annual revenue; the Moriscos, since it protected property for members of their families; and the lords of the Moriscos, since it preserved lands they had leased to their Morisco dependants.

The religious problem, and the activities of the Inquisition, aggravated the position of the Moriscos and provoked many of the conflicts of this period. Spanish writers later claimed that these events led logically to the decision to expel the Moriscos. In reality, expulsion was never inevitable. There was little difference between the tensions of the time and the equally tense convivencia of the Middle Ages. Islamic civilization was able to cope with the pressures placed on it. Christian society, for its part, regularly turned a blind eye to the Islamic activities of the Moriscos.

Though these still retained many of their old social customs, and fought to preserve their own religion, they gradually came to realize that some compromises would have to be made. Forced to conform to Christianity, they sought advice from their leaders. In about 1504 a mufti living in

Orán (north Africa) issued a *fatwa* or opinion on the situation of Muslims living in Spain. He ruled that in times of persecution Muslims could conform to virtually all outward rules of Christianity without defecting from their beliefs.[18] This ruling, which permitted *taqiyya* (dispensation from religious obligations when under persecution), circulated in text among the Moriscos in the 1560s. The practice made it possible for Moriscos to cling on to their religion. It also enabled them to live in their own country, Spain, on terms that they could in some measure decide for themselves.

In many parts of the peninsula, consequently, there continued to be a practical *convivencia* between Old Christians and New Christians of Muslim origin. The town of Arcos de Medinaceli, on the estates of the Duke of Medinaceli near the frontier of Castile with Aragon, was in the 1550s nine-tenths Morisco in population. The Moriscos played their due part in the financial and political administration of the town, sharing municipal posts equally with Old Christians.[19] When Moriscos were buried, Old Christians attended the funeral. It was a poor community, which may explain the absence of anything beyond the formal signs of Christianity in the religion of the Moriscos. But there was clear evidence that many of them, even though formally Catholic, also had special rites – in their fasts, their burials, their ablutions – that differentiated them from other Christians. None of this altered the tranquillity in which the communities in Arcos lived during the two generations before the 1568 revolt in Granada.

It was not a unique situation. Reading the times through the perspective of inquisitorial documents, one can be misled into imagining a permanent state of confrontation. Though there were important and periodic conflicts, what seems more striking is the absence of confrontation in many parts of Spain through much of the sixteenth century.[20] It was in this period too that the Christians could afford still to entertain a romanticized vision of their links with Moriscos, with the appearance in 1565 of the romance *Abencerraje y Jarifa*, a story of love between Christian and Muslim. Some Moriscos also took a universal view of religious truth. The Inquisition of Toledo tried one for saying 'that every one should be allowed to practise his own religion', another for maintaining 'that the Jew and the Muslim could each be saved in his own law'.[21]

The ability of the communities to coexist was recognized and welcomed by many, but did not alter the fact that as a whole the Moriscos refused assimilation.[22] Apart from culture, dress, and communal autonomy, the principal problem remained that of conversion, for they overwhelmingly rejected the type of Christianity offered to them.

In 1513 Archbishop Talavera of Granada, who had encouraged his Moriscos to sing Arabic hymns at mass, complained to the crown about cultural pressure upon them. Francisco Núñez Muley, a Morisco leader who in his youth was page to Talavera, recalled how the archbishop went through the mountains of Granada to preach and say mass. Since there was no organ for music he made the natives play the *zambra* (a traditional dance), and during mass always said his greeting 'The Lord be with you' in Arabic. 'I remember this', Núñez reminisced, 'as if it were yesterday'.[23] Many Christian nobles understood the need for some cultural tolerance. In 1514 the Count of Tendilla criticized Ferdinand's attempt to make Moriscos abandon their clothing: 'What clothing did we use to wear in Spain, how did we wear our hair, what sort of food did we eat, if not in the Morisco style?'[24]

But the early missionary efforts were fruitless. When he went to Granada in 1526, Charles V was informed that 'the Moriscos are truly Muslims: it is twenty-seven years since their conversion and there are not twenty-seven or even seven of them who are Christians'. In Granada and Valencia they held fast to their religion, observing prayers, fasts and ablutions, and were strengthened in their faith by their clergy, the alfaquis. Had religious practice alone been at issue, social tension might not have been so high. But in the everyday contact with Old Christians there was periodic irritation and conflict over dress, speech, customs and, above all, food. Moriscos slaughtered their animal meat ritually, did not touch pork (the meat most commonly eaten in Spain) or wine, and cooked only with olive oil whereas Christians cooked with butter or lard. They tended also to live apart in separate communities, which could lead to antagonism: for example, in Aragon there was friction between highland Christians (the *montañeses*) and Moriscos living in the plains. Even in Castile, where the older Morisco communities were more assimilated, there were cases such as Hornachos (Extremadura), a flourishing and almost entirely Morisco town of 5,000 people all of whom at the expulsion in 1610 emigrated to Morocco. Though religious zeal was weaker in Castile and in those parts of Aragon where coexistence with Christians had diluted traditional practices, Islam endured because of community solidarity. In general, Moriscos were strongly repelled by the doctrines of the Trinity and the divinity of Jesus, and felt extreme repugnance at the sacraments of baptism (families would wash the chrism off on returning home, and hold a Muslim ceremony), penitence and the Eucharist (Morisco irreverence at mass was proverbial).[25]

There were many attempts to catechize them.[26] From 1526, missionaries were sent out in Valencia and Granada. In the 1540s a Franciscan, Fray Bartolomé de los Angeles, missionized Valencia; in the 1560s further campaigns were conducted in Valencia by Jesuits and other clergy. In 1566 the archbishop of Valencia, Martín de Ayala, published his manual *Christian Doctrine in Arab and Castilian*. Ayala also tried, with little success, to find clergy who knew, or could learn, Arabic. Juan de Ribera, who became archbishop of Valencia in 1568, initiated a financial scheme to increase the stipends of priests and to make work among the Moriscos more congenial to the clergy. He also helped to found a seminary and a college for Morisco boys and girls. For the forty-three years that he held this see, Ribera made every effort to travel round his bishopric and attend to the needs of the Moriscos.

Considerable opposition to the missionary programme in the crown of Aragon came from the seigneurs, who had opposed the forced conversions of 1526 and at every stage fought the activities of the Inquisition. In 1561 in Valencia the inquisitor Miranda appointed members of the rich Morisco family of Abenamir as familiars of the Inquisition, but the Duke of Segorbe, their overlord, ordered them to give up the appointment since his protection was sufficient for them. In 1566 the Inquisition of Aragon complained that 'the seigneurs daily persecute the comisarios and familiars that the Holy Office has in their lands, expelling them and telling them that in their territory they want no Inquisition'.[27] It was in the nobles' interest to keep Morisco dependants under their control, since they were a substantial source of revenue. In various meetings of the Cortes they pressed continually for Moriscos to be free from inquisitorial confiscations, a concession granted in the 1571 concordia.

There were conflicts between nobles and the Inquisition. In 1541 a prominent Valencian grandee, the Admiral of Aragon, Sancho de Moncada, was reprimanded by the Inquisition for building a mosque for his Moriscos and telling them 'that they should pretend to be Christians externally but remain Muslims internally'. In 1569 he was placed under house-arrest for three years for persistently protecting his Muslim vassals against the Holy Office.[28] In 1571 the Grand Master of the Order of Montesa appeared in an auto de fe for protecting his Moriscos. In 1582 in Aragon when the lord of Ariza, Jaime Palafox, heard that the Inquisition had arrested three of his vassals he and his men burst into the house of a familiar and beat and stabbed him to death. The courts sent him for life to the north African fortress of Orán.[29]

Even had the nobles been more cooperative, it is unlikely that the Moriscos would have responded favourably to Christian overtures. Supported by the taqiyya, they defiantly maintained and proclaimed their separateness. María la Monja of Arcos in 1524 said 'that not for all the world would she cease saying that she had been a Muslim, so great a source of pride was it for her'.[30] The authorities, as the Granada regulations of December 1526 showed, were convinced that all Morisco customs were obstacles to the acceptance of Christianity. In 1538 a Morisco of Toledo was arrested by the Inquisition and accused of 'playing music at night, dancing the *zambra* and eating *couscous*', implying that these activities were heretical. In 1544 the synod of the bishopric of Guadix held that 'it is suspicious to take baths, specially on Thursday and Friday night'! Even the Morisco manner of sitting – never on seats but always on the ground – could be viewed as Islamic.

In several parts of Spain the Inquisition prosecuted Morisco religion when the occasion arose. In Daimiel (Ciudad Real), where the community had duly converted in 1502, a generation of tranquillity was interrupted by an important series of arrests and prosecutions around 1540.[31] The most intense period of religious pressure did not come until after the provincial Church councils of 1565. Attempts to Christianize Spaniards, the clergy felt, made no sense if not applied also to the Moriscos. In Granada the Church council demanded that radical measures be adopted. Philip II's chief minister, Cardinal Espinosa, agreed.

Tensions and conflicts were at their most intense in the most Islamic of the Morisco territories, Granada. When all the repressive legislation was repeated in a pragmatic of January 1567 in Granada, Francisco Núñez Muley drew up a memorial protesting against the injustices done to his people:

> Every day we are mistreated in every way, by both secular officials and clergy. all of which is so obvious that it needs no proof. ... How can people be deprived of their natural tongue, in which they were born and raised? The Egyptians, Syrians, Maltese and other Christian people speak, read and write in Arabic, and are still Christians as we are.

Two generations of tension exploded finally in the Morisco revolt that began on Christmas Eve of 1568 in Granada and spread to the Alpujarras.

It was a savage war between Christians and Muslims, with atrocities on both sides, and military repression was brutal. Thousands of Moriscos died. Over eighty thousand were forcibly expelled from the kingdom and made to settle in Castile. The end of the rebellion did little to solve the problem. The Granadans brought into Castilian communities an Islamic presence they had not hitherto known. Where Castile had had about twenty thousand Mudéjares, by the end of the century the numbers had swelled to over one hundred thousand, mostly Arabic in tongue and Muslim in culture. Moreover, the military threat was now obvious. Some four thousand Turks and Berbers had come into Spain to fight alongside the insurgents in the Alpujarras. Morisco banditry in the south reached its peak in the 1560s. There were millennarian hopes of liberation from oppression. Inevitably, seeing the obduracy of the Moriscos, the authorities reverted to a repressive policy.

The Granada war created a decisive change in attitudes. The excesses committed on both sides were without equal in the experience of contemporaries; it was the most savage war to be fought in Europe that century. Philip II was staggered by the massacres of priests committed by the rebels. The Moriscos, for their part, had suffered unspeakable atrocities. Apart from the deaths and expulsions, thousands were sold into slavery within Spain: in Córdoba alone, in 1573, there were over fifteen hundred Morisco slaves.[32]

From that period the attempts at conversion decreased and the repression intensified. Those expelled from Granada to the provinces of Castile took with them their Islamic beliefs and their hatred of Castile. In Arcos de Medinaceli the older community of integrated Moriscos were pressurized by the newcomers to declare themselves openly as Muslims.[33] From the 1570s in Aragon and Valencia Moriscos formed the bulk of Inquisition prosecutions.[34] In the tribunal of Granada itself, Moriscos represented 82 per cent of those prosecuted between 1560 and 1571.[35] In the tribunal of Cuenca the arrival of the Granadans quintupled the number of Moriscos prosecuted, strengthened the faith of the Castilian Muslims and provoked a wave of persecution by the Holy Office.[36] In the tribunal of Saragossa 266 Moriscos were tried over the years 1540–59; between 1560 and 1614 the total shot up to 2,371, a ninefold increase. In Valencia there were eighty-two Morisco prosecutions in the earlier period, but 2,465 in the latter – a thirtyfold increase. In the autos de fe in both tribunals in the 1580s, Moriscos constituted up to ninety per cent of all accused. The repression in Aragon was singularly harsh. Though the kingdom had only half as many Moriscos as Valencia, it suffered much higher rates of execution and condemnation to the galleys.[37]

It is true that the repression of the Moriscos was not strictly comparable to the severity meted out to judaizers and Protestants. In Cuenca only seven Moriscos were 'relaxed' in person out of 102 cases in the period 1583–1600, and in Granada only twenty were 'relaxed' out of 917 Moriscos appearing in autos in the years 1550–95.[38] This was because the Moriscos were not usually treated as heretics but rather as infidels to whom patience should be shown. However, there is no doubt that the patience of the Christian missioners had long since run out. Reporting from a visit to the Moriscos of Aragon in 1568 the bishop of Tortosa wrote: 'These people have me fed up and exasperated. ... they have a damnable attitude and make me despair of any good in them. ... I have been through these mountains for eight days now and find them more Muslim than ever and very set in their bad ways. I repeat my advice that they should be given a general pardon without insisting on confessions, for there is no other way (unless it be to burn them all).'[39] 'All of them live as Muslims, and no one doubts this', the Inquisition of Aragon had affirmed in 1565.[40]

Throughout Spain there was ample evidence that most Moriscos were proud of their Islamic religion and fought to preserve their culture. Oppression only strengthened their separateness. 'They marry among themselves and do not mix with Old Christians, none of them enters religion nor joins the army nor enters domestic service nor begs alms; they live separately from Old Christians, take part in trade and are rich', runs a report of 1589 made to Philip II on the Moriscos of Toledo.[41] By contrast, for Moriscos the inquisitors were 'thieving wolves whose trade is arrogance and greed, sodomy and lust, tyranny, robbery and injustice'. The Inquisition was 'a tribunal of the devil, attended by deceit and blindness'.[42] Even while the confrontation developed, in some parts of Spain there was peace between Christians and Muslims. In many communities, the continued coexistence of both cultures was accepted. In the area of La Sagra (Toledo), where Moriscos were some five per cent of the population, during the late sixteenth century there was 'a peaceful and fruitful coexistence'.[43] In the province of Cuenca, coexistence was positive.[44] In parts of Aragón, there was even occasional intermarriage between the communities.[45]

Some willingness to assimilate was demonstrated, moreover, by the case of the leaden tablets of Granada. In 1588 and particularly in 1595 the astonishing discovery was made in a cave at Sacromonte, Granada, of a number of tablets apparently engraved in ancient Arabic and claiming to add information to the Christian revelation.[46] Purporting to date from very early times, they depicted a form of Christianity in which features offensive to Muslims did not exist. A big controversy ensued, with many Christian authorities believing in their genuineness. A few Catholic scholars (such as the Hebraist Benito Arias Montano) had doubts. Only in 1682 did Innocent XI pronounce the tablets to be fakes. The fraud had in fact been perpetrated by two prominent Moriscos, Miguel de Luna and Alonso del Castillo, who hoped to syncretize Islamic culture and Christian faith. It was an attempt to claim a place for Arabic Christianity within the framework of Iberian Catholicism.

Despite continuing signs of convivencia, there were events which aggravated confrontation between Christian and Islamic civilization in Spain. In Granada Moriscos were now, after the expulsions, less than a tenth of the population;[47] and the centre of tension moved to the huge Morisco community of Valencia.[48] Here the military threat from the Ottoman empire, backed up by piracy and coastal raids, made the authorities take steps to restrict and disarm Moriscos. The Alpujarra crisis of 1568–70 was followed opportunely by victory over the Turkish fleet at Lepanto in 1571. But Lepanto did not end fears of invasion.[49] Morisco banditry in the south worsened after the 1570s. From this decade French Protestant leaders were in touch with Aragonese Moriscos. Street riots between the communities took place. In Córdoba there were serious incidents in August 1578, provoked in part by open Morisco rejoicing at the destruction of the Portuguese army in the battle of Alcazar el Kebir.[50] In 1580 at Seville a conspiracy abetting invasion from Morocco was discovered. In 1602 Moriscos were plotting with Henry IV of France. In 1608 the Valencian Moriscos asked for help from Morocco. The threat was powerful and real. 'Fear entered into the heart of Spain.'[51]

By the 1580s official opinion had moved in favour of a solution similar to that of 1492. In Lisbon in 1581 Philip II convened a special committee to discuss the matter. In September 1582 the council of state formally proposed a general expulsion. The decision was approved by both Church and Inquisition. It was warmly supported by Martín de Salvatierra, bishop of Segorbe, who had in 1587 drawn up a memorial favouring expulsion,[52] and by Archbishop Ribera who, seeing the failure of his zealous attempts to convert the Moriscos, turned into their most implacable enemy.

When Philip III came to the throne in 1598 it became clear that at all levels there were many who disagreed with the proposal of expulsion. No opinions in favour were expressed in the Cortes of Castile or in those of Valencia. Both the Duke of Lerma and the king's confessor in 1602 opposed expulsion since 'it would be terrible to drive baptized people into Barbary and thus force them to turn Muslim'. As late as 1607 the crown's highest ministers preferred a policy of preaching and instruction. The publicists (arbitristas) of the period were uniformly opposed to expulsion. González de Cellorigo in his *Memorial* (1600) denounced the idea. The nobility of the crown of Aragon were solidly against any measure that would deprive them of their labour force.

However, by 1609 the Duke of Lerma had changed his mind. He presented to the council of state a decision that the lords in Valencia – where his own estates lay – should be compensated by being given the lands of the expelled Moriscos. Opportunely, the lords were coming round to support expulsion. For years, their costs had been rising while the fixed rents from their Morisco vassals stagnated.[53] There were, moreover, fears for security. Morisco population growth seemed uncontrollable. Between Alicante and Valencia on one side and Saragossa on the other, a huge mass of 200,000 Muslim souls appeared to be threatening Christian Spain. In Granada there were further expulsions to counteract the rise in numbers. In Aragon there had been 5,674 Moriscos in 1495, but in 1610 they numbered 14,190 – a fifth of the population. In Valencia the results of censuses made in 1565 and 1609 suggested that the Old Christians might have increased by 44.7 per cent and the Moriscos by a remarkable 69.7 per cent. 'Their aim was to grow and multiply like weeds', claimed a writer in 1612.[54] Castration as a method of control was recommended in 1587 by Martín de Salvatierra.

The expulsion was eventually decreed on 4 April 1609, and took place in stages up to 1614. Operations commenced in Valencia, which contained half the Moriscos in the peninsula and was therefore potentially the most dangerous province. In all, about three hundred thousand Moriscos were expelled, from a peninsular population of some three hundred and twenty thousand.[55] Although the human losses of the expulsion represented little more than four per cent of Spain's population, the real impact in some areas was very severe. Where Moriscos had been a large minority, as in Valencia and Aragon, there was immediate economic catastrophe. But even where they were few in number, the fact that they had a largely active population, with no gentry or clergy or soldiers, meant that their absence could lead to dislocation. Tax returns fell and agricultural output declined.

The Inquisition also faced a bleak future. In 1611 the tribunals of Valencia and Saragossa complained that the expulsion had resulted in their bankruptcy, since they were losing 7,500 ducats a year which they had formerly received from ground-rents. The tribunal of Valencia at the same time acknowledged receiving some compensation, but claimed that a sum of nearly nineteen thousand ducats was still payable to it by the government to make up for what it had lost.[56] A statement of revenue drawn up for the tribunal of Valencia just before the expulsion of the Moriscos shows that 42.7 per cent of its income derived directly from the Morisco population. A similar statement drawn up for the Inquisition of Saragossa in 1612 showed that since the expulsion its revenue had fallen by over forty-eight per cent.[57]

Within a century, with the support of the Inquisition, the authorities had carried out a radical surgery to excise from Spain (in 1492 and in 1609) two of the three great cultures of the peninsula. Cardinal Richelieu in his memoirs described the Morisco expulsions as 'the most barbarous act in human annals'. Cervantes in his *Don Quixote* makes a Morisco character, Ricote, applaud the heroic act of Philip III, 'to expel poisonous fruit from Spain, now clean and free of the fears in which our numbers held her'.[58] Writers then and later closed their ranks and attempted to justify the operation. Many of the Valencian nobility had opposed expulsion, but Boronat, the leading historian of the Morisco question, glosses over their opposition and praises those few lords 'of pure blood and Christian heart' whose religion overrode their self-interest and made them support the measure. For the historian Florencio Janer the expulsion was the necessary excision of an 'enemy race' from the heart of Spain.[59]

These uncompromising statements do not necessarily reflect the real opinion of people at that time. The attitude of the Inquisition in particular was neither uniform nor always hard-line. In Valencia, for example, the inquisitors in 1582 were pessimistic about attempting to Christianize the Moriscos: 'in the six hundred years that they have lived in Spain we have seen few converted.' They consequently proposed 'to expel all of them from Valencia and settle them in Old Castile, but not to send them to the Levant or Barbary, because after all *they are Spaniards like ourselves*'.[60] By the end of that year the prospect of expulsion was already in sight. The Spanish Inquisition took no active part in the decision to expel, which was arrived at exclusively by a small group of court politicians. It continued, however, to act with severity against Moriscos accused of offences against religion, and after 1609 those still in its cells were given the unenviable choice of punishment or exile. Almost in its totality, Muslim Spain was rejected and driven into the sea: thousands for whom there had been no other home were expelled to France, Africa, and the Levant.[61] It was the last act in the creation of an orthodox society and completed the tragedy that had been initiated in 1492.

In perspective the expulsion seems to bear all the marks of inevitability. But despite official propaganda, there is little proof that it was supported unanimously by Spaniards. Opposition to the hard line was more widespread than is often assumed. The prominent writer Pedro de Valencia, writing before the decision had been taken, stated that 'expulsion is a harsh penalty and affects many innocent children, and no unjust course that offends God can be of benefit to the realm'.[62] 'It is a most malign policy of state', Fernández de Navarette, who attacked the expulsion of both Jews and Moriscos as ill advised, commented in 1626, 'for princes to withdraw their trust from their subjects'. Given the enormous controversy aroused within Spain by the expulsions, it is not surprising that as late as 1690 the Moroccan envoy in Madrid could report having heard officials denounce the Duke of Lerma's responsibility for the act.[63]

No exceptions on exclusively religious grounds were allowed. In 1611 when it was proposed to expel the Moriscos of the valley of Ricote, a community of six towns in Murcia, a special report pointed out that the 2,500 inhabitants were truly Christian. But the expulsion still went ahead. Even so, the realm was not as cleansed from Islamic heresy as the zealots would have wished. A small proportion of Moriscos managed to obtain special permission to remain: they consisted in part of the wealthy assimilated elite, and in part of slaves. The inquisitors themselves had allowed groups of apparently Christianized Moriscos to remain behind.[64] Between 1615 and 1700 prosecutions of Moriscos made up about nine per cent of cases tried by the Inquisition. The incidence varied from only one case in Valladolid to 197 in Valencia and 245 in Murcia.[65] There continued, moreover, to be startling cases in later years, such as the group of wealthy Morisco families brought to trial in Granada in 1728.[66] Many of those expelled also yearned to return home. An agent of the English government in Morocco in 1625 reported that the Moriscos in exile were offering to supply men for an invasion of Spain. 'Many have confessed to me that they are Christians. They complain bitterly of their cruel exile, and desire deeply to return under Christian rule'.[67] Convivencia had vanished from Spain. But had religious peace and unity been achieved?

11

RACIALISM AND ITS CRITICS

What plague could destroy a state more than this matter has destroyed the conscience of our Spain?

Fernando de Valdés, SJ (1632)

In late mediaeval Spain, social mobility was accompanied by mobility of ideals between upper and lower classes. A 'noble' attitude to life, for example, was not necessarily restricted to the noble elite. Members of the humblest professions, especially in northern Spain, could claim to be hidalgos and enjoy the privileges attached to rank. Rank demanded respect for one's integrity or 'honour'. In Old Christian society, honour had been earned not simply by personal integrity but also by demonstrating that one had achieved distinction, for example in battle. In time the respected ideals of society – valour, virility, piety, honest wealth – became the basis of 'honour' and 'reputation'. At its simplest level in the village, 'honour' was the opinion held of one by neighbours, and to compromise one's honour – by crime, by sexual misconduct – brought disgrace. At the apex of the social pyramid a noble was in danger of compromising his honour in many ways, but society allowed him several avenues of defence, because he had broader obligations to his kin, his dependants and sometimes his community. The violent methods of protecting honour – assassinating a seducer, duelling with someone who had spoken an insult – were punishable by law, though in many cases the law gave way to public opinion and let the perpetrator go free.

The concept of honour discriminated against the unsuccessful. The poor, mean and outcast were deemed incapable of honour. An hidalgo was permitted to obtain wealth, but not through vulgar means such as working for an employer. Those who did not share the same faith were likewise arguably out of the scope of honour. In Reconquest Spain this theoretically applied to Jews and Muslims, but in practice it applied only to the humbler social ranks. There is ample evidence of Jews and Muslims of the elite being treated on equal terms by Christians; and Christian writers also accepted this equality. By the fifteenth century the deterioration in the socio-political position of Jews and Muslims had significantly affected their capacity to obtain honour. The view that all Old Christians, by the mere fact of not being tainted by semitic blood, were honourable, was becoming widespread. 'Though poor', says Sancho Panza in *Don Quixote*, 'I am an Old Christian, and owe nothing to anybody.' It was felt that Spain, its traditions and faith, belonged exclusively to Old Christians. The heritage could not be shared with those who were outside the picture, whether Jews or Muslims or heretics. What had begun as social discrimination developed into social antagonism and racialism.

The concept of honour, pride and reputation was tending to become chauvinistic and exclusivist.[1] In the fifteenth century it was felt by some that the honour of faith and nation could be preserved only by ensuring that one's lineage was not contaminated by Jews and Muslims. Yet what if the highest ranks of the nobility had been penetrated by Jewish blood? It was notorious that the principal families of Aragon and Castile, and even the royal family, could trace their descent through conversos. Old Christian Spain would collapse if this process went on. A few zealous souls therefore considered that now was the time to stop the Jewish fifth column. With this we have the beginnings of a new stress on racial purity and the consequent rise of the cult of *limpieza de sangre* (purity of blood).

Unofficial attempts to marginalize Christians of Jewish or Muslim origin occurred in the early decades of the fifteenth century. In Barcelona in 1436 the city banned those of converso origin from acting as notaries within its jurisdiction. In Catalonia and Valencia that same year complaints were made to the pope that conversos were being excluded from office. In Lleida in 1437 the converso brokers fought successfully against attempts to exclude them.[2] In Castile the town of Villena obtained a royal privilege in February 1446 to exclude conversos from residence. These measures reflected specific local conditions and conflicts.

The discriminatory measures of the middle and late fifteenth century, by contrast, had a wider significance. In Castile in the 1440s and 1460s, and the crown of Aragon in the 1460s, the instability of royal power provoked disorder and rebellion. In Castile the king's unpopular chief minister, Alvaro de Luna, was of converso origin. Jews and conversos supported him and as a result earned the hostility of the minister's enemies. The most prominent of these was the chief magistrate of Toledo, Pero Sarmiento, inspirer of the famous Sentencia-Estatuto (see above, Chapter

Three). In the civil wars in Aragon, King Juan II received the support of both Jews and conversos. His opponents accordingly directed their attacks at these minorities. Later, in 1472, Juan II stated uncompromisingly that he had 'verified the fidelity of the conversos to his cause and his person, and had promoted them to the highest offices in his court'.[3] In both Castile and Aragon during these years of turmoil many measures were taken against minorities by opponents of the crown. Though obviously motivated by some element of anti-Jewish feeling, they did not necessarily represent the nature of popular opinion. Nor do they suggest that the position of Jews and conversos was worsening. After the return of peaceful conditions, in both realms the crown tried to revoke anti-converso measures.

The Toledo troubles, exceptionally, encouraged further discrimination. They touched such important issues of principle that an immediate controversy was aroused.[4]

One of the first attacks on the 1449 Sentencia-Estatuto was made by the distinguished legist Alfonso Díaz de Montalvo, who emphasized the common traditions and inheritance of Jews and Christians, and pointed out that a baptized Jew was no different from a baptized Gentile. The Mother of God, he said, and all the Apostles had been Jews. Those self-styled Christians who had drawn up the Sentencia were moved by material greed and were wolves disguised as sheep in the flock of Christ. At the same time the converso royal secretary Fernan Díaz de Toledo drew up a memorandum (*Instrucción*)[5] for his friend Lope de Barrientos, bishop of Cuenca and the king's chancellor. In this remarkable document, which openly defended his people, the secretary listed the Jewish origins of the chief families of Castile. On the basis of the memorandum, Barrientos (who was not a converso) wrote a passionate defence of the conversos.[6] Another distinguished intervention came from the Dominican Cardinal Juan de Torquemada, who was of distant converso origin, in his *Treatise against Midianites and Ishmaelites* (1449).[7] The most important refutation of the Sentencia came from the pen of the bishop of Burgos, Alonso de Cartagena, son of the converso Pablo de Santa María, his predecessor in the see. Holder of many high offices of state, in 1434 he led the Spanish delegation to the Church council at Basel, where in a famous speech he defended the international standing of Spain. In his *Defence of Christian Unity* (1449–50), he argued that the Catholic Church was properly the home of the Jews, and that Gentiles were the outsiders who had been invited in. His moderate arguments were continued by the General of the Jeronimites, Alonso de Oropesa, who in 1465 completed his *Light to*

Enlighten the Gentiles, which stressed the need for unity in the Church, and outlined the rightful place held in it by Jews.[8] The objections raised by these writers, and reflected in the hostility to the Sentencia shown both by the pope and the archbishop of Toledo, were not enough to prevail against political faction, demagogy and prejudice. By 1461 Alonso de Espina was pressing for an Inquisition to be established.

The Inquisition, from 1480 onwards, gave a major impetus to the spread of discrimination. The social antagonism of which Spaniards had long been aware was now heightened by the spectacle of scores of 'judaizers' being found guilty of heretical practices and sent to the stake. True religion, it seemed, must be protected by the exclusion of conversos from positions of importance. In 1483 a papal bull ordered that episcopal inquisitors should be Old Christians. In the same year the military orders of Alcántara and Calatrava adopted rules excluding all descendants of Muslims and Jews. Other religious bodies began to insert discriminatory clauses into their statutes.

The university college (Colegio Mayor) of San Bartolomé in Salamanca was the first institution in Spain to adopt a statute of exclusion. It did this at the time of the anti-converso hysteria which accompanied the founding of the Inquisition, around 1482.[9] At the same date the influential college of San Clemente in Bologna, to which many Castilians went to study, began excluding 'those who fled from Seville [in 1480] because they were not Old Christians'.[10] This exclusion had important features. It was directed only against those suspected of heresy, from one region alone, and did *not* apply to all conversos. Conversos therefore continued to attend the college tranquilly. But the murder of Pedro Arbués in 1485 changed all this. Arbués had graduated from the college only ten years before, and was highly regarded there. The result was a statute, formally adopted in 1488, excluding all conversos from entry.[11] The Colegio of Santa Cruz at Valladolid had a statute as part of its foundation rules in 1488. Other Valladolid colleges did not hesitate to modify the rules of their founders. That of San Ildefonso, founded by Cisneros in 1486, had no statutes against conversos, but after the cardinal's death the college adopted one in 1519. When he founded the great monastery of St Thomas Aquinas in Ávila, Torquemada applied to the pope in 1496 for a decree excluding all descendants of Jews.

Despite these moves, the number of institutions that practised exclusion was always small. It was not until 1531, over a generation later, that any other Dominican foundation followed Torquemada's lead. Persecution of judaizers was by then trailing off, and there was evidently no pro-limpieza craze in existence. The first cathedral chapter to adopt a limpieza statute was that of Badajoz in 1511. The cathedral chapter of Seville in 1515 adopted one on the initiative of its archbishop, the inquisitor Diego de Deza. The university of Seville, although it had been founded by a converso, in 1537 adopted a statute of limpieza after someone had carefully blotted out of the original charter the clause making the university open to all.[12]

The Inquisition obviously played an influential part in the process. But its own exclusion rules did not apply to conversos in general, *only* to those who had been penanced. From the beginning it was the rule, set out in Torquemada's Instruction issued at Seville in November 1484, that

> the children and grandchildren of those condemned [by the Inquisition] may not hold or possess public offices, or posts, or honours, or be promoted to holy orders, or be judges, mayors, constables, magistrates, jurors, stewards, officials of weights and measures, merchants, notaries, public scriveners, lawyers, attorneys, secretaries, accountants, treasurers, physicians, surgeons, shopkeepers, brokers, changers, weight inspectors, collectors, tax-farmers, or holders of any similar public office.[13]

This practice was upheld by the Catholic monarchs, who issued two decrees in 1501 forbidding the children of those condemned by the tribunal to hold any post of honour or to be notaries, scriveners, physicians or surgeons. The exclusion was strictly restricted to those who had been penanced in some way. It did not extend to conversos in general.

From the very beginning of the discriminatory process, then, there was a clear ambivalence in the rules. Even if it was their real intention to exclude conversos, discriminating institutions stopped short of it and only penalized families suspected of heresy. The exclusion process was, moreover, seldom taken seriously. In the Spanish college at Bologna conversos continued to enter without serious problems. The students even elected a converso rector in 1492.[14] In Seville cathedral the rules seem to have been repeatedly infringed, and in 1523 the canons had to petition the crown to confirm the validity of their statute, which, however, continued to be unobserved, as the canons complained to the government in 1586.[15]

The relative liberality of the Jeronimites, shown in the writings of Alonso de Oropesa, General of his order from 1457 and re-elected for four successive terms, appears to have attracted judaizers to become members. Officials resisted pressure to discriminate, but in 1485 a scandal broke over the mother house at Guadalupe, where it was alleged that a friar,

Diego de Marchena, had been accepted as a member though he had never been baptized, and had continued to practise (or so it was claimed, on the basis of events of eighteen years before!) Judaism within the protection of the monastery.[16] The chapter meeting of the order in 1486 adopted a statute excluding conversos,[17] which was later revoked after a special appeal by Ferdinand and Isabella. The trend towards exclusion was unfortunately reinforced by the discovery that year of a nest of judaizers in the Jeronimite monastery of La Sisla in Toledo. The prior, García de Zapata, used to say when elevating the Host at mass, 'Up, little Peter, and let the people look at you', and when in confession would allegedly turn his back on the penitent. The Inquisition of Toledo burnt him and four other monks of the monastery in 1486–7. The result was that in 1493 the order passed a rule (approved by the pope in 1495) that 'non recipiantur conversi'. In 1552 the exclusion was extended to all those of Muslim origin.

Other religious orders were, as it happens, slow to follow the Jeronimite example. Not until over thirty years later, in 1525, did the Franciscans adopt a statute of limpieza, doing so against strong internal opposition. The Dominicans began some form of discrimination from as early as 1489, and a limpieza statute was apparently adopted by them in Aragon. In practice, exclusion never became official policy in either order.[18]

The existence and growth of discrimination should not be misconstrued as a triumph of racialism in Spain.[19] The Sarmiento statute had been firmly rebutted by the highest authorities in Church and state, and never took effect in its home-town, Toledo. In the same way, subsequent expressions of racialism in Spain were regularly contested. Antisemitism continued to exist, but the zeal for limpieza was – despite mistaken affirmations to the contrary made by many writers – very strictly confined to a few institutions in a limited number of regions.

The introduction of limpieza rules in the half-century after the foundation of the Inquisition always encountered bitter opposition. The statute of 1488 in San Clemente in Bologna led to a decade of disturbances, including the murder of the college's rector in 1493.[20] When we look closer at some of the controversy aroused in Spain, unexpected questions arise which cast in doubt the common opinion that the country was somehow in the grip of a racialist frenzy. Why did so few public institutions adopt statutes? Why did they take so long to do so? Why, above all, did the Inquisition not exclude conversos? And why, once certain bodies adopted statutes, did they not observe them?

We shall return to these questions in a moment. They need to be considered in the light of the famous racialist statute adopted by Toledo cathedral in 1547.

The archbishop of Toledo had attempted unsuccessfully in 1536 to introduce a statute of limpieza. His successor in 1546, Juan Martínez Siliceo, did not mean to fail. Born of humble peasant stock, Siliceo had struggled upwards to carve out a brilliant career for himself. He had studied for six years at the university of Paris and later taught there for three. Called home to teach at Salamanca, he soon attracted enough attention to be appointed tutor to Charles V's son, Philip, a post he held for ten years. When the see of Toledo fell vacant in 1546 he was appointed to it. The new archbishop was preoccupied with more than just his freshly won dignity. He had been haunted all his life by the shadow of his humble origins, and drew his only pride from the fact that his parents had been Old Christians.

In his new post he felt in no mood to compromise with converso Christians whose racial antecedents were in his mind the principal threat to a secure and unsullied Church. When, therefore, in September 1546 he discovered that the pope had just appointed a converso, Dr Fernando Jiménez, to a vacant canonry in the cathedral, and that the new incumbent's father had once been condemned by the Inquisition as a judaizer, he refused to accept the appointment. Siliceo wrote to the pope protesting against his candidate, and sounding a warning that the first church in Spain was now in danger of becoming a 'new synagogue'. The pope withdrew his man, but Siliceo thought this was not enough and proceeded to draw up a statute to exclude all conversos from office in the cathedral. A chapter meeting was hurriedly convoked on 23 July 1547, and with ten dissentient votes against twenty-four the statute of limpieza was pushed through.

The voting figures show that not all the canons had been present at the meeting. An immediate protest was raised by the archdeacons of Guadalajara and Talavera, Pero González de Mendoza and Alvaro de Mendoza, both sons of the powerful Duke of Infantado, and both Old Christians. Condemning the injustice and impropriety of the statute, they criticized the archbishop for not calling all the dignitaries of the cathedral to his meeting, and also threatened to appeal to the pope. The controversy that followed gives us an invaluable summary of the views both of opponents and of supporters of the limpieza statutes.

According to the explanatory document drawn up by Siliceo,[21] the policy of limpieza was now practised in Spain by the military orders, by university colleges and by religious orders. The existence of a converso danger was proved by the fact that the Lutheran heretics of Germany were nearly all descendants of Jews. Nearer home, 'the archbishop has found that not only the majority but nearly all the parish priests of his archdiocese with a care of souls . . . are descendants of Jews.' Moreover, conversos were not content with controlling the wealth of Spain. They were now trying to dominate the Church. The size of the danger was shown by the fact that in the last fifty years over fifty thousand conversos had been burnt and penanced by the Inquisition, yet they still continued to flourish. To emphasize this argument, the archbishop demonstrated that of the ten who had voted against his statute, no fewer than nine were of Jewish origin, five of them coming from the prolific converso family to which Fray García de Zapata belonged.

Siliceo was not giving the whole picture. It is true that among the most hostile to the statute were the dean of the cathedral, Diego de Castilla, and the humanist Juan de Vergara, both conversos; but at least six other canons who shared their hostility were Old Christians. What distinguished these canons (two of whom were, as we know, of the noble house of Mendoza) and the dean was their irrefutably aristocratic lineage, in contrast to Siliceo, who was of humble origin. In the protest drawn up by the dissentient clergy[22] the complaint was made that, first, the statute was against canon law; second, it was against the laws of the kingdom; third, it contradicted Holy Scripture; fourth, it was against natural reason; and, fifth, it defamed 'many noble and leading people of these realms'. The sting lay in the fifth article. As Siliceo and his opponents well knew, few members of the nobility had not been tainted with converso blood. By promoting a limpieza statute, therefore, the archbishop was obviously claiming for his own class a racial purity that the tainted nobility could not boast.

There was immediate, highly placed opposition to the statute outside the cathedral. The city council of Toledo protested energetically against the measure, which (they said) threatened to bring back the civil wars of the Comunidades to the city. Previous archbishops, they added, had refused to exclude conversos, and Cardinal Travera in 1536 had ordered no action on a proposal to introduce a statute. If the present statute were allowed to proceed, it would arouse 'hatreds and long-standing enmities'. The councillors knew of what they spoke. Their petition, addressed to Prince Philip early in August 1547, managed to secure approval in the city council only after a heated debate. The prince, then ruling Spain in his father's absence, was deeply concerned. He sent a special judge to Toledo to look at the situation on the spot. He also asked the president of the council of Castile, the highest court in the land, to send him an opinion from both the judicial and the Church point of view. The council of Castile gave its legal verdict on 25 August. 'The statute', they ruled, 'is unjust and scandalous and putting it into effect would cause many problems.' They recommended that the prince order its suspension, for the moment. To obtain a Church point of view, the president of the council, who happened also to be bishop of Sigüenza, called a meeting of his clergy. They ruled that 'the statute in its present harsh form raises grave problems, and putting it into effect would cause even more'. It should be suspended until further consultation.[23]

The prince accordingly suspended the statute in mid-September 1547, and referred the matter to Charles V in Germany. Siliceo was furious. At the end of September he protested to his former pupil against the suspension 'decreed without hearing us'. For the moment, he was silenced. The statute was condemned by the university of Alcalá as a source of 'discord sown by the devil'. Toledo had a long history of conflict involving conversos, and officials were concerned to soothe passions.

Not till nine years later was the statute allowed to proceed. The pope issued a formal approval in 1555, and in August 1556 Philip, now king, ratified it.[24] Times had changed, and with them Philip's own views. However, there is no reason to believe that he had become an antisemite. The affirmation in one of his decrees that 'all the heresies which have occurred in Germany and France have been sown by descendants of Jews, as we have seen and still see daily in Spain', was in effect quoted from a petition by Siliceo, and not an expression of his own sentiments.[25] There is of course clear evidence that from this period the king accepted as fact the information that some of his advisers, of confirmed anti-converso views, were giving him. It is less well known that substantial elite opinion opposed such views. Philip's biographer Cabrera de Córdoba, in referring to the Siliceo statute as 'detested by those who decide the principles of good government', reported that the Cortes had an 'undying hatred' of the measure.[26] His statements are a reflection of the impressive opposition to limpieza.

Confirmation of the Toledo statute in 1556 came only a few months before Siliceo's death the following year. It coincided with a period of religious crisis and heightened suspicions of conversos. It was also the period when the Inquisition itself decided at last to enforce limpieza, through a royal order of December 1572. By the 1570s, ironically, the demand for proofs of purity had come to a virtual stop. The 'statute communities', as they were called, were at this period limited to the six university Colegios Mayores; some religious orders (Jeronimites, Dominicans and Franciscans); the Inquisition; and some cathedrals (Badajoz, Córdoba, Jaén, León, Osma, Oviedo, Seville, Sigüenza, Toledo and Valencia). Virtually only one secular sector was affected: the mediaeval military orders (the Order of Santiago adopted one as late as 1555), and their administrative organ, the council of orders. Private legal arrangements, such as entails (*mayorazgos*), might also lay down conditions of limpieza. A sprinkling of town councils and confraternities, mainly in Castile, also practised exclusion.

Though limited in number, some of these bodies were of crucial importance. From the sixteenth century, entry into a Colegio Mayor became the essential stepping-stone to a career in both Church and state in Castile.[27] If conversos were excluded, they would find the upper level of professions closed to them. In the same way the *encomiendas* of the military orders were one of the most desirable ways of attaining noble status. Exclusion from the orders would spell disaster to the social pretensions of a converso family. The panorama, evidently, looked bleak for them.

The real picture was more complex.[28]

First, the small number of institutions with statutes (less than a sixth of Spain's sees, for example) refutes any idea of a limpieza mania sweeping the country. Time and again, other bodies cited this fact in defence of their own refusal to follow the trend. The statutes, moreover, existed almost exclusively in Castile. In Catalonia, for example, limpieza rules were unknown before the period of the Counter Reformation, when they crept in together with the other baggage of Castilian ecclesiastics.[29] They were rarely found in Castilian city councils, despite considerable pressure in favour from anti-converso factions. In brief, the statutes were never part of the public law of Spain and never featured in any body of public law. Their validity was restricted only to those institutions which had them.

Second, they were always controversial and were never widely accepted. In Rome Pope Paul IV had approved the Toledo statute, but he did this out of policy and not principle. The same pope in 1565 refused to approve a new statute for the cathedral of Seville and condemned limpieza as contrary to canon law and ecclesiastical order. His successor Pius V was a consistent enemy of the statutes. In Spain a continuous debate, directed largely *against* the statutes, was unleashed. The tide of controversy was stemmed by the Inquisition, which in 1572 tried to forbid any writings either for or against the statutes.

Third, even where statutes existed Spaniards found it possible to impose them with a typical laxity that in many cases undermined their existence. Philip II was no exception. When he felt it necessary, he appointed converso Church dignitaries even if it contravened a statute. In some dioceses the rules were regularly by-passed. In Toledo in 1557, one year after the king confirmed the famous statute, a converso was appointed as canon of the cathedral.[30] In the see of Sigüenza in 1567 the bishop decided to ignore the statute in existence when making appointments.[31] In 1589 Philip II appointed a priest of known converso origin, Gabriel Márquez, to be his chaplain in the same cathedral of Sigüenza. When it was pointed out that the statute forbade this, Philip suspended the appointment but ordered that the statute be looked into.[32] In the Inquisition itself, the rules were often disregarded, and clergy of known converso origin were employed as assessors.[33] In the late sixteenth century familiars were often (cases are documented in Murcia and Barcelona) appointed without any proofs at all.

Despite the prohibitions in the military orders, known conversos were accepted. In 1552 Prince Philip, then regent of Spain, appointed his friend Ruy Gómez (not a converso) as president of the military Order of Calatrava. Ruy Gómez remarked confidentially to a friend that the current president of the Order of Alcántara 'is a New Christian'.[34] When king, Philip continued to tolerate an occasional converso in the military orders. He bestowed a knighthood of Santiago on a famous Flanders war veteran but ordered that no enquiry be made into his genealogy.[35] The few city councils with statutes seem not to have paid attention to the rules except when it served their purpose. Toledo city in 1566 adopted a statute that was expressly approved by Philip II. Despite it, converso families like the Franco, Villareal, Herrera and Ramírez continued freely throughout the period to occupy posts.[36] Philip subsequently refused to approve limpieza statutes for other cities. In Cuenca, which had a long history of antagonism to conversos, converso families during the late sixteenth century in fact occupied 50 per cent of the posts on the city council.[37] A leading judge of the time, Castillo de Bobadilla, observed that conversos in Castile had free access to municipal posts; and another jurist, Pedro Núñez de Avendaño, commented that conversos were sometimes in theory excluded from 'public offices, *although in practice they are freely admitted'*.[38] The gap was vast between adoption of statutes and their implication.

Fourth, where statutes existed those who wished to avoid them did so: by bribes or by fraudulent proofs. Rich conversos, complained some members of the Cortes of Madrid in 1551, 'obtain sanction from Your Majesty through bribes, and in this the state is much prejudiced'.[39] Bribes persisted at every level, but it was the false proofs that emerged as the biggest preoccupation. False proofs implied corruption and scandal. It was this, possibly more than any other single aspect, that excited elite opposition to the statutes.

Throughout these years, then, there was a profound ambivalence about the implementation of exclusion. It had been the practice in the early years of the Inquisition to 'rehabilitate'[40] conversos accused of lesser offences. Those who had completed their penances and paid a sum of money could obtain from the Inquisition a certificate restoring their former status. Since they had not been judged guilty of heresy, they did not incur any major penalties. It meant – despite a commonly held opinion to the contrary – that mere punishment by the inquisitors did not necessarily prejudice one's career. The practice coincided with an accepted principle of canon law.

Conversos, whether or not penanced by the Inquisition, might be in principle excluded from many important bodies; in practice, they were capable of acceding to most public offices in Spain. In 1522 the Inquisition stipulated that the universities of Salamanca and Valladolid should not grant degrees to conversos. But in 1537 Charles V decreed that in colleges where New Christians were being excluded, 'the constitutions of founders be respected'.[41] Throughout the period, conversos can be found both as students and as professors in the major universities. The situation in the provinces was no different. The father of the Murcian humanist Francisco de Cascales was burnt at the stake as an alleged judaizer in 1564. Cascales opportunely exiled himself from the city. In 1601, however, he returned to Murcia and was appointed to the chair of grammar there. Everybody knew about his origins but no questions were asked.[42]

A central figure in controversies at Salamanca University during the 1570s, Martín Martínez de Cantalapiedra, was a known converso who had been appointed to the chair of Hebrew there in 1559. The same university had not hesitated, a generation before (in 1531), to appoint the converso Pablo Coronel as professor of Hebrew. Although discrimination of some sort may have been practised at Salamanca, the university was always opposed to formal exclusion. When in 1562 the rector proposed introducing a limpieza statute, the university assembly voted that 'before introducing it we should consider carefully the many types of problems that might arise'. Finally, 'it was resolved that for the time being it should not be introduced'. When another attempt was made to introduce a statute in 1566, Philip II himself stepped in to prohibit it.[43]

Limpieza was seriously limited in its effectiveness, but there can be no doubt of the threat it could represent. Though practised in only a limited number of institutions, these were so significant that a barrier to status mobility was frequently created. In theory canon law limited the extent to which the sins of fathers could be visited on their sons and grandsons. Limpieza adopted no such limits. If it were proved that an ancestor on any side of the family had been penanced by the Inquisition or was a Muslim or Jew, the descendant could be accounted of impure blood and disabled from the relevant office. Applicants for many posts had to present genealogical proofs of the purity of their lineage. The fraud, perjury, extortion and blackmail that came into existence because of the need to prove limpieza was widely recognized as a moral evil. If pretendants to office could not offer convincing genealogical proofs, comisarios were appointed to visit the localities concerned and take sworn statements from witnesses about the antecedents of the applicant. The comisarios examined parish records and collected verbal testimony. In an age when written evidence was rare, the reputation of applicants lay wholly at the mercy of local gossip and hostile neighbours. Bribery became necessary. If an applicant was refused a post with the Inquisition the tribunal never gave any reason, with the result that the family of the man became suspected of impurity even if this was not the case. Some applicants had to go through legal processes which might last several years, with all the attendant expenses, before a proper genealogy could be drawn up. Others resorted to perjury to obtain posts, thus involving themselves and their witnesses in heavy fines and infamy when the tribunal discovered their offence. Frequently applicants would be disabled from employment simply by the malicious gossip of enemies, because 'common rumour' was allowed as evidence.[44] Genealogy became a social weapon.

It did not, however, create an insuperable barrier to entry into the nobility. Formal barriers, in reality, existed only for entry into the military orders of Castile. To obtain an encomienda in any of these, one had to have one's lineage checked by the council of orders in Madrid. This bureaucratic obstacle could be by-passed only if the king himself intervened (as, we have seen, he sometimes did). Otherwise it obviously opened up a hornet's nest of enquiries and slanders. Entry into the titled nobility, by contrast, was a process unbeset by any limpieza rules. The standard treatise on nobility, the *Summa nobilitatis* (1553) of Juan Arce de Otalora, affirmed expressly that all converts from Judaism and Islam 'may without any discrimination be admitted on equal terms to the rank and immunities of nobility'.[45] He pointed out that it was well known that many illustrious persons in Spain were of distant Jewish origin. However, he added, those among the converts who were guilty of heresy could be excluded.

'Infamy' affected the honour, religion and 'race' of a Spaniard. It could bring shame and disgrace upon himself, his family and all his descendants. This view was followed by a writer of the time of Philip IV, Juan Escobar de Corro, who in his *Treatise on the purity of the nobility* (c. 1632) equated the word 'purity' with 'honour', and considered death preferable to infamy. For Escobar the strain on an impure lineage was ineffaceable and perpetual.[46] This extreme and basically racialist doctrine (professed, it must be noted, at a time when the statutes of limpieza were in decay) meant that not even baptism was able to wash away the sins of one's fathers. The Inquisition helped powerfully to make such attitudes possible. Early in the sixteenth century the practice was begun of hanging up the sanbenitos of offenders after the period for which the garment had to be worn. This was standardized by the official Instructions of 1561, which stipulated that

> all the sanbenitos of the condemned, living or dead, present or absent, be placed in the churches where they used to live ... in order that there may be perpetual memory of the infamy of the heretics and their descendants.[47]

The declared aim of displaying the garments was therefore to perpetuate the infamy of condemned persons, so that from generation to generation whole families should be penalized for the sins of their ancestors. It became general practice to replace old and decaying sanbenitos with new ones bearing the same names of the offenders. The garments were widely hated not only by the families concerned but also by the districts on which they brought disrepute. The city of Logroño (Navarre) in 1570 successfully petitioned the Suprema to be allowed to remove from its churches the great number of sanbenitos belonging properly to churches in other regions.[48] In the rising against the Spanish government in Sicily in 1516, the sanbenitos in the churches were torn down and never replaced. In the peninsula, however, the tribunal took every care to ensure that they should be exposed ceaselessly, as they were in most regions until the end of the eighteenth century. In practice in the end it mattered not at all whether a man had been burnt or simply made to do penance in an auto de fe. Thanks to the sanbenito, his descendants could still suffer public disability.

Infamy was beyond doubt the worst punishment imaginable in those times. In the ordinary criminal courts, humiliating punishments that brought public shame (*vergüenza*) and ridicule were feared more than the death sentence,[49] since they ruined one's reputation for ever in the local community and brought disgrace on all one's family and relatives. In the Inquisition, similarly, one's 'honour' could be destroyed by humiliating penalties (such as flogging), but the gravest of all punishments was the sanbenito, since its duration could be perpetual. When young Anna Enríquez, daughter of the Marquesa of Alcañices and sister-in-law of Francisco Borja, was condemned by the Inquisition in 1559 to wear a sanbenito for her part in the Protestant group of Valladolid, Borja used his influence to have the sanbenito part of her sentence annulled: the 'honour' of her family was thereby saved.

Though the Holy Office was clearly responsible for perpetuating infamy, from very early on it also tried to restrict the rumour and slander associated with it, and in numerous cases prosecuted those who attempted to defame their neighbours. Ironically, it therefore became an offence, punishable by the Inquisition, to call someone a 'Jew'. In 1620, for example, Antonio Vergonyós, a familiar and priest of Girona, was banished for a year from his village for slandering a neighbour as a 'Jueu'.[50]

Spanish concern over infamy extended also to non-Judaic heresy. The violent reaction against the Valladolid Protestants was provoked in part by a curious popular pride that did not admit the possibility of Castilians becoming infected by heresy. 'Before that time', commented one contemporary, 'Spain was clean [*limpia*] of these errors.'[51] When Carlos de Seso and Fray Domingo de Rojas were being brought back to Valladolid, reported the Inquisitor General, 'in all the villages through which they passed, crowds of men, women and children came out to see them, calling for them to be burnt. The friar[52] was very afraid that his relatives would kill him on the journey.'[53] Rojas had good reason to fear. We know of the remarkable case of Juan Díaz – a Spanish friend of the reformer Bucer – who was assassinated in Germany by his own brother Alfonso, a Catholic who feared that his brother's heresy would bring shame on his family and on all Spain.[54] The Inquisition shared this attitude to the extent of trying to pursue Spanish heretics such as Miguel Servet even beyond the borders of Spain, for fear that their heresies would bring disgrace on the honour of the Spanish nation. The tradition was continued with some energy by the governments of both Charles V and Philip II. Philip's officials, as we have seen above, employed the heretic-hunter Alonso del Canto to bring back to Spain those who might bring ill fame on the country.[55]

The social consequences of limpieza were so corrosive that there was always strong opposition to it at all social levels. It became a continual source of friction between the Society of Jesus and the Inquisition. We have seen that Ignatius Loyola, when a student at Alcalá in 1527, fell under suspicion because of his strict religious practices. This was the very year that the province of Guipúzcoa made into law an earlier ordinance of 1483, forbidding entry to conversos. At this time Ignatius indignantly denied any knowledge of Judaism, since he was a noble from a province (Guipúzcoa) which had hardly known Jews. Some years later, however, he declared while dining with friends that he would have considered it a divine favour to be descended from Jews. When asked his reason for saying this, he protested, 'What! To be related to Christ Our Lord and to Our Lady the glorious Virgin Mary?' On another occasion a fellow Basque who was a friend of his had spat at the word 'Jew' when he mentioned it. Ignatius took him aside and said, according to his biographer, ' "Now, Don Pedro de Zárate, be reasonable and listen to me" – And he gave him so many reasons that he all but persuaded him to become a Jew'.[56] The incidents show that Ignatius had managed to free himself from one of the major social prejudices prevailing in Spain.

Like its founder, the Society of Jesus refused to associate itself with racialism. When in 1551 the Jesuits opened a college at Alcalá without the permission of Archbishop Siliceo, the latter issued an order forbidding any Jesuit to act as a priest without first being personally examined by him. It was no secret that the reason for this order was Siliceo's hostility to the presence of converso Christians in the college. Francisco Villanueva, rector of the college, wrote indignantly to Ignatius about this.

> It is a great pity that there seems to be nobody willing to leave these poor people anywhere to stay on earth, and I would like to have the energy to become their defender, particularly since one encounters among them more virtue than among the Old Christians and hidalgos.[57]

The first provincial of the Jesuits in Spain, Antonio de Araoz, impressed however upon Ignatius that Siliceo had promised to visit the order with great favours if it would only adopt a statute of limpieza. He also warned that the good name of the Society in Spain would be harmed by the knowledge that there were New Christians in its ranks. Despite this,

Ignatius refused to change his attitude. All through the controversy in Spain about the statutes of limpieza, and up to his death in 1556, he would not allow his order to discriminate against conversos. When conversos did apply to enter its ranks he advised them to join the Company in Italy rather than in Spain. When talking of the limpieza cult he would refer to it as 'el humor español' – (the Spanish whim); or, more bitingly on one occasion, 'el humor de la corte y del Rey de España' – (the whim of the Spanish king and his court).

All the generals of the order after Loyola were firm in their opposition to the statutes. The immediate successor of Ignatius was Diego Laínez, General from 1558 to 1565. The fact that he was a converso aroused opposition to his election from sectors of the Spanish Church. In a letter to Araoz in 1560 Laínez denounced limpieza as 'el humor o error nacional' (the national whim or error) and demanded total obedience from the Spanish Jesuits. In 1564 a Jesuit wrote from Seville to Laínez, lamenting the divisions within the order based on lineage. 'These distinctions do much harm, especially among those who recall that golden time of affection at the beginning'.[58] Laínez's successor was a Spaniard of unimpeachable Old Christian blood – Francisco Borja. On one occasion the Prince of Eboli, chief minister of Philip II, asked Borja why his Company allowed conversos in its ranks. Borja pointed out that the king himself employed known conversos:

> Why does the king keep in his service X and Y, who are conversos? If His Majesty disregards this in those he places in his household, why should I make an issue about admitting them into the service of that Lord for whom there is no distinction between persons, between Greek and Jew, or barbarian and Scythian?[59]

By the 1590s, however, the Jesuits in Spain found that recruits were falling off as the whispering campaign initiated by its enemies succeeded in presenting the Society as a party of Jews. Moreover, by a process of selection the chief posts in the Spanish province were going to Jesuits who favoured exclusion. The result was pressure for a modification to the constitution of the Society, and at the General Congregation held at Rome in December 1593 it was voted to give way to Spanish views and exclude conversos from membership in Spain. Among the few voices raised in protest in Spain was that of Father Pedro de Ribadeneira.[60] Due almost exclusively to his singlehanded efforts to keep the Society to the path laid down by Loyola, a reaction to the vote of 1593 took place in the order. It led to a decree in February 1608, by which all conversos who had been Christians for five generations were allowed to enter the Society. The 1608 decree was nominally only a concession, but in practice it involved the complete reversal of the decision of 1593, since most conversos in Spain had in fact been Christians for five generations, as a result of the compulsory conversions of 1492.

Another leading Jesuit, Juan de Mariana, had meanwhile in his treatise on *The king* (1599) penned an uncompromising attack on racial discrimination. 'The marks of infamy', he urged, 'should not be eternal, and it is necessary to fix a limit beyond which descendants must not pay for the faults of their predecessors'.[61] The opposition of the Jesuits was not unique. Though a few other sees followed Toledo in adopting limpieza, the statutes were never universally accepted. Of the sixty cathedrals in Spain, possibly no more than twelve ever had statutes. Many that had them never operated them. Leading clergy penned attacks on the system of limpieza. Melchor Cano appears to have criticized them in a paper of 1550, and another Dominican, Domingo de Valtanás, attacked them in a book published in Seville in 1556.[62] In Rome, prominent Spaniards spoke openly against limpieza. This persuaded Diego de Simancas, bishop of Zamora, to publish in about 1572 his *Defence of the Toledo Statute,* possibly the last substantial defence of the doctrines of Siliceo. By the end of the sixteenth century, there was widespread unease about limpieza in the upper levels of society. Enquiries into ancestry threatened the good name of the noblest families. For one member of a family to be refused a post because of alleged impurity, meant a stigma on the rest of the family. The practice of limpieza threatened to expose the entire nobility to infamy.

At this point a revolutionary *crise de conscience* occurred in the very citadel of orthodoxy, the Inquisition.[63] From about 1580, when Cardinal Gaspar de Quiroga was Inquisitor General, serious doubts about statutes were raised in the Holy Office. 'I was in the council of the Inquisition in 1580', reports a subsequent Inquisitor General, Niño de Guevara, 'and saw this matter proceed very far, with the council resolved to petition the king about it, and putting forward many pressing reasons.' Nothing more seems to have happened until the 1590s, when Philip II himself had second thoughts. The king, reports a later writer, 'was very attached to the statutes, but in the last days of his life, when experience had matured, he ordered a big committee to be set up specifically to discuss this matter, and all of them agreed with His Majesty that the statutes should be restricted to one hundred years', meaning that freedom from the taint of heresy for three generations should make any converso fit for office.

Because of the king's death, nothing came of the proposal, but the ground was prepared for the great attack on the statutes mounted by the noted Dominican theologian Agustín Salucio, whose *Discourse* on limpieza, which he had apparently discussed with Philip II, was published in 1599.[64] Salucio, then aged seventy-six (he died in 1601), felt that 'I could not be true to my conscience if I did not speak my opinion on so important a matter.' His book was supported by personal letters from the very highest authorities: the patriarch of Valencia, Juan de Ribera; the archbishop of Burgos; the Duke of Lerma.[65] Taking his stand on the innumerable abuses committed in the process of limpieza proofs – false testimony, bribery, forgery, lies – Salucio protested that 'the scandals and abuses ... have provoked a secret war against the authority of the statutes'. 'It is said', he commented, 'that there is no peace when the state is divided into two factions, as it is now divided almost in half, as in a civil war.' He presented two main objections of principle to the statutes: they had outlived their purpose; and whatever good they achieved was outweighed by the harm. 'It would be a great comfort to the assurance of peace in the realm', he summed up, 'to restrict the statutes so that Old Christians and Moriscos and conversos should all come to form one united body, and that all should be Old Christians and in peace.'

The work caused an immediate crisis in the Inquisition. The Suprema overruled the Inquisitor General and banned the book. However, deputies to the Cortes had been sent copies of the *Discourse* by wily old Salucio, and they at once insisted on debating the matter. On 11 February 1600 they presented a memorial to Philip III, petitioning 'how important it is to make a decision on this matter, because of the great offences caused to God every day'. At the same time they set up a committee to report on Salucio's paper. In a discussion paper sent by the Cortes to the committee, they complained that 'in Spain we esteem a common person who is *limpio* more than a hidalgo who is not *limpio*'.[66] As a result, the memorial continued, there were now two sorts of nobility in Spain, 'a greater, which is that of *hidalguia*; and a lesser, which is that of limpieza, whose members we call Old Christians'. Irrational criteria of purity had also come into existence: swordsmen were reputed *limpios* and physicians were reputed Jews; people from León and Asturias were called Old Christians and those from Almagro conversos. 'All this is so absurd that were we another nation we would call ourselves barbarians who governed themselves without reason, without law, and without God . . .'

Another evil effect, they said, was that because of rigorous genealogical proofs the state lost eminent subjects who had the talent to become great theologians and jurists but who did not follow these professions because they knew they would not be admitted to any honours. As a result, people of no rank and little learning had risen to high posts in the country, while true and learned nobility had been deprived of the chance to pursue their careers. Discrimination against Jewish blood would only make the conversos become more compact, defensive and dangerous; whereas in France and Italy the lack of discrimination had allowed them to merge peacefully into the community. The natural consequence of limpieza proofs would be that those who were irrefutably limpios (and hence alone capable of holding office) would soon be a tiny minority in the country with the great mass of the people against them, 'affronted, discontented and ripe for rebellion'.

In the summer of 1600 the Duke of Lerma asked the new Inquisitor General, Cardinal Niño de Guevara, to report on Salucio's book and various other documents. In August Guevara sent the king an astonishing report,[67] which contradicted the views of the majority of the Suprema and praised Salucio as 'a very learned friar to whom the whole Catholic Church and particularly the Holy See owe a great deal'. The split in the Inquisition was not resolved, and Salucio's book remained under ban. However, with so many eminent leaders of Church and state hostile to the statutes, the floodgates to public discussion had been opened. In about 1613 a New Christian of Portuguese origin, Diego Sánchez de Vargas, issued in Madrid an attack against the statutes. In 1616 the Madrid magistrate, Mateo López Bravo, complained in his *On the king* that for those excluded by the limpieza laws 'there remains no way of hope except the sowing of discord'. In 1619 Martín González de Cellorigo, now resident in Toledo and an official of the Inquisition, wrote a *Plea for Justice* on behalf of the New Christians: it was addressed to the Inquisitor General but not actually published.[68]

In about 1621 an inquisitor, Juan Roco Campofrío, bishop of Zamora and later of Soria, wrote a *Discourse*[69] against the statutes. According to him, the proofs of limpieza were a source of moral and political scandal in the nation. The stigma of impurity had divided Spain into two halves, one of which was constantly warring against the other. The outrages and quarrels provoked by the statutes had been responsible for over ninety per cent of the civil and criminal trials in Spanish courts. The racialism of the statutes was wrong, for many conversos and Moriscos had been more virtuous than so-called Old Christians, and many of those brought to trial by the Inquisition had in fact been true Christians and not Jews.[70] The great danger, the inquisitor went on, was that the greater part of the population of Spain would soon be branded as impure, and the only remaining guarantee of Old Christian blood would be one's plebeian origin. The inquisitor's tract was only one of the many written on the subject. A censor of the Inquisition, Francisco Murcia de la Llana, in a *Discourse* of 1624 condemned both the racialism and the xenophobia of his contemporaries:

> Look into yourself [he addressed Spain] and consider that no other nation has these statutes, and that Judaism has flourished most where they have existed. Yet if any of your sons marries a Frenchwoman or a Genoan or an Italian you despise his wife as a foreigner. What ignorance! What overwhelming Spanish madness![71]

In his famous *Conservation of monarchies* (1626) Pedro Fernández de Navarrete attacked discrimination against conversos and Moriscos, warning that 'all realms in which many are excluded from honours run a great risk of coming to ruin'.[72]

Though Lerma had been opposed to the statutes, he did little to change them. It was otherwise with Olivares, who came to power in 1621 at the accession of Philip IV. Olivares never made a secret of his hostility to limpieza. At his instigation, the Inquisition in 1626 issued perhaps the most remarkable document ever to proceed from the inner portals of the Holy Office.[73]

Conceding that there were now few or no judaizers in Spain, the Suprema in this 1626 document argued that 'it follows that since what gave rise to the statutes has totally ceased, it would be civic and political prudence that at least the rigour of their practice should cease'. Denouncing the widespread perjuries and forgeries involved, the inquisitors said: 'nobody can doubt this if he sees what goes on today in every city, town or village, even in the testimonials for familiars in any little hamlet. No one could better inform Your Majesty of this abuse, from direct experience, than the Holy Office.' After analysing in detail the evils of the system of genealogical proofs, the Suprema went on to argue that Hebrews no less than Gentiles were members of Christ's Church and that unity of all, without discrimination, was essential. In words that could have been written by Olivares himself, the council of the Inquisition stated that its aspirations were exactly those of Philip IV:

that your several kingdoms should act in conformity and unity for both good and ill, joining together in friendly equality, so that Castile should act with Aragon, and both with Portugal, and all of them with Italy and the other realms, to help and aid each other as though they were one body (fortunate enough to have Your Majesty as head). These considerations, so in keeping with God's intentions, are in large measure frustrated if there remain such odious divisions and such bloody enmities as those which exist between those held to be *limpios*, and those held to be stained with the race of Judaism.

In this favourable climate it was possible for the Committee for Reform (*Junta de Reformación*) in February 1623 to decree new rules modifying the practice of limpieza. One act (involving three positive proofs of limpieza in any one of the four lines of descent) was enough when applying for office and no others were needed when promoted or changing one's job. Verbal evidence was not admitted if unsupported by more solid proof, and 'rumour' was disallowed. All literature purporting to list the descent of families from Jews, such as the notorious Green Book of Aragon (Libro verde de Aragón), was ordered to be publicly destroyed and burnt. Although these measures aroused much opposition, they also released a flood of anti-limpieza writings which take their stand with the other literature that makes this reign a time of intellectual crisis in Spanish history. That the problem was appreciated in the highest circles is shown by the report given by one member of the Committee for Reform, who claimed that limpieza was

the cause and origin of a great multitude of sins, perjuries, falsehoods, disputes and lawsuits both civil and criminal. Many of our people, seeing that they are not admitted to the honours and offices of their native land, have absented themselves from these realms and gone to others, in despair at seeing themselves covered with infamy. So much so that I have been told of two eminent gentlemen of these realms who were among the greatest soldiers of our time and who declared on their deathbeds that since they were unable to gain entry into the orders of chivalry they had very often been tempted by the devil to kill themselves or to go over and serve the Turk, and that they knew of some who had done so.[74]

The reform of February 1623 was ordered to be observed 'by all the councils, courts, Colegios Mayores and statute communities'. In fact, it remained a dead letter and was not observed by a single body outside the government and the Inquisition. The latter, not surprisingly, soon ceased to observe the reform. Controversy therefore continued well into the seventeenth century. The Inquisitor General in 1623 commissioned a further reasoned attack on the statutes by Diego Serrano de Silva, a member of the Suprema.

From its inception in the 1580s, this impressive and astonishing campaign against the statutes of limpieza was led, at every stage, by Inquisitors General and officials of the Inquisition, supported by ministers of state such as Lerma and Olivares. Their view, as events showed, might have been powerful in elite circles but was a minority one within the Holy Office. By the 1630s confusion reigned once again in the limpieza rules. The Suprema by majority vote in 1628 declared that 'we are convinced that observance of the statutes of limpieza is both just and praiseworthy'.[75] Government ministers were concerned at the problems that would continue to rise in applications for posts and titles. Eventually in 1638 the crown issued yet another decree, reinforcing the reform of 1623.[76]

The predictable conservatism of the inquisitors was no guide to the state of informed opinion in Castile. Prominent individuals, both inside and outside the Holy Office, continued to express their disagreement with limpieza.[77] In his well-known *Five excellences of the Spaniards* (1629), Fray Benito de Peñalosa commented that 'when we come to the question of limpieza, there are things much to be lamented. . . . It is something absurd and most prejudicial'. He pleaded for reforms.[78] In 1632 a powerful and persuasive argument against limpieza was published by Fernando de Valdés, rector of the Jesuit seminary in Madrid and a consultant for the Inquisition. Basing himself on Salucio's discourse but going further in his attack on the statutes, Valdés summed up: 'Let the final and strongest argument against the statutes be that our republic has lost its respect for them.'[79] In 1635 the noted political writer Jerónimo de Zeballos, repeating arguments used by his predecessors, wrote his own *Discourse* against the practice of limpieza.[80]

The publication of these works, and indeed the half-century or so of open controversy over the question, demonstrates irrefutably that limpieza was never an untouchable theme. Numerous prominent intellectuals from the mid-sixteenth century onwards questioned it and attacked it. It was never accepted officially in Spanish law, nor in most of the institutions, churches and municipalities of Spain. It hurt most deeply and profoundly, as racial discriminations tend to do, in the sphere of status, rank and promotion. But at no point did it ever become a national obsession.[81]

On the other hand, it tended to survive precisely because struggles for status are a feature of the human condition. In mid-seventeenth-century Logroño, those who opposed the existing elite on the city council tried to base their campaign on the alleged lack of limpieza among the councillors.[82] In personal disputes and rivalries, insults used limpieza as the point of attack. 'Juan Ruiz de Vergara called another' who was competing for a post in a military order, 'commoner'; whereupon 'the other responded that if he was a commoner Ruiz was a converso'. In another case, 'the man called Juan de Clavijo a "Jew", but not because he was one.'[83]

The deliberate use of limpieza to discredit enemies and rivals ended only in discrediting limpieza itself. By the late seventeenth century the few remaining statutes were being openly ignored and contravened in every walk of life. In the reign of the last Habsburg, the converso Manuel José Cortizos, whose father was known to have been a practising Jew, was nevertheless elevated to the rank of marquis; and the Madrid society doctor Diego Zapata continued his career despite being imprisoned twice for judaizing.[84] The only exception to this strange mixture of persecution and tolerance occurred with conversos in the island of Mallorca. As late as the mid-eighteenth century, 'although good Catholics, their sons were denied entrance to the higher ranks of the clergy, and their daughters to the religious orders. They were forced to live in a restricted area in the city and the people calumniated them with the names *Hebreos, Judios, Chuetas*. Guilds, army, navy and public offices were closed to them.'[85] Despite various efforts by the government and some clergy, discrimination continued up to the end of the nineteenth century. In 1858 they were still 'refused all public offices and admission to guilds and brotherhoods so that they were confined to trading. They were compelled to marry among themselves, for no one would contract alliances with them nor would the ecclesiastical authorities grant licences for mixed marriages.'[86]

Echoes of limpieza practice continued in Spain through the eighteenth century. In 1751 a minister, José de Carvajal, thought the treatise of Agustín Salucio so convincing that he ordered a copy of it to be made for himself;[87] and the Count of Floridablanca considered the penalties for impurity unjust because 'they punish a man's sacred action, that is, his conversion to our holy faith, with the same penalty as his greatest crime, that is, apostasy from it'.[88] Despite such criticisms, limpieza as a concept survived the abolition of the Inquisition. So far did purity of blood cease to have any connection with the Jewish problem that in 1788 we find Charles III's minister Aranda using the phrase 'limpieza de sangre' in the sense of purity from any taint of servile office or trade, so that the synonymous term *limpieza de oficios* also came into existence by the end of the century.[89] Official recognition of its need ceased with a royal order of 31 January 1835 directed to the Economic Society of Madrid, but up to 1859 it was still necessary for entrance into the corps of officer cadets. The last official act was a law of 16 May 1865 abolishing proofs of purity for marriages and for certain government posts. The removal of legal barriers could not, evidently, wholly efface an attitude rooted in the practice of centuries. Blanco White, writing in the early 1800s, could recall how in his village near Seville even the children were capable of remembering the shame suffered by a certain family that had had a brush with the Inquisition several generations before.[90]

12

THE INQUISITION AND THE PEOPLE

The causes of the ruin of those people are: ignorance both in faith and in customs; not having anyone to teach them, since the parish priests are like the rest; not having the Inquisition...

Report to Philip II, 1581, on the people in the Spanish Pyrenees[1]

B ecause the Inquisition had been brought into existence to combat the 'heretical depravity' of judaizers, for a long time it paid little attention to other offences. Secondary offences were always listed in accusations, but mainly to back up the main crime. The Aragonese notary Dionis Ginot, burnt in effigy at Saragossa in 1486, was condemned for both Judaism and bigamy. Inevitably, judaizers were frequently accused of a wide range of other offences such as atheism and usury. When dealing with these matters, the Inquisition came into contact with the ordinary misdemeanours of the mass of the Spanish people.

Conversos were often accused of atheism, a perfectly credible accusation in view of the strange cultural situation in which many found themselves, living (in Pulgar's words) 'neither in one law nor the other'. If some were sceptical both of Judaism and of official Christianity, it is not surprising to find conversos like Alvaro de Lillo maintaining in 1524 that 'we are born and die and nothing more', or María de la Mota claiming that 'I'll look after myself in this world and you'll not see me badly off in the next.'[2] Both were tried by the Inquisition of Cuenca. As the Inquisition shifted its attention from conversos, it was to find that sentiments like these were common among Old Christians as well. Indeed, what was particularly alarming was not simply that true religion may have been perverted by heresy, but that in many parts of Spain it could be doubted whether there was any true religion at all.

It was this realization that moved one inquisitor to argue in 1572 that Galicia should have its own Inquisition:

If any part of these realms needs an Inquisition it is Galicia, which lacks the religion that there is in Old Castile, has no priests or lettered persons or impressive churches or people who are used to going to mass and hearing sermons. . . . They are superstitious and the benefices so poor that as a result there are not enough clergy.[3]

'If the Holy Office had not come to this realm', a local priest wrote later, 'some of these people would have been like those in England.'

The judgments of the inquisitor obviously called in question both the nature and the depth of religious belief in Spain. Centuries away from that time, it is difficult to assess the true situation. Over much of Spain Christianity was still only a veneer.[4] The religion of the people remained backward, despite gestures of reform by Cisneros and other prelates. It was still a period of vague theology, irregular religious practice, non-residence of both bishops and clergy, and widespread ignorance of the faith among both priests and parishioners. Over vast areas of Spain – the sierras of Andalusia, the mountains of Galicia and Cantabria, the Pyrenees of Navarre, Aragon and Catalonia – the people combined formal religion and folk superstition in their everyday attempt to survive against the onslaught of climate and mortality. The standard religious unit was the rural parish, coinciding normally with the limits of the village. Over four-fifths of Spain's population lived in this environment, beyond the reach of the big towns to which villagers only went on market days to sell their produce. As religious reformers and inquisitors quickly found out, the rural parishes were close-knit communities with their own special type of religion and their own saints.[5] They were also hostile to any attempt by outsiders – whether clergy or townspeople – to intrude into their way of life.

Clergy recognized that the people were lax in their observance of religion, and woefully ignorant about their faith. In Vizcaya in 1539 an inquisitor reported that 'I found men aged ninety years who did not know the Hail Mary or how to make the sign of the cross'.[6] In the town of Bilbao, stated another in 1547, 'the parish priests and vicars who live there report that one in twelve of the souls there never goes to confession'.[7] In the north of Aragon, reported another colleague in 1549, there were many villages 'that have never had sight of nor contact with Church or Inquisition'.[8]

The Holy Office was far from being the only institution interested in the religious life of Spaniards. Already by the late fifteenth century there had been three major channels through which changes were being introduced into peninsular religion: the reforms of religious orders, instanced on one hand by the remarkable growth of the Jeronimite order and on the other by imposition of the reformist Observance on the mendicant orders;

the interest of humanist bishops in reforming the lives of their clergy and people, as shown for example by the synodal decrees of the see of Toledo under Alonso Carrillo and Cisneros;[9] and the new literature of spirituality exemplified in García de Cisneros' *Exercises in the Spiritual Life* (1500). As elsewhere in Catholic Europe, humanist reformers were well aware that theirs was an elite movement that would take time to filter down into the life of the people. Efforts were, however, being made by the orders. From 1518 the Dominicans were active in the remote countryside of Asturias. The principal impulse to popular missions came from the growth of the Jesuits in the 1540s. At the same time, several reforming bishops tried to introduce changes into their dioceses. It was an uphill task. In Barcelona, Francisco Borja, at the time Duke of Gandía and viceroy of Catalonia, worked hand in hand with reforming bishops but commented on 'the little that has been achieved, both in the time of queen Isabella and in our own'.[10]

From the early century a patient effort of evangelization was made. In America in 1524 a group of Franciscan missionaries, numbering twelve in deliberate imitation of the early apostles, set out to convert Mexico. In 1525 the Admiral of Castile, Fadrique Enríquez, drew up a plan to recruit twelve apostles to convert his estates at Medina de Rioseco to Christianity.[11] The problem in both cases was perceived as being the same: there were 'Indies' of unbelief no less in Spain than in the New World. From the 1540s at least, the Church authorities became concerned not only with the problem of converting the Moriscos but also with that of bringing the unchristianized parts of the country back into the fold. In Santiago in 1543 the diocesan visitor reported that 'parishioners suffer greatly from the ignorance of their curates and rectors'; in Navarre in 1544 ignorant clergy 'cause great harm to the consciences of these poor people'. Many rural parishes lacked clergy, particularly in Catalonia and the Basque country, where ignorance of the language made it difficult for priests to communicate with their flock. The immense confusion of jurisdictions presented a major obstacle: churches, monasteries, orders, secular lords, bishops, towns, the Inquisition – all disputed each other's authority.

The piecemeal efforts to reform religion in the early century were given a unity of purpose by the coming of the Counter Reformation and the issue in 1564 of the decrees of Trent.[12] Concerned to keep religious change under his control, the king in 1565 ordered the holding of Church councils in the principal sees of the monarchy. Subsequent proposals for reform involved the collaboration of the Inquisition.

The visitations made by inquisitors were not an isolated effort. Over the same period many Spanish clergy also began carrying out visitations of their dioceses and religious houses. The tasks did not overlap. Bishops were primarily concerned with getting good clergy and decent churches; the Inquisition was concerned with getting orthodox worshippers. Jesuits made Spain into a mission field. 'This land', a canon of Oviedo wrote in 1568 to Borja, 'is in extreme need of good labourers, such as we trust are those in the Society of Jesus.' Another wrote in the same year: 'There are no Indies where you will suffer greater dangers and miseries, or which could more need to hear the word of God, than these Asturias.'[13] The mission field soon encompassed all of Spain. The Jesuit Pedro de León, who worked all over Andalusia and Extremadura, wrote that 'since I began in the year 1582, and up to now in 1615, there has not been a single year in which I have not been on some mission, and on two or three in some years'. The need was stressed by an earlier Jesuit, reporting on the inhabitants of villages near Huelva: 'many live in caves, without priests or sacraments; so ignorant that some cannot make the sign of the cross; in their dress and way of life very like Indians'.

By venturing into the mission field, the Inquisition began to take cognizance of some offences that had formerly been poorly policed. The diagram of prosecutions in Toledo (given in Chapter Nine) indicates beyond doubt that whereas in the first phase of its history the tribunal had been concerned almost exclusively with conversos, in the next century its attention was focused primarily on Old Christians. Nearly two-thirds of those detained by the Holy Office in this period were ordinary Catholic Spaniards, unconnected with formal heresy or with the minority cultures. The new policy of directing attention to Old Christians cannot be viewed cynically as a desperate move to find sources of revenue. The prosecuted were invariably humble and poor, and the tribunal's financial position was in any case better after the mid-sixteenth century.

The almost entire absence of heresy in much of Spain during the peak years of religious conflict in Europe, can be illustrated by the diagrams on page 259, showing the activity of the Inquisition among Catalans.

The Catalans represented just over half of the cases dealt with by the Inquisition in those years. Yet allegations of heresy were never made against them, only against the French and others of non-Catalan origin. A fifth of the Catalans were accused of sexual offences (mainly bigamy, bestiality and rash statements), 15 per cent were accused of blasphemy ('moral control'),

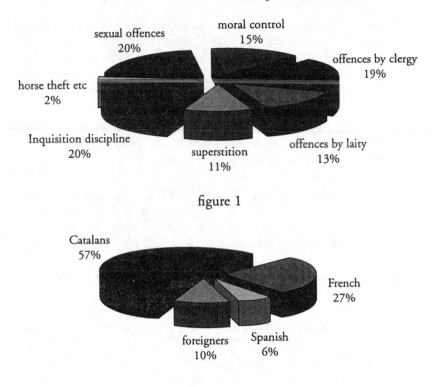

figure 1

figure 2

Tribunal of Barcelona, showing 1,735 cases tried over the years 1578–1635.[14]
Figure 1: the offences of 996 Catalans; figure 2: the 1,735 cases by national category

19 per cent were clergy who had seduced women or said offensive things in their sermons, 13 per cent were laymen who had made anticlerical statements or robbed churches, 11 per cent were people who had dabbled in witchcraft, a further 20 per cent represented officials of the Inquisition who had committed offences or laymen who had impeded them in their duties, and two per cent were guilty of stealing horses.

By its collaboration with the campaigns of bishops, clergy and religious orders among the native population, the Inquisition contributed actively to promoting the religious reforms favoured by the Counter Reformation in Spain. But its role was always auxiliary, and seldom decisive; it helped other Church and civil courts to enquire into certain offences, but seldom claimed exclusive jurisdiction over those offences. As a result, it is doubtful whether its contribution was as significant or successful as that of other branches of the Church. We have already seen that the attempt to make a direct impact through visitations was not fruitful. Because prosecutions in the Inquisition were initiated from below,[15] the tribunal was in a peculiarly strong position to affect and mould popular culture, and the volume of prosecutions in some areas may suggest that it was carrying out its task successfully. The Holy Office, however, suffered from at least one major advantage: it was always an alien body. Bishops, through their parish priests, were directly linked to the roots of community feeling, and were able to carry out a considerable programme of religious change based on persuasion. The Inquisition, by contrast, was exclusively a punishing body. It was operated, moreover, by outsiders (often unable to speak the local language), and though feared was never loved. As a result, its successes were always flawed.

When not directly occupied with the alleged heresies of conversos and Moriscos, the Holy Office during the sixteenth and seventeenth centuries dedicated itself in great measure to disciplining the Old Christian population. It paid attention, above all, to the attitudes, beliefs and actions of lay people; but it also looked at the role of the clergy in these same matters. Its activity was, in the Europe of that day, by no means exceptional. Many Protestant churches, above all the Calvinists, also tried to enforce norms of belief and conduct. Their methods were sometimes harsh, and often criticized as 'inquisitorial'.

The entry of the tribunal into the area of disciplining the laity can be dated with some precision. From the mid-sixteenth century reformist clergy in Spain, inspired in part by the Jesuits, became concerned about the low levels of moral and spiritual life. A few tribunals, led by that of Toledo, showed that they were willing to take action against non-Christian conduct. From the 1560s, prosecutions multiplied.

The overwhelming bulk of prosecutions was for purely verbal offences. The inquisitors themselves classified these as 'propositions'. Ordinary people who in casual conversation, or in moments of anger or stress, expressed sentiments that offended their neighbours, were likely to find themselves denounced to the Inquisition and correspondingly disciplined. A broad range of themes might be involved. Statements about clergy and the Church, about aspects of belief and about sexuality, were among the most common. In particular, persistent blasphemy and affirmations about 'simple fornication' were treated seriously. The offence arose less with the words than with the intention behind them and the implicit danger to faith and morals.

We should be clear about the place of verbal offences in traditional culture. In a large pre-literate age, all important social affirmations – such as personal pledges or court testimony – were made orally. 'Whole aspects of social life', it has been pointed out for mediaeval Europe, 'were only very imperfectly covered by texts, and often not at all ... The majority of courts contented themselves with purely oral decisions'.[16] A man's spoken word was his bond. Judicial evidence consisted of what some people said about others. By the same token, negative declarations – insults, slander – were usually verbal. Verbal statements directed against one's neighbours and against God or religion were treated with severity by both state and Church authorities, for they disturbed the peace of the community. All legal tribunals of the day, including the Holy Office, therefore paid attention to the consequences of the spoken word. The inquisitors never went out looking for 'propositions'. Their job was not the wholly impossible one of regulating what Spaniards said. Nor were they trying to impose a form of social control. In practice, it was members of the public who, out of malice or (very occasionally) out of zeal, took the trouble to report offensive statements. Nearly one-third of the 996 Catalans disciplined by the Inquisition between 1578 and 1635, were in trouble for what they had said rather than for anything they did.[17]

In many cases the Inquisition was called in as a social arbiter, to keep the peace or to resolve disputes. It was a valuable function that more normally was performed by the Church, but which in special cases might call for the intervention of the inquisitors. In 1632, for example, they were asked to intervene in a village near Montserrat (Catalonia), where bitter personal quarrels erupted one day into scandalous conduct at Sunday mass. In the same year they intervened in a quarrel between the parish priest of a village near Girona, and the local familiar. Both men were summoned and ordered to mend their conduct to each other.[18]

The Inquisition joined other Church authorities in demanding more respect for the sacred. Blasphemy, or disrespect to sacred things, was at the time a public offence against God and punishable by both state and Church. In time, the tribunal gave the term a very broad definition, provoking protests by the Cortes of both Castile and Aragon. The Cortes of Madrid in 1534 asked specifically that cases of blasphemy be reserved to the secular courts alone. The Holy Office continued, however, to intervene in the offence, punishing bad language according to the gravity of the context. Blasphemous oaths during a game of dice, sexual advances to a girl during a religious procession, refusal to abstain from meat on Fridays, obscene references to the Virgin, wilful failure to go to mass: these were typical of the thousands of cases disciplined by the Inquisition.[19]

Anticlerical statements were also punished. Among the accused we find Lorenzo Sánchez, notary in 1669 of the Inquisition, saying that 'tithes are ours, and the clergy are our servants, which is why we pay them tithes'. Active hostility to religion fell into the category of sacrilege, as in the case in 1665 of Francesc Dalmau, a farmer of Tarragona, who was accused of going into the pulpit fifteen minutes before mass began and preaching ridiculous and absurd things until the priest appeared; it was also said that he habitually left mass for the duration of the sermon and that he ridiculed Holy Week ceremonies.[20]

The attempt to discipline words and actions was time-consuming, and formed the principal activity of inquisitors during their visitations in this period. The problem was particularly grave in rural areas. In Galicia in 1585, for example, the inquisitors admitted that doubts about the presence of Christ in the sacrament were widespread, but 'more out of ignorance than malice', and that questioning of the virginity of Mary was 'through sheer thickheadedness rather than out of a wish to offend'. They had the case of the man in a tavern who, when a priest present claimed to be able to change bread into the body of Christ, exclaimed in unbelief, 'Go on! God's in heaven and not in that host which you eat at mass!'[21] In Granada in 1595, a shepherd from the village of Alhama claimed not to believe in confession and said to his friends: 'What sort of confession is it that you make to a priest who is as much of a sinner as I? Perfect confession is made only to God.' The inquisitors concluded that 'he seemed very rustic and ignorant and with little or no capacity of understanding', and sent him to a monastery to be educated.[22] Rather than making its sentences lighter because of the low degree of religious understanding in rural areas, the Inquisition increased its punishments in order to achieve greater disciplinary effect. Thus every type of expression, whether mumbled by a drunkard in a tavern or preached by an ignorant priest from the pulpit, that was considered offensive, blasphemous, irreverent or heretical, was – if denounced – carefully examined by the Holy Office. It was at the level of verbal offences rather than heretical acts that the Inquisition came most into contact with the ordinary people of Spain for the greater part of its history.

For those who were arrested instead of being simply penanced during a visitation, there was normally a close examination in the basic elements of belief.[23] Prisoners were asked to recite in Castilian the Our Father, Hail Mary, Credo, Salve Regina and the ten commandments, as well as other statements of belief. The interrogatory seems to have come into use in the 1540s, and provides useful evidence of the extent to which ordinary Spaniards were instructed in the faith. An analysis of 747 interrogations from the tribunal of Toledo[24] suggests, it has been argued, that there was an improvement in knowledge of the essentials during the late sixteenth century. Before 1550 only about forty per cent of those questioned were able to repeat the basic prayers; by the 1590s this had risen to nearly seventy per cent. Since the test was not carried out on the same people in both periods, however, no reliable comparison can be made. In default of statistical proof, we must fall back on simple impressions. Evidence from the Toledo Inquisition papers of the late seventeenth century suggests that levels of religious knowledge were fairly high. Scores of accused from the lower classes and from rural areas enjoyed a basic knowledge of the prayers of the Church, and all were able to recite the Our Father and Hail Mary. Among the few exceptions was Inés López, an illiterate fifty-year-old hospital nurse who in 1664 'crossed herself and recited the Our Father and Hail Mary well in Castilian, but did not know the creed, the Salve, the confiteor, the laws of God and of the Church, the articles of faith or the sacraments; the inquisitor warned her and ordered her to learn them, for she has an obligation to do so as a Christian'.[25]

If an improvement in elementary religious knowledge really happened, it was certainly not general. In parts of Spain that did not enjoy the density of clergy and schools to be found in Madrid and Toledo, ignorance was still the order of the day. The Church set up schools, made sermons obligatory and enforced recitation of prayers at mass. Even in its negative disciplinary role, the Inquisition made some contribution to the evolution of Spanish religion. It attempted to impose on Spaniards a new respect for the sacred, notably in art, in public devotions and in sermons. This can be seen in the other side of the tribunal's disciplining activity: its attempt to control the clergy.

Clergy were encouraged to put their churches in order. Diocesan synods at Granada in 1573 and Pamplona in 1591 were among those which ordered the removal and burial of unseemly church images. The Inquisition, likewise, attempted where it could to censor religious imagery.[26] In Seville in the early seventeenth century it recruited the artist Francisco Pacheco to comment on the suitability of public imagery. The attempt to regulate art was usually futile; there was no obvious way to influence taste.[27] As in other matters, the Inquisition had to put up with denunciations from ignorant people. In 1583 a Franciscan friar from Cervera denounced a painting he said he had seen in a church in Barcelona. It represented John the Baptist as eighty years old and St Elizabeth as twenty years old. This, he said, was incorrect and therefore heretical; and 'I suspect that the man who painted it was Dutch'.[28]

Public devotions were generally under the supervision of the bishops, but here too the Inquisition had a role. It helped to repress devotional excesses, such as credulity about visions of the Virgin.[29] The celebration of pilgrimages and of fiestas such as Corpus Christi was regulated by the episcopate. But written works, such as the text of *autos sacramentales* (plays performed for Corpus), normally had to be approved by the Inquisition, creating occasional conflicts with writers. On the other hand, the tribunal steadfastly refused to be drawn into the debate over whether theatres were immoral and should be banned. It is well known that substantial Counter-Reformation opinion, especially among the Jesuits, was in favour of shutting theatres; and indeed they were shut periodically from 1597 onwards. But theatres were normally under the control of the council of Castile, not of the Holy Office, and the only way the latter could express an opinion was when plays were printed. Even then it kept clear of the theatre, and the major dramatists of the Golden Age were untouched. No play by Lope de Vega, for example, was interfered with until 1801. When the Inquisition did tread into the field, by requiring expurgations (in the 1707 Index) in the Jesuit Camargo's *Discourse on the Theatre* (1689), it explained that the ban was 'until changes are made; but the Holy Office does not by prohibiting this book intend to comment on or condemn either of the opinions on the desirability or undesirability of seeing, reading, writing or performing plays'.[30]

A highly significant area of activity was sermons. No form of propaganda in the Counter Reformation was more widely used than the spoken word, in view of the high levels of illiteracy. Correspondingly, in no other form of communication did the Inquisition interfere more frequently. Sermons were to the public of those days what television is to the twentieth century: the most direct form of control over opinion. The impact of the Holy Office on sermons – among those denounced to it were sermons by Carranza and Fray Francisco Ortiz – was perhaps even more decisive than its impact on printed literature. Bishops normally welcomed intervention by the inquisitors, for they themselves had little or no machinery with which to control some of the absurdities preached from the pulpits of their clergy. Occasionally, inquisitorial intervention took on political tones. The tribunal of Llerena in 1606 prosecuted Diego Díaz, priest of Torre de Don Miguel, for preaching (in Portuguese) that God had not died for Castilians:[31] and the tribunal of Barcelona in 1666 prosecuted a priest of Reus for having declared that 'he would prefer to be in hell beside a Frenchman than in heaven beside a Castilian'.[32] More normally, the problem lay in preachers who got carried away by their own eloquence or who were shaky in their theology, such as the Cistercian Maestro Cortes who in 1683 put the glories of Mary above those of the Sacrament, or the priest in Tuy who on Holy Thursday told his flock that in the Sacrament they were celebrating only the semblance of God, whose real presence was above in heaven.[33]

Both laity and clergy were affected by another major sphere into which the inquisitors intruded: their sexual life. Bishops after the Council of Trent made extensive efforts in Spain to impose the official view on the sanctity of matrimony. In Barcelona after 1570, for example, licences to marry could not be issued without both parties being formally instructed in religion, and the bishops issued decrees against the common practice of young people living together after betrothal. The Inquisition, for its part, enforced post-Tridentine morality by attempting to stamp out the widespread conviction that 'simple fornication' was no sin, and it also prosecuted various sexual offences including bigamy.

'Simple fornication', in early modern Spain, was voluntary intercourse between two unmarried adults.[34] The Inquisition took an interest in this and other sexual questions not because of the sexual act in itself but because of the implied disrespect for the sacrament of matrimony. In pre-Tridentine Spain, a low level of religious awareness and the persistence of traditional moral practices combined to produce far greater sexual freedom among all age groups than is commonly imagined. This was reflected in the remarkably widespread view that sex ('simple fornication') was not wrong if it broke no rules. By extension, concubinage was not wrong, nor was it wrong for an unmarried adult to have sex with a prostitute. The absence of sexual guilt was shared by laity and clergy alike. The inquisitors of Toledo were actively preoccupied with the problem, and from 1573 the Suprema encouraged other tribunals to pursue the matter. In Toledo prosecutions for statements about simple fornication constituted a fifth of all prosecutions in 1566–70, and a quarter in 1601–5.[35] An indication that the imposition of the new morality was, in some measure, an imposition of urban rigour on rural laxity comes from Galicia, where propositions on fornication (such as that of Alonso de Meixide, who maintained 'that in his village it had never been a sin to have carnal intercourse between unmarried men and women') were more commonly found among the peasantry. This was so much the case that the inquisitors there explained in 1585 that 'the reason why we are less strict with fornicators is because we know from experience that most of those we arrest in these lands, where there is a great lack of doctrine especially in the rural areas, speak from stupidity and ignorance and not from a wish to commit heresy'.[36]

In Barcelona in 1599 a man warned a prostitute that what she did was a sin, to which she replied that 'it is no sin since we are both unmarried'. He promptly denounced her to the inquisitors, who dismissed the matter but warned her 'to learn the catechism and come to the Inquisition every two weeks until she has learnt it'. The problem, evidently, arose from the existence of brothels, which operated with public licence in most parts of Spain.[37] Since the city authorities continued to permit them, and they did their best business during religious festivals, all that the clergy could do was to try to convince both prostitutes and their customers of the sinfulness of their actions. It did not help when priests with ulterior motives told attractive women in the parish that 'fornication is no sin'.[38]

The Inquisition continued its sexual campaign with a drive against bigamy. Because the offence was normally punishable in civil and Church courts, there were constant protests against the Inquisition's interference. The Catalan concordia of 1512, for example, laid down that bishops alone should try bigamy cases unless heresy was involved. The Inquisition, however, argued that bigamy implied a measure of heresy, since it questioned the sacredness of matrimony; it therefore continued its activity despite repeated protests from the Cortes of Aragon. Nor was the Holy Office wasting its time on an offence of negligible importance. Bigamy was surprisingly frequent, possibly because it represented, in a society that did not permit divorce, one alternative to an unsatisfactory marriage. In most tribunals, about five per cent of cases tried by the Inquisition were for bigamy. From the mid-sixteenth century five years in the galleys became the standard punishment for men, a much lighter penalty than that meted out by secular courts. Women, no less than men, were frequent bigamists. Many did not feel they were committing wrong. When Francisco Cossio was arrested by the tribunal of Toledo in 1694, the evidence against him included a letter to his parish priest in which he said that 'it is true that marriage, in the opinion of those with whom I have discussed it, is valid; but in my case it was necessary to re-validate it in order to continue it'.[39]

The moral behaviour of clergy had preoccupied Church reformers through the centuries, and bishops were happy to obtain the cooperation of the Inquisition. The Council of Trent had placed clerical reform at the forefront of its programme. Bishops defined the duties of priests strictly and cut back their public role (they could no longer, for example, go to taverns or wedding-feasts). It was inevitably easier to pass decrees than to enforce them, and clergy continued to use their privileged position to disport themselves, break the laws and seduce parishioners.[40] They also continued the long-standing custom of keeping women. The problem, attended to by both Church courts and Inquisition, was insoluble. In the two years 1561–2 the vicar general of Barcelona had to issue fifty-seven warnings to clergy of the diocese over their concubines. In what appear to be the figures for a single year, 1613, the Inquisition of Catalonia disciplined seventy-seven of its familiars and comisarios for various offences. All the thirty-eight comisarios had one offence in common, 'matters to do with women'.[41]

The Inquisition was particularly interested in the problem of solicitation during confession.[42] The confession-box as we know it today did not come into use in the Church until the late sixteenth century, before which there was no physical barrier between a confessor and a penitent, so that occasions for sin could easily arise. The frequent scandals caused Fernando de Valdés in 1561 to obtain authority from Pius IV for the Inquisition to exercise control over cases of solicitation, which were interpreted as heresy because they misused the sacrament of penance. Though accused confessors were usually guilty it is quite clear that the confessant was sometimes to blame. Among curious cases of solicitation was that denounced by an elderly beata in Guissona (Catalonia) in 1581, against an itinerant Franciscan who 'told her she must accept the penance he imposed, and this startled her, and the friar said he had to give her a slap on her buttocks and he made her raise her skirts and gave her a pat on the buttocks and said to her, "Margarita, next time show some shame", and then he absolved her'.[43] In Valencia the parish priest of Beniganim was tried in 1608 for having solicited twenty-nine women, most of them unmarried, 'with lascivious and amorous invitations to perform filthy and immoral acts'.[44]

There were many cases of marginal sexuality in which the Inquisition also intervened. Sodomy was the most significant. Homosexuality in the Middle Ages was treated as the ultimate crime against morality: the standard definitions of it refer to the 'abominable' or the 'unspeakable' crime. The usual punishment was burning alive or, in Spain, castration and stoning to death. Under Ferdinand and Isabella the punishment was changed to burning alive and confiscation of property. Since the mediaeval Inquisition had exercised jurisdiction over sodomy, the Spanish tribunal seems to have begun to do so; but in 1509 the Suprema ordered that no action was to be taken against homosexuals except when heresy was involved. Here a curious split in policy seems to have occurred, because although the tribunals of Castile never again exercised jurisdiction over sodomy, the Inquisition in Aragon now officially adopted powers over this very crime. On 24 February 1524 the pope, Clement VII, issued a brief granting the Inquisition of the realms of Aragon jurisdiction over sodomy, irrespective of the presence of heresy. From this time onwards the Aragonese inquisitors kept their new authority,[45] which they never gave up, despite the typical complaints raised by the Cortes of Monzón in 1533. Aragon was unique in this matter, for not even the Roman Inquisition exercised jurisdiction over sodomy. The punishment laid down by the law, and rigorously enforced by the state, was death by burning.

The Inquisition was harsh to sodomizers (both men and women), but tended to restrict death by burning only to those aged over twenty-five. Minors, who were inevitably a high proportion of those arrested, were normally whipped and sent to the galleys. A certain liberality on the part of the Suprema can be seen in the fact that some death sentences were commuted, and mildness was also shown to clergy, who were always a high proportion of offenders. The treatment of bestiality, usually placed in the same category as homosexuality, altered this picture somewhat, for it was almost invariably punished ruthlessly. Those guilty of it were normally marginalized people of poor intelligence, but this appears not to have helped them. By contrast, some highly placed homosexual offenders were more favourably treated. The most famous case was that of the Valencian grandee Pedro Galcerán de Borja, grand master of the chivalric Order of Montesa.[46] In 1572 he was arrested by the Inquisition of Valencia on charges of sodomy. His case dragged on for some three years; he was heavily fined, but subsequently returned to active political life.

In general, the tribunals of the crown of Aragon had a record of great severity in the matter. The tribunal of Saragossa in the late sixteenth century stands out as exceptional. Between 1571 and 1579 over one hundred men were tried by it on bestiality or homosexuality charges, and at least thirty-six of them were executed. In total, between 1570 and 1630 the inquisitors here handled 543 cases, and executed 102 persons.[47] The tribunals of Barcelona and Valencia were considerably less rigorous. In overall perspective, punishment of sodomy may be seen as a preoccupation of both secular and ecclesiastical courts. In Seville and Madrid, where the Inquisition had no jurisdiction over the offence, secular courts were equally merciless with those it decided to castigate.[48]

The campaign against popular superstition was a broad one, marginal to the Inquisition's concerns in the sixteenth century but more significant in the seventeenth, when in some tribunals it accounted for a fifth of all prosecutions. Popular culture, especially in the rural areas, had always sought unorthodox cures to daily afflictions. Villages had their wise men or wise women (*curanderos*) who could offer medicinal ointments, find lost objects, heal wounded animals, or help a girl to win the affections of her loved one. Cures might take the form of potions, charms, spells or simply advice. It was a subculture that coexisted with and did not try to subvert official Catholicism, although in certain New Christian areas the Christian content of the spells was doubtful.[49] In rural areas the world of magic even entered the Church, with many clergy incorporating folk practices – rites, prayers, offerings, dances – into the normal liturgy. All this was stamped on firmly by reforming bishops, post-Tridentine clergy and the Inquisition. In the process of contrasting the dark world of primitive superstition with the illuminated world of the gospel, unfortunately, preachers and learned men unduly simplified the forces at work and helped to create fears of 'witchcraft'.

The role of the Inquisition in cases of witchcraft was much more restricted than is commonly believed. In 1370 and 1387 the laws of Castile declared that sorcery was a crime involving heresy, for which laymen would be punished by the state and the clergy by the Church. Well after the foundation of the Inquisition, jurisdiction over sorcery and witchcraft remained in secular hands: this is demonstrated by a decree of 1500 which ordered an investigation into sorcery but put the matter into the hands of corregidores and the civil courts.[50] The mediaeval Inquisition had likewise left such questions largely in secular hands, so that no change of policy was involved. By the early sixteenth century, when the Holy Office began enquiries into the heresy of witchcraft, repression of the offence was still normally in the hands of the state courts. The Inquisition's reluctance to interfere was motivated in part by doubts whether any heresy was involved. Certain types of popular superstition, 'sorcery', and the whole range of astrology, were ill-defined areas in which many learned men and clergy themselves dabbled. Astrology, for example, was on the university syllabus at Salamanca, but not until the late sixteenth century did the Inquisition, encouraged by the papacy, attempt to suppress it as a science. Quiroga's Index of 1583 followed Rome in banning occult arts and divination. This move (which preceded Sixtus V's bull of 1585 against magic, *Caeli et terrae*) confirmed the tribunal's concern to wipe out alternatives to the truths of Counter-Reformation religion.

Magic and witchcraft were not treated as a major problem until the late fifteenth century. In 1484 Pope Innocent VIII issued the bull *Summis desiderantes* which first recognized witchcraft as a disease to be rooted out. Two German Dominicans, Kramer and Sprenger, were sent to deal with the superstition in north and central Germany. Two years later they issued their handbook, the *Malleus Maleficarum* (*Hammer of Witches*). In this impressive compilation of case-histories the Dominicans argued that, far from witchcraft being a delusion, it was a practice based on actual commerce with Satan and the powers of darkness, and that witches did in fact eat and devour human children, copulate with devils, fly through the air to their meetings or 'sabbats', injure cattle, raise up storms and conjure down lightning. No book did more in its time to promote a belief it was allegedly fighting. The view of the *Malleus* was supported by subsequent decrees of popes and bishops. In Europe as a whole the witch-craze gained momentum, but there was always an important number of theologians and bishops in both Italy and Spain who considered that talk of flying through the air and copulation with the devil was a delusion to be pitied rather than punished.

Mediaeval secular practice had been that witches should be burnt, and the Inquisition at first followed suit. The Saragossa tribunal burnt one in 1498,[51] another in 1499 and three in 1500. From this time on, cases of witches were regularly reported, the first at Toledo being in 1513 and at Cuenca in 1515. At Cuenca the popular fear was fed by stories of children being found bruised and murdered, 'wherefore it is suspected they were wounded or killed by *xorguinos* and *xorguinas* [wizards and witches]'.[52] From 1520 edicts of faith in both Castile and Aragon began to add magic, sorcery and witchcraft to the list of offences implying heresy. However, the belief in the sabbat was still far from being accepted by learned opinion. At Saragossa in 1521 a theologian declared that the sabbat 'was a delusion and could not have occurred, so no heresy is involved'.

The Inquisition was not the only court concerned with prosecutions. In Navarre for most of the sixteenth century, witchcraft was examined not by the Inquisition but by the state. In 1525, for example, possibly thirty witches were burnt on the orders of the state prosecutor, Balanza, of the royal council of Navarre.[53] As late as 1568 the Suprema ordered the tribunal of Barcelona to hand back to the episcopal court a case of 'incantations'; and in Navarre in 1596 (the case of the witches of Araiz) the local inquisitor ordered that 'it is agreed not to deal with these matters in the Holy Office', and the prosecution reverted to the royal council of Navarre. Here, then, were two important aspects of the role of the Inquisition in witchcraft: some inquisitors were sceptical of the reality of diabolic witchcraft, and the tribunal made no claims to exclusive jurisdiction.

The subsequent policy of the Inquisition arose out of an historic meeting held at Granada in 1526.[54] As a result of the persecution of witches by secular authorities in Navarre that year, Inquisitor General Manrique delegated a committee of ten, which included the jurist Hernando de Guevara and the future Inquisitor General Valdés, to decide whether witches really did go to the sabbat. The discussion paper offered to the meeting stated that 'the majority of jurists in this realm agree that witches do not exist', because of the impossibility of the acts they claimed to do. A vote was taken and a majority – six – of those present decided 'that they really go' to the sabbat; a minority of four, including Valdés and Guevara, voted 'that they go in their imagination'. The meeting also decided that since the homicides to which witches frequently confessed might well be illusory, they should be tried by the Inquisition and not handed over to the civil authorities. If, however, the authorities had proof of homicide, they should be free to act on their own account.

Many of those on the committee were during those same weeks in Granada discussing the conversion of the Moriscos. In general the committee was concerned more to educate the so-called witches than to chastise them. The bishop of Mondoñedo, for example, suggested the following remedies: 'send preachers to those parts, to tell the people of the errors of the witches and how they have been deceived by the devil; the inquisitors and secular judges should proceed with caution; the monasteries of that region should be reformed'. One of the resolutions of the whole committee was that 'great care be taken to preach to them in their language', namely in Basque. The urgent need for rechristianization was noted subsequently by the theologian Alfonso de Castro in his *Adversus haereses* (1534), referring to 'Navarre, Vizcaya, Asturias, Galicia and other parts, where the word of God has seldom been preached. Among these people there are many pagan superstitions and rites, solely because of the lack of preachers.'

The persecution and execution of witches continued but the Holy Office, guided by the 1526 resolutions, played very little part in it. The 1526 decisions were communicated in detail to local tribunals. In Navarre, for example, the inquisitors were given strict instructions not to proceed in such cases without consulting the Suprema and the local judges.[55] Witch persecution is reported to have occurred in Navarre in 1527–8,[56] with the participation of the local inquisitor Avellaneda, and the execution of at least fifty witches on the authority of the royal council of Navarre. Since no convincing documents for this appear to have surfaced, however, it has been suggested that the whole affair was spurious and based on a forgery.[57] When further troubles occurred in Navarre in 1538 the then inquisitor, Valdeolivas, was instructed by the Suprema not to accept the confessions of witches literally, and to 'speak to the principal people and explain to them that the loss of harvests and other ills are either sent by God for our sins or are a result of bad weather, and that witches should not be suspected'.

In other Inquisitions of the peninsula a similar scepticism was the rule. The tribunal of Saragossa executed a witch in 1535,[58] but after protests by the Suprema executed no further witches throughout its history. In 1550 the inquisitor of Barcelona, Diego Sarmiento, was dismissed for having executed witches without referring the cases to the Suprema. The case began in 1548, when a Valencian called Juan Mallet was called in by various towns to identify witches in the Tarragona area. 'They took him through the villages', says a report of the Inquisition, 'and made the people come out of their houses so he could look at them and say which were witches, and those he pointed out were arrested without any other proof or information whatever'. The prosecutions were conducted by local justices. On this occasion inquisitor Sarmiento obtained custody of some of the arrested women, on the excuse that the Inquisition had jurisdiction. He was then faced with the problem of what to do with them. In June 1548 he organized a special conference in the palace of the Inquisition in Barcelona. Those attending were the bishop, the seven judges of the royal Audiencia, and nine leading prelates including the abbot of Montserrat. Sarmiento put to them exactly the question that had been debated in Granada in 1526. He asked whether 'the witches were able to go to the sabbat bodily and assume the form of animals, as some of them claim and confess'. The unanimous conclusion was that 'they were of the opinion that these witches can travel bodily because the devil takes them, and can do the ills and murders they confess and they should be firmly punished'. It was as a result of this decision that Sarmiento allowed seven of the women to be burnt early in 1549.

The Suprema in Valladolid was appalled. In May 1549 it sent inquisitor Francisco Vaca to make a report. Vaca ordered the immediate release of two witches still in the cells. He then sent to Valladolid one of the most damning denunciations of witchcraft persecution ever recorded. Half a century before inquisitor Alonso de Salazar Frias, Vaca condemned the witch-craze. He sent one of the documents in the case to the Suprema, with the comment: 'I believe that most of the other cases are as laughable as this one indicates'. He recommended freeing all those detained in the villages, and the return of all goods confiscated. Inquisitor Sarmiento was dismissed in 1550 for his part in the events. For the rest of its career the Inquisition in Catalonia punished no witches.[59]

Throughout the sixteenth century the Inquisition seems to have maintained its hostility to persecution of witches. Juana Izquierda, tried before the Toledo tribunal in 1591, confessed to taking part in the ritual murder of a number of children. Sixteen witnesses testified that the children had in fact died suddenly, and that Izquierda was reputed to be a witch. What would in any other European country have earned Izquierda the death sentence, in Spain earned her nothing more than abjuration de levi and 200 lashes.[60]

The only significant relapse from this good record occurred in Navarre, where the tribunal had for many years resisted pressure by the royal council to use the death penalty against witches.[61] The explanation for the relapse must be sought not in Spain but in France. Just across the frontier, in the Pays de Labourd, the Bordeaux judge Pierre de Lancre had conducted a horrendous witch-hunt in the autumn of 1609, during which he executed eighty witches. The campaign supplied most of the material for his famous book on witchcraft, *Tableau de l'Inconstance* (1612). The Labourd executions sent a shiver of terror through the Navarrese valleys and created a witch-scare in Spanish territory that swept along with it the inquisitors of Logroño, one of whom was Alonso de Salazar Frias.[62] A great auto de fe was held in the city on Sunday, 7 November 1610. So lengthy were the proceedings that the ceremony had to be continued into the following day. Of the fifty-three prisoners who took part in the auto, twenty-nine were accused of witchcraft and, of these, five were burnt in effigy and six in person.[63] This extreme measure produced a reaction in the Suprema, which in March the next year deputized Alonso de Salazar Frias to visit the relevant districts of Navarre, carrying with him an edict of grace to invite the inhabitants to repudiate their errors. Salazar's mission was to be an epoch-making one. He began work in May 1611 and ended his labours in

January 1612, but only on 24 March did he eventually present his report to the Suprema. During the time of his mission, Salazar declared, he reconciled 1,802 persons. Of these, 1,384 were children between the ages of nine and twelve in the case of girls, and between nine and fourteen in the case of boys. Of the others, 'several were old and even senile, over the age of seventy and eighty'. After close examination of all the confessions and evidence about murders, witch-sabbats and sexual intercourse with devils, Salazar came to his conclusion:

> I have not found the slightest evidence from which to infer that a single act of witchcraft has really occurred. Indeed, my previous suspicions have been strengthened by new evidence from the visitation: that the evidence of the accused alone, without external proof, is insufficient to justify arrest; and that three-quarters and more have accused themselves and their accomplices falsely.
>
> I also feel certain that under present conditions there is no need of fresh edicts or the prolongation of those existing, but rather that in the diseased state of the public mind every agitation of the matter is harmful and increases the evil. I deduce the importance of silence and reserve from the experience that there were neither witches nor bewitched until they were talked and written about.

Salazar's long memorial[64] was a victory neither for humanism nor rationalism, but quite simply for the laws of evidence. As a trained lawyer (letrado) he was interested less in the theological debate over the reality of witchcraft than in the material problem of having to arrest people on the basis of unsupported hearsay. 'There is no use in saying that the evidence for witchcraft is certain. Nobody doubts this. ... The real question is: are we to believe that witchcraft has occurred in a case simply because the witches say so?'

Salazar's report was contested by his colleagues but finally accepted by the Suprema. He was helped powerfully by the fact that, as he himself pointed out, the Inquisition since 1526 had turned its face against the traditional death sentence for witches; that more and more letrados, rather than theologians, were becoming inquisitors; and that the best informed opinion in Spain was in favour of scepticism over the reality of witchcraft. Even before the mission to Navarre, the Inquisitor General had commissioned a report from the scholar Pedro de Valencia. In his report, dated April 1611,[65] Valencia was careful not to deny the reality of witchcraft, but his conclusions suggested that there was a strong element of mental sickness in the Navarre events, and that exceptional care must be taken to prove offences. 'The accused must be examined first to see if they are in their right mind or possessed or melancholic.' Their conduct 'is more that of madmen than of heretics, and should be cured with whips and sticks rather than with sanbenitos'. Finally Valencia advised that 'one must look for evidence, according to law, of an offence having been committed'.

On 29 August 1614 the Suprema issued authoritative instructions that reaffirmed the policy of 1526 and were to remain the principal guide to the future policy of the Inquisition. Drawn up in thirty-two articles, the instructions adopted Salazar's scepticism towards the claims of witches, and advised caution and leniency in all investigations. Belated justice was done to the victims of the Logroño auto of 1610: their sanbenitos were not to be exposed, and no stigma was to attach to them or to their descendants. Although the Inquisition was still obliged to follow European opinion and regard witchcraft as a crime, in practice all testimony to such a crime was rejected as delusion, so that Spain was saved from the ravages of popular witch-hysteria and witch burnings at a time when they were prevalent all over Europe.

The decision of 1614 benefited those accused but placed the Inquisition in an ambiguous position in theory and in practice: in theory, because it admitted that diabolism was possible but denied any single instance of it; in practice, because it became reluctant to intervene in witchcraft cases and often conceded jurisdiction to the civil authorities. The Inquisition reverted to its practice of not burning, but continued to prosecute all types of superstition with vigour. In many tribunals in the seventeenth century this was the largest category of offences after 'propositions'.

Two cases from Barcelona show how the new attitude worked.[66] In 1665 the tribunal uncovered a group of middle-class diabolists who recited black masses, conjured up devils and beheaded a goat at one of their ceremonies. A priest in the group was suspended from holy orders for five years, and a surgeon was flogged and banished for the same length of time. In the same year Isabel Amada, a widow of Mataró, was denounced by shepherds who had refused to give her alms. Within three days, they said, 'two of their mules and thirty sheep died, and the accused claimed that she had done it with the help of the devil'. She was set free by the inquisitors. Such lenient verdicts would have been unthinkable in other European countries.

Had all tribunals, Church and secular, behaved in this way, the prosecution of superstition would have become in Spain what the Inquisition intended it to be: a means of disciplining the people into orthodox Christianity. The control of much jurisdiction over witchcraft by the secular power meant, however, that – contrary to what is frequently affirmed – witches continued to be executed in Spain. In the kingdom of Aragon, for example, the civil authorities continued in full possession of their jurisdiction over witchcraft and the Inquisition seems to have made no more than token efforts to assert its claims. At least as many witches were tried before non-inquisitorial courts in Upper Aragon in the early seventeenth century as before the Inquisition.[67] Witches in Aragon were hanged, not burnt, by the civil courts, but the number of those executed is not known. In Catalonia, likewise, executions continued. In the jurisdiction of Vic, forty-five witches were sentenced by the civil authorities in 1618–22. Dozens of witches were hanged in several towns throughout Catalonia, including some in the Pyrenees. The royal courts tried in vain to intervene: their efforts were blocked by the local and baronial jurisdictions in which the executions took place. The rector of the Jesuits in Barcelona, Pere Gil, penned a powerful plea to the viceroy to intervene, but with little result. The incidents declined in number after 1627.[68]

We have seen that a good part of the Inquisition's zeal for religion was little more than active xenophobia. This was ironic, since Spain's imperial expansion took thousands of Spaniards abroad and brought them in touch with the rest of the world on a scale unprecedented in their history. The imperial experience did nothing to change the xenophobia of the inquisitors. From 1558 the Lutheran scare was used as a disincentive against contact with foreigners. A common accusation levelled against many accused was that they had been to a *tierra de herejes*, which in inquisitorial parlance meant any country not under Spanish control.

All properly baptized persons, being *ipso facto* Christians and members of the Catholic Church, came under the jurisdiction of the Inquisition. Foreign heretics, therefore, appeared from time to time in autos held in Spain. The burning of Protestants at Seville in the mid-1500s shows a gradual increase in the number of foreigners seized, a natural phenomenon in an international seaport. Of those appearing in the Seville auto of April 1562, twenty-one were foreigners – nearly all Frenchmen. At the auto of 19 April 1564 six Flemings were 'relaxed' in person, and two other foreigners abjured de vehementi. At the one on 13 May 1565 four foreigners were 'relaxed' in effigy, seven reconciled and three abjured de vehementi. One Scottish Protestant was 'relaxed' at the Toledo auto of 9 June 1591, and another, master of the ship *Mary of Grace*, at the auto of 19 June 1594.

The harvest reaped by the Inquisition was by now greater from foreign than from native Protestants. In Barcelona from 1552 to 1578, the only 'relaxations' of Protestants were of fifty-one French people. Santiago in the same period punished over forty foreign Protestants. These figures were typical of the rest of Spain. The details given by Schäfer show that up to 1600 the cases of alleged Lutheranism cited before the tribunals of the peninsula totalled 1,995, of which 1,640 cases concerned foreigners. Merchants from countries hostile to Spain ran the risk of having their crews arrested, their ships seized and their cargoes confiscated. Of the two Englishmen 'relaxed' at the great Seville auto of 12 December 1560, one, Nicholas Burton, was a ship's master whose cargo was appropriated by the authorities.[69]

Foreign visitors who publicly showed disrespect to acts of Spanish religion (refusing to take off one's hat, for example, if the Sacrament passed in the street) were liable to arrest by the Inquisition. This happened so frequently that nations trading to Spain made it their primary concern to secure guarantees for their traders before they would proceed any further with commercial negotiations. England, being a market for Spanish materials, secured easier terms than might have been expected. In 1576 the Alba-Cobham agreement settled the position of the Inquisition *vis-à-vis* English sailors. The tribunal was allowed to act against sailors only on the basis of what they did *after* arriving in a Spanish port. Any confiscation was to be confined to the goods of the accused alone, and was not to include the ship and cargo, since these did not usually belong to him. Despite the outbreak of hostilities between England and Spain over the Dutch question, the agreement of 1576 continued to hold good for at least two decades after.[70] When peace eventually came under James I, the agreement was incorporated into the treaty of 1604.

In general, since the late sixteenth century the authorities in Spain's principal ports had turned a blind eye to the trading activities of foreign Protestants, mainly English, Dutch and Germans. The peace treaties with England in 1604 and with the Dutch in 1609 merely accepted the situation. Some French merchants continued to fall foul of the tribunal.[71] In broad terms, however, the resolution of the council of state in 1612, accepted by the Inquisition, was that English, French, Dutch and Bearnese Protestant merchants not be molested, 'provided they cause no public disturbance'.[72] Commercial realities imposed the need for toleration.

England secured a renewal of these guarantees after the war of 1624–30, in article nineteen of the peace treaty of 1630, which promised security to English sailors 'so long as they gave no scandal to others'. The proviso was not to the liking of the government of Oliver Cromwell, which took power in mid-century. In 1653 he proposed to Spain a treaty of alliance which would have given Englishmen virtual immunity from the Inquisition. The relevant articles would have allowed English subjects to hold religious services openly, to use Bibles freely, to be immune from confiscation of property and to have some Spanish soil set apart for the burial of English dead. So great was his prestige that the Spanish council of state was quite ready to concede the articles,[73] but the proposal was rejected because of the firm opposition of the Suprema, which refused to allow any compromise.

Foreign Protestants did not normally appear in autos de fe at the end of the seventeenth century, but the pressure on them continued, especially in the ports. Catalonia, for example, experienced the presence of foreigners in the form of sailors in the ports, soldiers in foreign regiments of the Spanish army and French immigration across the Pyrenees. The Barcelona tribunal had regular numbers of 'spontaneous' self-denunciations from foreigners wishing to become Catholics. In the 1670s and 1680s there were about a dozen cases a year, often outnumbering prosecutions of native Spaniards. In the record year 1676 no fewer than sixty-four foreigners came before the Inquisition there, renounced the heresies they had professed and asked to be baptized.[74] There were still unfortunate cases – such as the twenty-three-year-old Englishman who was arrested for public misbehaviour in Barcelona in 1689 and died in the cells of Inquisition – but in general the Holy Office was both lenient and tolerant. It is significant that after the long war of the Spanish Succession from 1705 to 1714, when thousands of heretical (Huguenot, English and German) troops had been captured by Spanish forces on Spanish territory, not a single fire was lit by the Inquisition to burn out any heresy that might have entered the country.

The fate of foreigners who fell into the hands of the Holy Office may best be examined in the well-documented history of the tribunal in the Canary Islands. The Canaries were a regular port of call for Englishmen, not only for direct trade (in wines) but also because they were a convenient halt before the long voyage across the Atlantic to Spanish America and the South Sea. Between 1586 and 1596 in particular, English traders and sailors were subjected to irregular persecution by the Spanish authorities, then at war with England. An auto de fe held at Las Palmas on 22 July 1587 included for the first time fourteen English seamen, one of whom – George Gaspar of London – was 'relaxed' in person, the only Englishman ever to suffer death in this tribunal. The next public auto, on 1 May 1591, included the burning of the effigies of four English seamen, two of whom had been reconciled in the previous auto. The auto de fe of 21 December 1597, apparently the last in which Englishmen appeared,[75] included eleven English sailors. This is not, of course, the total number of Englishmen who were captured by the Inquisition. The lists show that from 1574 to 1624 at least forty-four Englishmen were detained in the cells of the Canaries Inquisition. Many saved their skins by 'spontaneous' conversion. During the seventeenth century at least eighty-nine foreigners became Catholics in this way, and in the eighteenth century 214 did, of whom the English were a majority.[76]

The English sailors were particularly vulnerable to the Inquisition because many of them were old enough to have been baptized in the true faith under Queen Mary, and young enough to have conformed without difficulty to the Elizabethan settlement. They were consequently apostates and heretics, ideal material for the tribunal.

The long history of tolerance to traders, however, influenced the tribunal to take a more realistic attitude towards foreigners. When war broke out again in 1624 between England and Spain, the resident English were left unmolested, thanks to the inquisitors in the Canaries. Commercial reasons were the main motive behind the anxiety of the authorities not to persecute foreigners unnecessarily. The moderate attitude seems to have encouraged the traders, for by 1654 the number of Dutch and English residents in Tenerife alone was put at 1,500.[77] This happy state of affairs was almost immediately shattered by Cromwell's clumsy aggression against Hispaniola in 1655. The Spanish authorities undertook reprisals against the community of English merchants in the peninsula, who, forewarned of the Hispaniola expedition, got out of the country before the blow fell. Officials charged with carrying out the reprisals arrived too late. In Tenerife the confiscations 'in this island, in Canary, and in La Palma are of small consideration'. In the port of Santa María 'there was one Englishman, no more'. In Cadiz only the English Catholics remained. In San Lucar 'they were so forewarned that nothing considerable remains', and 'the majority of them and the richest have sold everything and left with the English fleet'.[78] They eventually came back, as they always did. By that time Protestant merchants had little to fear from the wrath of the Inquisition, which had grown to respect the existence of bona fide trading communities where religion counted far less than the annual profit. To this extent the Holy Office was moving out of an intolerant age into a more liberal one.

A kaleidoscopic survey of the Holy Office, such as the present one, runs the risk of presenting a view only from above. The presence, and therefore the impact, of the Inquisition appears unquestionable. It is logical to conclude (as some do)[79] that the Inquisition imposed fear and uniformity throughout Spain. The tribunal itself never ceased to proclaim its successes. At the auto de fe in Barcelona in 1602, reported the inquisitors with considerable satisfaction (but doubtful veracity), 'our procession caused terror in the people'.[80] Many historians have assumed that the Inquisition was an effective weapon of social control, keeping the population in its place and maintaining social and religious norms.

There is little evidence to support this contention. In their daily lives Spaniards, like others in Europe, had to deal with many authorities set over them. They contended with secular lords, royal officials, Church personnel, religious communities, and urban officials. The Holy Office also was one of these authorities. But except at times when the inquisitor came round on his visitation, the people had little contact with him. The presence of a local familiar or comisario did not affect the situation; their job was to help the inquisitor if he came, not to act as links in an information network.

The likely degree of contact, in a world where (unlike our own today) control depended on contact, is in effect a good guide to whether the Inquisition managed to have any impact on the ordinary people of Spain. The evidence from the tribunal of Catalonia is beyond question.[81] No proper visitations were made here by the inquisitors during the early sixteenth century. In the second half of the century sixteen visitations in all were made, but they were always partial visits done in rotation, and limited to the major towns. These towns might be visited once every ten years. The people out in the countryside, by contrast, were lucky if they managed to see an inquisitor in their entire lives. There were large areas of the principality that had no contact with the Inquisition throughout its three centuries of history. Three-quarters of all Catalans prosecuted by the Inquisition in the years 1578–1635 came from the capital, Barcelona. The activity of the tribunal, in short, was restricted to the city (where its influence was notoriously small). Out in the countryside it had neither activity nor influence. The degree of social control was negligible.[82]

After generations of living with the Holy Office the people accepted it. No demands for its abolition were made before the age of Enlightenment. In many cases, the existence of the Inquisition was even welcomed, for it offered a disciplinary presence not often found in the society of that time. People with grudges or complaints, particularly within families and within communities, could take their problems to the tribunal and ask for a solution. 'You watch out', an angry housewife in Saragossa screamed at her inn-keeper husband (in 1486), 'or I'll accuse you to the inquisitor of being a bad Christian!'[83] A court of this type could conceivably be welcomed by some Spaniards even in the twentieth century.[84] Acceptance was probably greater in the cities, where the numerous clergy gave it active support in their sermons and where the tribunal from time to time put on autos de fe to reaffirm its role. But even in the unexplored countryside it could sometimes have a positive role to play. The documents record many cases of village conflict and tension that in the last resort looked for a solution to one or other of the disciplinary tribunals in the city.

Hostility to the tribunal was, for all that, commonplace. There were three main reasons for this. First, the Inquisition was a disciplinary body, and therefore (like any similar body, even in the twentieth century) resented by ample sectors of the population. Its policing duties were modest, but excited the hostility of other policing officers from other jurisdictions; and of those who by definition did not like police intrusion. In moments of anger, such people could not refrain from cursing the Holy Office. Where possible, the Inquisition tried to protect its reputation against them. The 'propositions' that they prosecuted offer useful evidence of what some Spaniards felt. The archives contain hundreds of statements expressing rage or contempt, ample material with which to prove the hostility of the Spanish people. 'I don't give a damn for God or for the Inquisition!' 'I care as much for the Inquisition as for the tail of my dog!' 'What Inquisition? I know of none!' 'I could take on the whole Inquisition!' 'The Inquisition exists only to rob people!' The multitude of oaths, however, no more prove hostility than their absence in the late eighteenth century proves support. Enmity to the tribunal was common, but most oaths were uttered out of habit or when drunk or in moments of anger or stress. The brawling and the swearing demonstrate a lack of respect, but otherwise prove little more than that Spaniards have never inertly accepted the political or religious systems imposed on them.

The second reason for hostility was when jurisdictions clashed. No other tribunal in all Spanish history provoked so much friction with every other authority in both Church and state. The conflicts were particularly intense in the realms of the crown of Aragon. In Catalonia the inquisitors complained more than once, and apparently with good reason, that the Catalans wanted to get rid of them. In 1632 the inquisitors of Barcelona complained that 'among the travails suffered by this Inquisition and its officials the most serious are the contempt and scorn they face in public and in private, on every occasion and in every way'.[85] But, despite all the fury, its opponents never once questioned the religious rationale of the Holy Office.

In *ancien régime* Spain, no popular movements attacked the Inquisition and no rioters laid a finger on its property. The exceptions, to be found only in the fuero provinces of Spain, are notable. In 1591 the tribunal of Saragossa intervened rashly (as we have seen) in the Antonio Pérez affair and was directly attacked by the angry mob. In the revolutionary Barcelona of 1640 the mob, informed that Castilian soldiers were lodged in the Inquisition, burst into the building, smashed down the doors, threatened the inquisitors and took away documentation.[86] Especially in the crown of Aragon, the tribunal never ceased to be regarded as a foreign institution.

The third reason for hostility was the frequently alien character of the tribunal. The inquisitors were Castilians, unable to speak the languages or dialects of the rural communities into which they intruded. They were city men, unwelcome in the quite different environment of country villages. Their visits, we have seen, were very rare indeed. In contrast to the welcome they usually gave to wandering preachers, villages were seldom pleased to see an inquisitor. In sixteenth-century Galicia, a parish priest begged his congregation to be deaf and dumb when the inquisitors visited. 'Let us be very careful tomorrow', he said, 'when the inquisitor comes here. For the love of God, don't go telling things about each other or meddle in things touching the Holy Office.'[87] In seventeenth-century Catalonia the parish priest of Aiguaviva publicly rebuked the comisarios of the Inquisition when they came to check the baptismal records in order to carry out a proof of limpieza. 'He told them not to write lies, and that it would not be the first time they had done so, by falsifying signatures and other things'.[88]

The effective contact of the tribunal with the people was at all times, outside the big towns, marginal. In sixteenth-century Mexico, '95 per cent of the population never had any contact with the Inquisition'.[89] A similar situation can be found in much of Spain. In Catalonia, 'in over 90 per cent of the towns, during more than three centuries of existence, the Holy Office never once intruded'.[90] We have seen already that the rarity of visits through-out the countryside by inquisitors in effect cut off much of Spain from contact with the Inquisition. In the heartland of Castile, by contrast, com-munications were better and contact more effective. But even in Toledo five times as many townspeople as peasants were tried by the tribunal,[91] tes-timony to the difficulties of dominating the much larger rural population. Though the Inquisition was singularly effective in its initial campaign against alleged judaizers, therefore, there is good reason to conclude that it failed when it turned to matters that were not directly questions of heresy.

13

VISIONS OF SEFARAD

In a nation like Spain there are many nations, so intermingled that the original one can no longer be recognised. Israel, by contrast, is one people among many, one even though scattered, and in all places separate and distinct.

Isaac Cardoso, *The Excellence of the Jews*, 1679[1]

The large number of judaizing cases with which the Inquisition dealt in the early years of the sixteenth century marked the end of the generation of ex-Jews who had had direct acquaintance with the Mosaic law taught before 1492. Anyone punished for judaizing in 1532 at the age of fifty would have been ten years old in 1492, old enough to remember the Jewish environment and practice of his family. Approximately after the 1530s, this generation and its memories disappeared. The figures suggest that from 1531 to 1560 possibly only three per cent of the cases dealt with by the tribunal of Toledo concerned judaizers.[2]

For the rest of the sixteenth century Spain was no longer conscious of a judaizing problem. By the 1540s conversos had virtually disappeared from Inquisition trials.[3] In many sectors of public life, particularly in the early part of the century, there was little discrimination against conversos. Samuel Abolafia, who returned voluntarily to Spain in 1499 and became a Christian as Diego Gomez, became integrated into Old Christian society despite a brush with the Inquisition.[4] Feeling against Jews showed itself more in prejudice than in persecution. Antisemitism existed, but the discriminatory statutes of limpieza were losing their force and had little impact on conversos. There were attempts to restrict socially damaging aspects of antisemitism. It was, for example, a common insult in Spain to call someone a Jew. The Inquisition tried to stamp on the practice. The aggrieved party could take his case to the Holy Office as the body best qualified to examine his genealogy, disprove the accusation publicly, and thus uphold his 'honour'. By the 1580s, as the growing feeling against the doctrine of limpieza shows, antisemitic prejudice was itself being called in question. It was a key argument of Salucio that judaizers had almost totally disappeared from the realm, 'and although there are signs that some remain, it is undeniable that in general there is no fear or suspicion of them'. Other writers admitted that most conversos were now peaceful and reliable Christians. Diego Serrano de Silva in 1623 argued: 'we see by the experience of many years that families of this race are at heart thorough Christians, devout and pious, giving their daughters to convents, their sons to the priesthood'.

Many conversos, of course, retained their hatred for the Inquisition. In 1528 in Catalonia the tribunal arrested a man for distributing a manuscript which accused the Inquisition of lies, perjury, murder, robbery and raping women in prison. In 1567 in Badajoz the inquisitors seized a notice that had been posted up in public and which stated that 'the property of every New Christian is at risk, six years from today not a single one will be left to arrest'.[5]

But by and large the conversos were integrated. In 1570 when an inquisitor of Cuenca was asked to go on a visit of his district, he preferred not to go to the areas of Castile, 'where, by the grace of God, it is believed that there are no heretics', but instead to visit the Morisco areas near Aragon.[6] Most conversos felt no affinity with their distant origins. Occasional problems might be caused by the limpieza regulations, but these were commonly overcome. In Fregenal de la Sierra (Extremadura) most of the town were conversos and therefore conveniently swore to each other's Old Christian credentials. The inquisitor reported that the people apparently believed sincerely that baptism made one automatically into an Old Christian. During an inquisitorial visit in 1576, he said, over four hundred false witnesses to proofs of limpieza were found, and 'most of those who go to America from this district are conversos'.[7] Higher up in elite society, where there was more contempt for limpieza, false testimonials were winked at and some conversos had little difficulty in making their way. The wealthy Márquez Cardoso family, for example, employed agents of Old Christian origin and noble rank to swear to their limpieza.[8]

There continued, however, to be judaizers. For the most part, it is difficult to describe them as Jews, since their heresies owed more to strong family and community traditions than to active Jewish belief.[9] Most external signs of Judaism had disappeared. Circumcision was no longer practised, since children were liable to discovery; synagogues or meeting-places were no longer possible; the sabbath was normally not observed, though token observances might be made or observance even moved to a different day; the great festivals of the year were not celebrated, though there appears to have been a general preference to celebrate at least one – the fast of Esther. Many learnt to eat the forbidden foods since there was no better way of dissimulation. Judaizers of the late sixteenth and early seventeenth century were often unrecognizable as Jews. Those who clung fast to their identity, nevertheless, maintained an ineradicable faith in the one God of Israel, passed down from father to son the few traditional prayers they could remember, and used the Catholic Old Testament as their basic reading. Occasionally, the capacity to conserve age-old beliefs and customs was astonishing. One such survival group was discovered in 1588 in the heart of Castile, in and around the town of Quintanar de la Orden (La Mancha).[10] Over a period of several months, culminating in autos de fe in 1590–2, a hundred people here of pure Castilian origin were identified and punished as judaizers. They managed, without access to outside contact or their own sacred texts, to preserve faithfully (in Castilian) the key rituals and prayers of Judaism.

A number of other cases came to light in the south of the peninsula in the same decade. In 1591 a number of denunciations were made in the tribunal of Granada. 'In this case', the inquisitors reported, 'up to now 173 judaizers have been discovered, and every day more are being discovered'.[11] The accused were natives of the region and mostly women. Their Mosaic practices were purely residual, transmitted stubbornly over two generations by the women.[12] A large auto was held in Granada on 27 May 1593, with 102 penitents, eighty-nine of them alleged judaizers. Further accused from the same case were displayed in the auto there on 25 October 1595, with seventy-seven penitents of whom fifty-nine were alleged judaizers. An auto at Seville in 1595 included eighty-nine judaizers.[13]

However, the high degree of integration of conversos calls seriously in question any attempt to identify them as a separate entity within the population.[14] The Inquisition of this period, if we may judge by its edicts of faith, had a somewhat confused image of the type of offence committed by alleged judaizers. In the late fifteenth century and early sixteenth, edicts issued by distinct tribunals listed the offences that could be identified. By around 1630 the Holy Office settled for a single standard edict, common to all the tribunals.[15] The text of this edict, whether through the sloth or the ignorance of the inquisitors, described judaizing practices as they may possibly have been identified around the year 1490, but which a century and a half later were evidently no longer practised as stated. The edicts of the seventeenth century described full Jewish customs, when common sense indicated that only an utterly crazy judaizer would have openly practised any of them. A typical edict, evidently using text dating from a century before, contains the following passage inviting people to identify judaizers in their midst:

> If you know or have heard of anyone who keeps the Sabbath according to the law of Moses, putting on clean sheets and other new garments, and putting clean cloths on the table and clean sheets on the bed on feast-days in honour of the Sabbath, and using no lights from Friday evening onwards; or if they have purified the meat they are to eat by bleeding it in water; or have cut the throats of cattle or birds they were eating, uttering certain words and covering the blood with earth: or have eaten meat in Lent and on other days forbidden by Holy Mother Church; or have fasted the great fast, going barefooted that day; or if they say Jewish prayers, at night begging forgiveness of each other, the parents placing their hands on the heads of their children without making the sign of the cross or saying anything but, 'Be blessed by God and by me'; or if they bless the table in the Jewish way; or if they recite the psalms without the *Gloria Patri*; or if any woman keeps forty days after childbirth without entering a church; or if they circumcise their children or give them Jewish names; or if after baptism they wash the place where the oil and chrism was put; or if anyone on his deathbed turns to the wall to die, and when he is dead they wash him with hot water, shaving the hair off all parts of his body.

The references made, such as to the giving of Jewish names or the eating of 'meat prepared by Jewish hands', were evidently out of touch with reality, since Jewish names and Jewish butchers had not existed in Spain for a century and a half.[16]

The genuineness of some of the 'judaizing' of these years must, therefore, be called in question. The inquisitors were only too ready to identify a heresy where there was none. Quite apart from recording the animosity of hostile and ignorant witnesses, the Inquisition trial papers also record attitudes and statements that were not peculiar to conversos but were shared by broad sections of the Christian population. Insults to saints, the Virgin, priests, the mass, and Christ himself, were (as we have seen) commonplace among the Spanish people. It is possible that such insults were among the few options available to disgruntled conversos.[17] But they were no evidence of a tendency to judaize.

The degree of integration can be seen precisely in contexts which appear to show the contrary. The groups of families involved in the autos de fe in Granada in the 1590s were all from the well-to-do bureaucracy, occupying important posts in the city council and the high court (Chancillería). Though scores of their relatives were punished by the Inquisition (mostly the women), not a single male member of these families lost his job.[18] As in most of Spain, limpieza rules were a dead letter. The men freely went to university and occupied posts in every major institution. The 1590 cases were a mere hiccup. As the city of Granada stated, the hope was that soon all this would be a mere memory, as in the cases at Murcia in the 1560s, of which 'not a trace remains'.[19]

The relatively undisturbed life of Spanish conversos was transformed from the late 1580s by an influx of Portuguese conversos. Of the refugees who fled from Spain before and during 1492, a great number went to Portugal, swelling its Jewish community to about a fifth of the total population. Portugal did not yet have an Inquisition, so the trials now suffered by the Spanish exiles who had gone there were caused by the crown, the clergy and the populace. The permission which had been granted to Jews to reside (at the price of nearly a ducat a head) was limited to six months only, after which they were offered the same alternatives of conversion or expulsion. When the time was up the richer Jews bought themselves further toleration, but the poorer were not so lucky and many went into exile again, over the sea and across to Africa. The final imposition of conversion on the Jews in Portugal was modified in 1497 by the promise not to persecute conversos for a period of twenty years. Although the crown benefited from tolerating this active minority, communal hatreds were soon stirred up, and in 1506 Lisbon witnessed the first great massacre of New Christians. Despite such outbreaks, there was little official persecution until about 1530, so that the conversos in Portugal were flourishing undisturbed at precisely the time that their generation was being rooted out in Spain. In 1532 King João III determined to introduce an Inquisition on the Spanish model. The institution of this tribunal was delayed only by the powerful support commanded in Rome by wealthy New Christians.[20] Eventually in 1540 the Portuguese Inquisition celebrated its first auto de fe; but its powers were still not fully defined, thanks to the vacillation of Rome and the enormous bribes offered periodically by the conversos. Only on 16 July 1547 did the pope issue the bull which finally settled the structure of an independent Portuguese Inquisition.

The presence of a native Inquisition was one of the factors provoking a mass emigration of Portuguese New Christians back into Spain, which for many of them had been the land of their birth. In the three tribunals of the Portuguese Inquisition at Lisbon, Evora and Coimbra, there were between 1547 and 1580 thirty-four autos de fe, with 169 'relaxations' in person, 51 in effigy and 1,998 penitents.[21] This activity, for a country with so large a percentage of Jewish descendants, was arguably less intense than in the early years of the Spanish Inquisition; but had an impact nevertheless on those affected. The move of conversos back to Spain began around 1570,[22] before the union of the crowns in the person of Philip II in 1580. The union, which had as one consequence an increase in inquisitorial rigour, probably accelerated the return movement. In 1586 the cardinal Archduke Albert of Austria, who was also governor of Portugal, was named Inquisitor General of the country, with the result that within nineteen years (1581–1600) the three Portuguese tribunals held fifty autos de fe, in forty-five of which there was a total of 162 'relaxations' in person, 59 in effigy and 2,979 penitents.[23] It is small wonder that by the end of the reign of Philip II the Spanish Inquisition was alarmed to discover within Spain the existence of a new threat, this time from the Portuguese who had fled from their own Inquisition.

Having seen the hostility of the Inquisition to racial minorities, especially the Moriscos, and to foreigners in general, but especially to the French, it would be rash to imagine that the tribunal viewed Portuguese immigrants with equanimity. There is every reason to consider that their position as foreigners, even more than their lineage, made them an immediate focus of attention.

From the 1590s judaizers of Portuguese origin began to make a significant appearance in trials. In 1593 the inquisitors of Cuenca, alerted no doubt by the recent case of native judaizers in Quintanar, began a far-reaching enquiry into a group of Portuguese families in Alarcón.[24] In the 1600s the preponderance of Portuguese judaizers became clear and undeniable. To take a few examples at random: in the auto at Córdoba on 2 December 1625, thirty-nine of the forty-five judaizers penanced were Portuguese, and the four 'relaxations' were all Portuguese; another auto there on 21 December 1627 included fifty-eight judaizers, all of them Portuguese, and Portuguese represented all the eighteen 'relaxations', of which five were in person. An auto at Madrid on 4 July 1632 featured seventeen Portuguese among the forty-four accused, and similarly one at Cuenca on 29 June 1654 featured eighteen of the same nation out of fifty-seven cases. Finally, in the Córdoba auto of 3 May 1655 three out of five judaizers 'relaxed' were Portuguese, as were seven out of nine penanced, and almost all the forty-three reconciled were of the same nationality.[25]

The ebb of Castilian Jewry was replaced by a flood-tide of Portuguese New Christians who fed the flames and coffers of the Spanish monarchy. Of over two thousand two hundred persons prosecuted for judaizing by the Spanish tribunals between the 1660s and 1720s, 43 per cent were Portuguese by origin.[26]

Spanish converso families of the earlier generation were by now merged into Castilian society. The families around Ciudad Rodrigo, for example, were dedicated to the soil and to herding.[27] By contrast the newer immigrants, who had not yet had the opportunity of integrating, earned their living in commerce and the professions. The Portuguese newcomers around Ciudad Rodrigo and Badajoz were traders and administrators of taxes. Of 343 known occupations among judaizers tried in Granada during the seventeenth century, just over half were traders, with shopkeeping, medicine and tax-collecting figuring prominently among the professions.[28] In the Cuenca area the new immigrants were small traders and dealers in money. Their aptitude for business prompted Spaniards in the area to claim, in a phrase that explains much about the subsequent persecution, that they were 'very rich and grasping people' and 'ate in style and did much business'.[29]

The return of the Portuguese signified the emergence of a new tendency in the life of peninsular Jews. Till then the general trend had been towards emigration or integration. Since well before 1492, conversos and Jews had fled abroad. Now the yearning for Sefarad brought a new generation back to the land of their fathers.[30] Some returned from abroad, some simply crossed over into Spain from Portugal. Several lived to regret having come back. One such was Baltasar López, arrested in Santiago in 1677, who regretted that he had not stayed in Bayonne (France), where he had his home and his wife and had at least been able to 'live freely as a Jew'.[31]

The immigrants brought a new perspective into the life of the Inquisition, which now found that it had to struggle against the royal wish to tolerate such wealthy subjects as the Portuguese. Just after 1602 the Portuguese offered Philip III a gift of 1,860,000 ducats (not to mention enormous gifts to the royal ministers) if the crown would issue a general pardon to judaizers of their nation for past offences. That the conversos could afford so great a sum is clear from their own admission that they were worth 80,000,000 ducats all told. Royal penury gave way before such a magnificent offer, and application was made to Rome. The papal decree for a pardon was issued on 23 August 1604 and published on 16 January

1605; on the latter date the three Portuguese tribunals released a total of 410 prisoners.[32] By this astonishing agreement the Spanish crown revealed its own financial bankruptcy and its willingness to jettison religious ideals when the profits from a bribe exceeded those from confiscation.

This did not mean any more than a temporary respite in the work of the Inquisition, which resumed activity in both Portugal and Spain as soon as the terms of the pardon had been worked off. In Portugal particularly, the Inquisition resumed work with a thoroughness it had not shown in the old days, and when in 1628 the prelates of Portugal proposed new measures to be enforced against the New Christians, the latter paid Philip III another handsome sum, probably well over eighty thousand ducats, to allow them to leave for Spain. The emigrants, however, left not only for Spain but also for foreign lands of the dispersion, so swelling the numbers of the Jewish communities in France, Holland and England. It was perfectly obvious to everyone that such emigration was a grave loss to Spain, and the matter was discussed with the royal ministers by the Portuguese residing in Spain under Philip IV. A memorandum sent to the king by the New Christian merchants claimed that they were the financial mainstay of the crown, since their contribution lay in

> sending to the East Indies countless ships laden with merchandise, whose customs duties maintain the navy and enrich the kingdom; supporting Brazil and producing the machinery to obtain sugar for all Europe: maintaining the trade to Angola, Cabo Verde and other colonies from which Your Majesty has obtained so many duties; delivering slaves to the Indies for their service, and journeying and trading from Spain to all the world. Finally, the New Christians are today in Portugal and Castile those who maintain commerce, the farming of the revenues to Your Majesty, and the agreements to supply money outside the realm.[33]

Because of emigration, they claimed, the advantages of their services were being lost and Rouen, Bordeaux, Nantes and Florence were benefiting from it. The Spanish authorities were susceptible to this kind of argument, and to stories that the commercial powers – particularly Holland and, after Cromwell's day, England – were controlled by Jews. The Portuguese merchants must therefore be retained in the peninsula. This became easier after the first state bankruptcy of Philip IV's reign, in 1626: the losses suffered by the Genoese bankers created a vacuum into which Portuguese financiers moved, although not without great protests from contemporaries. One of these, the writer Pellicer de Ossau, in 1640 put his objections in this way:

> It was thought that the evils brought about by the Genoese financiers could be cured by resorting to the Portuguese, for since they were at the time subjects of the crown, to make use of them would also benefit the crown. But this was only to go from bad to worse. For since most of the Portuguese merchants were Jews, fear of the Inquisition made them establish their main trading houses in Flanders and cities of the north, keeping only a few connections in Spain. The result was that far from Spain benefiting, most of the profits went to the Dutch and other heretics.[34]

The count Duke of Olivares, prime minister of Philip IV, saw matters in quite a different light. He ignored any protests which might interrupt his plans to use Jewish finance to restore the fortunes of the monarchy, and the years of his ministry in Spain were those when converso bankers flourished most.[35]

His modification of the statutes of limpieza in 1623 was the first public break to be made with official antisemitism. In 1634, and again in 1641, he is said to have opened negotiations with the exiled Jews in Africa and the Levant, to persuade them to return to Spain under guarantees which would reverse the negative consequences of their expulsion. This radical and certainly unpopular policy seems to have contributed eventually to the downfall of Olivares.

In 1628 Philip IV granted the Portuguese financiers freedom to trade and settle without restriction, hoping thereby to win back from foreigners a section of the Indies trade. Thanks to this, the New Christians extended their influence to the principal trading channels of Spain and America. However successful they may have been in business, nevertheless they could not escape the consequences of their cultural origin, and several of them had to suffer the rigours of the Inquisition. From the 1630s to the 1680s some of the wealthiest men in Spain were ruined in fame and fortune by the Holy Office. The Portuguese financiers among them were, in addition, tarnished by identification with their nation, which was in revolt against Madrid after 1640; and with the disgrace of Olivares in 1643 their last great protector disappeared.

In 1636 the Inquisition brought the financier Manuel Fernández Pinto to trial for judaizing. On one occasion during his career he had lent Philip IV the sum of 100,000 ducats. Now the tribunal extorted from him the enormous sum of 300,000 ducats in confiscations.[36] Even more prominent than Pinto was Juan Núñez Saravía,[37] whom we first meet as contributor, with nine other Portuguese financiers, to a loan of 2,159,438 ducats made to Philip IV in 1627. In 1630 Saravía was denounced to the Inquisition as a judaizer and protector of judaizers. No action was taken by the tribunal, which continued to accumulate evidence from France and America showing that, besides his religious errors, Saravía was also guilty of exporting bullion to his coreligionaries abroad and importing base money in its place. Early in 1632 Saravía and his brother Enrique were arrested, and after the usual delays of the Inquisition Juan was finally in 1636 put to mild torture under which he admitted nothing. He was condemned to abjure de vehementi and fined 20,000 ducats, appearing with his brother and other judaizers in the Toledo auto of 13 December 1637. From men of Saravía's standing the tribunal could expect to make large profits, and besides the fine on Juan it is estimated that his brother Enrique was condemned to confiscations which amounted to over three hundred thousand ducats. Juan Saravía was no doubt ruined by a case which had destroyed his good name and obliged him to fritter away five years in an inquisitorial prison, for he never makes any further appearance among the number of bankers who served the crown.

After 1640, as we have observed, the Portuguese financiers in Spain were in a different position, without a native country and without official support, particularly after the fall of Olivares.[38] The wealthier among them were eliminated one by one. In 1641 a probable relative of Saravía called Diego de Saravía was tried by the Inquisition and suffered the confiscation of 250,000 ducats in gold, silver and coin. In 1646 the aged financier Manuel Enrique was arrested and condemned, and in 1647 another financier not named in the records was tried at Toledo. The records bring out the close connections between the accused. In 1646, for instance, the property of the wealthy financier Esteban Luis Diamante was sequestrated by the Inquisition. Diamante was a colleague in the banking firm of his brothers-in-law Gaspar and Alfonso Rodríguez Pasarino, of whom the latter was in prison accused of judaizing, while the former had saved himself by flight. Alfonso had a daughter named Violante who was married to the eminent banker Simon de Fonseca Piña, an astute and wealthy businessman who seems never to have come into conflict with the Holy Office. The property confiscated from the Pasarinos on this occasion probably exceeded a hundred thousand ducats.[39]

Apart from the wealthy few, there were whole families of ordinary conversos living in Madrid who suffered from the renewal of persecution.

The 1650s saw the beginning of wholesale arrests and trials which turned into a reign of terror for the Portuguese converso minority in Spain. A contemporary living in Madrid in mid-century supplies us with a dramatic account of facts and rumours about arrests.[40] 'No one trusts the Portuguese financiers any more. They are going bankrupt and fleeing from the Inquisition. I have been assured that after the auto at Cuenca over two hundred families took to flight during the night. This is what fear can do' (22 August 1654). 'In Seville at the beginning of April four wealthy Portuguese merchants were seized at night by the Inquisition' (17 May 1655). 'The Cardosos have fled to Amsterdam, taking 200,000 ducats in wool and 250,000 in gold. It is said this was because the Inquisition wished to arrest them, and so they are in search of a land where one lives in greater freedom than in Spain' (2 June 1655). The wealthy Cardoso brothers, who administered taxes in several provinces, fled because a blackmailer had threatened to testify that they were judaizers unless they paid for silence. Faced with the possibility of having to prove their case against false testimony, 'they preferred to fly from punishment rather than remain in gaol until the truth was established' (29 May 1655). The diarist thought it a serious matter that lying witnesses should be able to ruin the lives of prominent men like these.

> The fact is that if it is the practice in the Holy Office, as they say it is, not to punish false witnesses because no one would denounce if they did so, then that is terrible and even inhuman, to leave the life, honour and property of one who may be innocent to the mercy of his enemies. Every day we see many people like this emerging from their travails after great sufferings and years of prison.

'On Monday the thirteenth at midnight the Inquisition seized fourteen Portuguese traders and financiers, in particular two tobacco merchants. These people sprout like mushrooms' (15 September 1655). 'Since last Saturday the Inquisition in Madrid has imprisoned seventeen Portuguese families. . . . In the street of the Peromostenses they are hurriedly building a prison big enough to hold all the people that fall every day into the trap. It is said for certain that there is not a Portuguese of high or low degree in Madrid who does not judaize' (18 September 1655). 'There is not a single tobacco merchant in Madrid whom the Inquisition hasn't arrested. The other day they took away two entire families, both parents and children. Many others are fleeing to France' (23 October 1655).

The condemnation of judaizers and the flight of wealthy fugitives brought about precisely the situation Olivares had attempted to avoid: bankruptcies among the trading classes of Madrid and other cities, leading to a collapse of confidence in some leading financiers and a consequent contraction in the size of the group of bankers on whom the crown could ultimately rely. Heads continued to roll. 'There has been an auto at Cuenca. Brito abjured *de vehementi*; he was condemned to the sanbenito, banishment and to pay 6,000 ducats. Montesinos met the same fate, but the fine was higher: 10,000 ducats. Blandon, 4,000. El Pelado, 300. . . . All were from Madrid and had lived years there; very rich men' (8 January 1656). Brito was the financier Francisco Díaz Méndez Brito, who was made to do penance there once, and then again at a later date imprisoned by the Inquisition. Montesinos was the banker and merchant Fernando de Montesinos Téllez, a prominent financier who at the age of sixty-six was imprisoned together with his wife Serafina de Almeida in 1654, by the Inquisition of Cuenca. Serafina was a cousin of the Cortizos family, whom we shall meet presently. Fernando was a man of enormous fortune. His assets at the time of his arrest amounted to 567,256 ducats; of this sum a substantial part was tied up in Amsterdam, so that his effective assets were put at 474,096 ducats. His household goods alone, worth 10,000 ducats, were a testimony to his affluence,[41] yet the Inquisition penalized the couple only, and left the fortune undisturbed. Fernando and Serafina were fined a total of 8,000 ducats. After this 'he went to Amsterdam to live there freely, terrified of being burnt if he returned. He left his sons behind, having given them all his property. It is said that they will send the property over there bit by bit, and then one day do the same as he' (22 November 1656). Montesinos, therefore, apparently returned to the open practice of Judaism in Amsterdam. But his sons, far from following his example, continued the family's financial services to the crown. The great deflation of 1680 began their ruin as bankers, and by the beginning of the eighteenth century they had gone into liquidation.

The liberal attitude of the Inquisition towards Montesinos' fortune was not dictated by unselfishness. The fact was that so many wealthy financiers were appearing before the tribunal that the government took alarm at the possible threat to the financial stability of Spain. On 7 September 1654 the council of finance came to an agreement with the Inquisition that the latter was to attend only to the personal property of those accused, and that money which was involved in official contracts was to be dealt with by the former. The agreement had the virtue of differentiating between a financier and his firm. As a result we find that the imprisonment of principals such as Fernando Montesinos did not automatically lead to the dissolution of their business.

The auto de fe held at Cuenca on 29 June 1654 included among its victims the financier Francisco Coello, administrator of taxes in Malaga.[42] In 1658 Francisco López Pereira, administrator of taxes in Granada, who had once before been tried by the Inquisition of Coimbra in 1651, made another appearance before the tribunal in Spain but had his case suspended. Diego Gómez de Salazar, administrator of the tobacco monopoly in Castile and a fervent judaizer, was reconciled in the auto held at Valladolid on 30 October 1664 and almost all his family suffered condemnation in due course.

Among the most prominent conversos in mid-century was the financier Manuel Cortizos de Villasante, born in Valladolid of Portuguese parents.[43] His astuteness and financial dealings raised him to the highest ranks in the kingdom, and he had become by the end of his life a knight of the Order of Calatrava, Lord of Arrifana, a member of the council of finance and secretary of the Contaduría Mayor de Cuentas, the principal department of the treasury. All this occurred at a time when the statutes of limpieza were in full force. Suddenly, after his death in 1650, it was discovered that he had been a secret judaizer and had been buried according to Jewish rites. The discovery would normally have led to the ruin of his family, but their rank and influence saved them from disaster. Indeed, notwithstanding the strong suspicion that other members of family were secret Jews, Manuel's son Sebastian was in 1657 appointed Spanish ambassador to Genoa; while another son, Manuel José Cortizos, continued his father's work as a financier of the crown, obtained the title of Viscount of Valdefuentes in 1668 and shortly afterwards that of Marquis of Villaflores. Throughout the reign of Charles II, Cortizos was second to none in the financial services he rendered the crown. In 1679, thanks to defaulting by his creditors, he was obliged to ask for a moratorium on his transactions, even though his assets were worth several million ducats.

Another tobacco administrator in a high social position, Luis Márquez Cardoso, was reconciled together with his wife at an auto in Toledo in November 1669. In August 1691 Simon Ruiz Pessoa, a leading Portuguese financier who had managed the customs duties of Andalusia from 1683 to 1685, was arrested by the Inquisition in Madrid. In 1694 Francisco del Castillo, a member of the Contaduría Mayor de Cuentas, born in Osuna and resident in Ecija, was arrested in Seville by the tribunal.

The most eminent Portuguese financier to suffer in this reign was

Francisco Báez Eminente. He took no part in international exchange but restricted his considerable fortune to the administration of the customs duties of Andalusia, Seville and the Indies (the *almojarifazgos*), as well as provisioning the royal army and navy in Andalusia. During his term of administration in 1686 such severe measures were taken against smugglers that, according to one source, 'we came to experience what was held to be impossible in Cadiz, namely that there should be no smuggling'. Eminent was a member of the Contaduría Mayor, and in view of the fact that a good part of Castile's trade passed through Andalusia, his work was of the highest importance to the crown, which he served, as the government later admitted, 'for over forty years with credit, industry and zeal that were well known'. Despite this long service and his advanced years, on 6 December 1689 he was suddenly arrested by the Inquisition in Madrid. His colleague Bernardo de Paz y Castañeda was arrested at about the same time. The arrests made no difference to the firm of Eminente, which had been handed over to his son Juan Francisco in April 1689, and continued successfully under him well into the next century.

Thus, once again in the seventeenth century, judaizers were the main preoccupation of the Inquisition: in the tribunal of Toledo they made up nearly half of all cases. In the 1670s in Andalusia there was a notable increase in prosecutions.[44]

The more active Judaism of the Portuguese brought new life to the conversos of Spain. It also helped to create a wholly new Judeo-converso consciousness in western Europe.

The consciousness, ironically, had its roots in Spain. Within the peninsula most conversos remained cut off from the development of international Jewry. It is remarkable, for instance, that the millennarian movement of Sabbatai Zvi, which shook the entire Jewish world and found its ablest controversialist in the north African rabbi Jacob Saportas,[45] seems to have caused no tremor in Spain, even though the Inquisition was aware of the phenomenon and warned its tribunals to keep a watch at the ports for any unusual emigration of conversos. Likewise, there was little active development of Judaic thought within Spain.

But a feeling for Sefarad permeated the thought of western European Jews and helped to stimulate developments in thought and literature. Ironically, the conversos who lived abroad felt that they were different from others, and different even from other Jews, precisely because they were from Sefarad. The cultivation of Iberian cultural habits became a distinguishing feature of the communities of exiles.[46] Amsterdam afforded liberty of printing to those who wished to publish. But Sefarad was still home, and many were deeply conscious of their roots there. Among them was the young Spinoza, of Spanish origin even though he lived all his life outside the peninsula. The peninsula itself did not provide congenial ground for Jewish speculative thought, a fact that prompted the exile of one of the best-known converso figures of the period. Isaac Cardoso (d. 1680), professor of Madrid and Valladolid and physician to Philip IV, left the country in 1648 and went to live as a Jew in Venice. Here he published his *Philosophia libera* (1673), which was an exposition of atomist philosophy based on Gassendi and owed little to Judaism.[47]

A few other intellectuals also exiled themselves, but reluctantly. Enriquez Gómez (b. Cuenca, 1600), whose parents had been tried by the Inquisition and who himself became a Jew in France, remained so attracted by the pull of Sefarad – the only land that could provide him with a public for the language in which he wrote – that he returned to Spain in 1650 and wrote for thirteen years in Seville under the pseudonym Fernando de Zárate. While abroad in Rouen in 1647 Gómez wrote the second part of his *Política Angélica*, a reasoned programme for reform of the Inquisition: he asked for the identification of witnesses, the suppression of confiscations, a ban on sanbenitos, and speedy trials. He reserved his harshest strictures for the practice of limpieza, which he called 'the most barbarous seed sown by the devil in Christendom. ... Because of it the best families have left the realm; it has created thousands of godless, has injured neighbourly love, has divided the people and has perpetuated enmities.'[48] While in Seville he had the unusual opportunity to see himself burnt in effigy in an auto there in April 1660. The inquisitors eventually caught up with him. He was arrested in September 1661 and died of a heart attack in the cells in March 1663. In July that year he was once again condemned in effigy in an auto.[49]

A more determined exile was Gaspar Méndez, who fled to Amsterdam, where he changed his name to Abraham Idana and in 1686 wrote a stinging attack on the Inquisition for 'using unheard-of tortures to force many to confess what they have not done, this being the cause why many who have been arrested and have entered the prisons without knowing anything other than that they are Christians, have come out as Jews. This is the reason why I left a country where such a tribunal holds sway.'[50]

Iberia, despite the echoes of the Inquisition, gave to Jewish and converso exiles a common bond that made them all 'men of the nation'. Even those who were no longer practising Jews felt a profound kinship, based less on religion than on origins, with the converso world from which they had emerged.[51] A few of those who contributed to the new brand of converso consciousness in Europe broke firmly with orthodox Judaism. They included Uriel da Costa, Isaac Orobio de Castro and, at one remove, Spinoza. Orobio, born 1617 in Portugal, moved with his parents around mid-century to Málaga.[52] He studied medicine at the university of Osuna. In 1654 he and his family were arrested by the Inquisition of Seville on a charge of judaizing. They appeared in an auto de fe but were lightly punished and eventually, in 1658, released. A couple of years later they left Spain. Orobio arrived in 1662 in Amsterdam, where he participated in the rich intellectual world of the Jews. In the background of the thinking of the Sephardic diaspora, there always remained the memory of Spain. Through men such as Orobio, 'the social thinking of Spain found its way into the writings of the Jews of Amsterdam'.[53]

The closing years of the seventeenth century, still mistakenly viewed by many as years of decay, were thus a period when conversos not only looked to new horizons, but also contributed to new trends of thought. In the peninsula, conversos emerged into public life. Tolerance for them was, however, balanced by residual surges of persecution in several tribunals of the peninsula, notably in the Balearic islands. The French ambassador, the Marquis of Villars, was a witness to this blend of tolerance and persecution. He was present at the great auto of June 1680, and observed that 'these punishments do not significantly diminish the number of Jews in Spain and above all in Madrid where, while some are punished with great severity, one sees several others employed in finance, esteemed and respected though known to be of Jewish origin'.[54]

Among the most significant conversos of the late century, and a man whose career aptly illustrates the strange mixture of tolerance and intolerance of those days, was Dr Diego Mateo Zapata.[55] Born of Portuguese parents in Murcia in 1664, Zapata was brought up by his mother as a secret Jew. In 1678 she was arrested, tortured and emerged in an auto de fe in 1681. His father was arrested on suspicion, but set free. Zapata went to the university of Valencia to study medicine, and then to Alcalá, where he was befriended by Francisco Enríquez de Villacorta, a doctor of Jewish origins. He moved to Madrid and thanks to his connections managed to prosper. In 1692 he was arrested in Madrid by the Inquisition on charges of Judaism, and spent a year in the cells of the tribunal at Cuenca; the prosecution was suspended, and he was released in 1693. In 1702 he was elected president of the Royal Society of Medicine in Seville. The early eighteenth century found him rich and successful in Madrid, in possession of a large library that included the works of Bacon, Gassendi, Bayle, Paracelsus, Pascal and other philosophers. In 1721 he was suddenly arrested again on charges of Judaism, and appeared in an auto de fe in Cuenca in 1725, condemned to ten years' banishment and the loss of half his goods. He returned to active work in Madrid, helped to found the Royal Academy of Medicine in 1734, and died in 1745.

His posthumously published *Sunset of the Aristotelian Forms*, which appeared in 1745, was a radical departure from his earlier devotion to the principles of Galen which still dominated orthodox medicine in Spain. Zapata shares with Dr Juan Muñoz Peralta the sad fame of being among the last men of medicine to suffer at the hands of the Inquisition.[56] Peralta was distinguished enough to have been physician to the king and queen in the War of Succession, and was subsequently summoned to Versailles to attend to Louis XIV himself. In 1700 he was elected first president of the Royal Medical Society of Seville. Tried and imprisoned by the Inquisition shortly before 1724, he never returned to practise as a royal physician.

Conversos predominated in the autos of the late seventeenth century. In the Granada auto de fe of 30 May 1672 there were seventy-nine judaizers out of ninety victims, fifty-seven of them being Portuguese. The great Madrid auto of 30 June 1680 included 104 judaizers, nearly all Portuguese. The Córdoba auto of 29 September 1684 included thirty-four judaizers (some of them cried out 'Moses, Moses,' as they perished in the flames) among the forty-eight penitents.[57] Autos de fe after the 1680s show a definite decline from these numbers, indicating that the first generation of Portuguese conversos had been wiped out as surely as the native conversos had been at the beginning of the sixteenth century.

A special exception to this decline of persecution must be noted in Mallorca, where the burnings erupted only in the closing years of the seventeenth century. Mallorca followed a slightly different development from the rest of Spain. The mediaeval Inquisition had existed there since 1232 and the new tribunal was introduced only in 1488. Even before this, the island had a Jewish problem which paralleled that on the mainland. The great massacres of 1391 were repeated here in riots in August 1391, and Vincent Ferrer extended his proselytizing activities to the island in 1413. By about 1435 it was reckoned that the whole Jewish population had embraced Christianity, but as in Spain it was found necessary to introduce the Inquisition to root out the doubtful cases. The first autos de fe showed the existence of a problem. In 1489 there were fifty-three 'relaxations' of conversos, most of whom were burnt in effigy as fugitives. On 26 March 1490, after 424 conversos had responded to the terms of clemency offered in an edict of grace, eighty-six conversos were reconciled; and on 31 May 1490 there were thirty-six 'relaxations' and fifty-six reconciliations. Up to September 1531 every person 'relaxed' in the Mallorcan Inquisition was of Jewish origin, and the total number of 'relaxations' to that date was 535.[58] By the 1530s the same phenomenon that we have noted for peninsular Spain occurred: the number of converso victims declined sharply and a whole generation of judaizers ceased to exist. Now, however, the Morisco problem took its place, aggravated by the fact that Morisco refugees from Valencia often chose to flee to the Balearic islands. Mass reconciliations of Moriscos occurred in Mallorca from the 1530s, and the first 'relaxations' took place in the auto of 10 July 1535. Between 1530 and 1645 there were ninety-nine Moriscos reconciled in Mallorca, twenty-seven of them in 1613 alone.[59] The corresponding absence of judaizers is shown by the fact that between 1535 and 1645 only ten people were 'relaxed', and of these seven were Moriscos. The absence of judaizers at this particular period, when they proliferated in Spain, is evidence that the Portuguese emigrants did not make their way to the Balearics in any numbers.

After a lull of well over a century, the storm burst eventually over the Mallorcan converso descendants – the Chuetas – in 1675, when a young man of nineteen years, Alonso López, was burnt in the auto of 13 January.[60] With him were burnt the effigies of six Portuguese judaizers, indicating that persecution in the Spanish peninsula had at last driven the Portuguese out into the Mediterranean. Repercussions from this case led in 1677 to a general arrest of conversos, and by 1678 the Inquisition had arrested 237 people on the charge of complicity in what seems to have been a genuine plot to assert their political and human rights. Now followed two great waves of persecution in 1679 and 1691. In the spring of the former year no fewer than five autos de fe were held in Mallorca, with a total of 221 reconciliations. As we have seen, the confiscations made at these autos reached a record total of well over two and a half million ducats. Crushed by these events, the conversos waited ten years before they could stir again. In 1688 some of them, led by Onofre Cortes and Rafael Valls, attempted to recoup all in a plot which fell through and led directly to the four autos de fe held in 1691, at which thirty-seven prisoners were 'relaxed' in person;

those reconciled or burnt in effigy increased this figure to a total of eighty-six converso victims. After this great suppression, the conversos of Mallorca made no further attempt to improve their position. They remained into modern times a depressed community, subjected to calumny and discrimination.

Throughout Spain, then, the seventeenth century closed with a holocaust of conversos. The eighteenth century opened with a new dynasty and an apparently new outlook on religion. Philip V seemed to mark the change to a new era by refusing to attend an auto de fe held in his honour at the beginning of the reign. With elimination first of the native judaizers and then of the Portuguese immigrants, it appeared that the converso problem had at last been solved. All this was a delusion. Philip V grew to learn that he must live according to the customs of his subjects, and did not subsequently refuse to attend autos. The change of dynasty involved very little change in religious practice, and the persistence of judaizers in Spain was treated with almost as much severity as in the preceding century. A final wave of repression occurred in the early 1720s.[61]

Meanwhile there were promising signs for Spanish Jews, thanks in part to the capture of Gibraltar by the English in 1704 and its cession to England by the peace of Utrecht (1713). Spain laid down a condition 'that on no account must Jews and Muslims be allowed to live or reside in the said city of Gibraltar'. The English made no attempt to observe these discriminatory demands, and very rapidly the Jewish community grew. By 1717 there were 300 Jewish families there, with their own synagogue, and by the nineteenth century Jews were a tenth of the population on the Rock.

The toll of judaizers in the 1720s, though very substantial, represented the tail-end of a long history of persecution. There were several important autos in 1720 in Madrid, Mallorca, Granada and Seville, but the real wave of repression broke out in 1721 and lasted to the end of the decade. The peak years were 1721–5, when sixty-six autos appear to have been held. Between 1726 and 1730 possibly another eighteen were celebrated. The persecution of the 1720s was directed almost exclusively against immigrants of Portuguese origin, accused of judaizing; they made up nearly eighty per cent of the cases of those years.[62] Over the whole period from the 1660s to the 1720s, the Spanish tribunals prosecuted over two thousand two hundred persons for judaizing.[63] Some three per cent of these were burnt at the stake (in the 1720s the incidence was higher, over eight per cent[64]). The majority – over three-quarters – spent a few years in prison.

In the years after 1730 the number of autos and of accused declined rapidly, and by mid-century the converso community had ceased to be a major religious issue. With this last great persecution the practice of Judaism in Spain crumbled and decayed. Cases were rare in the latter half of the eighteenth century, the last one to occur at Toledo being in 1756. Among more than five thousand cases coming before the tribunals between 1780 and 1820 when the Inquisition was suppressed, there were only sixteen cases of judaizing, and of these ten were of foreigners whilst the remaining six were prosecuted only on suspicion.[65] The Jews had been to all appearances eliminated from Spain, the last prosecution being the case of Manuel Santiago Vivar at Córdoba in 1818.

All this did not mean a relaxation of antisemitism. When in 1797 finance minister Pedro Varela resurrected the long-forgotten idea of Olivares and attempted to bring the Jews back into Spain, his suggestions were firmly rejected by Charles IV. As late as 1802 the crown was issuing threats against those of its subjects who were shielding Jews from the Inquisition. In 1804 a French-Jewish merchant of Bayonne was molested by the tribunal, whereupon the indignant French ambassador intervened to say 'that the exercise of international rights ought not to depend on an arbitrary distinction about the religion in which a man was born and the religious principles he professed'.[66] The struggle continued into the opening decades of the twentieth century, where it merged into problems that are part of contemporary history.

To antisemites among the new generation of Spaniards, Jews were the dark stain on the history of their country. The shadow of the Jews was everywhere present, yet they themselves were extinct. The only surviving memory of them was in the sanbenitos that foreign travellers reported having seen hung in churches in the peninsula well into the nineteenth century. But if the Inquisition could claim to have rid Spain of the Jewish menace, it was still partly to blame for the bitter legacy of antisemitism in the country. The political right wing in nineteenth-century Spain and Europe adopted the Jew as its prototype enemy, sometimes distinct from and sometimes identified with the freemason. The Jew, who had now become a myth and no more, became identified in certain minds with all that was hostile to the tradition represented by the Inquisition. To be a Jew meant not being a Catholic, therefore not to be a Catholic meant being a Jew: one result of this popular reasoning meant that 'Jews and freemasons', 'Jews and Protestants' and 'Jews and foreigners' became self-explanatory identifications. In the constant struggle waged by the right wing to preserve Catholic Spain, all that was hostile and sinister became personified in the Jew who was on the other side. The aberrations of the nineteenth century found their last heyday in the racist literature circulated in Spain during the Second World War.

Speculation and curiosity still hang around the issue of Jewish survivals in the nineteenth century. The question was put at its most dramatic by George Borrow during his indefatigable travels with the Bible round western Spain. In 1836 he was riding by night on his *burra* through Old Castile, when about two leagues before Talavera he fell into conversation with a figure making the same journey on foot.

> Hardly had a few words been exchanged than the man walked on about ten paces, in the same manner as he had previously done: all of a sudden he turned, and taking the bridle of the *burra* gently in his hand, stopped her. I had now a full view of his face and figure, and those huge features and Herculean form still occasionally revisit me in my dreams. I see him standing in the moonshine, staring me in the face with his deep calm eyes. At last he said:
>
> 'Are you then *one of us?*'[67]

In this way, in the middle of the nineteenth century, Borrow claimed to have come upon one of the few remaining communities of secret Jews in Spain. The incident has been fiercely attacked by writers of all shades of opinion, and there is little doubt that the speeches Borrow puts into the mouth of his new friend Abarbanel verge on fantasy. Yet there seems no reason to doubt that Borrow did meet Spaniards – as he later met an ex-inquisitor – who claimed to know of secret judaizers in the country. Several other travellers made similar reports. One of his predecessors, Joseph Townsend, reported in 1787 after travelling through the country:

> Even to the present day both Mahometans and Jews are thought to be numerous in Spain, the former among the mountains, the latter in all great cities. Their principal disguise is more than common zeal in external conformity to all the precepts of the Church: and the most apparently bigoted, not only of the clergy, but of the inquisitors themselves, are by some persons suspected to be Jews.[68]

Whatever the truth of the matter, the fact remains that Judaism continued to be an issue in Spain long after the last heretic had died at the stake. On the one hand, there was a legacy of suspicion and fear based on antisemitism – the willingness to blame the secret and concealed enemy for all the evils of policy and history. On the other, there was a distinct atmosphere of racialism which persisted into modern times. On both counts the Inquisition had some part to play and some responsibility to bear in the tragedy of a hunted people.

During the last decades of the eighteenth century the Inquisition became openly political in its hostility to the Enlightenment, and lost the little support it had enjoyed among the progressive elite in Spain. In the epoch following the French Revolution, one of the first acts of the French regime that occupied Spain in 1808 was to abolish the Holy Office on 4 December. The patriotic forces in the country were represented at the Cortes of Cadiz (1810), which on 22 February 1813 also decreed the abolition of the Inquisition, by a margin of ninety votes against sixty. It was an act that provoked considerable opposition from traditionalists, and on 21 July 1814 Ferdinand VII restored the tribunal, but in name rather than in reality. Effectively the Holy Office was now moribund. On 9 March 1820 the king was forced by liberal opposition to abolish it yet again. The final decree of suppression, issued by the government of Queen Isabella II on 15 July 1834, was little more than a formality. From this date the Inquisition ceased to exist in the Spanish monarchy.

Long before that, it had entered the realm of mythology. Since the sixteenth century, opponents of the tribunal had taken the initiative in attacking it through the useful medium of the printing press. The Holy Office, clinging to its rule of secrecy, refused to get drawn into any public debate. It thereby left the field wide open to its enemies, who set about 'inventing' their own image of the Inquisition.

14

INVENTING THE INQUISITION

... a wild monster, of such strange form and horrible mien that all Europe trembles at the mere mention of its name.

Samuel Usque, in the sixteenth century[1]

From its very inception, the Inquisition in Spain provoked a war of words.[2] Its opponents through the ages contributed to building up a powerful legend about its intentions and malign achievements. Their propaganda was so successful that even today it is difficult to separate fact from fiction.

The first period of myth-building, in the sixteenth century, had nothing to do with the sufferings of the conversos. Spain's championship of the Catholic cause, and the persecution of Protestants in Castile in 1559–62, gave birth to a number of writings that presented the Inquisition as a threat to the liberty of western Europe. Bearing in mind the very small number of Protestants ever executed by Spanish tribunals, the campaign against the Inquisition can be seen as a reflection of political and religious fears rather than as a logical reaction to a real threat.

The printing-press, one of the most powerful weapons taken up by the Reformation, was used against the tribunal. For the first time, in the 1560s images of the dreaded (and, we have seen, newly elaborated) auto de fe were reproduced as proof of the terrible fate awaiting the enemies of Rome.[3] Protestant pens depicted the struggle of heretics as one for freedom from a tyrannical faith. Wherever Catholicism triumphed, they claimed, not only religious but civil liberty was extinguished. The Reformation, according to this interpretation, brought about the liberation of the human spirit from the fetters of darkness and superstition. Propaganda along these lines proved to be strikingly effective in the context of the political conflicts of the period, and there were always refugees from persecution to lend substance to the story.

In England John Foxe warned his contemporaries that

> this dreadful engine of tyranny may at any time be introduced into a country

where the Catholics have the ascendancy; and hence how careful ought we to be, who are not cursed with such an arbitrary court, to prevent its introduction.[4]

For Foxe and others the Inquisition was a typical example of the evils of Rome. In their works it was presented as the supreme institution of intolerance:

When the inquisitors have taken umbrage against an innocent person, all expedients are used to facilitate condemnation; false oaths and testimonies are employed to find the accused guilty; and all laws and institutions are sacrificed to satiate the most bigoted vengeance.

As late as the mid-nineteenth century one of the best examples of such propaganda could be found in John Motley's brilliant history of *The Rise of the Dutch Republic*, first published in London in 1855. Motley adhered close enough to the truth to appear convincing, yet writing half a century after Llorente he could say this of the Spanish Inquisition:

It taught the savages of India and America to shudder at the name of Christianity. The fear of its introduction froze the earlier heretics of Italy, France and Germany into orthodoxy. It was a court owning allegiance to no temporal authority, superior to all other tribunals. It was a bench of monks without appeal, having its familiars in every house, diving into the secrets of every fireside, judging and executing its horrible decrees without responsibility. It condemned not deeds but thoughts. It affected to descend into individual conscience, and to punish the crimes which it pretended to discover. Its process was reduced to a horrible simplicity. It arrested on suspicion, tortured till confession, and then punished by fire. Two witnesses, and those to separate facts, were sufficient to consign the victim to a loathsome dungeon. Here he was sparingly supplied with food, forbidden to speak, or even to sing – to which pastime it could hardly be thought he would feel much inclination – and then left to himself till famine and misery should break his spirit. When that time was supposed to have arrived, he was examined. Did he confess and forswear his heresy, whether actually innocent or not, he might then assume the sacred shirt, and escape with confiscation of all his property. Did he persist in the avowal of his innocence, two witnesses sent him to the stake, one to the rack. He was informed of the testimony against him, but never confronted with the witness. The accuser might be his son, father, or the wife of his bosom, for all were enjoined, under the death penalty, to inform the inquisitors of every suspicious word which might fall from their nearest relatives. The indictment being thus supported, the prisoner was tried by torture. The rack was the court of justice: the criminal's only advocate was his fortitude – for the nominal counsellor, who was permitted no communication with the prisoner, and was furnished neither with documents nor with power to procure evidence, was a puppet, aggravating the lawlessness of the proceedings by the mockery of legal forms. The torture took place at midnight, in a gloomy dungeon, dimly lighted by torches. The victim – whether man, matron, or tender virgin – was stripped naked and stretched upon the wooden bench. Water, weights, fires, pulleys, screws – all the apparatus by which the sinews could be strained without cracking, the bones bruised without breaking, and the body racked exquisitely without giving up its ghost – was now put into operation. The executioner, enveloped in a black robe from head to foot, with his eyes glaring at his victim through holes cut in the hood which muffled his face, practised successively all the forms of torture which the devilish ingenuity of the monk had invented. The imagination sickens when striving to keep pace with these dreadful realities.[5]

One of the most significant sources for a Protestant image of the tribunal was the *Sanctae Inquisitionis Hispanicae Artes*, published in Heidelberg in 1567. The author's pseudonym was Reginaldus Gonzalvus Montanus, but the work seems in reality to have been written jointly by two Spanish Protestant exiles, Casiodoro de Reina and Antonio del Corro.[6] They supplied, for perhaps the first time, a full description of the functioning of the Inquisition and its persecution of Protestants in Spain. Their first-hand knowledge gave authority to the account and turned it into an international success. Between 1568 and 1570 it was issued in two editions in English, one in French, three in Dutch, four in German and one in Hungarian. From that time, Protestant Europe could see beyond any doubt that its most deadly enemy was the terrible Inquisition of Spain. No mention was made, either by Montanus or by other polemicists, that the principal victims of the Spanish tribunal had been not Protestants but people of Jewish and Muslim origin.

As time went on, the anti-Inquisition legend grew, thanks to the efforts of zealous Protestants to keep alive the cause for which their martyrs suffered. To a nineteenth-century edition of Foxe's *Book of Martyrs*, a certain Reverend Ingram Cobbin MA added the following account of the Inquisition, enlivening it with detailed falsehoods with which even Foxe had not sullied his original narrative. During the Napoleonic wars in

Spain, the Reverend Cobbin assured his readers, the French troops of liberation broke into the secret cells of the tribunal in Madrid:

> There they found the instruments of torture, of every kind which the ingenuity of men or devils could invent. The first instrument noticed was a machine by which the victim was confined and then, beginning with the fingers, all the joints in the hands, arms and body were broken and drawn one after another, until the sufferer died. The second [was the water torture]. The third was an infernal machine, laid horizontally, on which the victim was bound: the machine then being placed between two scores of knives so fixed that by turning the machine with a crank the flesh of the sufferer was all torn from his limbs into small pieces. The fourth surpassed the others in fiendish ingenuity. Its exterior was a large doll, richly dressed and having the appearance of a beautiful woman with her arms extended ready to embrace her victim. A semicircle was drawn around her, and the person who passed over this fatal mark touched a spring which caused the diabolical engine to open, its arms immediately clasped him, and a thousand knives cut him in as many pieces.[7]

A second major source of anti-Inquisition propaganda was, by contrast, Catholic in origin. From 1494 onwards, Spanish troops had intervened in Italy to check the expansion of French influence. But they came to stay. Ferdinand the Catholic had been king of Sicily; he now also took over the kingdom of Naples. Under Charles V, Spaniards in addition took over the duchy of Milan and established their power firmly in the peninsula. The peoples of Italy, including the papacy, quickly came to view the Spaniards as oppressors. They cultivated an unfavourable image, a 'Black Legend', about Spain that extended itself also to the Spanish Inquisition.[8]

It was in the Italian provinces of the Spanish crown that the greatest and most successful revolts against the Inquisition occurred. There were risings in 1511 and 1526 in Sicily, caused partly by popular hatred of the tribunal's familiars. Ferdinand the Catholic attempted to introduce the Spanish Inquisition into Naples, which already had its own episcopal Inquisition, but effective protests blocked his bid. The issue did not subside; both in 1547 and 1564 there were risings in the province because of rumours that the Spanish tribunal was going to be established. In reality, as Philip regularly insisted to his own ministers, he had no intention of exporting the Spanish tribunal to any of his non-Spanish realms.

Italians distrusted these assurances. They continued to cultivate their own vision of Spanish policy. When Italian diplomats, whether from independent states (such as Venice) or from the papacy, came to visit the peninsula, they saw little to praise. The reports they sent home described a poor and backward nation dominated by a tyrannical Inquisition. In 1525 the Venetian ambassador Contarini claimed that everyone trembled before the Holy Office. In 1557 ambassador Badoero spoke of the terror caused by its procedure. In 1563 ambassador Tiepolo said that everyone shuddered at its name, as it had total authority over the property, life, honour and even the souls of men. 'The king', he wrote, 'favours it, the better to keep the people under control'.[9] In 1565 ambassador Soranzo reported that its authority transcended that of the king. In the crown of Aragon, he reported, 'the king makes every attempt to destroy the many privileges they have, and knowing that there is no easier or more certain way of doing it than through the Inquisition, never ceases to augment its authority'.[10] Francesco Guicciardini, as Florentine ambassador to Ferdinand, was also representative of Italian opinion when he described Spaniards as 'very religious in externals and outward show, but not so in fact'.[11] Almost the same words were used by the Venetian Tiepolo in 1563. Italians felt that Spanish hypocrisy in religion, together with the existence of the Inquisition, proved that the tribunal was created not for religious purity, but simply to rob the Jews. Similar views were certainly held by the prelates of the Holy See whenever they intervened in favour of the conversos. Moreover, the racialism of the Spanish authorities was scorned in Italy, where the Jewish community led a comparatively tranquil existence. As the Spanish ambassador at Rome reported in 1652: 'In Spain it is held in great horror to be descended from a heretic or a Jew, but here they laugh at these matters, and at us, because we concern ourselves with them.'[12]

The next important source for the 'invention' of the Inquisition came with the political struggle against Spain in western Europe. A leading part in the propaganda war was played by the Dutch and the English, who opportunely possessed the most active printing-presses. The Dutch revolt against Spain, and subsequently the English campaign against the projected Armada invasion, were the focal points of the anti-Spanish campaign.

In the Netherlands it was feared that Spain intended to introduce the Inquisition as a means of subduing the country. During the religious wars in France, the Huguenots feared that Henry III, in concert with Philip of Spain, planned to establish a native Inquisition. William of Orange and the Count of Egmont were so disturbed about this that they asked Cardinal

Granvelle in 1561 to deny the report. Philip II assured Granvelle unequivocally that the Spanish model of Inquisition was unsuitable for export to the Netherlands or Italy.[13] Even in England, where he had exercised some influence as husband of Mary Tudor, no steps were ever taken to introduce the tribunal. Indeed, during that period Philip attempted to restrain the Marian persecution of heretics. The truth was that most European countries already had their own machinery for dealing with heretics and had no need for outside help. Besides this, the Spanish tribunal was not by nature a primarily anti-Protestant body, and would have needed substantial modification if introduced into some European states. Finally, the foreign policy of Philip II was by no means consistently anti-Protestant, so that the picture of Spain as a rabidly Catholic power distorts the reality of sixteenth-century international politics.[14]

The Netherlands already possessed an Inquisition of its own which Philip II confessed was 'more merciless than the one here'. At the very time that magistrates in Antwerp were objecting to the possibility of a Spanish tribunal, they themselves were executing heretics. The Antwerp courts between 1557 and 1562 executed 103 heretics,[15] more than died in the whole of Spain in that period. Rumours of Spain's intentions were a legend employed to discredit Spain and support resistance. William of Orange in his famous *Apology* of 1581, written in reply to a decree outlawing him, turned the issue into a brilliant exercise in anti-Spanish propaganda. The execution of heretics, he claimed, was a natural occupation for blood-thirsty Spaniards: 'the brightness of the fires wherein they have tormented so many poor Christians, was never delightful or pleasant to mine eyes, as it hath rejoyc'd the sight of the Duke of Alba and the Spaniards'. 'I will no more wonder', he added, 'at that which all the world believeth: to wit, that the greatest part of the Spaniards, and especially those that count themselves noblemen, are of the blood of the Moors and Jews'.[16]

The preparation of the Spanish Armada likewise encouraged the English government to launch a propaganda war against Philip II.[17] The continuous anti-Spanish attitude of radical Protestants was now fortified by political support from the government, which financed propaganda leaflets, among them *A Fig for the Spaniard* (1591). English sailors who had spent time in the cells of the Inquisition were given help with publishing their stories. Antonio Pérez, resident at this time in England, contributed to the campaign by his own writings, published in England from the 1590s, and by his authorship of the leaflet *A treatise Paraenetical* (1598).

*

Not until the nineteenth century was there a serious assessment of the antisemitic phase of the Spanish Inquisition. This development seems to have first taken place in England in the 1830s. Historians and novelists, conscious of the movements for emancipation of Catholics and Jews in England, 'began to use fifteenth-century Spain as a paradigm for the birth of a nation based on racial and religious homogeneity'.[18] They were influenced by the novels of Sir Walter Scott, notably his *Ivanhoe*, which had a Jewess as its heroine. American works such as Washington Irving's imaginative *Conquest of Granada* (1829), and Prescott's masterly *History of Ferdinand and Isabella* (1837) were also influential. The public, which had hitherto thought of the Inquisition only in terms of the persecution of Protestants, was able through such publications to appreciate the key role of the Jews in Spain. Prescott informed his readers that 'the fires of the Inquisition, which were lighted exclusively for the Jews, were destined eventually to consume their oppressors'.

The new awareness of the Jewish role gave rise to a number of important studies, both in Spain (the publications of Amador de los Ríos) and outside it (the pioneering researches of Yitzhak Baer). The terrible reality that most of the mortal victims of the Spanish Inquisition were of Jewish origin, left an uneffaceable memory of the tribunal in the minds of the Jewish people. Descendants of those who survived the great diaspora of 1492 considered the Inquisition to be their own special historical nightmare. Samuel Usque in the sixteenth century painted, with good reason, a terrifying picture of the Inquisition as a monster that

> rises in the air on a thousand wings ... wherever it passes its shadow spreads
> a pall of gloom over the brightest sun ... the green grass which it treads or
> the luxuriant tree on which it alights, dries, decays and withers ... it
> desolates the countryside until it is like the Syrian deserts and sands ...[19]

This vision created a powerful mythology about the Inquisition that rooted itself in the perception of those who felt that they were better equipped than anyone to understand how it operated. A respected Jewish scholar has argued that the Inquisition 'maintained its hold on the Iberian population through its terrorist methods, the dependence of royal power on its support, and the apparent absence of any alternative to combat heresy', and that 'practically no one was safe from its grasp'.[20] More recently, historians have extended the mythology in other directions, by projecting the image of a whole people driven into exile ('the entire Jewish population left Spain ... some 200,000'), and a Spain reduced to slavery ('under the iron grip of an institution that was feared and abhorred').[21] These presentations were obviously deeply influenced by the Jewish experience in twentieth-century Europe.

Among non-Jewish historians the perception of the Inquisition has been complex.[22] After generations of uninformed prejudice on the part of both defenders and critics of the Inquisition, the first real approach to a documented survey was begun by Juan Antonio Llorente, one of the last officials and the first modern historian of the tribunal. A supporter of the reforming pro-French party in Spain in the opening years of the nineteenth century, Llorente held various posts in the Inquisition, including (for two years) that of secretary of the Madrid tribunal. When the French occupiers of Spain abolished the Holy Office, he was entrusted with care of its papers. On the basis of this documentation, some of which he took into exile with him to France, Llorente prepared a history of the Inquisition, which was not published until 1817, in French and in Paris. Llorente's lengthy work, the first account to be based on original documentation, was epoch-making. It also had many faults, which subsequent scholars as well as those of a different ideological persuasion did not easily forgive. For a very long time, however, Llorente's account dominated the field; and even today his work is recognized as a classic.[23]

Llorente was one of the sources used by the American historian W. H. Prescott for his three-volume unfinished study of the reign of Philip II (1855). In this work Prescott found himself fascinated by the Inquisition, and developed a particularly negative image of Inquisitor General Valdés, who was made responsible for the intellectual harm done to Spain by the Holy Office, 'the malignant influence of an eye that never slumbered, an unseen arm ever raised to strike'.[24] Prescott's striking vision of the Inquisition may have contributed in part to the powerful image of the Grand Inquisitor created by Fyodor Dostoyevsky (who read Prescott in Russian in 1858)[25] in his novel *The Brothers Karamazov*.

The decisive step for Inquisition studies came in the 1870s, when the American scholar Henry Charles Lea began collecting material for a proposed history of the Inquisition in Spain. His work, published in four volumes in 1906–8 (but not consulted by Spanish scholars until nearly eighty years later), remains still the definitive history of the tribunal. Though Lea had strong prejudices that he expressed uncompromisingly, his work once and for all rescued the tribunal from the make-believe world of invented history, and placed it firmly in the arena of documented fact. Lea's work illuminated very many aspects of the Inquisition, but study of the documents did not guarantee an end to debate. Two major scholarly trends of controversy, founded on great learning but also on highly sub-jective intuitions, have had an important influence on literary and historical experts in the twentieth century.

The first of these trends, already touched on above, was in literature. Pioneered by Américo Castro, it developed a number of theses that inspired a generation of scholars but at the same time provoked hard-hitting criticisms from others. Central to the beliefs of the Castro school was a vision of the Inquisition as the great oppressor of creativity in Spain, precisely because they saw most creativity as Jewish. Some adepts of the school, going further than this, visualized a Spain in which every aspect of thinking and printing was directly controlled by the Holy Office. The second of the trends has been influential among some Jewish scholars who, inspired by the pioneering researches of Yitzhak Baer, have logically emphasized the anti-Jewish character of the Inquisition. In the process they have developed stimulating but controversial theses, of which the best-known is the affirmation that conversos and Jews in Spain were one people.

At about the same time that Prescott and Motley published their work, a mythology of Spain's decline began to be created among French and Spanish historians, and with it an insistence on the Inquisition's responsibility for economic and cultural decay. Spanish condemnation was uncompromising. Nineteenth-century liberals, the first proponents of the 'decline' theory, were ready to blame every failure in Spanish history on the Inquisition. The economic problems of the country were attributed to the Holy Office.[26] Subsequently, other western historians took up the theme. The persecution of conversos and the expulsion of the Jews led, apparently, to the impov-erishment and decay of Spain, and the destruction of its middle class. Religious persecution led to the decay of trade with Protestant powers and thus to a collapse in Spanish power and wealth.

None of these propositions, still widely current, has ever been supported by evidence of any sort. The Inquisition was particularly careful never to interfere in trade policy. Nor did the tribunal have any influence on industrial policy: foreign Protestant manufacturers were as a rule forbidden to settle in Spain, but numerous Flemish and other Catholic manufacturers were actively encouraged.

In the short term, there were often some highly negative aspects. The flight of conversos during the early years of the Inquisition in the 1480s, gave rise to complaints from civil authorities in both Andalusia and Catalonia. Problems of this nature continued in later periods. A Mallorcan noble in 1679 protested that the persecution of the Chuetas 'would result in the gravest damage to and destruction of the commerce that used to exist in Mallorca'. In 1683 the city of Murcia complained of 'the scarcity suffered in this city from all the property of merchants, the houses and revenue confiscated by the Holy Office'. In 1694 the town of Antequera claimed that 'the Inquisition had driven out considerable capital by castigating those who owned it'.[27] Even if such complaints could be substantiated, it would be difficult to prove any long-term damage to the economy.

Spaniards always had their own attitudes and mythology about the Inquisition. The people as a whole gave their support to its existence. The tribunal was, after all, not a despotic body imposed on them tyrannically, but a logical expression of the social prejudices prevalent in their midst. It was created to deal with a problem of heresy, and as long as the problem was deemed to exist people seemed to accept it. At every moment the inquisitors were convinced that the people were with them, and they were not necessarily wrong. 'It is only the lords and leading persons who wage this war against the Holy Office', they complained in Aragon in 1566, 'and not the people.'[28] At no time in *ancien régime* Spain – neither in the Castilian revolts of 1520 nor the Andalusian urban risings of 1648 nor in any other act of social unrest – did the populace attack the Inquisition as a religious institution. In 1640 in Barcelona they scared the Castilian inquisitors out of the country, but it was no more than a prelude to setting up a native non-Castilian Inquisition. Only in March 1820 in Madrid did the mobs for the first time break with intent into the tribunal's palaces, by now half-empty buildings from which a handful of startled prisoners were liberated.

Support for the tribunal was, however, always modified by considerable reserve. 'It is fine', a Catalan noble said in 1586, 'for the Holy Office to look into questions of faith and punish bad Christians; but as for other matters, they should be dealt with when the Cortes meets'.[29] Like others, he saw clearly that there were matters in which the Inquisition had no business to meddle. And indeed the Inquisition meddled very much less than we might think. Both defenders and opponents of the Inquisition have accepted without question the image of an omniscient, omnipotent tribunal whose fingers reached into every corner of the land. The extravagant rhetoric on both sides has been one of the major obstacles to understanding. For the Inquisition to have been as powerful as suggested, the fifty or so inquisitors in Spain would need to have had an extensive bureaucracy, a reliable system of informers, regular income and the co-operation of the secular and ecclesiastical authorities. At no time did it have any of these. From what we have seen of the often flimsy network of familiars and comisarios, the financial difficulties of the inquisitors and the perennial conflicts with all other jurisdictions (especially in the fuero realms), we can conclude that the real impact of the Inquisition was, after the first crisis decades, so marginal to the daily lives of Spaniards that over broad areas of Spain – principally in the rural districts – it was little more than an irrelevance. In Catalonia, beyond the major cities a town might see an inquisitor maybe once every ten years, or even once in a century; many never saw one in their entire history.[30] Central Castile excepted, this picture is probably valid for much of Spain. The people supported the tribunal, on this showing, not because it weighed on them heavily and oppressed them, but for precisely the opposite reason: it was seldom seen, and even less often heard. It has frequently been suggested that the survival of the proverb 'Con el Rey y con la Santa Inquisición, chitón!' ('On the king and the Holy Office, not a word!'[31]) is testimony to the power of the Holy Office to silence criticism. The suggestion not only betrays a curious belief that Spaniards are unable or unwilling to criticize those who rule over them: it is also unhistorical. The archives of the Inquisition contain thousands of cases of forthright criticism by ordinary Spaniards, not subversive radicals wishing to abolish the institution (though many did so wish) but ordinary citizens objecting to bullying familiars, greedy inquisitors and corrupt personnel. Very many Spaniards, neither of Jewish nor of Muslim origin, hated the Holy Office. Like any police system, it was not loved; but most Castilians, and many Spaniards, seem to have felt that its continuation was a guarantee of the everyday framework in which they lived.

The absence of real contact with the tribunal can be illustrated by the mythical image of it retained in the folk memory of country people. For the older generation of Galician peasants, as narrated to a researcher earlier this century,[32] the Inquisition experienced by their forefathers was still a living and frightening memory. The inquisitors came in the night in carriages specially fitted with rubber wheels that would make no noise; they listened at doors and windows to hear what people were saying; they took away beautiful girls; their favourite torture – on this there was absolute unanimity among those interviewed – was to sit their victim down and drip boiling oil on his head until he died. The persistence of this bizarre and completely fantastic image among the peasants was, one may presume, evidence of the enormous gap that had opened up between the Inquisition and the society it purported to defend.

There was, from generation to generation, no lack of criticism and opposition. Early critics such as Pulgar and Talavera could remember the tolerant aspects of convivencia. Alonso de Virués, humanist and bishop, also subsequently (in 1542) criticized intolerance and those 'who spare neither prison nor knout nor chains nor the axe; for such is the effect of these horrible means, that the torments they inflict on the body can never change the disposition of the soul'.[33] Luis de Granada for his part criticized (in 1582) those Spaniards who 'through misdirected zeal for the faith, believe that they commit no sin when they do ill and harm to those who are not of the faith, whether Moors or Jews or heretics or Gentiles'.[34] Juan de Mariana, a supporter of the Inquisition, criticized both forced conversion[35] and the belief in limpieza. By the eighteenth century, inquisitors like Abad y Sierra were convinced that fundamental changes in structure were needed. There was no wholly unquestioning support, either at the popular or the elite level.

Contact with the outside world was one of the most potent causes of growing disillusion with the Inquisition. Spaniards came to realize that coercion was not inevitable in religion, and that other nations seemed to exist happily without it. We have the opinion of a pharmacist arrested by the Inquisition at Laguna (Tenerife) in 1707. He is reported to have said

> that one could live in France because there there did not exist the poverty and subjection that today exists in Spain and Portugal, since in France they do not try to find out nor do they make a point of knowing who everyone is and what religion he has and professes. And so he who lives properly and is of good character may become what he wishes.[36]

A generation later, in 1741, another native of the Canaries, the Marquis de la Villa de San Andrés, echoed precisely the same sentiments when he praised Paris, where life was free and unrestricted 'and no one asks where you are going or questions who you are, nor at Easter does the priest ask if you have been to confession'.[37] In 1812 in the Cortes of Cadiz, the priest Ruiz Padrón, who had travelled in the United States and knew Benjamin Franklin, rejected the Inquisition on the grounds that it was unnecessary to the practice of the faith. This was the spirit that threatened to splinter the defences of a traditionalist society. It was, in one way, an urge to freedom, but in another way it was a demand for justice. The fate of the Jews and Moors continued to be on the conscience of intelligent statesmen. When José Carvajal began to interest himself in the attacks directed by Salucio against the statutes of limpieza, his main preoccupation was 'the cruel impiety with which they have treated those who were outside the Catholic religion, barring all human doors of entry against them'.[38] This was in 1751. A similar approach was adopted by the great statesman of the Spanish Enlightenment, Jovellanos, in 1798. For him the primary reason for criticizing the Inquisition was the fate of the conversos:

> From this arose the infamy that covered descendants of these conversos, who were reputed infamous by public opinion. The laws upheld this and approved the statutes of *limpieza de sangre*, which kept out so many innocent people not only from posts of honour and trust but also from entering churches, colleges, convents and even unions and trade guilds. From this came the perpetuation of hatred not only against the Inquisition but against religion itself.[39]

Jovellanos argued that the injustices committed against a whole section of society by the Inquisition now needed to be remedied. The tribunal had lost all theoretical justification for its existence, since the modern threat to religion came no longer from Jews and Moriscos and heretics but from unbelievers. Against these the tribunal would be of little avail, since its ministers were ignorant and incapable. The time had come to get rid of such a superfluous body, to right the injustices of history, and to restore to the bishops their old powers over heresy.

Despite this, Jovellanos and his other Catholic colleagues in the government and in the ranks of the nobility were not radical revolutionaries. Their desire for reform and for changes in society was limited by the concern for stability. The Catholic liberals who opposed the Inquisition were unwilling to look too far. Jovellanos wrote to his friend Jardine: 'You approve of the spirit of rebellion; I do not. I disapprove of it openly and am far from believing that it carries the seal of merit.'[40] Because of this the attitude of Catholics as such towards the Inquisition ceased to be of great consequence, and was lost among the waves of turbulence created by those whose hatred of the Holy Office was only part of their distrust of organized religion.

Because the Inquisition was a conflictive institution its history has always been polemical. The rule of secrecy, unfortunately, gagged the mouths of its own spokesmen and aided those of its detractors, with the result that for its entire career the propaganda war was won effortlessly by its enemies. The discovery of the riches of inquisitorial documentation has helped to restore the balance of information but also created new dangers. Ease of access to the archives has encouraged some scholars to rely exclusively on the Inquisition for their information, as though the Inquisition were a uniquely reliable source. As a result an enormous amount of data has been produced by researchers, but only limited progress has been made towards understanding the social or ideological conditions in which the Holy Office operated. In some respects, we have advanced little beyond the situation that impelled Menéndez Pelayo to satirize those who identified the tribunal with all the ills of Spain:

> Why was there no industry in Spain? Because of the Inquisition. Why are we Spaniards lazy? Because of the Inquisition. Why are there bull-fights in Spain? Because of the Inquisition. Why do Spaniards take a *siesta*? Because of the Inquisition.[41]

Undue concentration on the institution of the Holy Office, to the exclusion of other relevant social aspects, now constitutes the biggest single obstacle to understanding the phenomenon. The Inquisition, like any other policing body, needs to be studied within the broader context that it occupied in history: its significance can be grossly distorted if we rely only on its own documentation for information. Moreover, we too often assume that it had a special philosophy of its own. In reality, as the preceding pages have argued, the Inquisition was only a product of the society it served, and evolved in tune with that society.

Once the facile use of the Inquisition as an explanation for all the good or ill in Spanish history has been removed, the challenge to explain the cultural evolution of Spain becomes sharper. The decay in the universities, for example, clearly owed little to the Inquisition. Theology fell into a rigid Thomist and scholastic mould. 'If they prove to me that my faith is founded on St Thomas', exclaimed 'El Brocense', 'I'll shit on it and find another!' But by the seventeenth century Aquinas and Aristotle were the unshakeable pillars of philosophy in Spain. Population decline played a part in the declining intake of Castilian universities, where matriculations reached their peak in around 1620 and declined continuously into the eighteenth century. No new universities were founded in Castile between 1620 and the early nineteenth century. As in all periods of economic recession, preference went to 'useful' rather than speculative studies and the lack of prospects in certain subjects effectively doomed them. By 1648 it was proposed at Salamanca to suppress the chairs of Greek, Hebrew, mathematics and other subjects: Greek and Hebrew had not been taught since the 1550s.[42] For none of this can the Inquisition be blamed. In area after area of Spanish culture it is increasingly obvious that factors were at work which it would be grotesque to try to attribute to the Inquisition.

Aware that it was unreasonable to castigate the tribunal for all Spain's failures, Juan Valera in 1876 asked whether it was not something in Spain's own character that was culpable. He identified the cause as religious fanaticism: 'a fever of pride, a delirium of vanity ... We thought we were the new people of God, and confused religion with patriotic egoism ... Hence our divorce and isolation from the rest of Europe.'[43] Subsequent writers likewise looked at the problem in broader terms. Claudio Sánchez Albornoz saw the seeds of future conflict in the massive rejection by Spain of its Jewish and Arabic culture: 'we had no religious wars in the sixteenth century, but we have had them in the twentieth'.[44] The contradictions within Spain which had apparently been reconciled by the imposition of religious uniformity were to break out again. For Ramón Menéndez Pidal the reconciliation had never taken place, and there always existed a struggle – often mute, never suppressed – between Two Spains.[45] The interplay between African and European Spain, isolationist and international Spain, liberal and reactionary Spain, caused the tensions that explained the strife in Spanish history. The Two Spains followed 'the fated destiny of the two sons of Oedipus, who would not consent to reign together and mortally wounded each other'. Menéndez Pidal looked forward to an age when reconciliation would eventually occur, and reintegration would lead to unity of purpose in a tolerant society.

The Inquisition, by its very nature, had been opposed to a tolerant society. Its introduction by Ferdinand and Isabella brought an end to the society of convivencia and provoked relentless opposition from New Christians who recognized its capacity for evil. The problem did not, however, start with the Inquisition. For a generation before its introduction, the polarization of Spanish society between rival clans based on cultural antecedents had threatened political stability. New Christians featured both as victims and as aggressors. Discrimination on grounds of race had also existed long before the Inquisition. The tribunal, therefore, created no new problems and merely intensified old ones. Some Christian conversos were able sincerely to support the activities of the Holy Office but sought ways to mitigate its antisemitic tendencies and financial irregularities. This attempt at a compromise position turned out to be a costly illusion.

The Inquisition helped to institutionalize the prejudices and attitudes that had previously been commonplace in society. Like all police forces that operate in secrecy and are not publicly accountable, it began to enjoy the arrogance of power. As the society of conflict developed, the Inquisition found itself at the centre of communal tensions. The people accepted it because its punishments were directed not against them but against the scapegoats and the marginalized: heretics, foreigners, deviants. Outside the crisis years of the mid-sixteenth century, few intellectuals felt threatened. From the early eighteenth century onwards many felt that the Inquisition could be rendered harmless if subjected entirely to government control. Not until the end of that century did the tribunal show itself to be clearly out of step with opinion in both Church and state.

Even when all explanations have been offered, the questions remain. How could a society as apparently tolerant as Castile, in which the three great faiths of the West had coexisted for centuries and into which the mediaeval Inquisition had never penetrated, change its ideology in the fifteenth century, against the instincts of many great men in both Church and state? How could a clergy and population that had never lusted for blood except in war (Queen Isabella thought even bullfighting too gory), gaze placidly upon the burning alive of scores of their fellow Spaniards for an offence – prevarication in religion – that had never hitherto been a crime? How could the Spanish people – who were the first Europeans to broaden their vision by travelling the oceans and opening up the New World – accept without serious opposition the mental restrictions proposed by the Inquisition? The preceding pages have tried to offer the elements of an answer, but it is in the nature of the inquisitorial phenomenon that no answer can match the complexity of the questions. Even today in the twentieth century other nations have had and continue to have their Inquisitions: the human condition is subject to frailties that are not limited to any one people or faith and that regularly reverse the gains made in previous generations by 'civilization' and 'progress'.

LIST OF ABBREVIATIONS

ACA:CA	Archivo de la Corona de Aragón, Barcelona, section Consejo de Aragón
AE:CP, MD	Archives des Affaires Etrangères, Paris, section Correspondance Politique, Mémoires et Documents
AEM	*Anuario de Estudios Medievales*
AGS	Archivo General de Simancas
AGS:CJH	AGS section Consejo y Juntas de Hacienda
AGS:E	AGS section Estado
AGS:E/K	AGS section Estado K
AGS:PR	AGS section Patronato Real
AHN Inq	Archivo Histórico Nacional, Madrid, section Inquisición
AHR	*American Historical Review*
AHSI	*Archivum Historicum Societatis Iesu*
AR	*Archiv für Reformationsgeschichte*
ARSI Epist Hisp	Archivum Romanum Societatis Iesu, Epistolae Hispaniae
BH	*Bulletin Hispanique*
BHR	*Bibliothèque d'Humanisme et de la Renaissance*
BHS	*Bulletin of Hispanic Studies*
BL	British Library, London
BL Add	BL Additional manuscripts
BL Eg	BL Egerton manuscripts
BN	Biblioteca Nacional, Madrid
BRAE	*Boletín de la Real Academia Española*
BRAH	*Boletín de la Real Academia de la Historia*
BZ	Biblioteca Zabálburu, Madrid
CHE	*Cuadernos de Historia de España*
CHR	*Catholic Historical Review*
CODOIN	*Colección de Documentos Inéditos para la Historia de España*
EconHR	*Economic History Review*
Favre	Collection Favre, Bibliothèque Publique et Universitaire, Geneva

HAHR	*Hispanic American Historical Review*
HR	*Hispanic Review*
HS	*Hispania Sacra*
IMH	Institut Municipal d'Història, Barcelona
JEH	*Journal of Ecclesiastical History*
JQR	*Jewish Quarterly Review*
leg.	legajo (file)
MCV	*Mélanges de la Casa de Velázquez*
MLR	*Modern Language Review*
MP	*Modern Philology*
NRFH	*Nueva Revista de Filología Hispánica*
P&P	*Past and Present*
PAAJR	*Proceedings of the American Academy for Jewish Research*
PAPS	*Proceedings of the American Philosophical Society*
RABM	*Revista de Archivos, Bibliotecas y Museos*
REJ	*Revue des Etudes Juives*
RF	*Razón y Fe*
RFE	*Revista de Filología Española*
RH	*Revue Historique*
RI	*Revista de la Inquisición*
SCJ	*Sixteenth Century Journal*

NOTES

Chapter 1: A Society of Believers and Unbelievers (pp. 1–7)

1 AHN Inq lib. 733, f. 352.
2 Cited in Castro, p. 221.
3 Castro, p. 225.
4 Denis Menjot, 'Les minorités juives et musulmanes dans l'économie murcienne au bas Moyen-Age', in *Minorités et marginaux en Espagne et dans le Midi de la France (VIIe–XVIIIe siècles)*, Paris, 1986.
5 Adeline Rucquoi, 'Juifs et musulmans dans une ville de la Castille septentrionale', ibid.
6 C. Carrete Parrondo, 'Los judaizantes castellanos', in *Inquisición y conversos*, p. 201.
7 Cited in C. Carrete Parrondo, *El judaismo español y la Inquisición*, Madrid, 1992, p. 103.
8 Baer, I, chaps 5–6.
9 C. Carrete Parrondo, 'Nostalgia', p. 33.
10 Felipe de Meneses, *Luz del alma cristiana* (1554), ed. Madrid, 1978, pp. 317, 321.

11 This is the argument in Kamen 1993a.
12 The practice in the diocese of Toledo may be gauged by the prohibitions issued by the provincial council of Aranda in 1473: J. Tejada y Ramiro, *Colección de cánones y de todos los concilios*, 6 vols, Madrid, 1859, V, p. 24.
13 IMH Consellers C.XVIII, vol. 8, f. 95; AHN Inq lib. 731, f. 172.
14 *Fontes*, II, p. 120.
15 *Fontes*, II, p. 122.
16 C. Carrete Parrondo, ' "Duelos os dé Dios, e avrá Christiandad": nueva página sobre el criptojudaísmo castellano', *Sefarad*, ii, 1992, 369.
17 Monter, p. 24.
18 M.A. Fernández García, *Inquisición, comportamiento y mentalidad en el reino de Granada (1600–1700)*, Granada, 1989, pp. 110, 246.

Chapter 2: The Great Dispersion (pp. 8–27)

1 *Fontes*, II, p. 153.
2 'La Biblia de Mosé Arragel de Guadalfajara', cited in Castro, p. 489.
3 Cf. Angus Mackay, 'The Jews in Spain during the Middle Ages', in Kedourie, p. 33.
4 Mackay, ibid., in Kedourie, p. 34.
5 A.A. Neuman, *The Jews in Spain. Their social, political and cultural life during the Middle Ages*, 2 vols, Philadelphia, 1994, II, p. 184.
6 Cited by Pilar Pérez Viñtuales in *Destierros aragoneses*, p. 131.
7 Baer, II, pp. 95–134; P. Wolff, 'The

1391 pogrom in Spain. Social crisis or not?', *P&P*, 50, 1971; A. Mackay, 'Popular movements and pogroms in 15th-century Castile', *P&P*, 55, 1972.
8 Cited in Roth, p. 34.
9 Cited in E. Gutwirth, 'Towards expulsion: 1391–1492', in Kedourie, p. 54.
10 I here accept, in part, Roth, pp. 34–5.
11 Some writers equate the word with 'pig', but this is etymologically undocumented. By contrast there are several examples of the word being used

to refer to one who 'mars', i.e. spoils, the Christian faith. Thus Carrete Parrondo in *Fontes*, II, p. 53, cites a converso of 1497 saying 'Bien me llaman a mí marrano, pues que marré en volverme de la buena ley a la mala'.

12 Cf. David Romano, 'Rasgos de la minoría judía en la Corona de Aragón', in *Xudeus e Conversos*, II, pp. 229–30.

13 Neuman, II, p. 217; Castro, pp. 491–6; Caro Baroja, II, pp. 162–90.

14 M.A. González and P. de Forteza, 'Los médicos madrileños a fines del siglo XV', *Torre de los Lujanes*, 31, 1996, 225.

15 Monsalvo Antón, pp. 70–84.

16 Castro, p. 499.

17 Neuman, II, p. 187.

18 M.A. Ladero Quesada, 'Los judíos en el arrendamiento de impuestos', *Cuadernos de Historia*, anexos de *Hispania*, 6, 1975.

19 Carlos Alvarez García, 'Los judíos y la hacienda real bajo el reinado de los Reyes Católicos. Una compañía de arrendadores de rentas reales', in *Tres culturas*, p. 88.

20 This is the argument followed by Baer.

21 Bernáldez, chap. 43, p. 98.

22 Asunción Blasco, 'Los judíos en Aragón durante la baja Edad Media', in *Destierros aragoneses*, p. 57.

23 Pilar León Tello, *Judíos de Toledo*, 2 vols, Madrid, 1979, II, pp. 549–607.

24 F. Cantera Burgos and C. Carrete Parrondo, 'La judería de Buitrago', *Sefarad*, 32, 1972.

25 F. Cantera Burgos and C. Carrete Parrondo, 'La judería de Hita', *Sefarad*, 32, 1972.

26 A.A. Bel Bravo, *Los Reyes Católicos y los Judíos Andaluces (1474–1492)*, Granada, 1989, p. 128.

27 David Romano, 'Judíos hispánicos y mundo rural', *Sefarad*, ii, 1991, 364.

28 J. Cabezudo Astraín, 'La judería de Sos del Rey Católico', *Sefarad*, 32, 1972.

29 P. León Tello, 'La judería de Avila durante el reinado de los Reyes Católicos', *Sefarad*, 23, 1963.

30 M.F. Ladero Quesada, 'Judíos y cristianos en la Zamora bajomediaeval', in *Proyección histórica de España en sus tres culturas*, 3 vols, Valladolid, 1993, Vol. I, pp. 159–64.

31 Roth, p. 66.

32 For arguments against a decline, see E. Gutwirth, in Kedourie, pp. 54–68.

33 M.A. Motis Dolader, 'La expulsión de los judíos aragoneses', in *Destierros aragoneses*, p. 84.

34 C. Alvarez García, 'Los judíos y la hacienda', pp. 94–5.

35 Baer, II, pp. 70–243.

36 Riera Sans, pp. 76–7.

37 Riera Sans, p. 77.

38 Cited in Roth, p. 66.

39 E. Cantera Montenegro, 'El apartamento de judíos y mudéjares en las diócesis de Osma y Sigüenza a fines del siglo XV', *AEM*, xvii, 1987.

40 Carlos Barros, 'La tolerancia hacia los judíos en la Edad Media gallega', in *Xudeus e Conversos*, I, p. 103.

41 Motis Dolader, 'Los judíos zaragozanos', pp. 394–5.

42 Riera Sans, p. 79.

43 A possible total of seventy people, since not every taxpayer represented a full family.

44 Sources cited in J. Valdeón, 'Motivaciones socioeconómicas de las fricciones entre viejocristianos, judíos y conversos', in Alcalá 1995, p. 75.

45 Suárez Fernández, p. 16.

46 Suárez Fernández, p. 15.

47 Suárez Fernández, p. 33.

48 Motis Dolader, 'Los judíos zaragozanos', p. 397.

49 Cf. the details in Monsalvo Antón, pp. 148–80.

50 Cited by Angeles Navarro, 'La literatura y pensamiento de los hispanohebreos en el siglo XV', in *Expulsión de los judíos de España. II Curso de Cultura hispano-judía y sefardí*, Toledo, 1993, p. 57.

51 Cited by Valdeón, p. 76, in Alcalá 1995.

52 Cf. Roth, pp. 74–8. Also Kriegel, in

Xudeus e Conversos, I, p. 185: 'la plus
grosse partie de la documentation
témoigne indiscutablement d'une
solidarité des Juifs avec les conversos'.
53 'The majority of Jews had no love for
the conversos': Roth, p. 215.
54 E. Marín, 'Inventario de bienes
muebles de judíos en 1492', *Sefarad*, 48,
ii, 1988, n. 65.
55 *Fontes*, II, p. 77. The statement is of
1502.
56 Cited in Roth, p. 241.
57 *Fontes*, II, p. 23.
58 C. Carrete Parrondo, 'Los judaizantes
castellanos', in *Inquisición y conversos*, p.
198.
59 Cited in Roth, p. 214.
60 Fidel Fita, 'Nuevos datos para escribir
la historia de los judíos españoles: la
Inquisición en Jérez de la Frontera',
BRAH, 15, 1889.
61 Roth, pp. 283–4.
62 Motis Dolader, 'Los judíos
zaragozanos', p. 405.
63 Suárez Fernández, p. 41.
64 Suárez Fernández, p. 20.
65 W.H. Prescott, *History of the reign of
Ferdinand and Isabella*, 3rd edn, London,
1841, p. 269, n. 1.
66 J. Meseguer Fernández, 'La
Inquisición en Granada', in *Nueva visión*,
p. 386.
67 Stephen Haliczer, 'The Castilian
urban patriciate and the Jewish
expulsions of 1480–92', *AHR*, 78, Feb.
1973.
68 Cf. Maurice Kriegel, 'La prise d'une
décision: l'expulsion des juifs d'Espagne
en 1492', *RH*, 260, 1978.
69 Netanyahu 1968, pp. 54–6.
70 Printed in R. Conde, *La expulsión de
los judíos de la Corona de Aragón*,
Saragossa, 1991, doc. 1; also in Alcalá
1995, p. 129.
71 Pilar León Tello, *Judíos de Toledo*, I, p.
347.
72 M.A. Motis Dolader, in *Destierros
aragoneses*, p. 105.
73 *Fontes*, I, p. 137.
74 I adopt the form used by Roth,

p. 80. The sources refer to Seneor as chief
'rab' or 'rabbi', but he was obviously a
political rather than a religious figure.
75 Fidel Fita, 'La verdad sobre el
martirio del Santo Niño de La Guardia',
BRAH, 11, 1887; H.C. Lea, 'El Santo
Niño de La Guardia', in *Chapters from the
religious history of Spain*, Philadelphia,
1890, pp. 437–68; Baer, II, pp. 398–
423.
76 Danièle Iancu, *Les juifs de Provence
1475–1501: de l'insertion à l'expulsion*,
Aix, 1986; Shlomo Simonsohn, *The Jews
in the duchy of Milan*, 2 vols, Jerusalem,
1982, I, p. xxiv.
77 Motis Dolader, in *Destierros aragoneses*,
p. 111.
78 Cited by Maurice Kriegel, 'El edicto
de expulsión: motivos, fines, contexto',
in Alcalá 1995, p. 142.
79 C. Carrete Parrondo, 'Movimientos
mesiánicos en las juderías de Castilla',
in *Tres Culturas*, p. 68; J.N. Hillgarth,
*The Spanish Kingdoms 1250–1516. vol.
II: 1410–1516*, Oxford, 1978, pp. 419,
451.
80 Alain Milhou, *Colón y su mentalidad
mesiánica*, Valladolid, 1983, p. 305.
81 Mariana, bk 26, chap. 1.
82 Raphael, p. 53.
83 Henry Kamen, 'The Mediterranean
and the expulsion of Spanish Jews in
1492', *P&P*, 119, May 1988, 34–5;
Ladero Quesada, 'Las juderías de Castilla
según algunos "servicios" fiscales',
Sefarad, 31, 1971.
84 Riera Sans, p. 78.
85 Kamen, 'The Mediterranean', p. 37,
suggests 10,000. Riera suggests a total
of some nine thousand.
86 José Hinojosa Montalvo, 'La
demografía de la aljama judía de
Sagunto', *Sefarad*, 55, 1995, 274.
87 Bernáldez, chaps 110, 112.
88 Solomon Ibn Verga, in Raphael,
p. 97.
89 Joseph Ha Cohen and Rabbi Capsali,
in Raphael, pp. 17, 106.
90 For Aragon, A. Blasco, 'Los judíos del
reino de Aragón. Balance de los

estudios', *Actes del 1r col.loqui d'Història dels jueus a la Corona d'Aragó*, Lleida, 1991.

91 Carrete Parrondo, 'Nostalgia', p. 35.

92 Cf. Motis Dolader, 'Las comunidades judías en la corona de Aragón', in Alcalá 1995, pp. 32–54.

93 Rabbi Capsali, for instance (Raphael, p. 18), does not list Turkey as one of the immediate destinations of the exiles. Only later, he says (Raphael, pp. 20, 26), did some Jews from Naples go there.

94 Cited by Robert Bonfil, 'Italia: un triste epílogo', in Alcalá 1995, p. 249.

95 Rabbi Ha Levi, in Raphael, p. 87.

96 *Fontes*, I, p. 133, order of 25 June 1492.

97 Ladero Quesada 1988, p. 255.

98 Ladero Quesada 1988, p. 253.

99 *Fontes*, I, p. 75.

100 Cf. Raphael, p. 43.

101 The point, well known to specialists in the period, is reaffirmed by Roth, p. 313.

102 J. Gómez-Menor, 'Un judío converso de 1498. Diego Gómez de Toledo (Semuel Abolafia) y su proceso inquisitorial', *Sefarad*, 33, 1973.

103 *Fontes*, I, p. 75.

104 M.A. González and P. de Forteza (see n. 14 above), p. 223.

105 My conclusion, affirmed long ago, is now supported by Roth, p. 315. 'The truth is that the monarchs had no master plan for unification of the faith'; and by Kriegel, in *Xudeus e Conversos*, I, p. 188: 'aucun document rédigé à l'inspiration des souverains ne fait référence à la notion de la désirabilité d'une liquidation du pluralisme religieux'.

106 The point, made thirty years ago by Domínguez Ortiz and by myself, has now been reaffirmed by a Jewish scholar: Roth, pp. 272–5.

107 Suárez Fernández, p. 41.

108 E. Gutwirth, 'Reacciones ante la expulsión', in Alcalá 1995, p. 207.

109 Raphael, pp. 17, 43.

110 Jerónimo de Zurita, *Historia del rey Don Hernando el Catholico*, 6 vols, Saragossa, 1610, I, p. 9.

111 Luis de Páramo, *De origine et progressu Officii Sanctae Inquisitionis*, Madrid, 1598, chap. 6, p. 165.

112 For the expulsions from Orán in 1669, see Kamen 1981, pp. 492–3.

113 Bernáldez, chap. 112, p. 262.

Chapter 3: The Coming of the Inquisition (pp. 28–65)

1 *Fontes*, II, p. 56.

2 F. Márquez Villanueva, 'Conversos y cargos concejiles en el siglo XV', *RABM*, 63, ii, 1957.

3 Cited by J. Valdeón, 'Fricciones entre viejocristianos, judíos y conversos', in Alcalá 1995, p. 83.

4 P.L. Lorenzo Cadarso, 'Oligarquías conversas de Cuenca y Guadalajara (siglos XV y XVI)', *Hispania*, 186, 1994, 59.

5 Lorenzo Cadarso, 'Oligarquías conversas', p. 58.

6 Outline of the family in Roth, pp. 136–50. Also L. Serrano, *Los conversos D. Pablo de Santa María y D. Alfonso de Cartagena*, Madrid, 1942, pp. 23–4.

7 By contrast, there is no reason whatever for supposing – as is often done – that the first archbishop of Granada, Hernando de Talavera, was of converso origin.

8 Ladero Quesada 1984, p. 47.

9 'Copia de los sanvenitos que corresponden a la villa de Aguilar de la Frontera', BL Add 21447, fos. 137–9.

10 Cantera Burgos and León Tello, pp. xi–xii.

11 A. Rodríguez Moñino, 'Les Judaisants à Badajoz de 1493 à 1599', *REJ*, 15, 1956.

12 Juan Blázquez Miguel, *La Inquisición en Cataluña*, Toledo, 1990, p. 40.

13 M.A. Ladero Quesada, 'Sevilla y los

conversos: los "habilitados" en 1495',
Sefarad, ii, 1992, 438–9.

14 Domínguez Ortiz 1955,
pp.217–19.

15 For Quevedo, the Jewish conspiracy,
and Olivares, cf. J.H. Elliott, *The Count-
Duke of Olivares*, London and New
Haven, 1986, pp. 11, 556, 558.

16 Caro Baroja, II, pp. 162–244.

17 Inquisitors to Suprema, 28 Apr. 1579,
AHN Inq leg. 2704.

18 Chap. 11 below.

19 Published by R. Amador de los Ríos
in the *Revista de España*, vols. 105–6,
1885.

20 Printed in Caro Baroja, III,
pp. 287–99.

21 Caro Baroja, II, p. 264.

22 Good details in Roth, chap. 6.

23 B. Netanyahu, 'Fray Alonso de
Espina: was he a New Christian?',
PAAJR, 43, 1976.

24 Beinart 1981, p. 20.

25 E. Benito Ruano, *Toledo en el siglo XV*,
Madrid, 1961, appendices 16, 18, 19,
22, 44.

26 L. Delgado Merchán, *Historia
documentada de Ciudad Real*, Ciudad
Real, 1907, p. 419.

27 Caro Baroja, III, pp. 279–81.

28 Ladero Quesada 1984, p. 30.

29 Ladero Quesada 1984, p. 31.

30 For tensions in Córdoba, cf. John
Edwards, 'The Judeoconversos in the
urban life of Córdoba, 1450–1520',
Villes et sociétés urbaines au moyen age,
Paris, 1994.

31 S. Haliczer, cited in chap. 2, n. 67.

32 Netanyahu 1995, pp. 208–9; Roth,
p. 32.

33 Roth, p. 40.

34 I follow the excellent discussion in
Netanyahu 1995, p. 848 ff, though I do
not accept his dating the document to
1467.

35 Baer, II, p. 424.

36 Beinart 1981, p. 242.

37 José Faur, 'Four classes of conversos: a
typological study', *REJ*, 149, 1990,
113–24, appears to me a sensible

analysis that admits four varieties of
converso.

38 Cited in Netanyahu 1995, p. 410.

39 *Fontes*, II, p. 58.

40 E. Gutwirth, 'Elementos étnicos e
históricos en las relaciones judeoconversos en Segovia', in Yosef Kaplan,
p. 97.

41 A fair summary of such doubts is in
Roth, pp. 216–21.

42 Netanyahu 1995, p. 853.

43 Beinart, I, p. 339. Beinart's edition of
these documents is invaluable; however,
his own commentary on them is open to
dispute.

44 C. Carrete Parrondo, 'Los judaizantes
castellanos', in *Inquisición y conversos*, p.
197.

45 *Fontes*, II, pp. 37, 137.

46 Cf. John Edwards, 'Religious faith
and doubt in late medieval Spain',
P&P, 120, Aug. 1988, 13. See also chap.
12 below.

47 Both cited in Carrete Parrondo,
'Nostalgia', pp. 37–8.

48 Beinart, I, p. 371.

49 Beinart, I, pp. 311, 330.

50 *Fontes*, II, pp. 27, 45.

51 Cf. Edwards, 'Religious faith', p. 24.

52 Beinart, I, p. 481.

53 E. Gutwirth, 'Relaciones judeoconversos en Segovia', in Kaplan, p. 101.

54 *Fontes*, II, pp. 130, 98, 108.

55 Francesc Carreres i Candi,
'L'Inquisició barcelonina, substituïda
per l'Inquisició castellana (1446–1487)',
Institut d'Estudis Catalans, 1909–10,
p. 163.

56 Beinart, I, p. 82.

57 Cf. Netanyahu 1995, p. 1047.

58 Excellently summarized in
Netanyahu 1995, pp. 995–6, from
whom I take the examples that
follow.

59 Riera Sans, p. 84.

60 Riera Sans, p. 85.

61 Alonso de Palencia, *Crónica de Enrique
IV*, 4 vols, Madrid 1904–8, III, p. 108;
Bernáldez, p. 599.

62 Roth, p. 203, mistakenly dates the

foundation of the Inquisition to 1179.
No such body existed then.

63 Cf. Monter, p. 4, n. 3.

64 C. Carrete Parrondo, 'Los converos jerónimos', p. 101.

65 Azcona, p. 379.

66 Roth, p. 229, identifies Hojeda as 'head inquisitor' of Seville in 1478. I have found no evidence for this.

67 A good sketch of their measures is given in Tomás y Valiente, pp. 28–42.

68 Cf. Tomás y Valiente, pp. 157–60. The enquiries were known as 'inquisitio' in Latin, 'pesquisa' in Castilian.

69 The bulls of the early years are printed (with some errors) in Bernardino Llorca SJ, *Bulario Pontificio de la Inquisición Española en su período constitucional* (1478–1525), vol. 15, Miscellanea Historiae Pontificae, Rome, 1949.

70 Azcona, p. 387.

71 Cited in Netanyahu 1995, p. 853.

72 This last argument is the central thesis of Netanyahu's substantial study.

73 Cf. A. Cascales Ramos, *La Inquisición en Andalucía. Resistencia de los converos a su implantación*, Seville, 1986, pp. 57–69.

74 *Relación histórica de la Judería de Sevilla*, Seville, 1849, p. 24.

75 Bernáldez, chap. 44, p. 99.

76 Cf. Roth, pp. 244–6; Netanyahu 1995, pp. 1149–54.

77 Pulgar, V, p. 337.

78 I follow the convincing arguments in Netanyahu 1995, pp. 1155–64.

79 For the date 1488, see p. 138.

80 Lea, I, p. 587.

81 Lea, I, p. 233.

82 Lea, I, p. 590, appendix 11.

83 Quoted in Llorente 1812, p. 90.

84 Lea, I, p. 247.

85 Antonio C. Floriano, 'El Tribunal del Santo Oficio en Aragón. Establecimiento de la Inquisición en Teruel', *BRAH*, 86–7 (1925) and 88 (1926). Floriano's basic documentation, and other original sources, are published in the excellent compilation by Sesma Muñoz.

86 Sesma Muñoz, pp. 97–100.

87 Sesma Muñoz, p. 20.

88 Carreres i Candi, pp. 134–7.

89 Sesma Muñoz, p. 23.

90 Figures from the basic source for the early years of the Catalan Inquisition: Pere Miquel Carbonell, in *Colección de documentos inéditos del Archivo de la Corona de Aragón*, Barcelona, 1864–5, vols 27–8.

91 García-Cárcel 1976, p. 50.

92 García-Cárcel 1976, p. 60.

93 Previous murders of inquisitors, notably by the Cathars in France in 1243, had always provoked a severe reaction. Other assassinated inquisitors included Conrad of Marburg (Germany) in 1233 and Peter of Verona (Italy) in 1252.

94 He was popularly venerated as 'el Santo martyr', and was assigned a feast day in Spain in the sixteenth century. But a reluctant Rome did not canonize him until 1867.

95 Netanyahu 1995, pp. 1164–72, has some interesting arguments in this respect.

96 Netanyahu sees Ferdinand as the hammer of the conversos.

97 Jordi Ventura, 'A l'entorn del judaisme de les famílies Santangel i Sánchez', in *XIII Congrés d'Història de la Corona d'Aragó*, Palma, 3 vols, 1990, vol. III, p. 47.

98 Jordi Ventura, 'Els inicis de la Inquisició espanyola a Mallorca', *Randa*, 5, 1977.

99 Lea, I, pp. 167, 183, 267.

100 Figures for Barcelona from Carbonell, for Valencia from García-Cárcel 1976, p. 195.

101 For the edict in general, see chap. 8.

102 Lea, I, p. 169.

103 This is my translation of a particularly difficult phrase.

104 C. Carrete Parrondo, 'Los judaizantes castellanos', in *Inquisición y conversos*, p. 197.

105 Ibid., p. 196.

106 See chap. 9 below.

107 There were always exceptions: cf. *Historia de la Inquisición*, II, pp. 347–57.

108 Lea, I, pp. 169–70.

109 Ladero Quesada 1984, p. 41, suggests that most conversos did not reappear before the Inquisition, a conclusion I accept. García-Cárcel 1976, p. 180, by contrast, claims (without evidence) that in Valencia only 12 per cent of the hundreds who came forward escaped later prosecution.

110 Pulgar, p. 336.

111 Bernáldez, chap. 44, p. 101.

112 Diego Ortiz de Zúñiga, *Anales de Sevilla*, Madrid, 1677: year 1524, p. 482. The figures are certainly exaggerated. More recently it has been suggested that deaths did not exceed 248: Klaus Wagner, 'La Inquisición en Sevilla (1481–1524)', *Homenaje al Profesor Carriazo*, 3 vols, Seville, 1973, vol. III.

113 Dedieu, p. 242.

114 Monter, pp. 15, 21. The diagram of cases in Aragon in Motis Dolader, p. 402, suggests even fewer executions, but his data are evidently incomplete.

115 The figures given in García-Cárcel 1976, p. 174, according to which some seven hundred people were executed, are unproven. Monter 1990, p. 21, n. 36, concludes that García-Cárcel's figures are 'inaccurate'.

116 Monter, p. 21. This figure is supported by the painstaking work of Blázquez Miguel, who suggests fourteen executions of conversos up to 1499, and around twenty in the subsequent period: Blázquez Miguel, *Cataluña*, pp. 38, 51.

117 Some likely figures were published in the 1985 edition of my book. Roth, p. 265, curiously enough, printed my data but omitted the supporting references, and then concluded that I had not read the references.

118 Fidel Fita; Fita also suggests that 500 were burnt in effigy.

119 Monter, p. 53, makes a lower estimate of 1,500 executions.

120 Carrete Parrondo, 'Nostalgia', p. 40.

121 Carreres i Candi, p. 160.

122 IHM Consellers C. XVIII–6.

123 García-Cárcel 1976, p. 171.

124 Roth, p. 222: 'the desire to totally eradicate the converso class and also to enrich by the confiscation of as much property as possible'.

125 Text published by Azcona, in *Nueva visión*, p. 127.

126 Samuel Usque, in Raphael, p. 137.

127 And that many historians appear to have accepted unquestioningly.

128 Cf. J. Jiménez Lozano, 'The persistence of Judaic and Islamic cultemas in Spanish society', in Alcalá 1987, p. 407, who also cites Llorente in this respect.

129 Beinart, I, pp. 16–21.

130 Beinart, I, pp. 163–80. Even Beinart is forced to comment that the 'Jewish' practices of Chinchilla seem 'unimpressive'.

131 *Fontes*, II, pp. 19, 21.

132 *Fontes*, II, p. 32.

133 Beinart, I, p. 193.

134 Beinart, I, p. 116.

135 Beinart, I, p. 92.

136 Beinart, I, p. 404.

137 *Fontes*, II, p. 24. The testimony was given by a Jew in 1490.

138 Reading through the case histories now, this point appears quite obvious to me. It was only the reading of Netanyahu's forceful *Origins* (1995) that obliged me to rethink the whole question. Subsequently, I found support in Roth, pp. 217–20, 268.

139 Anonymous chronicler, *c.* 1495, in Raphael, p. 133.

140 Netanyahu 1995, p. 928.

141 Netanyahu 1995, p. 929.

142 *Fontes*, II, pp. 107, 149.

143 This view is echoed by one of the experts on the period, Tarsicio de Azcona. He refers to the post-1492 years as those of 'la supresión de los conversos' (in *Nueva visión*, p. 120).

144 All quotations that follow come from Carrete Parrondo, 'Nostalgia'. Carrete, however, does not distinguish between pre-1480 and post-1492 conversos.

145 Rabbi Capsali, in Raphael, p. 44.

Chapter 4: A Continuing Opposition (pp. 66–82)

1 Inquisitors to Suprema, 1618 AHN Inq lib. 743, f. 95.
2 'What we cannot doubt, is that in the fifteenth and sixteenth centuries the immense majority of the Spanish people, with their kings, magistrates and bishops leading them, gave their decisive support to the proceedings of the Inquisition': Bernardino Llorca SJ, *La Inquisición en España*, Barcelona, 1936, p. 166.
3 Llorente 1812, p. 37.
4 For pre-Inquisition trials in one city see Beinart 1981, p. 78.
5 The non-Spanish character of the Inquisition has prompted both Américo Castro and Claudio Sánchez Albornoz (the latter in *España, un enigma histórico*, 2 vols, 2nd edn, Buenos Aires, 1956, chap. I, n. 4) to argue that it was of Jewish origin.
6 Mariana, XXXI, p. 202.
7 J. Vicens Vives, *Ferran II i la ciutat de Barcelona 1479–1516*, 2 vols, Barcelona, 1936, I, p. 376.
8 Miguel Avilés, 'Motivos de crítica a la Inquisición en tiempos de Carlos V', in *Nueva Visión*, p. 187.
9 Mariana, XXXI, p. 202.
10 Vicens Vives, *Ferran II*, I, p. 382.
11 BN MS. 1517. For Pulgar's general position see F. Cantera Burgos, 'Fernando de Pulgar y los conversos', *Sefarad*, 4, 1944.
12 Cited in Márquez 1980a, p. 25; cf. Azcona, p. 399.
13 'Baptizati invite non recipiunt Sacramentum nec characterem baptismalem, sed remanent infideles occulti': Páramo, *De origine* (cited in chap. 2, n. 111), p. 165.
14 José de Sigüenza, *Historia de la Orden de San Jerónimo*, 2 vols, Madrid 1907 (Nueva Biblioteca de Autores Españoles, vols 8, 12) II, p. 306.
15 *Católica impugnación*, ed. F. Martín, introd. by F. Márquez Villanueva, Barcelona, 1961, p. 68.
16 Márquez 1980a, p. 233.
17 Bernáldez, chap. 44.
18 H. Graetz, 'La police de l'Inquisition d'Espagne à ses débuts', *BRAH*, 23, 1893.
19 Beinart 1981, p. 134.
20 Cf. J. Edwards, 'Trial of an Inquisitor: the dismissal of Diego Rodríguez Lucero, inquisitor of Córdoba, in 1508', *JEH*, 37, ii, Apr. 1986.
21 Tarsicio de Azcona, in *Nueva Visión*, p. 144.
22 Luis Ramírez y Las Casas Deza, *Anales de Córdoba*, in *CODOIN*, CXII, p. 279.
23 R. Gracia Boix, *Colección de documentos para la Historia de la Inquisición de Córdoba*, Córdoba, 1982, pp. 86, 96, 103; Tarsicio de Azcona, in *Nueva Visión*, p. 145.
24 T. Herrero del Collado, 'El proceso inquisitorial por delito de herejía contra Hernando de Talavera', *AHDE*, 1969.
25 Text (of May 1507) published by Azcona in *Nueva visión*, p. 130.
26 C. Fernández Duro, 'Vida y obras de Gonzalo de Ayora', *BRAH*, 17, 1890.
27 AGS:PR leg. 28, f. 39.
28 Lea, I, p. 211.
29 Lea, I, p. 211.
30 AGS:PR Inq leg. 28, f. 16.
31 AHN Inq leg. 4724², no. 8.
32 P. Gayangos and Vicente de la Fuente, *Cartas del Cardenal Don Fray Francisco Jiménez de Cisneros*, Madrid, 1867, p. 261.
33 Lea, I, p. 215.
34 All foregoing details from Llorente 1812, pp. 119–31.
35 AGS:PR Inq leg. 28, f. 45.
36 Llorente 1812, p. 156.
37 Joseph Pérez, *La Révolution des 'Comunidades' de Castille (1520–1521)*, Bordeaux, 1970, p. 509.
38 For all this, J.I. Gutiérrez Nieto, 'Los conversos y el movimiento comunero', *Hispania*, 94, 1964; and Pérez, *La Révolution*, pp. 507–14, 549–52.
39 BL Eg. 1832, fos 37–40.

40 Colas Latorre and Salas Auséns, p. 505.
41 Pérez, *La Révolution*, p. 551, n. 117.
42 Monter, p. 324.
43 Reguera, p. 121.
44 Comisario to inquisitors, 14 Sep. 1574, AHN Inq lib. 738, f. 5.
45 Kamen 1993a, p. 260.
46 Monter, p. 322.
47 In the 140 years between 1536 and 1675 the Inquisition of Mallorca, for example, did virtually nothing. This fascinating inactivity also has its interest for the social historian.

Chapter 5: Excluding the Reformation (pp. 83–102)

1 Bataillon, p. 490.
2 Bataillon, pp. 110, 454. For an overview of the impact of the Reformation on Spain, see H. Kamen, 'Spain', in B. Scribner, R. Porter and M. Teich, eds, *The Reformation in national context*, Cambridge, 1994.
3 Bataillon, p. 280.
4 Bataillon, p. 240. The basic document in the debate has been printed by M. Avilés, *Erasmo y la Inquisición*, Madrid, 1980.
5 Bataillon, p. 277.
6 Helen Nader, *The Mendoza family in the Spanish Renaissance*, New Brunswick, 1979.
7 For a comment on the 'depressing' state of Spanish humanism, see Jeremy Lawrance, 'Humanism in the Iberian peninsula', in A. Goodman and A. MacKay, *The Impact of Humanism on Western Europe*, London, 1990, pp. 248–54.
8 On the state of spoken Latin, Gil Fernández, pp. 30–5.
9 Cardinal Mendoza to king, 20 Sep. 1561, AGS:E leg. 142.
10 Márquez 1980b, prints the edict, pp. 229–38.
11 There is a splendid study by Angela Selke, *El Santo Oficio de la Inquisición. Proceso de Fr. Francisco Ortiz (1529–1532)*, Madrid, 1968.
12 John E. Longhurst, *Luther and the Spanish Inquisition: the case of Diego de Uceda 1528–1529*, Albuquerque, 1953.
13 Baer, II, p. 275.
14 Baer, II, p. 350–6.
15 Cf. the comments of J.L. González Novalín, discussing the views of
Márquez, in García-Villoslada, III, ii, pp. 153–4.
16 M. Ortega Costa, *Proceso de la Inquisición contra María de Cazalla*, Madrid, 1978.
17 A good summary of the principal trials by Melquiades Andrés in *Historia de la Inquisición*, I, pp. 488–520.
18 Isabel was released in December 1538, Alcaraz in February 1539. A late casualty of the alumbrado trials was the Old Christian Rodrigo de Bivar, chaplain to the duke of Infantado, arrested in 1539 but released: see Alastair Hamilton, *El proceso de Rodrigo de Bivar (1539)*, Madrid, 1979.
19 Juan de Avila, *Avisos y Reglas Cristianas sobre aquel verso de David: Audi, Filia*, ed. L. Sala Balust, Barcelona, 1963, p. 32.
20 Angela Selke, 'Vida y muerte de Juan López de Celaín in *BH*, 62, 1960.
21 Bataillon, pp. 438–70.
22 Description of his death made to Francisco Borja: ARSI Epist Hisp 103, f. 231.
23 J.E. Longhurst, *Erasmus and the Spanish Inquisition: the case of Juan de Valdés*, Albuquerque, 1950; J.C. Nieto, *Juan de Valdés (1509?–1541)*, Michigan, 1968; M. Bataillon, *Erasmo y el Erasmismo*, Barcelona, 1977, pp. 245–85; Carlos Gilly, 'Juan de Valdés: Übersetzer und Bearbeiter von Luthers Schriften in seinem *Diálogo de Doctrina*', AR, 74, 1983.
24 Bataillon, pp. 476–7.
25 J. Goñi Gaztámbide, 'El impresor Miguel de Eguía procesado por la Inquisición', HS, 1, 1948.

26 Lea, III, p. 419.
27 Bataillon, p. 490.
28 Bataillon, p. 545.
29 Schäfer identifies only thirty-two cases; but very many more (cf. M. Jiménez Monteserín, 'Los luteranos ante el tribunal de la Inquisición de Cuenca 1525–1600', in *Nueva visión*, p. 695) can be found.
30 J.I. Tellechea, 'Biblias secuestradas por la Inquisición española en 1552', *BH*, 64, 1962.
31 J.L. González Novalín, *El inquisidor general Fernando de Valdés*, 2 vols, Oviedo, 1968.
32 Soto to emperor, 25 Aug. 1552, AGS:E leg. 89, f. 68.
33 For Egidio and other 'Protestants' see Edward Boehmer, *Bibliotheca Wiffeniana: Spanish Reformers of two centuries, from 1520*, 3 vols, London, 1864–1904.
34 Cf. Alvaro Huerga, *Predicadores, alumbrados e Inquisición en el siglo XVI*, Madrid, 1973. In a careful study, Robert C. Spach, 'Juan Gil and sixteenth-century Spanish Protestantism', *SCJ*, 26, iv, 1995, inclines to the view that Egidio was neo-Protestant; but I am not convinced of this.
35 A. Gordon Kinder, 'Cipriano de Valera, Spanish reformer', in *BHS*, 46, 1969; and his *Cassiodoro de Reina*, London, 1975. For the Seville community, Schäfer, I, pp. 345–67; II, pp. 271–426.
36 Schäfer, I, pp. 233–48; III, pp. 1–813.
37 Leonor de Vivero was the wife of Pedro de Cazalla of Valladolid. Both had been patrons in 1520 of Francisca Hernández, and were related to María de Cazalla, the alumbrada of Guadalajara. Of the ten children of Leonor and Pedro, four were burnt by the Inquisition (the three priests Agustín de Cazalla, Francisco de Vivero and Pedro de Cazalla). Leonor's bones were exhumed, and the family house razed.
38 On Rojas and Seso see Tellechea 1977; and 'El clima religioso español en 1550', in Tellechea 1968, I, pp. 105–239.
39 J.E. Longhurst, 'Julian Hernández', and E. Droz, 'Note sur les impressions genevoises transportées par Hernández', *BHR*, 22, 1960.
40 Tellechea 1968, II, p. 241, n. 21.
41 AGS:PR leg. 28, f. 37.
42 Lea, III, p. 571, appendix VIII.
43 Tellechea 1968, I, p. 147.
44 Diego Suárez to Laínez, Seville, 23 Aug. 1559, ARSI Epist Hisp 96, f. 398.
45 Schäfer, II, pp. 286–8.
46 Dead and absent accused were represented at autos by figures or effigies which were burnt in their stead: hence the need to talk of others being burnt in person.
47 BN MS. 9175, fos 258–60.
48 Schäfer, II, p. 107.
49 Huerga, p. 9.
50 Both cases cited in Jiménez Monteserín, 'Los luteranos', in *Nueva visión*, pp. 724–7.
51 Valdés to Philip, AGS:E leg. 129, f. 128.
52 Cf. Monter, p. 43; J. García Servet, *El humanista Cascales y la Inquisición murciana*, Madrid, 1978, J. Contreras, *Sotos contra Riquelmes*, Madrid, 1992.
53 'Lo que parece convernia proveerse', AGS:E leg. 129, f. 112.
54 Cf. Monter, p. 50: 'after 1570 great autos were rarely held in Castile'. He sees 'an increase in pomp and solemnity around 1570', p. 51. For further discussion of autos, see chapter 9 below.
55 The exact number is uncertain. For the figures in this paragraph I have been guided in part by W. Monter, 'Heresy executions in Reformation Europe, 1520–1565', in O.P. Grell and B. Scribner, *Tolerance and intolerance in the European Reformation*, Cambridge, 1996.
56 Philip to Valdés, 23 Aug. 1560, Favre, vol. 29, f. 4.
57 A. Gordon Kinder, 'A hitherto unknown group of protestants in

sixteenth-century Spain', *Cuadernos de Historia de Jerónimo Zurita*, 51–2, 1985, 140–1.

58 Christine Wagner, 'Los Luteranos ante la Inquisición de Toledo en el siglo XVI', *HS*, 94, xlvi, 1994, 480.

59 Cf. Bataillon, p. 728; Monter, p. 130.

60 Eugenio Asensio, 'Pedro de Orellana, minorita luterano', in *Nueva visión*, pp. 785–95.

61 Quadra to king, London, 11 Oct. 1561, AE:CP, MD vol. 234, f. 105.

62 Guzmán de Silva to king, London, 26 Apr. 1565, *CODOIN*, XXVI, p. 540.

63 Canto's detailed memorandum of 1563, in AGS:CJH leg. 55, f. 174, gives a good sketch of Spanish heretics in Europe.

64 Canto to Eraso, Brussels, 12 May 1564, AGS:E leg. 526, f. 125.

65 Reguera, p. 145.

66 Klaus Wagner (cited above, chap. 3, n. 112), III, p. 490.

67 Werner Thomas, *Een spel van kat en muis. Zuidnederlanders voor de Inquisitie in*

Spanje 1530–1750, Brussels, 1991, p. 151.

68 Letter to Suprema, 23 Oct. 1560, AHN Inq lib. 730, f. 23.

69 Schäfer, II, pp. 1–106.

70 Reguera, p. 70.

71 Monter, p. 236. Figures are rounded off.

72 I can recall sitting through a sermon in Valladolid in the 1960s, when the preacher denounced foreign Catholics for their liberal tendencies.

73 Reguera, p. 163.

74 Kamen 1993a, p. 220.

75 Philip to Requesens, Jan. 1569, cited in L. Serrano, *Correspondencia diplomática enre España y la Santa Sede*, 4 vols, Madrid 1914, III, p. cii.

76 Álava to Philip II, AGS:E/K 1502, fos 9, 15; 1503, f. 22.

77 Álava to Philip II, Feb. 1565, AGS:E/K 1503, f. 37.

78 Álava to Philip II, June 1565, AGS:E/K 1504, f. 6.

79 AGS:E/K 1503, f. 76.

Chapter 6: The Impact on Literature and Science (pp. 103–36)

1 Araoz to Diego Laínez, ARSI Epist Hisp 96, f. 430.

2 Text in Bujanda, V, pp. 121–2.

3 Cf. Bujanda, V, p. 44.

4 The law is printed in Bujanda, V, pp. 122–7.

5 Kamen 1993a, p. 396.

6 Kamen 1993a, p. 397.

7 Bujanda, V, p. 125; Kamen 1993a, p. 397.

8 Bujanda, V, p. 124.

9 Kamen 1993a, chap. 8.

10 Most of what follows is drawn from Kamen 1993a, pp. 388ff.

11 G. Antolín, 'La librería de Felipe II', *BRAH*, 90, 1927, 341.

12 Cf. Kamen 1993a, pp. 388 ff.

13 AHN Inq leg. 2155¹.

14 Kamen 1993a, p. 398. There were theoretical controls on some reprints, e.g. in 1569 the royal council claimed

the sole right to relicense Church publications.

15 T.S. Beardsley Jr., 'Spanish printers and the classic, 1482–1599', *HR*, 47, 1979, 30.

16 Cf Kamen 1993a, pp. 389–95.

17 Kamen 1993a, p. 393.

18 Jaime Moll, 'Problemas bibliográficas del libro del Siglo de Oro', *BRAE*, 59, 1979; also his 'Valoración de la industria editorial española del siglo XVI', in *Livre et lecture en Espagne et en France sous l'Ancien Régime*, Paris, 1981.

19 Cited in Kamen 1993a, p. 398.

20 Tellechea 1968, II, pp. 241, 255.

21 J.M. López Piñero, *Ciencia y Técnica en la Sociedad española de los siglos XVI y XVII*, Barcelona, 1979, pp. 141–4.

22 Francés de Álava to king, Montpellier, 18 Dec. 1564, AGS:E/K leg. 1505, f.

28; Toulouse, 18 Jan. 1565, ibid., leg. 1503, f. 20.

23 Kamen 1993a, p. 396.

24 BZ 130, f. 12.

25 Report of Jan. 1585, BZ 130, f. 12.

26 For the Indices in general, see Heinrich Reusch, *Der Index der verbotenen Bücher*, 2 vols, Bonn, 1883–5.

27 *Tres índices expurgatorios de la Inquisición española en el siglo XVI*, Madrid, 1952.

28 Cf. Bujanda, V, pp. 63–76.

29 J.I. Tellechea, 'Biblias publicadas fuera de España secuestradas por la Inquisición española en 1552', *BH*, 64, 1962.

30 Monter, p. 238.

31 Bujanda, V, pp. 77–90, 148–62.

32 Bujanda, V, p. 162, sees the 1554 censorship of Bibles as still 'fruit d'un certain oecuménisme'.

33 Cf. Bujanda, V, p. 110.

34 Calculated from the analysis in Bujanda, V, pp. 164–91.

35 Kamen 1997, chap. 2.

36 Mario Scaduto SJ, 'Laínez e l'Indice del 1559', *AHSI*, 24, 1955.

37 Cf. Otis H. Green, *Spain and the western tradition*, 4 vols, Madison, 1963–6, IV, p. 140.

38 Cf. Bataillon, pp. 734–6.

39 Cf. Márquez 1980a, pp. 151–2, 233–5.

40 Discussed above, chap. 5.

41 Justo Cuervo, 'Fray Luis de Granada y la Inquisición', *Homenaje a Menéndez Pelayo*, 2 vols, Madrid, 1899, I, pp. 733–43.

42 Cándido de Dalmases SJ, 'San Francisco de Borja y la Inquisición española, 1559–61', *AHSI*, 41, 1972.

43 Juan Suárez to Laínez, 20 Oct. 1559, ARSI Epist Hisp 96, f. 444.

44 Huerga, *passim*.

45 Cited by C. Carrete Parrondo, 'Los judaizantes castellanos ante la Inquisición 1482–1505', in *Inquisición y conversos*, p. 194.

46 Cf. Bujanda, V, p. 74.

47 V. Pinto Crespo, *Inquisición*

y control ideológico en la España del siglo XVI, Madrid, 1983, pp. 166–9, shows that not all the books were in fact burnt.

48 Kamen 1993a, p. 223.

49 V. Pinto Crespo, 'Nuevas perspectivas sobre el contenido de los Indices inquisitoriales hispanos del siglo XVI', *HS*, xxxiii, 1981, 616.

50 Pinto Crespo, *Inquisición y control*, p. 182.

51 Philip II to Alba, 24 Dec. 1569, AGS:E leg. 542, f. 4.

52 Bujanda, VI, pp. 38–9, offers this valuable suggestion to explain the delay in the Index.

53 Felix Asensio SJ, 'Juan de Mariana ante el Indice quiroguiano de 1583–4', *Estudios Bíblicos*, 31, 1972.

54 Bujanda, VI, p. 76.

55 Bujanda, VI, pp. 76–82.

56 Bujanda, VI, pp. 100–8.

57 Text in *RABM*, 8, 1903, 218–21. On the authorship, P.E. Russell, 'Secular literature and the censors: a sixteenth-century document re-examined', *BHS*, 69, 1982.

58 Cf. the memoir printed in Bujanda, VI, pp. 55–63.

59 Pinto Crespo, *Inquisición y control*, p. 56.

60 Cf. *Perfiles jurídicos*, p. 390.

61 Miguel Avilés, 'La censura inquisitorial de "Los seis libros de la República" de Jean Bodin', *HS*, 76, xxxvii, 1985.

62 See the sharp protest by the seventeenth-century inquisitorial censor Murcia de la Llana when Rome banned a book by a Jesuit friend: 'it is incredible that a book should be totally banned from Rome after circulating for many years among Spaniards without causing any offence': AHN Inq lib. 1231, fos 672–3.

63 J. Pérez Villanueva, 'Baronio y la Inquisición española', *Baronio storico e la Controriforma, Atti di convegno di studi, Sora 1979*, Sora, 1982.

64 Kamen 1993a, p. 228.

65 Sources for this paragraph in Kamen 1993a, pp. 225–6.

66 Cited in Pinto Crespo, *Inquisición y control*, p. 104. Marcus Pérez, a Calvinist, was of Spanish converso origin.

67 'Sobre visitas de navios', AHN Inq lib. 1275, f. 123.

68 A. Redondo, 'Luther et l'Espagne de 1520 à 1536', *MCV*, I, 1965.

69 J. Pardo Tomás, *Ciencia y Censura. La Inquisición Española y los libros científicos en los siglos XVI y SVII*, Madrid, 1991, p. 30.

70 Reguera, pp. 140–2.

71 AHN Inq lib. 737, f. 343.

72 AHN Inq lib. 1233, f. 209.

73 AHN Inq lib. 743.

74 AHN Inq leg. 2155¹.

75 Order of Mar. 1606, AHN Inq lib. 743.

76 AHN Inq lib. 737, f. 73.

77 AHN Inq leg. 4470¹, no. 3.

78 Pinto Crespo, *Inquisición y control*, p. 128.

79 Kamen 1993a, p. 224.

80 AHN Inq lib. 731, f. 166.

81 Kamen 1993a, p. 223.

82 AHN Inq leg. 4470¹, no. 3.

83 C. Péligry, 'Les difficultés de l'édition castillane au XVIIe siècle', *MCV*, 13, 1977.

84 Pinto Crespo, *Inquisición y control*, p. 641.

85 Kamen 1993a, p. 223.

86 Cf. Kamen 1993a, p. 228.

87 AHN Inq leg. 4517¹, no. 1.

88 AHN Inq leg. 4470¹, no. 4; leg. 4517¹, no. 1. Cf. also Pardo Tomás, *Ciencia y Censura*, pp. 289–91.

89 M. Agulló y Cobo, 'La Inquisición y los libreros españoles en el siglo XVII', *Cuadernos Bibliográficos*, 28, 1972.

90 See Bujanda, V, pp. 127–31.

91 Fidel Fita SJ, 'Los tres procesos de San Ignacio de Loyola en Alcalá de Henares', *BRAH*, 33, 1898.

92 Dalmases, 'San Francisco de Borja', p. 64.

93 Gil Fernández, p. 447.

94 Llorente 1817, I, pp. 343–5; Márquez 1980a, pp. 40–2; Bataillon, p. 164.

95 Lea, III, pp. 149–62; Luis Alonso Getino OP, 'La causa de Fr Luis de León', *RABM*, 9, 1903 and 11, 1904; *CODOIN*, XI, Madrid, 1847.

96 Miguel de la Pinta Llorente OP, *Proceso contra el hebraista Martín Martínez de Cantalapiedra*, Madrid, 1946, p. 392.

97 B. Rekers, *Benito Arias Montano*, London, 1972, chap. 3. This interesting study has several important slips, including the claim that 'the whole of Montano's work was prohibited' by the Inquisition (p. 68); on this point see J.A. Jones, 'Pedro de Valencia's defence of Arias Montano: the expurgatory indexes of 1607 (Rome) and 1612 (Madrid)', *BHR*, 40, 1978. Rekers also accepts the claim by Sicroff (Sicroff, p. 269) that Montano was of converso origin.

98 *CODOIN*, XLI, pp. 316, 387.

99 Gregorio de Andrés, *Proceso inquisitorial del Padre Sigüenza*, Madrid, 1975.

100 A. Tovar and M. de la Pinta Llorente, *Procesos inquisitoriales contra Francisco Sánchez de las Brozas*, Madrid, 1941, p. xliv.

101 Américo Castro, 'Erasmo en tiempo de Cervantes', *RFE*, 18, 1931, 364.

102 Ibid., 366.

103 Juan de Mal Lara, *Filosofía vulgar*, ed. A. Vilanova, 3 vols, Barcelona, 1958–9, I, p. 29.

104 Miguel de la Pinta Llorente, *La Inquisición Española y los problemas de la Cultura y de la Intolerancia*, Madrid, 1953, p. 152.

105 Cited in Márquez 1980a, p. 83.

106 Cited in part in Bataillon, p. 727.

107 Enrique Llamas, *Santa Teresa de Jesús y la Inquisición Española*, Madrid, 1972, p. 99. See also F. Márquez Villanueva, *Espiritualidad y Literatura en el siglo XVI*, Madrid, 1968, pp. 145–52, 179–86. The interesting study by Carole Slade, *St Teresa of Avila. Author of a heroic life,*

Berkeley, 1995, suggests that Teresa's Inquisition experiences influenced all her writing.

108 Alvaro Huerga, *Predicadores, alumbrados e Inquisición en el siglo XVI*, Madrid, 1973; *Los Alumbrados de Baeza*, Jaén, 1978; *Historia de los Alumbrados (1570–1630)*, 2 vols, Madrid, 1978.

109 An entertaining critique of Castro's views is given by Eugenio Asensio, 'Notas sobre la historiografía de Américo Castro', *AEM*, 8, 1972–3.

110 Cf. the entertaining essay by Nicholas Round, 'La "peculiaridad" literaria de los conversos. ¿Unicornio o Snark?', in Alcalá 1995, p. 557.

111 The observations by Márquez 1980a, pp. 46–8, have never been refuted.

112 A partial list of possible conversos in J.-C. Gómez-Menor, 'Linaje judío de escritores religiosos y místicos españoles del siglo XVI', in Alcalá 1995, p. 587.

113 Miguel de la Pinta Llorente and J.M. de Palacio, *Procesos inquisitoriales contra la familia judía de Juan Luis Vives*, Madrid, 1964.

114 See Kamen 1993a, p. 271, and sources there cited.

115 Menéndez y Pelayo, V, p. 482.

116 Lea, IV, p. 528.

117 Lord Acton, *Essays on Church and State*, London, 1952, p. 393.

118 Américo Castro, *España en su historia. Cristianos, moros y judíos*, Buenos Aires, 1948, p. 598.

119 Pardo Tomás, *Ciencia y Censura*, p. 65.

120 Pardo Tomás, *Ciencia y Censura*, p. 49.

121 Kamen 1993a, pp. 418, 421.

122 Maxime Chevalier, *Lectura y lectores en la España del siglo XVI y XVII*, Madrid, 1976.

123 López Piñero, *Ciencia y Técnica*, pp. 147–8.

124 'The mechanisms of censorship were of limited significance in altering intellectual development': R.A. Houston, *Literacy in early modern Europe. Culture and Education 1500–1800*, London, 1988, p. 165.

125 Cf. Kamen 1993a, p. 401.

126 Márquez 1980a, pp. 189–200.

127 A. Paz y Meliá, *Papeles de Inquisición*, 2nd edn, Madrid, 1947, pp. 23, 69, 71.

128 'Las obras de caridad que se hazen tibia y flojamente no tienen mérito ni valen nada': *Quijote*, book 2, chap. 36. See A. Castro, 'Cervantes y la Inquisición', *MP*, 27, 1929–30.

129 Márquez 1980a, pp. 168–9.

130 Paul F. Grendler, *The Roman Inquisition and the Venetian Press, 1540–1605*, Princeton, 1977, p. 162.

131 Alfred Soman, 'Press, Pulpit and Censorship in France before Richelieu', *PAPS*, 120, 1976, 454.

132 Pardo Tomás, *Ciencia y Censura*, however, feels (p. 269) that 'the efficiency of control was considerable' up to the seventeenth century. His view is based exclusively on the Inquisition's own papers, which are obviously optimistic about the success achieved.

133 Angel Alcalá, in 'Inquisitorial control of writers', in Alcalá 1987, p. 321, places emphasis on the word 'control'. Elsewhere (same volume, p. 617) he states that 'the inquisitorial system kept Spain in chains for three hundred and fifty years'.

134 The view of Pinto Crespo, 'Thought control in Spain', in Haliczer, p. 185.

135 Pardo Tomás, *Ciencia y Censura*, p. 87, expresses this opinion because a report of the Inquisition in 1632 stated that 'very few books by heretics enter Spain'. The report needs to be compared with what we know of the availability of foreign books.

136 Cf. John Gascoigne, 'A reappraisal of the role of the universities in the Scientific Revolution', in David Lindberg and Robert Westman, eds, *Reappraisals of the Scientific Revolution*, Cambridge, 1990, p. 250.

137 Pardo Tomás, *Ciencia y Censura*, pp. 220–7.

138 Pardo Tomás, *Ciencia y Censura*, pp. 151–83.

139 For the context of this, see Kamen 1981, p. 512.

140 Cf. the opinion of R.O. Jones in 1971: 'The Spain of Philip II remained closed to new currents of thought beyond its frontiers': R.O. Jones, *Historia de la literatura española. Siglo de Oro: prosa y poesía*, Barcelona, 1974, p. 124.

141 The view of Carlos Eire, in his stimulating and scholarly study, *From Madrid to Purgatory. The art and craft of dying in sixteenth-century Spain*, Cambridge, 1995, p. 512.

142 Cited by L. Hanke, 'Free speech in sixteenth-century Spanish America', *HAHR*, 26, 1946.

143 David C. Goodman, *Power and penury. Government, technology and science in Philip II's Spain*, Cambridge, 1988.

144 The view of D.W. Cruikshank, ' "Literature" and the book trade in Golden Age Spain', *MLR*, 73, 1978. Cf. Kamen 1993a, pp. 389–93 and authorities cited there.

145 Cf. Kamen 1997, chap. 7.

Chapter 7: Structure and Politics (pp. 137–73)

1 Inquisitors to Suprema, 1623, AHN Inq lib. 744, f. 146.

2 Sesma Muñoz, p. 229.

3 This date, suggested by J.A. Escudero ('Los orígenes del Consejo de la Suprema Inquisición', in Alcalá 1984), revises the date 1483 given by Lea.

4 Lea, I, p. 174.

5 García-Cárcel 1976, p. 135; García-Carcel 1980, p. 127.

6 AHN Inq lib. 1275, f. 169.

7 Nicolau Eimeric and Francisco Peña, *Le manual des inquisiteurs*, ed. L. Sala-Molins, Paris, 1973.

8 For one view of the instructions, see J.L. González Novalín, 'Reforma de las leyes del Santo Oficio', in *Nueva visión*, pp. 211–17.

9 AHN Inq lib. 497.

10 Cited by R. López Vela, in *Historia de la Inquisición*, II, 105.

11 In fact, for Aragon, Italy, Navarre and America.

12 *Historia de la Inquisición*, II, pp. 112–6.

13 Lea, II, pp. 168–78. A recent study of the case is the Madrid thesis by Chicha Gómez.

14 I here follow J. Contreras and J.P. Dedieu, 'Geografía de la Inquisición española: la formación de los distritos 1470–1820', *Hispania*, 40, 1980; but their information should be balanced against the exhaustive listing in Lea, I, pp. 541–55.

15 It is possible to offer alternative dates, depending on what one means by 'establishment'.

16 Toledo had four: see R. Pérez-Bustamante, 'Nóminas de inquisidores', in *Nueva visión*, p. 261.

17 Cf. J. Caro Baroja, *El señor inquisidor y otras vidas por oficio*, Madrid, 1970, pp. 20, 31.

18 J.-P. Dedieu, in Bennassar, p. 84.

19 Rules of 1560 and 1573 required that they be married, peaceable and of non-converso origin, with a minimum age of twenty-five: Lea, II, pp. 275, 279.

20 Philip II to Quiroga, 16 July 1574, BL Eg. 1506, f. 21v.

21 Lea, I, p. 447.

22 Report of 13 May 1628, AHN Inq leg. 2155[1].

23 The totals are given by the Inquisition. Contreras, p. 77, suggests that the tribunal was not telling the truth.

24 Contreras, pp. 90–2.

25 R. García-Cárcel, 'Número y sociologia de los familiares de la Inquisición valenciana', in *Nueva visión*, p. 277.

26 AHN Inq leg. 2155[2].

27 García-Cárcel, 'Número y sociologia', p. 279. In Valencia and Granada the Inquisition also appointed Moriscos as familiars.

28 For familiars in Catalonia, see Kamen 1993a, pp. 265–70, a picture that corrects the presentation given by Contreras in Alcalá 1987, p. 151, of Catalan familiars as having 'a predominance of the middle classes'.

29 Lea, I, p. 416.

30 Inquisitors to Suprema, 24 June 1597, AHN Inq leg. 2707¹.

31 Contreras, pp. 90–2, 129–30.

32 An excellent analysis of comisarios in the diocese of Cuenca is given by Sara Nalle, 'Inquisitors, priests and people during the Catholic Reformation in Spain', *SCJ*, 18, iv, 1987. She exaggerates, however, the ability of the comisario network to control the lives of Spaniards.

33 S. Nalle, 'Inquisitors', p. 584.

34 Reguera, p. 57.

35 In the first edition of this book, I affirmed that the Inquisition 'was never given a regular income on which to subsist'. I have since been convinced by the diligent research of José Martínez Millán (see *Historia de la Inquisición*, II, pp. 972–8) to change my views.

36 Hernando del Pulgar, *Los claros varones de España*, Madrid, 1747, p. 252.

37 Diego Ortiz de Zúñiga, *Annales de Sevilla*, Madrid, 1677, p. 389.

38 C. Carrete Parrondo, 'Los judaizantes castellanos', in *Inquisición y conversos*, p. 196.

39 Cited by Amando Represa, 'El miedo y la huida ante la Inquisición', in *Proyección histórica de España en sus tres culturas*, Valladolid, 1993, I, pp. 259–64.

40 Beinart, I, p. 391.

41 Copy of petition by Consellers to king, IMH Consellers C.XVIII–6.

42 Fidel Fita, 'La Inquisición en Guadalupe', *BRAH*, 23, 1893, 283–8.

43 Cf. Pilar Huerga, 'La Hacienda de la Inquisición aragonesa durante el reinado de Fernando el Católico', *Jerónimo Zurita*, 63–4, 1991 (publ. 1994).

44 Cf. Azcona, p. 422; Lea, II, pp. 367, 371.

45 García Ivars, p. 221.

46 AHN Inq legs 4776–9.

47 Pedro Sanahuja OFM, *Lérida en sus luchas por la fe*, Lleida, 1946, p. 162.

48 Azcona, p. 418.

49 Lea, II, p. 403.

50 Ladero Quesada 1984, p. 40.

51 Ladero Quesada 1984, p. 41.

52 *Historia de la Inquisición*, II, p. 909.

53 Lea, I, p. 329.

54 Lea, I, p. 330.

55 To emperor, 25 Jan. 1547: AGS:E leg. 75, f. 302.

56 M. Avilés, 'Motivos de crítica', in *Nueva visión*, p. 191.

57 AHN Inq leg. 2700.

58 AHN Inq leg. 2702.

59 AHN Inq leg. 4760¹.

60 AHN Inq leg. 4723³.

61 Cited in J. Fernández Nieva, *La Inquisición y los Moriscos extremeños (1585–1610)*, Badajoz, 1979, p. 87.

62 For 1618, from García-Cárcel 1980, p. 177; for 1671–8, from AHN Inq leg. 4994¹; for 1705, from AGS:GJ leg. 622.

63 AHN Inq leg. 4723³.

64 AHN Inq leg. 4723³; Fernández Nieva, *La Inquisición*, p. 16.

65 'Memoria de los salarios que tienen', AHN Inq lib. 1232, fos 205–9.

66 AHN Inq leg. 4724¹, exped. 1.

67 Henry Kamen, 'Confiscations in the economy of the Spanish Inquisition', *EconHR*, 18, iii, 1965.

68 AHN Inq leg. 4597².

69 Lea, II, p. 433.

70 AHN Inq leg. 4760¹; also M.I. Pérez de Colosia and J. Gil, *Málaga y la Inquisición (1550–1600)*, no. 38 of *Jábega*, 1982, p. 13.

71 Fernández Nieva, *La Inquisición*, p. 87.

72 Lea, II, p. 438.

73 Kamen 1981, p. 360.

74 G. Cerrillo, 'Los familiares de la Inquisición en la época borbónica', *RI*, 4, 1995.

75 *Historia de la Inquisición*, II, p. 1059.

76 Lea, II, p. 110.

77 In BN MS. 718, fos 108–10, 'Remisiones de causas hechas por los sumos Pontífices a la Inquisición de España', there are examples of twenty-one such appeals referred back between 1569 and 1608.

78 Lea, II, p. 8.

79 A. Astraín, *Historia de la Compañía de Jesús en la asistencia de España*, 7 vols, Madrid, 1902–25, I–III.

80 A prosecution paper is published by C. Carrete Parrondo as *Fontes*, III.

81 This brief account, virtually unchanged from my first edition, is based on Menéndez y Pelayo, V, pp. 9–82; G. Marañón, 'El proceso del arzobispo Carranza', *BRAH*, 127, 1950, 135–78; Lea, II, pp. 48–86; and Tellechea 1968, I, pp. 23–6. The various studies by Tellechea on Carranza are definitive; but there is still no adequate biography.

82 Cf. J.I. Tellechea, in *Historia de la Inquisición*, I, p. 566 (a useful summary of the case). This corrects the picture, given in my first edition, of a Carranza rotting in the cells of the Inquisition.

83 Marañón, 'El proceso', p. 145.

84 Lea, I, pp. 567–9, appendix I.

85 A point made by R. López Vela in *Historia de la Inquisición*, II, pp. 88, 100.

86 AHN Inq lib. 1262, fos 138–47.

87 AHN Inq lib. 1275, f. 232.

88 'Justicias reales castigados por el Sancto Oficio', AHN Inq lib. 1275, fos 1–8.

89 Cited in Carrasco Urgoiti, p. 151; my italics.

90 AHN Inq leg. 1592¹, no. 2.

91 Kamen 1993a, p. 218.

92 Cited in Carrasco Urgoiti, p. 142.

93 AHN Inq leg. 2155¹.

94 Consulta of Aragon, 22 Aug. 1587, ACA:CA leg. 262, f. 4.

95 'Exemplares de haverse mandado borrar de libros de Audiencias y Consejos cedulas dadas contra el estilo de la Inquicisión', AHN Inq lib. 1275, f. 203, is taken up almost wholly with conflicts with Barcelona.

96 Menéndez y Pelayo, VI, p. 56.

97 Junta on Aragon to Philip II, 14 July 1591, BZ 186, f. 15.

98 Cited by Gregorio Marañón, *Antonio Pérez (El hombre, el drama, la época)*, 2 vols, Madrid, 1947, II, p. 605.

99 Kamen 1993a, p. 261.

100 AGS:E/K 1505, nos. 46–7.

101 What follows is drawn from Kamen 1981, pp. 364–9.

102 This quotation, and the Sanz case, are detailed in Kamen 1981, pp. 366–7.

103 'Consulta que hizo la Junta que mandó formar el Señor Rey Don Carlos 2° a Su Magd para reformar abusos de Inquisición', Real Academia de la Historia, MS.Est.23.gr.5.a.B, no. 129, fos 308–52.

104 This is the claim put forward by Bennassar, p. 373; and Domínguez Ortiz, 'Regalismo y relaciones Iglesia-Estado', in García-Villoslada, IV, pp. 113–21.

105 Cf. Netanyahu 1995, p. 1023, who likewise rejects the idea that Ferdinand used the Inquisition to establish absolutism.

106 Cf. R. López Vela in *Historia de la Inquisición*, II, p. 117.

107 Lea, II, pp. 133–57.

108 Luciano Serrano, *Correspondencia diplomática entre España y la Santa Sede*, 4 vols, Madrid, 1914, III, p. lxx.

109 E.g. by Lea, in general; also by Monter, p. 27.

110 BN MS. 2569.

111 Quoted thus in Sánchez Albornoz, II, p. 563. Lea, IV, p. 250 quotes it as four clerics. The origin of the quote is unknown.

112 Cited by J. Contreras, 'La Inquisición aragonesa', *HS*, xxxvi, 76, 1985, 516–17.

113 Contreras, ibid., pp. 516–17.

114 Here I use quotations from the one-volume English edition of Marañón, *Antonio Pérez*, published in London, 1954, pp. 11, 13.

115 My own view of the Pérez case is presented in part in Kamen 1997.

116 Marañón 1954, p. 53.
117 Marañón 1954, p. 276. The word 'liberty' here meant expressly 'the laws of Aragon', and not the general concept

of liberty.
118 Isabel Martínez Navas, 'Proceso inquisitorial de Antonio Pérez', *RI*, 1, 1991, 191.

Chapter 8: How it Operated (pp. 174–92)

1 Inquisitors of Barcelona to Suprema, AHN Inq leg. 1592[1].
2 Baer, II, p. 343; Lea, I, p. 169. Since not all parishes figure in this total, the real number of penitents may have been much higher.
3 García-Cárcel 1980, p. 192.
4 Carrasco, pp. 203–5.
5 An edict of faith of 1624 is printed in M. Jiménez Monteserín, *Introducción a la Inquisición española*, Madrid, 1980, pp. 503–35.
6 Contreras, in *Historia de la Inquisición*, I, p. 755, makes this undocumented claim on the terror caused in Galicia by edicts.
7 Cf. Kamen 1993a, p. 247.
8 Amando Represa, 'El miedo y la huida ante la Inquisición', in *Proyección histórica de España en sus tres culturas*, Valladolid, 1993, vol. I, pp. 254–64.
9 Tomás y Valiente, pp. 167–70.
10 Angela Selke, *Vida y muerte de los Chuetas de Mallorca*, Madrid, 1980.
11 Cited by Represa, 'El miedo', pp. 259–64.
12 Huerga, p. 13.
13 *Records of the Spanish Inquisition, translated from the original manuscripts*, Boston, 1828, p. 27.
14 Birch, I, pp. 103, 112.
15 Lea, II, p. 99.
16 AHN Inq leg. 218, no. 20, case of 1674.
17 García Ivars, p. 231.
18 This useful point is made by Dedieu, p. 108.
19 Avilés, (cited Chap. 4, n. 8), p. 190.
20 Cited by Vincent, p. 142.
21 Kamen 1993a, pp. 256, 260.
22 Kamen 1993a, p. 260.
23 'La orden que ha de guardar el inquisidor que huviera de salir a visitar

de la Inquisición de Llerena', AHN Inq lib. 1229, fos 168–79.
24 In what follows the evidence for Llerena comes from AHN Inq leg. 2700; for Toledo from J. P. Dedieu, 'Les inquisiteurs de Tolède et la visite du district. La sédentarisation d'un tribunal (1550–1630)', *MCV*, 13, 1977; for Galicia from Contreras, pp. 476–511.
25 AHN Inq leg. 2706[1], no. 33.
26 AHN Inq lib. 730, f. 108.
27 Contreras, p. 488.
28 Cf. García-Cárcel 1980, p. 190: 'the response to the edict was almost always silence'. He shows that visitations in 1589 and 1590 brought in only sixteen and thirty-eight denunciations respectively: p. 189.
29 'Memoria de las villas y lugares que visitó el Dr Juan Alvarez de Caldas', AHN Inq leg. 2155[1].
30 AHN Inq lib. 731, fos 10, 23.
31 Inquisitors to Suprema, 15 July 1623, AHN Inq leg. 2155[2].
32 Dedieu, p. 253. High figures for arrests normally meant a find of heretics: e.g. the Llerena tribunal arrested 130 'judaizers' in Badajoz in 1567.
33 *Records of the Spanish Inquisition*, pp. 78–113.
34 Lea, III, p. 552, analysing the manuscript from the university of Halle.
35 Lea, II, p. 572.
36 AGS:PR leg. 28; cf. Lea, I, p. 585.
37 I am now unable to locate my source for this. Cf. Caro Baroja, II, p. 187.
38 Kamen 1993a, p. 471, n. 220.
39 *CODOIN*, CXII, pp. 264–5, 270.
40 AHN Inq leg. 2701.
41 Iñaki Reguera, 'Las cárceles de la Inquisición de Logroño', in *Perfiles*, p. 437.
42 'Extracts from a narrative of the

Persecution of Hippolyto Joseph da Costa Pereira', in the English version of Philip Limborch's classic *The History of the Inquisition*, London, 1816, pp. 521–30.

43 Escamilla-Colin, I, p. 678.
44 M. de la Pinta Llorente, *Las cárceles inquisitoriales españolas*, Madrid, 1949, p. 115.
45 Birch, I, pp. 367–8.
46 Pinta Llorente, *Las cárceles*, p. 102.
47 B. Vincent, 'La prison inquisitoriale au XVIe siècle', in A. Redondo, *Les problèmes de l'exclusion en Espagne (XVIe–XVIIe siècles)*, Paris, 1983, p. 117.
48 Birch, I, p. 235.
49 Lea, II, p. 534.
50 Escamilla-Colin, I, p. 696.
51 Kamen 1993a, p. 218.
52 AHN Inq lib. 497, f. 45.
53 What follows is a radical revision of my previous conclusion that torture was seldom used.

54 Beinart 1981, p. 120.
55 García-Cárcel 1980, p. 199.
56 Bennassar, pp. 115–16.
57 Lea, III, p. 33.
58 Escamilla-Colin, I, p. 599.
59 Escamilla-Colin, I, p. 593.
60 Dedieu, pp. 80–2, by contrast, believes that inquisitors and Chinese Communists 'appliquaient des techniques semblables'.
61 The *potro* was virtually the only torture used by the tribunal in the seventeenth century. A detailed account of torture methods at that epoch is given in AHN Inq lib. 1226, fos 605–9.
62 Inquisitors to Suprema, 1 Apr. 1579, AHN Inq leg. 2704.
63 Cases of the 1660s cited by Escamilla-Colin, I, pp. 593–7.
64 For a case of 1648 in a secular court, cf. Tomás y Valiente, p. 414.
65 Lea, III, p. 25.
66 Birch, I, 381.

Chapter 9: *Trial and Punishment (pp. 193–213)*

1 Cited in Kamen 1981, p. 489.
2 Lea, III, p. 46.
3 See chap. 5 above.
4 Lea, III, p. 68.
5 AHN Inq leg. 1679, no. 3.
6 AHN Inq leg. 37, no. 1.
7 J.-P. Dedieu, 'L'Inquisition et le droit. Analyse formelle de la procédure inquisitoriale en cause de foi', *MCV*, 23, 1987, gives a schematic explanation of trial procedure.
8 Kamen 1993a, p. 255.
9 To Suprema, 2 May 1590, AHN Inq leg. 2706[1], no. 33. The Morisco was Gonzalo Bejarano, a convicted thief, whose vengeful revelations began the last great prosecution against the Moriscos of Hornachos.
10 Lea, III, p. 79.
11 The most ambitious were the figures offered by G. Henningsen and J. Contreras, 'Forty-four thousand cases of the Spanish Inquisition (1540–1700)', in Henningsen and Tedeschi, pp. 100–29.

12 In the tribunal of Murcia, where the Contreras figures offered a total of 1,735 cases between 1562 and 1682, the real total of cases was 2726, or over fifty per cent more: J. Blázquez Miguel, *El tribunal de la Inquisición en Murcia*, Murcia, 1986, p. 274. In the tribunal of Granada, where the Contreras figures offered 538 cases for the period 1550–1700, the real total was 1,187 persons tried, or over one hundred per cent more: Blázquez Miguel, 'Algunas precisiones sobre estadística inquisitorial', *HS*, 40, 1988, 137. For the tribunal of Barcelona, there are major disparities between the Contreras figures and the real number of cases: cf. Kamen 1993a, p. 259.
13 A term used by some scholars when tackling the figures.
14 Dedieu, pp. 240–1, tableaux 34 and 35.
15 García-Cárcel 1980, p. 212. A closer look at these cases (and those from Galicia) may well produce a different

analysis, but the figures can serve to give an idea of the balance between different penalties.

16 Contreras, p. 550.

17 Beinart, I, p. 607.

18 Escamilla-Colin, I, p. 830.

19 Cf. Dedieu, 'L'Inquisition et le droit' (n. 7 above), p. 247.

20 Lea, III, p. 156.

21 Monter, p. 32. Monter has the best available study of this punishment.

22 In reality, even in state tribunals 'life' meant a maximum of ten years: Kamen 1981, p. 266.

23 Vincent, p. 141.

24 Monter, p. 35.

25 BN MS. 9475.

26 Cf. Bennassar, p. 118.

27 Letter of 11 May 1573, AHN Inq leg. 2703.

28 Llorente 1817, IV, p. 92.

29 The fullest study is Consuelo Maqueda Abreu, *El auto de fe*, Madrid, 1992; there is also a good perspective in Bethencourt, chap. 7.

30 Jean Lhermite, *Le Passetemps*, 2 vols, Antwerp, 1890–6, I, p. 113.

31 Bethencourt, p. 406, refers to the painting as 'fondatrice d'un genre'.

32 Maqueda Abreu, *El auto de fe*, p. 20.

33 Bethencourt, p. 288, cites the important cases of the autos in Lisbon in 1728 and Palermo in 1724.

34 Bethencourt, p. 406.

35 Dedieu sees a decline in autos after 1580: Dedieu, p. 276.

36 Kamen 1993a, p. 45.

37 Monter, pp. 50, 52.

38 Cited in Escamilla-Colin, I, p. 180.

39 Fita, 'La Inquisición Toledana'.

40 A full account exists, by M. V. Caballero, 'El Auto de Fe de 1680', *RI*, 3, 1994, 69–140.

41 *An authentick Narrative of the origin, establishment and progress of the Inquisition*, London, 1748, pp. 35–9. The original account is Joseph del Olmo, *Relación Histórica del Auto General de Fe que se celebró en Madrid este año de 1680*, Madrid, 1680.

42 Fidel Fita, 'La Inquisición de Logroño y un judaizante quemado en 1719', *BRAH*, 45, 1904.

43 J. Simón Díaz, 'La Inquisición de Logroño (1570–1580)', *Berceo*, 1, 1946.

44 AHN Inq leg. 4696².

45 AHN Inq leg. 5047³.

46 AHN Inq leg. 4724¹, no. 1.

47 Inquisitors to Suprema, 23 Oct. and 21 Nov. 1560, AHN Inq lib. 730 fos 23, 26.

48 To Suprema, 13 Aug. 1622, AHN Inq leg. 2155².

49 Victoria González de Caldas, 'The auto de fe', in Alcalá 1987, p. 288.

Chapter 10: *The End of Morisco Spain (pp. 214–29)*

1 Cited by Luce López-Baralt, in *The Legacy of Muslim Spain*, p. 551.

2 Cisneros to the chapter of Toledo, 3 Feb. 1500, in Ladero Quesada 1988, p. 427.

3 Cited by Ladero Quesada 1988, p. 305, n. 66.

4 Royal letter of 12 Oct. 1501, in Ladero Quesada 1988, p. 478.

5 Quoted by L. P. Harvey, in *The Legacy of Muslim Spain*, p. 219.

6 My view, repeated over the years, is now reinforced by the work of Mark D. Meyerson, 'Religious change,

regionalism, and royal power in the Spain of Fernando and Isabel', in L. J. Simon, ed., *Iberia and the Mediterranean World of the Middle Ages*, vol. I, Leiden, 1995, pp. 101–2.

7 On this, cf. B. Vincent, 'Los moriscos y la circuncisión', in Vincent.

8 H. C. Lea, *The Moriscos of Spain: their conversion and expulsion*, London, 1901, pp. 409–14.

9 A. Redondo, *Antonio de Guevara (1480?–1545) et l'Espagne de son temps*, Geneva, 1976.

10 M. A. Ladero Quesada, *Los Mudéjares*

del reino de Castilla en tiempo de Isabel I, Valladolid, 1969.

11 Jacqueline Fournel, 'Le livre et la civilisation écrite dans la communauté morisque aragonaise (1540–1620)', *MCV*, 15, 1979.

12 Monter, p. 212.

13 G. Colás Latorre, 'Los moriscos aragoneses y su expulsión', in *Destierros aragoneses*, pp. 203–5.

14 M. C. Anson Calvo, in *Destierros aragoneses*, p. 309.

15 Cf. Mikel de Epalza, 'Les Morisques', in *Les Morisques et leur temps*, Paris, 1983, pp. 38–9.

16 Cf. Mikel de Epalza, in *Destierros aragoneses*, p. 225.

17 G. Colás Latorre, in *Destierros aragoneses*, p. 199.

18 Leila Sabbagh, 'La religion des Moriscos entre deux fatwas', in *Les Morisques et leur temps*, p. 49.

19 Carrasco, p. 198.

20 G. Colás Latorre, 'Cristianos y Moriscos en Aragón', *MCV*, 29, 2, 1993.

21 Peter Dressendörfer, *Islam unter der Inquisition. Die Morisco-Prozesse in Toledo 1575–1610*, Wiesbaden, 1971, p. 64, n. 171.

22 R. Carrasco, 'Le refus d'assimilation des Morisques: aspects politiques et culturels d'après les sources inquisitoriales', in *Les Morisques et leur temps*.

23 A. Fernández de Madrid, *Vida de Fray Fernando de Talavera*, Granada, 1992, p. lix.

24 Quoted in Helen Nader (cited chap. 5 above, n. 6), p. 187.

25 Cardaillac, *passim*. A good survey also is Anwar G. Chejne, *Islam and the West: the Moriscos*, New York, Albany, 1983.

26 Domínguez Ortiz and Vincent, 1978, chap. 5; R. Benítez and E. Ciscar, 'La Iglesia ante la conversión y la expulsión de los Moriscos', in García-Villoslada, IV, pp. 255–307.

27 Carrasco Urgoiti, p. 149.

28 Cf. Monter, p. 133.

29 J. Contreras, 'La Inquisición de Aragón: estructura y oposición (1550–1700)', *Estudios de Historia Social*, 1, 1977.

30 M. García-Arenal, *Inquisición y moriscos. Los procesos del tribunal de Cuenca*, Madrid, 1978, p. 84.

31 J.-P. Dedieu, 'Les Morisques de Daimiel et l'Inquisition', in *Les Morisques et leur temps*.

32 J. Aranda Doncel, 'La esclavitud en Córdoba', in *Córdoba, apuntes para su historia*, Córdoba, 1981.

33 Carrasco, p. 205.

34 Cf. Monter, chap. 9, with useful new perspectives.

35 Vincent, p. 125.

36 García-Arenal, *Inquisición y moriscos*, pp. 11, 23, 39.

37 Monter, p. 189.

38 García-Arenal, *Inquisición y moriscos*, p. 39; García Fuentes, p. xxxiii.

39 Bishop of Tortosa to Cardinal Espinosa, 28 July 1568, AHN Inq leg. 2155[1].

40 Carrasco Urgoiti, p. 148.

41 L. García Ballester, *Medicina, ciencia y minorías marginadas: los Moriscos*, Granada, 1977.

42 Cardaillac, p. 100.

43 J. M. Magán García and R. Sánchez González, *Moriscos Granadinos en La Sagra de Toledo 1570–1610*, Toledo, 1993, p. 82.

44 García-Arenal, *Inquisición y moriscos*, p. 117.

45 Monter, pp. 224–6.

46 D. Cabanelas, 'Intento de supervivencia en el ocaso de una cultura: los libros plumbeos de Granada', *NRFH*, 30, 1981. Also L. P. Harvey, in *The Legacy of Muslim Spain*, pp. 228–9.

47 B. Vincent, 'Los moriscos del reino de Granada después de 1570', *NRFH*, 30, 1981.

48 T. Halperin Donghi, 'Les Morisques du royaume de Valence au XVIe siècle', *Annales*, 1956; Halperin Donghi, 'Un conflicto nacional en el siglo de oro', *CHE*, 23–4, 1955, and 25–6, 1957.

49 A. Hess, 'The Moriscos: an Ottoman fifth column', *AHR*, 74, 1968–9.

50 J. Aranda Doncel, 'Cristianos y Moriscos en Córdoba', *Les Morisques et leur temps*, p. 263.

51 Braudel, p. 591.

52 BN MS. 721, fos 39–46.

53 This conclusion, drawn from research by James Casey, is summarized in Henry Kamen, *Spain 1469–1714. A society of conflict*, London, 1991, p. 221.

54 In reality, in Valencia at least, Morisco growth was already falling off: James Casey, 'Moriscos and the depopulation of Valencia', *P&P*, 50, 1971.

55 Domínguez Ortiz and Vincent 1978, chap. 9.

56 BL Eg MS. 1151, fos 323, 336. Cf. Pascual Boronat, *Los Moriscos españoles y su expulsión*, 2 vols, Valencia, 1901, II, pp. 657–61.

57 AHN Inq leg. 4671¹.

58 On Cervantes' views, cf. F. Márquez Villanueva, *Personajes y temas del Quijote*, Madrid, 1975.

59 Boronat, *Los Moriscos españoles*, II, pp. 196–7; F. Janer, *La condición social de los moriscos de España*, Madrid, 1857, pp. 114, 116.

60 García-Cárcel 1980, p. 102 [italics added].

61 For the emigration in general, Henri Lapeyre, *La Géographie de l'Espagne morisque*, Paris, 1959; for the exiles to Africa, Martine Ravillard, *Bibliographie commentée des Morisques*, Algiers, 1979.

62 Boronat, *Los Moriscos españoles*, II, pp. 68–93.

63 Kamen 1981, p. 487.

64 Alcalá 1987, p. 83.

65 Figures (probably insecure) as given by Contreras, in Henningsen and Tedeschi, p. 119.

66 AHN Inq leg. 5126¹. This case is virtually unstudied.

67 Cited in G. Gozalbes Busto, *Los Moriscos en Marruecos*, Granada, 1992, p. 115.

Chapter 11: Racialism and its Critics (pp. 230–54)

1 For a criticism of Américo Castro's view that exclusivism had Jewish origins, see B. Netanyahu, 'Américo Castro and his view on the origins of *pureza de sangre*', *PAAJR*, 46–7, 1979–80.

2 All cases cited in Riera Sans, p. 87.

3 Riera Sans, p. 89.

4 See the splendid chapter, titled 'The Great Debate', in Netanyahu 1995, pp. 351–661.

5 Nicholas Round, 'Politics, style and group attitudes in the Instruccion del Relator', *BHS*, 46, 1969, 289–319.

6 Cf. Roth, p. 92.

7 Juan de Torquemada, *Tractatus contra Madianitas et Ismaelitas*, ed. N. López Martínez, Burgos, 1957.

8 Alonso de Oropesa, *Luz para conocimiento de los Gentiles*, ed. Luis A. Díaz y Díaz, Madrid, 1979.

9 B. Cuart Moner, 'Los estatutos del Colegio de San Clemente', in E. Verdera y Tüells, ed., *El Cardenal Albornoz y el Colegio de España*, 6 vols, Bologna, 1979, IV, p. 602. This corrects the common error which dates the statute to 1414.

10 Cuart Moner 1991, p. 11.

11 Cuart Moner 1991, p. 17.

12 Domínguez Ortiz 1955, p. 58.

13 AHN Inq lib. 497, f. 22.

14 Cuart Moner 1991, p. 32.

15 Copy of letter from Charles V, 26 Nov. 1523, in BZ 140, f. 278.

16 Cf. discussion in Roth, pp. 233–6, using other published sources.

17 C. Carrete Parrondo, 'Los conversos jerónimos', pp. 97–116.

18 Domínguez Ortiz 1955, pp. 67–70, gives some details of the contradictory regulations adopted in the orders.

19 Repeating an opinion to be found in numerous well-known works, Netanyahu 1995 states (p. 1063): 'The limpieza movement progressed until it

dominated all Spanish ecclesiastical organizations and a major part of Spain's public opinion'. Neither of the affirmations in the passage is correct.

20 Cuart Moner 1991, p. 30.

21 'Sobre el Estatuto de limpieza de la Sancta Iglesia de Toledo', BN MS. 13267, f. 278.

22 'La contradicion hecha por algunas dignidades', BN MS. 1703, fos 1–17.

23 The president of Castile was Hernando Niño de Guevara. All documents here are in AGS Cámara de Castilla leg. 291, f. 1.

24 Sicroff, p. 137.

25 The passage is cited as being Philip's opinion by Sicroff, p. 138. However, it is not taken from any original document but from a copy. In the first edition of this book I relied too trustingly on Sicroff. Subsequent historians have since then followed me and quoted these extravagant antisemitic words as though they were Philip's. The passage may be found in Siliceo's memoir to Philip in BN MS. 13, 267, f. 281.

26 L. Cabrera de Córdoba, *Filipe Segundo, rey de España*, 4 vols, Madrid, 1876–7, I, p. 47.

27 R. Kagan, *Students and society in early modern Spain*, Baltimore, 1974, p. 94.

28 Sicroff offers a completely misleading image (chap. 3 of his book) of a limpieza 'officially supported by Church and state'. He omits to state that it was 'supported' *only* in the controversy in the cathedral of Toledo, and even then never observed.

29 Kamen 1993a, p. 271.

30 Kamen 1993b, VII, p. 7.

31 Domínguez Ortiz 1955, p. 65.

32 BL Add 28263, fos 491–2.

33 Cf. cases cited in Kamen 1993b, VII, p. 24, n. 27.

34 Ruy Gómez to Francisco de Eraso, 25 Nov. 1552, AGS:E leg. 89, f. 123.

35 The captain was Julián Romero: Cabrera de Córdoba, *Felipe Segundo*, II, p. 429.

36 Linda Martz, 'Pure blood statutes in sixteenth-century Toledo: implementation as opposed to adoption', *Sefarad*, 64, i, 1994, 91–94.

37 P. L. Lorenzo Cadarso, 'Oligarquías conversas de Cuenca y Guadalajara (siglos XV y XVI)', *Hispania*, 186, 1994, 79.

38 Both cited in B. González Alonso, *Sobre el Estado y la Administración de la Corona de Castilla en el Antiguo Régimen*, Madrid, 1981, p. 71 [italics added].

39 Cited Kamen 1993b, VII, p. 3.

40 Cf. my references in chap. 3 of this book.

41 Cited in Sicroff, p. 94, n. 125.

42 Domínguez Nafría, p. 64.

43 C. Carrete Parrondo, *El judaismo español y la Inquisición*, Madrid, 1992, p. 155; Gil Fernández, p. 470.

44 For examples of all this, Lea, II, pp. 300–6.

45 *Summa nobilitatis*, Salamanca, 1559 edn, p. 186.

46 J. Edwards, 'From anti-Judaism to anti-semitism: Juan Escobar del Corro's Tractatus', *Ninth World Congress of Jewish Studies* (1986), division B, vol. 1, pp. 143–50.

47 AHN Inq lib. 497, f. 50.

48 N. Hergueta, 'La Inquisición de Logroño. Nuevos datos históricos', *BRAH*, 45, 1904.

49 Cf. the case in Valencia in 1691 cited in Kamen 1981, p. 267.

50 AHN Inq leg. 1586, no. 8.

51 Tellechea 1968, II, p. 241, n. 21.

52 Rojas was the son of the Marquis of Poza.

53 Tellechea 1977, p. 53.

54 M. Bataillon, 'Honneur et Inquisition', *BH*, 27, 1925.

55 R. Truman and A. G. Kinder, 'The pursuit of Spanish heretics in the Low Countries: the activities of Alonso del Canto, 1561–1564', *JEH*, 30, 1979.

56 Eusebio Rey, 'San Ignacio de Loyola y el problema de los "Cristianos Nuevos" ', *RF*, 153, 1956.

57 Cited in Sicroff, p. 272.

58 Father Baptista to Laínez, 31 Aug. 1564, ARSI Epist Hisp 101, f. 286.

59 Eusebio Rey, 'San Ignacio de Loyola', p. 190.
60 It has been argued that Ribedeneira was of converso origin; see J. Gómez-Menor, 'La progenie hebrea del padre Pedro de Ribadeneira S.I.', *Sefarad*, 36, 1976.
61 *Obras*, Madrid, 1872, chap. 4, p. 540.
62 Domínguez Ortiz 1955, p. 43.
63 A fuller version of what follows is available in English as 'A crisis of conscience in Golden Age Spain: the Inquisition against "limpieza de sangre"', in Kamen 1993b, chap. 8.
64 Fray Agustín Salucio, *Discurso sobre los estatutos de limpieza de sangre*, Cieza, 1975 edn.
65 BN MS. 17909/5.
66 'Papel que dio el Reyno de Castilla a uno de los Sres ministros de la Junta diputada para tratarse sobre el Memorial presentado por el Reyno a S.M. con el libro del Pe Mro Salucio', BN MS. 13043, fos 116–27.
67 AHN Inq leg. 2156'.
68 I. S. Révah, 'Le plaidoyer en faveur des "Nouveaux-Chrétiens" portugais du licencié Martín González de Cellorigo (1619)', *REJ*, 122, 1963.
69 'Discurso de un inquisidor sobre los estatutos de limpieza', BN MS. 13043, fos 132–71.
70 A belated acceptance of the argument presented above in chap. 3!
71 'Discurso politico del desempeño del Reyno', in Caro Baroja, III, pp. 318–20.
72 *Conservación de monarquías*, Madrid, 1626, discourse VII.
73 'El Inquisidor General y Real Consejo de la Suprema', AHN Inq lib. 1240, fos 6–11.
74 Domínguez Ortiz 1955, appendix IVe, p. 233.
75 Kamen 1993b, VII, p. 18.
76 J. A. Martínez Bara, 'Los actos positivos en las pruebas genealógicas en el siglo XVII', in *Nueva visión*, p. 313.
77 The controversy refutes the claim by Sicroff (p. 265) that 'it was forbidden in Spain to question the basis of the statutes'.
78 *Libro de las cinco excelencias del Español*, Pamplona, 1629, p. 100.
79 Cf. Kamen 1993b, VII, pp. 20–1.
80 Domínguez Ortiz 1955, pp. 245–7.
81 The wholly undocumented image of 'obsession' continues to survive among some literary scholars, and among historians who adopt an ethnicist view of the conversos. For a comment on this situation, see H. Kamen, '*Limpieza* and the ghost of Américo Castro: racism as a tool of literary analysis', *Hispanic Review* (Philadelphia), autumn 1995.
82 F. M. Burgos Esteban, 'Los estatutos de limpieza y sus pruebas en el siglo XVII', in *Xudeus e Conversos*, I, p. 370.
83 *Xudeus e Conversos*, I, p. 371.
84 Kamen 1981, pp. 489, 493.
85 Braunstein, p. 123.
86 Cited in Lea, II, p. 314.
87 Carvajal to Joseph de Luyando, 28 Sep. 1751, BN MS. 13043, f. 130.
88 Domínguez Ortiz 1955, p. 129, n. 14.
89 Domínguez Ortiz 1955, p. 130.
90 Cited by Teófanes Egido, in *Historia de la Inquisición*, I, p. 1402.

Chapter 12: The Inquisition and the People (pp. 255–82)

1 Cited in Kamen 1993a, p. 86.
2 Cited in J. Caro Baroja, *Las formas complejas de la vida religiosa*, Madrid, 1978, p. 197.
3 Contreras, pp. 461, 463.
4 The more commonly held view differs from mine. 'Ces espagnols sont profondément chrétiens', says Dedieu, p. 43.
5 This theme is dealt with extensively in Kamen 1993a.
6 Reguera, p. 28.
7 M. Angeles Cristóbal, 'La Inquisición de Logroño', in *Inquisición española:*

nuevas aproximaciones, Madrid, 1987, p. 141.

8 J. Contreras, 'La Inquisición aragonesa', *HS*, xxxvii, 76, 1985, 522.

9 José Sánchez Herrero, *Concilios provinciales y sínodos Toledanos de los siglos XIV y XV*, La Laguna, 1976.

10 Borja to Ignatius Loyola, 7 June 1546, in *Monumenta Historica Societatis Jesu: S. Franciscus Borgia*, 5 vols, Madrid, 1896–1908, II, p. 520.

11 Melquiades Andrés, in *Historia de la Inquisición*, I, p. 505.

12 This sentence is, of course, a simplification. There was no concrete movement known as the 'Counter Reformation', and the decrees of Trent had in fact been trickling out for many years before.

13 J. L. González Novalín, 'Religiosidad y reforma del pueblo cristiano', in García-Villoslada, III–1, pp. 351–84, gives a good summary of the missionary problem in Spain.

14 Data are taken from Kamen 1993a, pp. 263–4.

15 As in rural England: see K. Wrightson in *Journal of Peasant Studies*, 5, 1977.

16 Marc Bloch, *Feudal society*, 2 vols, London, 1965, I, pp. 109, 113.

17 Kamen 1993a, pp. 263–4.

18 AHN Inq lib. 733, fos 367v, 383v.

19 An interesting discussion of blasphemy as an expression of anger rather than irreligion, based on cases tried by the Inquisition, is given in Maureen Flynn, 'Blasphemy and the play of anger in sixteenth-century Spain', *P&P*, 149, 1995.

20 The cases cited here and in the previous paragraph come from Kamen 1981, pp. 476–86.

21 Contreras, pp. 561, 667.

22 García Fuentes, p. 445.

23 Cf. Kamen 1981, p. 480.

24 J. P. Dedieu, ' "Christianisation" en Nouvelle Castille. Catéchisme, communion, messe et confirmation dans l'archevêché de Tolède, 1540–1650', *MCV*, 15, 1979.

25 AHN Inq leg. 79, no. 24, f. 38. My conclusions for Toledo are based on cases in AHN Inq legs. 24, 27, 41, 90.

26 V. Pinto Crespo, 'La actitud de la Inquisición ante la iconografía religiosa', *HS*, 31, 1978.

27 A good recent study on this complex subject is Palma Martínez-Burgos, *Ídolos e Imágenes. La controversia del arte religioso en el siglo XVI español*, Valladolid, 1990. I am grateful to the author for sending me a copy.

28 AHN Inq leg. 1592¹, no. 15.

29 Cf. William A. Christian Jr., *Apparitions in Late Medieval and Renaissance Spain*, Princeton, 1981.

30 R. María de Hornedo, 'Teatro e iglesia', in García-Villoslada, IV, p. 330.

31 Isabel Testón and Mercedes Santillana, 'El clero cacereño durante los siglos XVI al XVIII', in *Historia Moderna. Actas de las II Jornadas de Metodología y Didáctica*, Cáceres, 1983, p. 466.

32 AHN Inq lib. 735.

33 AHN Inq leg. 217, no. 12; Contreras, p. 561.

34 Any other sort of intercourse implied an offence. Involuntary intercourse was rape, and between married adults (i.e. married to another) voluntary intercourse was adultery.

35 J.-P. Dedieu, in Bennassar, p. 327.

36 Contreras, pp. 628–30.

37 For this and the cited case, see Kamen 1993a, pp. 320–1.

38 AHN Inq leg. 2155¹.

39 AHN Inq leg. 24, no. 7.

40 For the scandalous life of the clergy in Coria in 1591 see A. Rodríguez Sánchez, 'Inmoralidad y represión', in *Historia Moderna. Actas*, Cáceres, 1983, pp. 451–62.

41 Kamen 1993a, p. 324.

42 The most recent studies are by Adelina Sarrión Mora, *Sexualidad y confesión: la solicitación ante el tribunal del Santo Oficio (siglos XVI–XIX)*, Madrid, 1994; and Stephen Haliczer, *Sexuality in the confessional*, New York, 1996.

43 AHN Inq leg. 2155¹.

44 García-Cárcel 1980, p. 285.
45 The best survey of this development is Monter, chap. 13.
46 Monter, pp. 134–7.
47 Monter, p. 288.
48 Monter, pp. 289–90.
49 Morisco sorcery was a dimension of belief in relevant areas. See García-Cárcel 1980, p. 249; J. Caro Baroja, *Vidas mágicas e Inquisición*, 2 vols, Madrid, 1967, I, pp. 49–52.
50 Lea, IV, p. 183.
51 Cf. Monter, p. 255.
52 S. Cirac Estopañán, *Los procesos de hechicerías en la Inquisición de Castilla la Nueva*, Madrid, 1942, p. 196.
53 F. Idoate, *Un documento de la Inquisición sobre brujería*, Pamplona, 1972, p. 13.
54 Not, as Novalín has it (*Valdés*, p. 63), in 1525; nor, as Caro Baroja (*Vidas mágicas*, II, p. 60) claims, in 1529. The notes of the meeting are in AHN Inq lib. 1231, fos 634–7, 'Dubia quae in causa praesenti videntur'. There is a copy in the Bodleian, Oxford, Arch.Σ.130. Cf. Lea, IV, pp. 212–14.
55 Reguera, pp. 197–8.
56 The Basque cases emboldened Fray Martín de Castañega, *Tratado de supersticiones*, Logroño, 1529, to explain that women were more likely than men to be witches because they were, among other things, 'more talkative and cannot keep secrets'.
57 Monter, p. 262.
58 See Monter, p. 264.
59 Kamen, 1993a, pp. 237–8.
60 Lea, IV, p. 223.
61 Monter, pp. 268–9.
62 On the Navarre context, Gustav Henningsen, *The Witches' Advocate. Basque Witchcraft and the Spanish Inquisition*, Reno, 1980; and J. Caro Baroja, *Inquisición, Brujería y Criptojudaismo*, Barcelona, 1974, pp. 183–315.
63 BN MS. 718, f. 271.
64 G. Henningsen, *The Witches' Advocate*; Lea, IV, pp. 231–4.
65 'Acerca de los cuentos de las bruxas.

Discurso de Pedro de Valencia', AHN Inq lib. 1231, fos 608–29.
66 AHN Inq lib. 735.
67 Angel Gari, *Brujería e Inquisición en el Alto Aragón en la primera mitad del siglo XVII*, Saragossa, 1991, pp. 240–1. The Inquisition tried 121 cases in that period (mostly men), and the secular courts 64 (mostly women). In addition, cases were tried by the episcopal courts, a subject being studied by María Tausiet, who has come up with 32 Aragonese cases so far.
68 On all this, Kamen 1993a, pp. 239–45.
69 Lea, III, p. 447.
70 Albert Loomie SJ, 'Religion and Elizabethan commerce with Spain', *CHR*, Apr. 1964.
71 Cf. Monter, pp. 248–9.
72 Cited in M. Angeles Cristóbal, 'La Inquisición de Logroño' (cited above, n. 7), p. 145.
73 Consulta of State, 31 Mar. 1653, AGS:E leg. 2528.
74 AHN Inq lib. 735, f. 176.
75 L. de Alberti and A. B. Wallis Chapman, eds, *English Merchants and the Spanish Inquisition in the Canaries*, London, 1912, p. 80, n. 1.
76 F. Fajardo Spinola, *Reducciones de protestantes al catolicismo en Canarias durante el siglo XVIII: 1700–1812*, Gran Canaria, 1977, pp. 48, 51.
77 Alberti and Chapman, *English Merchants*, p. x.
78 AGS:E leg. 2981.
79 A view of 1993: 'el temor mas viscoso ... miedo, temor y estigma son los medios empleados para uniformar a todos': J. Contreras in *Historia de la Inquisición*, II, p. 606.
80 Kamen 1993a, p. 257.
81 Kamen 1993a, chap. 5.
82 Inquisition/citizen contact was, of course, higher in towns like Toledo and Madrid. Further studies, along the lines adopted for Catalonia, would clarify the issue of contact.
83 Sesma Muñoz, p. 23.

84 I refer to a report in today's newspaper (*El País*, 13 November 1996) of a woman in Pontevedra who went to the local police and denounced her husband for not performing his sexual duties towards her.
85 AHN Inq lib. 746, f. 179.

86 Kamen 1993a, p. 262.
87 Contreras, p. 683.
88 AHN Inq lib. 735, f. 349.
89 Richard Greenleaf, cited in *Historia de la Inquisición*, II, p. 665.
90 Kamen 1993a, p. 436.
91 Dedieu, p. 260.

Chapter 13: Visions of Sefarad (pp. 283–304)

1 Cited in Y. H. Yerushalmi, *From Spanish Court to Italian Ghetto. Isaac Cardoso: a Study in Seventeenth-Century Marranism and Jewish Apologetics*, New York, 1971, p. 392.
2 Dedieu, p. 254. I presume I have read his figures rightly.
3 Cf. Monter, p. 37.
4 See chap. 2 above, n. 102.
5 1528 prosecution of Gaspar Mercader, AHN Inq leg. 2155¹; the Badajoz case in AHN Inq leg. 2701.
6 Cited in R. Carrasco, 'Preludio al siglo de los portugueses', *Hispania*, 166, 1987, 523.
7 Licenciado Montoya to Suprema, 11 Jan. 1581, AHN Inq leg. 2705¹, no. 21.
8 Caro Baroja, III, p. 51.
9 The debate over the religion of these conversos is qualitatively different from that over the religion of the anusim of the fifteenth century. For some aspects of converso religion, see Cecil Roth, 'The religion of the Marranos', *JQR*, xxii, 1931; Braunstein; and I. S. Révah, 'Les Marranes', *REJ*, 1959, 54.
10 Charles Amiel, 'El criptojudaismo castellano en La Mancha a finales del siglo XVI', in Alcalá 1995, pp. 503–12.
11 García Ivars, p. 205.
12 García Ivars, pp. 236–8.
13 BN MS. 721, fos 127–31; García Fuentes; Lea, III, p. 267.
14 It consequently seems inadvisable to isolate them as a historical phenomenon, as though they were a separate race (which they were not) or a separate religion (which they were not either).

This ethnicist approach, confusing together both pre-1492 and post-1492 conversos, and those of Spanish and Portuguese origin, on the premise that all had a common nature, is the basis of some current research (cf. J. Contreras, 'The Judeo-Converso minority in Spain', in M. E. Perry and A. J. Cruz, *Cultural encounters*, Berkeley, 1991).
15 Charles Amiel, 'Crypto-judaisme et Inquisition. La matière juive dans les édits de foi', *Revue de l'Histoire des Religions*, 210, ii, 1993, 157.
16 A typical edict is reproduced in photocopy in Caro Baroja, I, pp. 440–1.
17 As suggested by David Gitlitz, 'Las presuntas profanaciones judías del ritual cristiano', in Alcalá 1995, pp. 156–63.
18 García Ivars, p. 243.
19 García Ivars, p. 221.
20 Lea, III, p. 239ff; A. Herculano, *Historia da origem e estabelecimento da Inquisiçao em Portugal*, 3 vols, Lisbon, 1907, I, pp. 228–86.
21 Lea, III, p. 259.
22 R. Carrasco, 'Preludio' (as above, n. 6), p. 540.
23 Lea, III, p. 265.
24 R. Carrasco, 'Preludio', p. 524.
25 Bodleian Library, Oxford, Arch.Σ.130, no. 8; Gaspar Matute y Luquín, *Colección de los Autos generales i particulares de Fe celebrados por el Tribunal de la Inquisición de Córdoba*, Córdoba, 1840, pp. 65, 127; BN MS. 718, f. 375, and MS. 6751, f. 53.
26 Escamilla-Colin, I, p. 266.

27 Pilar Huerga Criado, *En la raya de Portugal. Solidaridad y tensiones en la comunidad judeoconversa*, Salamanca, 1993.

28 J. Blázquez Miguel, 'Algunas precisiones sobre estadística', *HS*, 40, 1988, 138.

29 R. Carrasco, 'Preludio', p. 556.

30 Cf. Yosef Kaplan, 'The travels of Portuguese Jews from Amsterdam to the "lands of idolatry" (1644–1724)', in Kaplan.

31 Escamilla-Colin, I, p. 348.

32 Lea, III, pp. 267–70.

33 Elkan Adler, 'Documents sur les Marranes d'Espagne et de Portugal sous Philippe IV', *REJ*, 49, 1904.

34 Caro Baroja, II, pp. 56–7.

35 Cf. J. H. Elliott, *The Count-Duke of Olivares*, London and New Haven, 1986, pp. 300–4.

36 Caro Baroja, II, p. 59.

37 A. Domínguez Ortiz, 'El proceso inquisitorial de Juan Núñez Saravía, banquero de Felipe IV', *Hispania*, 61, 1955.

38 Cf. James C. Boyajian, *Portuguese bankers at the court of Spain 1626–1650*, New Brunswick, 1983, pp. 118–21.

39 The accounts of the firm are in AHN Inq leg. 5096².

40 The source is Barrionuevo's *Avisos*.

41 The Montesinos' accounts are in AHN Inq leg. 4971¹.

42 BN MS. 718, f. 375.

43 This and the following cases, from Kamen 1981, pp. 489–91.

44 García Ivars, p. 250.

45 For Sabbatai, see the masterly work of Gerschom Scholem, *Sabbatai Zevi: the mystical Messiah 1626–1676*, Princeton, 1973.

46 Miriam Bodian, ' "Men of the nation": the shaping of converso identity in early modern Europe', *P&P*, 143, 1994, 66.

47 Y. H. Yerushalmi, *From Spanish Court to Italian Ghetto* (cited n. 1 above).

48 I. S. Révah, 'Un pamphlet d'Antonio Enríquez Gómez', *REJ*, 121, 1962.

49 See N. Kramer-Hellinx, 'Antonio Enriquez Gómez: desafío de la Inquisición', in *Xudeus e Conversos*, I, pp. 289–307.

50 Maxim Kerkhof, 'La "Inquisición de Luzifer y visita de todos los diablos" ', *Sefarad*, 38, 1978.

51 M. Bodian, 'Men of the nation', pp. 70–2.

52 Details from the superb study by Yosef Kaplan, *From Christianity to Judaism. The story of Isaac Orobio de Castro*, Oxford, 1989.

53 Y. Kaplan, *Orobio de Castro*, p. 323.

54 Cited in Kamen 1981, p. 489.

55 J. B. Vilar Ramírez, *El Dr Diego Mateo Zapata (1664–1745)*, Murcia, 1970.

56 For both men, see A. Domínguez Ortiz, *Hechos y figuras del siglo XVIII español*, Madrid, 1973, pp. 159–91.

57 BN MS. 9475; Joseph del Olmo, *Relación* (cited in chap. 9, n. 41); Matute y Luquín, *Colección de los Autos*, p. 210.

58 *Inquisición de Mallorca. Reconciliados y Relajados 1488–1691*, Barcelona, 1946, pp. 201–75.

59 *Inquisición de Mallorca*, pp. 109–99.

60 Braunstein.

61 For repression in Cuenca see R. de Lera García, 'La última gran persecución inquisitorial contra el criptojudaismo: el tribunal de Cuenca 1718–1725', *Sefarad*, 47, i, 1987.

62 Teófanes Egido, in *Historia de la Inquisición*, I, p. 1386.

63 Escamilla-Colin, I, p. 874.

64 Teófanes Egido, in *Historia*, I, p. 1397.

65 Lea, III, p. 311.

66 G. Desdevises du Dézert, 'Notes sur l'Inquisition espagnole au dix-huitième siècle', *RH*, 6, 1899.

67 *The Bible in Spain*, London, 1930 edn, p. 155.

68 *A journey through Spain in the years 1786 and 1787*, 3 vols, London, 1792, III, p. 84.

Chapter 14: Inventing the Inquisition (pp. 305–20)

1 Raphael, p. 136.

2 The title of this chapter was decided before I had occasion to refer to Edward Peters, *Inquisition*, Berkeley, 1989, which has a similar title for its chap. 5. His very interesting discussion ranges more widely than my own.

3 Bethencourt, p. 406.

4 *The Book of Martyrs*, London, 1863 edn, p. 153.

5 London, 1912 edn, p. 165.

6 Nicolas Castrillo, *El 'Reginaldo Montano': primer libro polémico contra la Inquisición Española*, Madrid, 1991, p. 31.

7 *The Book of Martyrs*, London, 1863 edn, p. 1060.

8 Sverker Arnoldsson, *La Leyenda Negra: estudios sobre sus orígenes*, Göteborg, 1960.

9 Eugenio Alberi, *Relazioni degli ambasciatori veneti al Senato*, Florence, 1839–40, serie I, vol. 5, p. 22.

10 E. Alberi, *Relazioni*, serie I, vol. 5, p. 85.

11 'Relazione di Spagna', *Opere*, Bari, 1929–36, X, p. 131.

12 M. de la Pinta Llorente, *Aspectos históricos del sentimiento religioso en España*, Madrid, 1961, p. 37.

13 L. P. Gachard, *Correspondance de Philippe II sur les affaires des Pays-Bas*, 6 vols, Brussels, 1848–79, I, p. clxxvi.

14 For all these points, see Kamen 1997.

15 F. E. Beemon, 'The myth of the Spanish Inquisition and the preconditions for the Dutch revolt', *AR*, 85, 1994, 255.

16 *An Apology or Defence of William the First of Nassau, Prince of Orange*, London, 1707 edn, pp. 497, 530.

17 H. Kamen and J. Pérez, *La imagen internacional de la España de Felipe II*, Valladolid, 1980, p. 56; William S. Maltby, *The Black Legend in England*, Durham, N.C., 1971, pp. 76, 84.

18 Michael Ragussis, *Figures of conversion. 'The Jewish Question' and English national identity*, Durham, N.C., 1995, p. 127.

19 Raphael, pp. 136–7.

20 Salo Baron, *A Social and Religious History of the Jews*, 17 vols, 2nd edn, New York, 1952, XV, p. 174.

21 H. Beinart, in Kedourie, pp. 107, 114.

22 The best survey is Edward Peters, *Inquisition*.

23 For some evaluations, cf. Antonio Márquez's introduction to J. A. Llorente, *Noticia biográfica*, Madrid, 1982; and E. Peters, *Inquisition*, pp. 278–83.

24 Cited by E. Peters, *Inquisition*, p. 286.

25 E. Peters, *Inquisition*, p. 261.

26 Cf. the summary of the 1813 Cortes debates by S. Haliczer, in Alcalá 1987, p. 526.

27 Kamen 1981, p. 363.

28 Carrasco Urgoiti, p. 156.

29 AHN Inq lib. 731, f. 4.

30 Kamen 1993a, p. 437.

31 Gonzalo Correas, *Vocabulario de refranes*, Madrid, 1924, p. 124.

32 Carmelo Lisón Tolosana, 'Breve Historical Brujesco Gallego', *Ensayos de Antropología Social*, Madrid, 1973, esp. pp. 193–7. The material quoted here is taken from Kamen 1981, p. 471.

33 *Philippicae disputationes*, Antwerp, 1542, p. 157.

34 *Introduction del Symbolo de la Fe*, Barcelona, 1597 edn, part IV, trat. 1, p. 493.

35 Mariana, book 26, chap. 13.

36 Birch, II, p. 905.

37 Quoted in J. Vicens Vives, ed., *Historia de España y América*, 5 vols, Barcelona, 1957, IV, p. 247.

38 Carvajal to Luyando, 28 Sep. 1751, BN MS. 13043, f. 130.

39 'Representación a Carlos IV sobre lo que era el Tribunal de la Inquisición', *Obras* (Biblioteca de Autores Españoles, vol. 87, Madrid, 1956), p. 333.

40 Jean Sarrailh, *L'Espagne éclairée de la seconde moitié du 18e siècle*, Paris, 1954, p. 317.

41 M. Menéndez y Pelayo, *La Ciencia*

Española, Madrid, 1953 edn, p. 102.

42 R. Kagan, *Students and Society in early modern Spain*, Baltimore, 1974, p. 217.

43 'Del influjo de la Inquisición y del fanatismo religioso en la decadencia de la literatura española', *Disertaciones y Juicios literarios*, Madrid, 1878, p. 107.

44 Sánchez Albornoz, II, p. 563.

45 *The Spaniards in their history*, London, 1950, pp. 204–45.

SELECT BIBLIOGRAPHY

(This is limited to frequently cited works. Items which are cited within one chapter alone appear in the notes of that chapter.)

Alcalá, Angel, ed., *The Spanish Inquisition and the inquisitorial mind*, Boulder, 1987. (In Spanish: *Inquisición española y mentalidad inquisitorial*, Barcelona, 1984.)

Alcalá, Angel, ed., *Judíos, sefarditas, conversos*, Valladolid, 1995.

Azcona, Tarsicio de, *Isabel la Católica*, Madrid, 1964.

Baer, Yitzhak, *A History of the Jews in Christian Spain*, 2 vols, Philadelphia, 1966.

Bataillon, Marcel, *Erasmo y España*, Mexico, 1966.

Beinart, Haim, *Conversos on Trial. The Inquisition in Ciudad Real*, Jerusalem, 1981.

Beinart, Haim, ed., *Records of the trials of the Spanish Inquisition in Ciudad Real*, 3 vols, Jerusalem, 1974 (cited as Beinart).

Bennassar, Bartolomé, *L'Inquisition espagnole XVe–XIXe siècle*, Paris, 1979.

Bernáldez, Andrés, *Memorias del reinado de los reyes Católicos*, ed. M. Gómez-Moreno and J. M. de Carriazo, Madrid, 1962.

Bethencourt, Francisco, *L'Inquisition à l'époque moderne. Espagne, Portugal, Italie, XVe–XIX siècle*, Paris, 1995.

Birch, W. de Gray, *Catalogue of a collection of original manuscripts . . . of the Inquisition in the Canary Islands*, 2 vols, London, 1903.

Boehmer, Edward, *Bibliotheca Wiffeniana: Spanish Reformers of two centuries, from 1520*, 3 vols, London, 1864–1904.

Braudel, Fernand, *La Méditérranée et le Monde méditerranéen à l'époque de Philippe II*, Paris, 1949.

Braunstein, Baruch, *The Chuetas of Majorca. Conversos and the Inquisition of Majorca*, New York, 1972.

Bujanda, J. M. de, *Index des livres interdits*; vol. V: *Index de L'Inquisition espagnole, 1551, 1554, 1559*, Geneva, 1984; vol. VI: *Index de l'Inquisition espagnole, 1583, 1584*, Geneva, 1993.

Cantera Burgos, F. and León Tello, P., *Judaizantes del arzobispado de Toledo habilitados por la Inquisición en 1495 y 1497*, Madrid, 1969.

Cardaillac, Louis, *Morisques et Chrétiens. Un affrontement polémique (1492–1640)*, Paris, 1977.

Caro Baroja, Julio, *Los Judíos en le España moderna y contemporánea*, 3 vols, Madrid, 1962.

Carrasco, Raphael, 'Morisques anciens et nouveaux Morisques dans le district inquisitorial de Cuenca', *MCV*, 22, 1986.

Carrasco Urgoiti, M. S., *El problema morisco en Aragón al comienzo del reinado de Felipe II*, Madrid, 1969.

Carrete Parrondo, C., 'Los conversos jerónimos ante el estatuto de limpieza de sangre', *Helmantica*, 26, 1975.

Carrete Parrondo, C., 'Nostalgia for the past among Christian judeoconversos', *Mediterranean Historical Review*, vol. 6, no. 2, Dec. 1991.

Castro, Américo, *The Structure of Spanish History*, Princeton, 1954.

Colas Latorre, G. and Salas Auséns, J. A., *Aragón en el siglo XVI. Alteraciones sociales y conflictos políticos*, Saragossa, 1982.

Contreras, Jaime, *El Santo Oficio de la Inquisición de Galicia*, Madrid, 1982.

Cuart Moner, Baltasar, *Colegiales Mayores y limpieza de sangre durante la edad moderna*, Salamanca, 1991.

Dedieu, J.-P., *L'administration de la foi. L'Inquisition de Tolède (XVIe–XVIIIe siècle)*, Madrid, 1989.

Destierros aragoneses: judíos y moriscos, Saragossa, 1988.

Domínguez Nafría, J. C., *La Inquisición de Murcia en el siglo XVII: el licenciado Cascales*, Murcia, 1991.

Domínguez Ortiz, Antonio, *Los conversos de orígen judío después de la expulsión*, Madrid, 1955.

Domínguez Ortiz, Antonio and Bernard Vincent, *Historia de los Moriscos*, Madrid, 1978.

Escamilla-Colin, Michèle, *Crimes et châtiments dans l'Espagne inquisitoriale*, 2 vols, Paris, 1992.

Fita, Fidel, 'La Inquisición toledana. Relación contemporánea de los autos y autillos que celebró desde el año 1485 hasta el de 1501', *BRAH*, XI (1887).

Fontes Iudaeorum regni Castellae, ed. Carlos Carrete Parrondo, vol. I: *Provincia de Salamanca*, Salamanca, 1981; vol. II: *El Tribunal de la Inquisición en el Obispado de Soria (1486–1502)*, Salamanca, 1985; vol. III: *Proceso inquisitorial contra los Arias Dávila*, Salamanca, 1986.

García Fuentes, J. M., *La Inquisición en Granada en el siglo XVI*, Granada, 1981.

García Ivars, F., *La represión en el tribunal inquisitorial de Granada 1550–1819*, Madrid, 1991.

García-Cárcel, R., *Orígenes de la Inquisición española. El tribunal de Valencia, 1478–1530*, Barcelona, 1976.

García-Cárcel, R., *Herejía y Sociedad en el siglo XVI. La Inquisición en Valencia 1530–1609*, Barcelona, 1980.

García-Villoslada, Ricardo, *Historia de la Iglesia en España*, 5 vols, Madrid, 1980.

Gil Fernández, Luis, *Panorama social del humanismo español (1500–1800)*, Madrid, 1981.

Haliczer, Stephen, ed., *Inquisition and Society in early modern Europe*, London, 1987.

Henningsen, G. and Tedeschi, J. (eds), *The Inquisition in Early Modern Europe. Studies in Sources and Methods*, De Kalb, Illinois, 1985.

Historia de la Inquisición en España y América, 2 vols, ed. J. Pérez Villanueva and B. Escandell Bonet, Madrid, 1984–93.

Huerga, Alvaro, *El proceso de la Inquisición de Sevilla contra el maestro Domingo de Valtanás*, Jaén, 1958.

Inquisición y conversos. III Curso de cultura hispano-judia y sefardi, Toledo, 1994.

Kamen, Henry, *La España de Carlos II*, Barcelona, 1981.

Kamen, Henry, *The Phoenix and the Flame. Catalonia and the Counter Reformation*, London and New Haven, 1993 (cited as Kamen 1993a).

Kamen, Henry, *Crisis and change in early modern Spain*, Aldershot, 1993 (cited as Kamen 1993b).

Kamen, Henry, *Philip of Spain*, London and New Haven, 1997.

Kaplan, Yosef, ed., *Jews and Conversos. Studies in society and the Inquisition*, Jerusalem, 1985.

Kedourie, Elie, ed., *Spain and the Jews*, London, 1992.

Ladero Quesada, M. A., 'Judeoconversos andaluces en el siglo XV', in *Actas III Coloquio de Historia Medieval Andaluza. Minorías étnico-religiosas*, Jaén, 1984.

Ladero Quesada, M. A., *Granada después de la conquista*, Granada, 1988.

Lea, Henry Charles, *A History of the Inquisition of Spain*, 4 vols, New York, 1906–8.

Legacy of Muslim Spain, The, Leiden, 1992.

Llorente, Juan Antonio, *Memoria Histórica sobre cual ha sido la opinión nacional de España acerca del tribunal de la Inquisición*, Madrid, 1812.

Llorente, Juan Antonio, *Histoire Critique de l'Inquisition d'Espagne*, 4 vols, Paris, 1817–18.

Mariana, Juan de, *Historia General de España*, Biblioteca de Autores Españoles, vols XXX–XXXI, Madrid, 1950.

Márquez, Antonio, *Literatura e Inquisición en España 1478–1834*, Madrid, 1980 (cited as Márquez 1980a).

Márquez, Antonio, *Los Alumbrados. Orígenes y filosofía (1525–1559)*, Madrid, 1980 (cited as Márquez 1980b).

Menéndez y Pelayo, Marcelino, *Historia de los Heterodóxos Españoles*, 8 vols, Buenos Aires, 1945 (first edn was 1881).

Monsalvo Antón, J. M., *Teoría y evolución de un conflicto social. El antisemitismo en la Corona de Castilla en la Baja Edad Media*, Madrid, 1985.

Monter, William, *Frontiers of Heresy. The Spanish Inquisition from the Basque lands to Sicily*, Cambridge, 1990.

Motis Dolader, M. A., 'Los judíos zaragozanos en la época de Fernando II de Aragón', *Minorités et marginaux en Espagne et dans le Midi de la France (VIIe–XVIIIe siècles)*, Paris, 1986.

Netanyahu, Benzion, *Don Isaac Abravanel, statesman and philosopher*, Philadelphia, 1968.

Netanyahu, Benzion, *The Origins of the Inquisition in fifteenth-century Spain*, New York, 1995.

Nueva visión, nuevos horizontes. La Inquisición española, ed. J. P. Villanueva, Madrid, 1980.

Perfiles jurídicos de la Inquisición española, ed. J. A. Escudero, Madrid, 1989.

Pulgar, Hernando del, *Crónica de los Reyes Católicos* (vols V–VI, Colección de Crónicas Españolas), Madrid, 1943.

Raphael, David, ed., *The Expulsion 1492 Chronicles*, Hollywood, 1992.

Reguera, Iñaki, *La Inquisición española en el País Vasco*, San Sebastian, 1984.

Riera Sans, Jaume, 'Judíos y conversos en los reinos de la Corona de Aragón durante el siglo XV', in *La Expulsión de los judíos de España. II Curso de Cultura hispano-judía y sefardí*, Toledo, 1993.

Roth, Norman, *Conversos, Inquisition and the Expulsion of the Jews from Spain*, Madison, 1995.

Sánchez Albornoz, Claudio, *España, un enigma histórico*, 2 vols, 2nd edn, Buenos Aires, 1956.

Schäfer, Ernst, *Beiträge zur Geschichte des spanischen Protestantismus und der Inquisition im sechzenten Jahrhundert*, 3 vols, Gütersloh, 1902.

Sesma Muñoz, J. Angel, *El establecimiento de la Inquisición en Aragón (1484–1486). Documentos para su estudio*, Zaragoza, 1987.

Sicroff, A., *Les controverses des statuts de 'pureté de sang' en Espagne du XVe au XVIIe siècle*, Paris, 1960.

Suárez Fernández, Luis, ed., *Documentos acerca de la Expulsión de los Judíos*, Valladolid, 1964.

Tellechea, J. I., *El arzobispo Carranza y su tiempo*, 2 vols, Madrid, 1968.

Tellechea, J. I., *Tiempos recios*, Salamanca, 1977.

Tomás y Valiente, F., *El derecho penal de la monarquía absoluta (siglos XVI–XVII–XVIII)*, Madrid, 1969.

Tres culturas en la corona de Castilla y los sefardíes, Las, Salamanca, 1990.

Vincent, B., *Minorías y marginados en la España del siglo XVI*, Granada, 1987.

Xudeus e Conversos na Historia, ed. C. Barros, 2 vols, Santiago, 1994.

INDEX

The frequently used terms Aragon, Barcelona, Castile, Cortes, Granada, Madrid, Saragossa, Seville, Toledo, Valencia, are not indexed